Handbook of Challenging Behavior:
Mental Health Aspects of Mental Retardation

Steven Reiss

Nisonger Center
The Ohio State University

IDS Publishing Corporation
Worthington, Ohio

This book is dedicated to Margaret Reiss

———————————

Copyright (c) 1994 by IDS Publishing Corporation

All rights reserved. No part of the material protected by this copyright notice may be reproduced or utilized in any form by any means, electronic or mechanical, without prior written consent from the publisher.

The author is Professor of Psychology and Psychiatry at The Ohio State University and also Director, Nisonger Center, The Ohio State University.

The Nisonger Center is a member of the federal network of "University-Affiliated Programs" (UAPs) in mental retardation. The UAP network is the leading program for training professionals in mental retardation.

The scientific editor for this volume was Leonard W. Sushinsky, Ph.D.

The author would like to thank the members of his 1994 dual diagnosis class at OSU for their many comments on early versions of this work. The author also would like to thank Richard J. McNally for his comments on Chapter 2, Barry Zvolenski for general assistance, and Susan Havercamp for proof-reading.

This book was printed on acid-free paper.

Library of Congress Catalog Card Number: 94-77561
ISBN 0-9642598-1-8
Printed in the United States of America

CHAPTER 1. INTRODUCTION 1
I.   TERMINOLOGY 2
II.   SIGNIFICANCE OF CHALLENGING BEHAVIOR 4
    A. CONSEQUENCES OF MENTAL HEALTH DISORDERS 4
    B. MENTAL HEALTH DISORDERS OVER TIME 5
    C. PREVALENCE 6
       C1. STUDIES COMPARING PEOPLE WITH MR AND NO-MR 10
       C2. RESIDENTIAL SETTINGS 12
       C3. TYPES OF PSYCHIATRIC DISORDERS 12
       C4. MENTAL DISORDERS VS. OTHER DISORDERS 15
       C5. DEFINITION OF MENTAL RETARDATION 16
       C6. EFFECTS OF AGE 16
       C7. LEVEL OF MENTAL RETARDATION 18
       C8. DOWN SYNDROME 19
III.   DETERMINANTS OF CHALLENGING BEHAVIOR 19
    A. BIOLOGICAL RISK FACTORS 19
    B. PSYCHOSOCIAL RISK FACTORS 22
       B1. PROLONGED EXPOSURE TO NEGATIVE SOCIAL CONDITIONS 22
       B2. AWARENESS OF NEGATIVE SOCIAL CONDITIONS 26
       B3. INADEQUATE SOCIAL SUPPORT 27
       B4. SOCIAL SKILLS 28
       B5. SELF-CONCEPT 29
       B6. EXPECTATIONS OF FAILURE 29
       B7. VULNERABILITY TO STRESS 29
       B8. REINFORCER RESPONSIVENESS 30
    C. DEVELOPMENTAL FACTORS 31
       C1. PSYCHODYNAMIC MODELS 31
       C2. PERSONALITY DEVELOPMENT 32
       C3. POOR COMMUNICATION SKILLS 34
IV.   UNDERSERVED POPULATION 35
    A. DIAGNOSTIC OVERSHADOWING 35
    B. ISSUE AVOIDANCE 38
V.   CONCLUDING COMMENT ON MENTAL HEALTH 39

CHAPTER 2. PSYCHOPATHOLOGY 41
I.   DEVELOPMENTAL VS. CLINICAL APPROACHES 41
II.   ANXIETY DISORDERS 44
    A. EPIDEMIOLOGY 45
    B. SPECIFIC AND SOCIAL PHOBIAS 45
    C. PANIC DISORDER 46
    D. POSTTRAUMATIC STRESS DISORDER (PTSD) 47
    E. OBSESSIVE-COMPULSIVE DISORDER (OCD) 48
    F. GENERALIZED ANXIETY DISORDER (GAD) 49
III.   MOOD DISORDERS 50
    A. RECOGNITION OF OCCURRENCE 50
    B. MOODS 51
    C. TYPES 51
       C1. EPIDEMIOLOGY 52
       C2. PRESENTATION IN MENTAL RETARDATION 53
       C3. RESEARCH 54

IV.   SUICIDE 59
     A. EPIDEMIOLOGY 60
     B. PRESENTATION IN MENTAL RETARDATION. 60
     C. RESEARCH 60
V.   SCHIZOPHRENIA 61
     A. EPIDEMIOLOGY 63
     B. PRESENTATION IN MENTAL RETARDATION. 63
     C. SCHIZOPHRENIA AND MILD MENTAL RETARDATION 64
     D. SCHIZOPHRENIA IN SEVERE MENTAL RETARDATION 64
     E. RESEARCH 66
VI.   PERSONALITY DISORDERS 68
     A. EPIDEMIOLOGY 69
     B. SUBTYPES. 69
           B1. AVOIDANT PERSONALITY DISORDER 70
           B2. DEPENDENT PERSONALITY DISORDER 70
           B3. PARANOID PERSONALITY DISORDER 71
           B4. ANTISOCIAL PERSONALITY DISORDER 71
           B5. BORDERLINE PERSONALITY DISORDER. 72
           B6. HISTRIONIC PERSONALITY DISORDER 72
     C. PRESENTATION IN MENTAL RETARDATION 72
VII. SEVERE BEHAVIOR DISORDERS 73
     A. AGGRESSION. 73
     B. PSYCHOPATHOLOGY 75
     C. PSYCHOLOGICAL APPROACHES TO STUDY OF AGGRESSION 75
           C1. INFORMATION PROCESSING AND AGGRESSION 76
           C2. BEHAVIOR ANALYSIS 76
     D. CRIMINAL OFFENDERS 76
     E. SELF-INJURIOUS BEHAVIOR (SIB) 77
           E1. PSYCHOLOGICAL MOTIVATION OF SIB. 78
           E2. SIB AND PSYCHOPATHOLOGY 78
VIII. SEXUAL DISORDERS 81
     A. EPIDEMIOLOGY 82
     B. PRESENTATION IN MENTAL RETARDATION. 82
IX.   SOMATOFORM DISORDERS 83
     A. EPIDEMIOLOGY 83
     B. PRESENTATION IN MENTAL RETARDATION 84
X.   ATTENTION-DEFICIT/HYPERACTIVITY DISORDER (ADHD) 84
     A. EPIDEMIOLOGY 85
     B. PRESENTATION IN MENTAL RETARDATION. 85
     C. RESEARCH 85
XI.   SUBSTANCE ABUSE 86
XII. DISSOCIATIVE DISORDERS. 87
XIII. EATING AND SLEEP DISORDERS 88

CHAPTER 3. DIAGNOSIS & ASSESSMENT 91
I.   AAMR CLASSIFICATION SYSTEM 91
     A. PURPOSE OF NEW DEFINITION 91
     B. IMPLEMENTATION OF AAMR DEFINITION 92
     C. CRITICISMS OF NEW AAMR DEFINITION 93
     D. IMPLICATIONS FOR PEOPLE WITH CHALLENGING BEHAVIOR 95

II.	IDENTIFYING PRIMARY VS. SECONDARY DISABILITIES	95
III.	THE STIGMA OF PSYCHIATRIC DIAGNOSIS	97
IV.	PSYCHIATRIC DIAGNOSIS	97

A. RELIABILITY OF PSYCHIATRIC DIAGNOSIS 98
B. PSYCHIATRIC DIAGNOSIS AND MENTAL RETARDATION 100
    B1. APPLICABILITY OF PSYCHIATRIC DIAGNOSIS 100
    B2. MR FACTORS LIMITING PSYCHIATRIC DIAGNOSIS................... 100
C. DIAGNOSTIC GUIDELINES 102
    C1. DIAGNOSE PATTERNS OF SYMPTOMATOLOGY 102
    C2. DIAGNOSE CHANGES IN BEHAVIOR 102
    C3. MAKE ALLOWANCES FOR THE IMPACT OF
         INTELLECTUAL DISABILITY AND PSYCHOSOCIAL MASKING 103
    C4. ADMIT LIMITATIONS OF KNOWLEDGE 103
D. SOURCES OF ASSESSMENT INFORMATION........................... 103
    D1. CASE RECORDS 104
    D2. OBSERVATIONS OF BEHAVIOR.................................. 104
    D3. CLIENT INTERVIEWS.. 104
    D4. STAFF INTERVIEWS 105
    D5. PSYCHOLOGICAL INSTRUMENTS AND BIOLOGICAL MARKERS........ 105

V.	EVALUATING PSYCHOMETRIC INSTRUMENTS	105

A. PSYCHOMETRIC EVALUATION CRITERIA 105
    A1. TYPES OF RELIABILITY 105
    A2. INTERNAL VS. INTERRATER RELIABILITY......................... 106
    A3. r VS. PERCENT EXACT AGREEMENT SCORES...................... 106
    A4. VALIDITY STATISTICS 107
    A5. FACTOR VS. FACTOR CONTENT VALIDITY 108
    A6. CONSTRUCT VALIDITY 109
    A7. SUGGESTED PSYCHOMETRIC CRITERIA........................... 109
B. SELF-REPORT VS. INFORMANT MEASURES 110

VI.	GENERAL PSYCHOPATHOLOGY INSTRUMENTS	112

A. REISS SCREEN 115
B. REISS SCALES.. 117
C. PIMRA.. 119
D. ABC 122
E. DASH 123
F. PROUT AND STROHMER INSTRUMENTS............................. 124
G. EDRS AND DD-CBCL 126
H. COMPARATIVE RESEARCH 126

VII.	DIAGNOSTIC INSTRUMENTS	127

A. ANXIETY DISORDERS 127
B. MOOD DISORDERS... 127
C. SCHIZOPHRENIA 130
D. AUTISM 130
E. PERSONALITY DISORDERS 131
F. SEVERE BEHAVIOR DISORDERS................................... 131
G. SEXUAL DISORDERS 132
H. ATTENTION-DEFICIT DISORDER................................... 132

VIII.	PROJECTIVE ASSESSMENT OF PERSONALITY	133

A. FACTORS INFLUENCING STORIES 133
B. APT 134

	C. APT/MR	134
	D. HAND-TEST	135
IX.	OTHER INSTRUMENTS	135
X.	BIOLOGICAL TESTS	137

CHAPTER 4. TREATMENT APPROACHES 139

I.	PSYCHODYNAMIC THERAPY	139
	A. GENERAL MODELS	139
	A1. PSYCHOANALYSIS	139
	A2. CLIENT-CENTERED MODEL	141
	B. APPLICATIONS FOR MENTAL RETARDATION	142
	B1. PSYCHOTHERAPY AND MENTAL RETARDATION	142
	B2. COUNSELING, GROUP THERAPY, AND MENTAL RETARDATION	144
	B3. CLIENT-CENTERED THERAPY AND MENTAL RETARDATION	144
	B4. PLAY THERAPY AND MENTAL RETARDATION	145
	B5. ART, MUSIC, DANCE THERAPY, AND MENTAL RETARDATION	146
	C. EVALUATION OF PSYCHODYNAMIC THERAPIES	146
II.	BEHAVIORAL APPROACHES	149
	A. GENERAL MODELS	149
	A1. APPLIED PAVLOVIAN MODEL (BEHAVIOR THERAPY)	150
	A2. APPLIED OPERANT MODEL (BEHAVIOR ANALYSIS)	150
	B. APPLICATIONS TO MENTAL RETARDATION	151
	B1. STIMULUS-BASED TREATMENT	151
	B2. CONDITIONING	151
	B3. SKILLS TRAINING	151
	B4. EXTINCTION AND PUNISHMENT	152
	B5. FUNCTIONAL ANALYSIS	153
	C. COMMUNICATION THEORY	153
	D. EVALUATION	155
	D1. PERCENT OF CASES RESPONDING TO THERAPY	156
	D2. LONG-TERM BENEFITS	156
	D3. GENERALIZATION ISSUES	156
	D4. SIDE EFFECTS	157
	D5. ETHICS AND NONAVERSIVE THERAPY	158
	D6. OUTDATED PAVLOVIAN PRINCIPLES	158
III.	COGNITIVE APPROACH	159
	A. GENERAL MODELS	159
	A1. RATIONAL-EMOTIVE THERAPY	159
	A2. COVERT SENSITIZATION	160
	A3. COGNITIVE THERAPIES FOR DEPRESSION	160
	B. APPLICATIONS TO MENTAL RETARDATION	160
	B1. ANGER MANAGEMENT TRAINING (AMT)	161
	B2. PROBLEM-SOLVING APPROACH	162
	C. EVALUATION	163
IV.	PSYCHIATRIC DRUGS	163
	A. GENERAL MODEL	164
	B. APPLICATIONS TO MENTAL RETARDATION	164

	B1. NEUROLEPTICS (MAJOR TRANQUILIZERS)	165
	B2. ANTIDEPRESSANTS	166
	B3. ANTIMANICS	166
	B4. ANXIOLYTICS	167
	B5. ANTICONVULSANTS	167
	B6. STIMULANTS	167
	B7. OPIATE BLOCKERS	168
	B8. BETA BLOCKERS	168

    C. BEST PRACTICES FOR MENTAL RETARDATION. 169
    D. EVALUATION 171
        D1. OVERMEDICATION 171
        D2. UNKNOWN EFFECTS 171
        D3. BEST PRACTICES SOMETIMES NOT FOLLOWED 173
        D4. SIDE EFFECTS. 173
        D5. POLYPHARMACY 175
        D6. INADEQUATE TRAINING. 175
        D7. THE NISONGER-THE Arc INTERNATIONAL
            CONSENSUS STUDY. 175

V.   DIAGNOSTIC CONDITIONS 176
    A. ANXIETY DISORDERS. 176
    B. MOOD DISORDERS 177
    C. SCHIZOPHRENIA. 177
    D. PERSONALITY DISORDERS 178
    E. SEVERE BEHAVIOR DISORDERS. 178
    F. EATING DISORDERS 179
    G. OTHER DISORDERS. 179
VI. CONCLUSIONS. 179

CHAPTER 5. COMMUNITY INTEGRATION 181
I.   SERVICE BARRIERS 182
    A. HISTORICAL BARRIERS 182
        A1. CREATION OF STATE MR UMBRELLA AGENCIES 182
        A2. HISTORY AT FEDERAL LEVEL 183
    B. CURRENT BARRIERS 185
        B1. INADEQUATE COMMITMENT 185
        B2. INADEQUATE RESOURCES 186
        B3. ORGANIZATIONAL RESISTANCE TO CHANGE 186
        B4. PROFESSIONAL OPPOSITION 186
        B5. DIFFICULTY FINDING RESIDENTIAL PLACEMENTS. 186
        B6. LOW STATUS. 186
        B7. TWO LANGUAGES 187
    C. INTERNATIONAL SYSTEMS BARRIERS 187
II. OVERCOMING SERVICE BARRIERS. 187
    A. GOALS AND OBJECTIVES 188
        A1. GETTINGS' SUGGESTIONS. 188
        A2. ILLINOIS STATE TASK FORCE. 188
    B. CONSUMER ADVOCACY. 189
        B1. PARENT GROUPS AND CHALLENGING BEHAVIOR. 189
        B2. SELF-ADVOCACY AND CHALLENGING BEHAVIOR 190
    C. CREATING NEW SERVICES 191

	C1. CONFRONT HISTORY	192
	C2. ADEQUATE RESOURCES	192
	C3. REALISTIC TIME PERSPECTIVE	193
	C4. SUMMARY	193
III.	SERVICE MODELS	193
	A. SPECIALIZED VS. GENERIC SERVICES	194
	B. FAMILY SERVICES	195
	C. CRISIS INTERVENTION	197
	D. OUTPATIENT MODEL	198
	E. DAY SERVICES	200
	F. INPATIENT UNITS	201
	G. HOUSING AND SUPPORTED LIVING	203
	H. PERSONAL FUTURES PLANNING	204
	H1. EVALUATION OF PERSONAL FUTURES PLANNING	206
IV.	PROFESSIONAL TRAINING	207
	A. UAPs	208
	B. NADD	209
V.	BRIEFLY NOTED	210
	A. LEGAL ISSUES	210
	B. PREVENTION	211

PREFACE

SUMMARY — This book is intended as a comprehensive synthesis of what is known about the co-occurrence of mental health disorders and mental retardation. The intent is to provide a scholarly review of the relevant professional and research literatures. The book is written for a broad audience of researchers, professionals, and university students. Parents and family members may find portions of the book useful as an authoritative summary of current knowledge, although the book was not written for this audience and includes many discussions of research methods and clinical diagnoses.

New ideas sometimes move fields forward and stimulate a fair amount of professional and academic activity. Historically, the field of mental health disorders in people with mental retardation has seen two major new ideas in the course of this author's career. In the 1960s clinicians explored the idea that challenging behavior can be analyzed as functional behaviors and treated by systematic manipulation of antecedents and consequents. This idea, which is known as behavior analysis, revolutionized the treatment of challenging behavior and led to important clinical improvements in cases that were previously untreatable.

In the 1980s another new idea took hold — the idea that people with mental retardation are vulnerable to the full range of mental health disorders. This idea, which is known as "dual diagnosis," has led to the diagnosis and treatment of many disorders that had been previously neglected. Today, it is undeniable that virtually all mental health disorders seen in the general population can co-occur with mental retardation.

Interest in dual diagnosis has grown significantly since the early 1980s. In the United States, hundreds of service programs were created. Many training seminars and professional conferences have been held. The National Institutes of Health and the National Institute of Mental Health have jointly and individually held national conferences. The National Association for the Dually Diagnosed has sponsored annual conferences.

A review of the literature on the mental health aspects of mental retardation is timely. There is a need to summarize the growing literature on dual diagnosis. Also, the field has reached a point where academic issues need to be debated. The leaders of the field have been too polite with each other — there is too little in the way of constructive criticism.

PURPOSES OF BOOK

The three main purposes of this book are as follows:

1. To summarize and synthesize what is known about the co-occurrence of mental health disorders and mental retardation;

2. To provide a critical evaluation of research and theory on challenging behavior;

3. To suggest ideas and hypotheses for future research and/or professional activity.

SUMMARIZE/SYNTHESIZE LITERATURE

The literature on mental health disorders in persons with mental retardation has become sufficiently large to create a need for summary and synthesis. More than 700 publications are reviewed in this book. The intent was to provide an exhaustive review of the literatures on epidemiology, psychopathology, and assessment, and a representative review of the literatures on treatment and community integration. However, the literature has been growing so rapidly that the goal of an exhaustive review for certain topics could not be met.

Much of the literature on the co-occurrence of mental health disorders and mental retardation consists of professional or clinical reports. Many studies report observations of fewer than ten clients. Regarding the academic articles, a large percentage are theoretical in nature and include little or no original data. A relatively small percentage of the literature consists of controlled scientific studies.

In this book, an effort is made to understand psychopathology research in the context of research on personality, developmental psychology, and biological risk factors. The general points are as follows.

- People with mental retardation experience prolonged exposure to the negative social conditions known to cause psychological adjustment issues and psychopathology.

- People with mental retardation are vulnerable to the full range of psychopathology. Dual diagnosis represents a broadening of the range of clinical phenomena recognized for mental retardation. An excellent example of this was the recognition of the occurrence of depression in people with mental retardation.

- Large numbers of people with mental retardation have a mental health disorder.

- Researchers need to develop standard methods of assessment and diagnosis.

- Researchers need to develop effective therapies and to compare the effectiveness of alternative therapies.

- Administrators need to overcome the systems barriers to services.

CRITICAL EVALUATION

This book is intended to begin to meet the need for critical discussions and debate on substantive issues. Many dual diagnosis publications were not peer-reviewed prior to publication. Moreover, there are many thorny and complex issues in the dual diagnosis area that need to be debated and critically analyzed.

One common shortcoming in the dual diagnosis literature is a reliance on outdated theories of psychopathology. Two examples of this are favorable comments in the dual diagnosis literature regarding the learned helplessness theory of depression and the Pavlovian conditioning theory of phobia. Today, learned helplessness is no longer considered a viable model of affective disorder or even depression. Contiguity theories of Pavlovian conditioning are no longer considered viable models of phobias. The dual diagnosis literature needs to be brought up to date with respect to theories of psychopathology.

Another common shortcoming in the dual diagnosis literature is inadequate attention to critical diagnostic criteria. An excellent example of this is the recent tendency for some authors to assume that self-injurious behavior (SIB) is obsessive-compulsive behavior (OCD). In order to make this assumption, it is essential that the SIB be shown to be motivated by a reduction in anxiety, tension, or stress. At a minimum, the possibility that SIB is motivated by pleasure must be considered and rejected before serious consideration can be given to the possibility that the SIB is an example of OCD.

Good critical evaluations strengthen professional activity and research. Academic authorities should not hesitate to discuss ideas, methods, and findings in a frank, open manner. If a work cannot survive critical evaluation, everybody is better off finding out sooner rather than later.

Although there are a number of shortcomings in the dual diagnosis literature — too many publications were not peer reviewed; too many outdated theories are cited favorably; inadequate attention is sometimes given to diagnostic criteria — overall there is much to admire. There is a refreshing creativity in the

literature, especially from some American psychiatrists. A number of impressive scholarly reviews have been published, especially from some of the British psychiatrists, but also from American and Canadian authors. Some skilled clinicians have published on dual diagnosis.

SUGGEST NEW IDEAS

A number of new ideas are presented in this book. Some of these are hypotheses that need to be evaluated by future research, whereas others concern research methods or statistics. For example, in Chapter 1 the following hypothesis is proposed: High prevalence rates for mental health disorders in people with mental retardation are associated with research methods that involve the collection of new data, whereas low rates are associated with reviews of previously collected data. In Chapter 2 it is suggested that a "Darwinian" methodology is needed to address the thorny problems of diagnosing psychopathology in severe mental retardation. In Chapter 4 it is suggested that the data supporting the communication hypothesis of severe behavior disorders can be reinterpreted in terms of individual differences in need for attention and/or sensitivities to aversive stimuli. In Chapter 5 it is suggested that there is a close and previously unrecognized similarity between Carl Rogers' views and the philosophy that community integration has curative effects for people with challenging behavior.

In Chapter 3 the author's new (and likely controversial) ideas are presented regarding psychometrics. The present author believes that the psychometric approach used for IQ tests has been extended to psychopathology and behavior rating scales without adequate consideration of the differences between measuring abilities versus behavioral tendencies. Consequently, some psychometric criteria are vastly overrated in significance when psychopathology instruments are considered, and others are significantly underrated. These ideas are almost certain to elicit some criticism because they provide a basis for questioning the statistics in numerous research studies.

USES OF BOOK

This book is intended to have the following uses:

- Professional book to be used by psychologists, psychiatrists, behavior pediatricians and others working in the field of mental retardation;

- Textbook, or supplemental textbook, for college courses;

- Sourcebook for qualified mental retardation professionals, unit managers, parents, and family members;

- Sourcebook for researchers and graduate students seeking ideas for possible future study.

CALL FOR REPRINTS

The author intends to update this book on a periodic basis. Researchers and professionals are requested to send reprints and preprints of relevant work to the author at the Nisonger Center, Ohio State University, 1581 Dodd Drive, Columbus, Ohio 43210-1296.

CHAPTER 1. INTRODUCTION

Mental illness and mental retardation are two different disabilities (Bialer, 1970; Sarason & Doris, 1969; Tarjan, 1977). Mental illness is a psychological disability associated with emotional, social, and personality dysfunctioning. Mental retardation is a cognitive disability caused by the interaction of a person with limited intellectual functioning with his/her living environments (Luckasson, Coulter, Polloway, Reiss, Schalock, Snell, Spitalnik, & Stark, 1992). Most people who have a mental illness do not have mental retardation, and most people who have mental retardation do not have a mental illness. However, some people have both mental retardation and a mental illness (Balthazer & Stevens, 1975; Myers & Pueschel, 1991).

People with mental retardation are vulnerable to the full range of mental illnesses. As George Tarjan and Herbert Grossman were fond of saying, "Mental retardation is not an antidote for mental illness." That is, the same mental illnesses seen in the general population are seen in people with mental retardation. People with mental retardation can develop a psychosis, such as schizophrenia, or an anxiety disorder, such as an obsessive-compulsive disorder. They can become depressed and develop a mood disorder. They also are vulnerable to abnormal personality traits such as excessive dependency, suspiciousness, or impulsivity.

People who have both mental retardation and a mental health disorder constitute one of the most underserved populations in the United States (Reiss, Levitan, & McNally, 1982). For a number of reasons discussed later in this book, these people rarely receive the mental health services they need. They have difficulty obtaining adequate residential, mental health, and educational services. There are few advocates for this population. Although there are many more services today than there were in 1980, the vast majority of people with both mental retardation and a mental illness still do not receive minimally adequate services.

This book is about the joint occurrence of mental health disorders and mental retardation. The main points advanced in this introductory chapter are as follows:

1. The occurrence of mental illness in people with mental retardation is a significant social issue. As many as one to two million Americans may have both mental retardation and a mental illness on any given day. Significant emotional suffering often is involved for both the individual and family. Mental illness can last for significant periods of time if untreated. Some mental illnesses are difficult to treat and can last for lifetimes. Others are episodic, with episodes lasting for periods of weeks or months.

2. Many instances of challenging behavior are multi-determined by biological, psychological, social, and developmental factors. Especially noteworthy is the role played by negative social conditions such as stigmatization, segregation, and restricted opportunities.

3. Inadequate attention has been paid to the mental health aspects of mental retardation. This is partially explained by the diagnostic overshadowing phenomenon in which the presence of mental retardation decreases the diagnostic significance of psychiatric symptoms (Reiss, Levitan, & Szyszko, 1982). Another factor is avoidance of the issues — the field does not want to deal with the fact that many people with mental retardation are self-aware.

I. TERMINOLOGY

An outline of the terminology used in this book is provided in Table 1-1. The reader may wish to refer to this table periodically until he or she is familiar with how the terms are used throughout the book.

Mental disorders (or *clinical syndromes*) have onsets and are associated with significant deteriorations in functioning called *regressions*. Examples include anxiety disorder, somatoform disorder, mood disorder, schizophrenia, and dissociative disorder.

Personality disorders are deeply ingrained, chronic patterns of maladaptive behavior with no definite period of onset. Examples include conduct disorder, avoidant personality disorder, borderline personality disorder, and paranoid personality disorder.

Severe behavior disorders are severe conduct problems, including self-injurious behavior, severe destructive behavior, and stereotypic behavior. Depending on the individual case, the occurrence of a severe behavior disorder may or may not be associated with a mental disorder and/or a personality disorder.

In this book, mental disorders and personality disorders will be considered as two types of *mental illnesses*. Although severe behavior disorders may be associated with mental illness, by themselves severe behavior disorders are not considered examples of mental illnesses. For example, Anxiety Disorder will be considered an example of mental illness; Paranoid Personality Disorder will be

TABLE 1-1. TERMINOLOGY USED IN THIS BOOK

CHALLENGING BEHAVIOR
(Mental Health Disorders)
(Dual Diagnosis[1])
(Aberrant Behavior)
(Maladaptive Behavior)

Psychopathology
(Mental Illness)
(Psychiatric Disorder)

Severe Behavior Disorders[2]

Mental Disorders[2] (Clinical Syndromes)	Maladaptive Traits & Personality Disorders[2]	
Anxiety Disorder	Avoidant Personality Disorder	Aggressive Behavior
Mood Disorder	Dependent Personality Disorder	Self-Injurious Behavior
Suicide	Paranoid Personality Disorder	Stereotypies
Schizophrenia	Antisocial Personality Disorder	Rumination
Sexual Disorder	Borderline Personality Disorder	Other
Somatoform Disorder	Histrionic Personality Disorder	
Attention-Deficit Disorder		
Substance Abuse		
Dissociative Disorder		
Eating Disorder		
Sleep Disorder		

[1] The term *dual diagnosis* is included in this table to show where it fits. In this book, the term *challenging behavior* is used instead of *dual diagnosis*.
[2] Descriptions of the various mental disorders, maladaptive personality traits, personality disorders, and severe behavior disorders are presented in Chapter 2.

considered an example of mental illness; but self-injurious behavior will not be considered an example of mental illness. The reason self-injurious behavior is not considered an example of mental illness is to allow for the theoretical possibility that the behavior sometimes might occur for genetic, neurological, or medical reasons unrelated to the occurrence of mental illnesses.

The terms *psychopathology* and *psychiatric disorder* will be used interchangeably with the term *mental illness*. Generally, psychologists prefer the term *psychopathology,* and psychiatrists prefer the terms *psychiatric disorder* or *mental illness*.

The terms *mental health disorder, maladaptive behavior,* and *aberrant behavior* will be used interchangeably. As shown in Table 1-1, the three types of mental

health disorders are mental disorders, personality disorders, and severe behavior disorders. In the past, people with both mental retardation and a mental health disorder were said to have a *dual diagnosis*. The phrase *dual diagnosis,* however, has fallen into disfavor because of concerns about possible negative connotation (Szymanski & Grossman, 1984). The term dual diagnosis is not used in this book — the term challenging behavior is used instead. In this book, the term challenging behavior means "mental health disorder in a person with mental retardation." This is very different from the way many authors use the term challenging behavior, which is to refer to severe behavior disorders. In this book, however, the term challenging behavior refers generically to all mental health disorders — severe behavior disorder, mental disorder, and personality disorder — and it always implies a reference to people with mental retardation. The reason it is desirable to have a term that always implies a reference to mental retardation is that people first language is especially awkward when referring to a person with multiple disabilities.

II. SIGNIFICANCE OF CHALLENGING BEHAVIOR

Having defined our terminology, we now consider research on the importance of mental health disorders in people with mental retardation. This research has documented that mental health disorders can have significant adverse consequences, last for long periods of time, and affect large numbers of people.

A. CONSEQUENCES OF MENTAL HEALTH DISORDERS

Mental health disorders have a number of unfortunate consequences for people with mental retardation. They impair the individual's quality of life by delaying personal growth and creating barriers to social integration (Larson & Lakin, 1992; Schalock & Keith, 1993). They often cause a deterioration in overall adaptive functioning called a *regression*. In some cases, intellectual functioning is impaired (Russell & Tanguay, 1981).

Some mental health disorders are associated with emotional suffering. For example, Anxiety Disorder may lead to experiences of intense fear, repeated panic attacks, and chronic anxiety states. Mood Disorders may lead to experiences of despair, hopelessness, and self-hatred. Schizophrenia may lead to withdrawal from the interpersonal environment and overwhelming feelings of resentment. Paranoia may lead to intense jealousies and imagined slights and rejections. Personality Disorders may lead to suicidal attempts, alcoholism, pros-

titution, and crime. Severe behavior disorders may lead to self-injury, self-mutilation, chronic pain, irritability, and overactivity.

Mental health disorders also can lead to family anguish. Families often experience considerable frustration trying to find appropriate residential and support services. If their loved ones are terminated from service programs because of behavioral episodes, the frustrating process of finding an appropriate residential program begins anew.

Mental health disorders create barriers toward integration in educational, social, employment, and community settings. Antisocial and aberrant behavior is a major factor in the institutionalization and reinstitutionalization of persons with mental retardation (e.g., Beier, 1964; Eyman & Borthwick, 1980; Eyman & Call, 1977). Scheerenberger (1980) found that behavior problems were the primary obstacle to community placement of hospital residents. Maladaptive behavior is a major cause of failure in community placements (Bruininks, Hill, & Morreau, 1988). Poor social skills and maladaptive behavior also lead to failure in employment settings (Greenspan & Shoultz, 1981; Schalock & Harper, 1978).

B. MENTAL HEALTH DISORDERS OVER TIME

Mental health disorders in persons with mental retardation can persist for years with little change. Reid, Ballinger, Heather, and Melvin (1984) found considerable persistence of behavioral abnormalities among people with severe mental retardation over a six-year period. James (1986) reported a number of elderly persons with an IQ of less than 50 who had behavioral or affective problems for decades. Linden and Forness (1986) found poor adjustments in about 70 percent of a sample of 40 people with mild mental retardation ten years after treatment for various psychiatric disorders.

Gillberg and Steffenburg (1987) found a high degree of persistence of symptomatology in a group of 46 children with autism or psychosis. In this study, the children were assessed prior to the age of six and after the age of 16. Negative outcomes, which were found for 59 percent of the sample, were indicated by aloof behavior and low intellectual functioning. About 50 percent of the sample showed a temporary increase of hyperactivity, aggressiveness, and destructiveness during puberty. Thirty-five percent of the sample developed epilepsy at age 16-23.

Eyman, Borthwick, and Miller (1981) studied changes in the maladaptive behavior of clients served by a California regional center between 1974 and 1976. Of 2,736 total clients, 426 were available for follow-up two years after the intake assessment. The sample included 214 clients who had been admitted to a

state institution and 212 clients who had been referred to various community agencies. As measured by the AAMR Adaptive Behavior Scales (Nihira, Foster, Shellhass, & Leland, 1975), the study found few changes in maladaptive behavior over the two-year period.

Laman (1989) found evidence of the stability of depressed mood over a time period of 14 to 30 months. The subjects were 36 adults with mental retardation who had been administered the informant-rated version of the depression scale from the *Psychopathology Inventory for Mentally Retarded Adults* (Matson, 1988) and the *Illinois-Chicago Informant Rating Scale for Depression* (Reiss & Benson, 1985). There was a significant correlation over time of .40, $p < .01$.

Matson, Gardner, Coe, and Sovner (1991) evaluated 506 residents of four institutions in two states for frequency, severity, and duration of behavior problems. They found that 91.6 percent of maladaptive behaviors had been evident for at least 12 months.

The findings that behavior problems persist through time provide additional evidence of the need for services. Researchers have found that challenging behavior has the potential for creating devastating effects on both the individual and the family over periods of years. Without services, these problems rarely are resolved. Even when appropriate services are provided, the effect may be only to minimize the suffering because in many cases there is no complete cure.

C. PREVALENCE

Researchers have found that perhaps as many as one-third or more of all people with mental retardation have a significant behavioral, mental, or personality disorder requiring mental health services (Nezu, Nezu, & Gill-Weiss, 1992). Given a prevalence rate of mental retardation of about one to two percent of the total population — or about three to six million people in the United States — there may be as many as one to two million Americans who have both mental retardation and a mental health disorder. This estimate, moreover, reflects only the one-day prevalence rate — that is, the rate of mental health disorders on any given day. Because some people who are mentally healthy today may develop a mental health disorder in the future, the percentage of people with mental retardation who will need a mental health service at some point in their lives is likely to be much higher than the estimated one-day prevalence rates. Unfortunately, there is no research on lifetime or even one-year prevalence rates for mental health disorders in persons with mental retardation.

TABLE 1-2. EPIDEMIOLOGY STUDIES

Study	N	Ages	Sample	Comments/Method
FINDINGS 0% TO 15%				
Borthwick-Duffy & Eyman (1990)	76,603	0-65+	California DD system	Survey case records — all conditions
McQueen et al. (1987)	221	7-10	Sample from Canadian registry	Case files; high rate for behavior problems; 9% psychiatric disorder
Reiss (1985)	5,637	5-21	All Illinois school children	IEP evaluations statistics — all handicaps
Wright (1982)	1,507	adults	U.K mental handicap institution	Survey case records for serious illness
Heaton-Ward (1977)	1,251	adults	U.K. mental hospitals	Survey case records for serious illness
FINDINGS 16% TO 25%				
Lewis et al. (1988)	1,201	18-80	Survey Montana state & cmty	Make-shift rating instrument
Ferrell & Madison (1986)	not reported	adults	Survey caseload of four counties in California facilities	Survey case managers
Einfeld (1984)	4,461	5-20	Large sample of children seen at Australian diagnostic clinic	Professional interviews and clinical assessments
Eaton & Menolascino (1982)	798	6-51+	Participants in cmty. MR/DD program	Professional evaluation; high rate for personality disorder
Jacobson (1982a,b)	30,578	0-65	NYS DD system	Rating scale omitted some disorders
Dupont (1980)	6,000	0-65+	All persons in Denmark in institutions	Computer survey case files; rate for neurosis + psychosis
Szymanski (1977)	132	0-55+	Consecutive referrals to DD clinic	Psychiatric evaluation
FINDINGS 26% TO 35%				
Day (1985)	357	40+	Long-stay residents in MR hospital (U.K.)	Case records
Lund (1985a)	302	20+	Sample from Danish National Registry (Denmark)	Professional evaluation/rating scales
Hill & Bruininks (1984)	2,271	1-65+	Survey of 236 public and cmty. agencies	Staff interviews (ICAP categories); rates higher for public vs. community

Study	N	Ages	Sample	Comments/Method
Menolascino (1965)	576	0-8	Referrals to MR center	Professional evaluation
FINDINGS 36%+				
Chitty et al. (1993)	71	1-79	Survey of Canadian institutions	Reiss Screen & professional evaluations
Goldberg et al. (1992)	382	adults	Referrals for psychiatric services	Test battery and professional interviews
Reiss (1990)	205	12-65+	Random sample community services	2 step: screening & professional evaluation
Lakin et al. (1989)	3,618	0-63+	Survey of 691 mental retardation facilities	ICAP rating scale
Gilson et al. (1987)	5,005	18+	Survey Colorado cmty. agencies	Make-shift instrument
Reid & Ballinger (1987)	100	21-81	100 randomly selected adults, IQ>36, severe personality disturbance	Rating scale for personality
Gillberg et al. (1986)	143	13-17	Epidemiology study in area of Sweden	Psychiatric interviews
Gostason (1985)	102	20-60	Epidemiology study in area of Sweden	Psychiatric interviews, personality tests, case files
Koller et al. (1983)	221	22	All subjects who had been identified MR in study in an area of Scotland between 1951 and 1952	Extensive interviews with subjects and parents
Corbett (1979)	402	15+	Camberwell Register, England	Screening + professional interviews
Philips & Williams (1975a,b)	100	0-17	Consecutive admissions to mental retardation diagnostic clinic	Comprehensive professional evaluations
Chess & Hassibi (1970)	52	5-12	Selected from middle-class special classes	Comprehensive professional evaluations
Rutter et al. (1970) & Rutter et al. (1976)	2,199	9-11	all school children Isle of Wight	2 step: screen + professional evaluation
Craft (1959)	314	16+	Survey English mental hospital	Case files + professional evaluations
Dewan (1948)	30,247	18-40	Canadian army records	Based on psychiatric interviews and case history data
Weaver (1946)	8,000	adults	Survey of army inductees	Assessed under stress (wartime)

A summary of 33 studies on the prevalence of challenging behavior is presented in Table 1-2. The table shows wide variation in reported rates from under 15 to over 35 percent. A number of factors have been suggested as possible explanations for this variation (e.g., Borthwick-Duffy, 1994; Nezu et al., 1992; Russell, 1988). These factors include differences in sampling techniques (Jacobson, 1988), differences in classification systems (Borthwick-Duffy, 1994), and differences in the comprehensiveness of rating instruments (Reiss, 1990). Reiss (1990) has suggested that low prevalence estimates were obtained in studies that relied on surveys of case files, whereas high prevalence estimates were obtained in studies that used professional interviewers.

Table 1-2 suggests a strong correlation between method and results. Of five studies that reported overall prevalence rates of 15% or less for mental health disorders, all five involved the survey of case files that had existed prior to the start of the research. In contrast, Table 1-2 lists 17 studies that obtained overall prevalence rates of 36 percent or higher. In 14 of these studies, new data were collected as part of the research study; in 12 of these studies, the new data included comprehensive professional interviews.

The data reported in Table 1-2 support Reiss' (1990) hypothesis that mental health disorders are under-recorded in case files. For every individual who has a mental health disorder recorded in his or her case file, there are an estimated two to three who have an undiagnosed mental health disorder. At least three factors may account for this apparent underdiagnosis of mental health disorders in persons with mental retardation:

1. The vulnerability of people with mental retardation to psychopathology was not fully recognized prior to the mid-1980s. Consequently, there were many people with mental health disorders who were not referred for a psychiatric evaluation. In such cases, the mental health disorder would be detected in a research study in which the subjects were interviewed but perhaps not in a research survey of historical case files.

2. There has been a severe shortage of trained psychiatrists interested in working with people with mental retardation. There were many instances in the past in which psychiatric diagnoses were not made simply because there were no available psychiatrists to evaluate the individuals. In such cases, psychopathology might be detected in a research study in which the subjects were interviewed by psychiatrists or psychologists but not in a research survey of historical case files.

3. The phenomenon of *diagnostic overshadowing* (Reiss, Levitan, & Szyszko, 1982), which is discussed later in this chapter, suggests a general tendency

to underdiagnose mental health disorders in persons with mental retardation. In diagnostic overshadowing, professionals presume that the behavioral problems of people with mental retardation are a consequence of the mental retardation rather than evidence of a separate mental illness. Because of diagnostic overshadowing, there could be many people with mental retardation who had psychiatric and behavioral disorders that were not diagnosed separately from the condition of mental retardation. A survey of the case files of such people would obtain an artificially low estimate of the prevalence of mental health disorders.

Evidence supporting the hypothesis that case file data undercount mental health disorders was obtained in a study by Reiss (1990). In this study, psychologists evaluated the mental health status of 59 people with mental retardation. About 20 percent of the sample was found to have psychopathology that had not been previously recorded in the subjects' case files. The 20 percent finding is sufficiently large to explain much of the discrepancy between prevalence estimates based on case files (about five to 15 percent) and those based on professional interviews (about 35 percent).

C1. STUDIES COMPARING PEOPLE WITH MR AND NO-MR. There is a literature dating back to the 1920s on the relationship between intelligence and neurosis. Eysenck (1943) quoted Hollingworth as having administered hundreds of IQ tests to soldiers with neurosis and finding that, in general, they had below average scores. However, Eysenck (1943) examined data on 3,000 people and questioned the validity of this conclusion, suggesting instead that people with neurosis had either above or below average IQ scores. Both Hollingworth and Eysenck agreed that there were an unusual number of people with low IQ test scores who were highly anxious (neurotic), but they disagreed regarding the numbers of people with high IQ scores.

A number of studies directly compared the rates of psychopathology for persons with and without mental retardation. The best known of these studies is the research conducted on the Isle of Wight in the United Kingdom (Rutter, Tizard, Yule, Graham, & Whitmore, 1976). This research was based on a survey of the entire population of children aged 9, 10, and 11 in the Isle of Wight. A two-step methodology was used. In Step 1, screening questionnaires were completed by teachers and parents. In Step 2, interviews and other data were collected. The rate of mental health disorders in people with mental retardation was estimated at 30 percent based on parent interviews and at 42 percent based on teacher ratings. This compared with an overall rate of only seven percent for the general population. Thus, the Isle of Wight studies found that prevalence rates were five to seven times higher for children with mental retardation than for children with

no mental retardation.

Cullinan, Epstein, and Olinger (1983) compared ratings on the *Behavior Problem Checklist (BPC)* for 146 school girls with mild mental retardation and 228 school girls with no mental retardation. All of the children were between the ages of seven and 18.9 years. The group with mild mental retardation was given higher ratings for conduct problems, personality problems, social inadequacy, and social delinquency. In a followup study, Epstein, Cullinan, and Polloway (1986) compared ratings on the *BPC* for 360 students with educable mental retardation (EMR) and 360 students with no mental retardation. The students with EMR had significantly higher scores on the *BPC* factors of aggression, attention disorder, anxiety-inferiority, and social incompetence.

Koller, Richardson, Katz, and McLaren (1983) evaluated 221 people with mental retardation, aged 22. The study classified behavior problems in terms of emotional disturbance, hyperactive behavior, aggressive behavior, and antisocial behavior. Compared to matched peer controls, people with mental retardation were found to be two and one-half times more likely to have a behavior disturbance and seven times more likely to have a severe behavior disturbance.

Dewan (1948) surveyed the records of the Canadian army for 2,055 men with mental retardation and 28,192 men with no mental retardation. The men varied in age from 18 to 40 (average 25). An equivalent IQ score was obtained from the Canadian army M test; ratings of emotional instability were made by psychiatrists who interviewed the recruits and who had access to historical data, including previous medical and psychiatric records. The study found that 47.7 percent of the men with mental retardation, versus 19.7 percent of men with no mental retardation, were rated as emotionally unstable by psychiatrists. Thus, the prevalance of emotional instability was twice as great for men with mental retardation compared with the control peers.

Two surveys of state mental hospitals found that people with mental retardation are overrepresented in mental institutions. Duncan, Penrose, and Turnbull (1936) found that 17.8% of 2,000 mental patients could be certified as having mental retardation compared with about eight percent of the total population. Pollock (1945) surveyed first admissions to mental hospitals in the state of New York during the period of 1940 to 1942. By dividing the total number of first admissions by the estimated numbers of people with and without mental retardation in the state of New York, Pollock estimated that people with mental retardation were seven times more likely to be admitted to a mental hospital.

These studies provide support for the hypothesis that people with mental retardation are especially vulnerable to developing mental health disorders. In each of the studies in which the same assessment methods were applied to samples of people with and without mental retardation, rates for psychopathology were much higher for the people with mental retardation.

C2. RESIDENTIAL SETTINGS. There has been interest in the question of challenging behavior in various residential settings. This interest was an outgrowth of priorities during the 1970s and 1980s concerning community integration and residential alternatives.

A large body of data indicates that challenging behavior increases referral to institutions and creates barriers to community and social integration (Eyman & Borthwick, 1980; Bruininks, Hill, & Morreau, 1988). For these reasons, the rate of challenging behavior is very high in state-operated, institutional environments.

B. K. Hill, Robert Bruininks, and Charles Lakin have conducted a series of comprehensive studies on the prevalence of severe behavior disorders in persons living in various residential settings (e.g., Hill & Bruininks, 1984; Lakin, Hill, Hauber, Bruininks, & Heal, 1983). This research, which was national in scope, analyzed behavior problems in terms of frequency, severity, and consequences. The data were summarized in terms of the aberrant behavior categories of *injures self, injures other people,* and *destructive to property* (Bruininks, Hill, Weatherman, & Woodcock, 1986). The research found very high rates of challenging behavior in large state-operated facilities (White, Latkin, Bruininks, & Li, 1991). Only three states had rates of less than 30 percent, whereas 20 states had rates of 50 percent or more.

Although most studies have found that rates for challenging behavior in noninstitutional settings are much lower than those seen in large state institutions, the rates are still significant. White *et al.* found that rates for behavior that is hurtful to self varied from ten percent for semi-independent living environments to 31.0 percent for group homes. Similarly, rates for behavior that is hurtful to others varied from 14.1 percent for semi-independent living to 35.6 percent for group homes. In these findings, the rates for family and foster care living arrangements were in between those for semi-independent living and institutions.

Although most researchers found higher rates for institutional versus group homes, the Cunningham and Mueller (1991) National Medical Expenditure Survey was an exception. According to this survey, in the United States on January 1, 1987, there were 80,700 people with mental retardation in state institutions and another 111,000 in other residential facilities, including approximately 45,200 in small group homes. One or more mental health problems were reported for 25.6 percent of those surveyed. Approximately equal percentages of residents of group homes and state institutions had a mental health problem.

In conclusion, the available research suggests that the symptoms of mental health disorders are seen in people residing in all types of residential programs. In most research studies, however, the highest rates have been reported for institutional settings.

C3. TYPES OF PSYCHIATRIC DISORDERS. In one of the more influential

TABLE 1-3. PREVALENCE OF SYMPTOMS IN A COMMUNITY SAMPLE[1]

GROUPING (SYMPTOM)	% PROBLEM	% MAJOR PROBLEM
Poor Social Skills		
Social Inadequacies	36.5	8.9
Maladaptive Traits		
Attention-Seeking	27.9	11.9
Dependent	18.1	7.4
Nonassertive	27.3	4.0
Severe Behavior Disorder [2]		
Aggressive	21.1	4.4
Hostile	14.2	4.4
Temper Tantrum	13.8	5.4
Anxiety		
Anxious	31.4	6.4
Body Stress	21.6	5.4
Fearful	16.7	3.9
Depression		
Crying Spells	13.7	1.5
Sadness	14.3	3.4
Schizophrenia (Psychosis)		
Hallucination	2.9	2.9
Delusion	6.9	3.9
Regressive Behavior	5.9	2.0
Other		
Drug Abuse	2.0	0.0
Sexual Problem	11.5	1.5
Suicide	1.5	0.5

[1] Based on survey of a random sample of 205 persons served by community agencies in the Chicago metropolitan area (Reiss, 1990). Data entries indicate the percent of people in the sample for whom the symptom was rated as a *current* major problem (or problem).

[2] Rates for self-injurious behavior (SIB) and stereotypies were much lower.

reports on challenging behavior, Philips (1967) summarized the results of his work with 227 children with mental retardation. All of the children and their families had been referred to the Langley Porter Neuropsychiatric Institute in San Francisco:

> At the beginning of our program we hoped to see retarded children whose intellectual deficits were not complicated by emotional disorder . . . . It was uncommon, however, to see a retarded child who presented no emotional maladjustment as part of his clinical picture (Philips, 1967, p. 67).

Philips (1967) described a number of children who showed symptoms of sadness, withdrawal, phobic fears, and other maladaptive behavior. He concluded that maladaptive behavior appeared to result from an interaction of delayed development and negative social conditions.

Eaton and Menolascino (1982) summarized the results of psychiatric work with 798 persons with mental retardation seen at the Nebraska Psychiatric Institute. The subjects ranged in age from six to 76. Using the *DSM-II* psychiatric categories, the researchers found high rates for personality disorder (27.2 percent) and psychotic reactions (29.8 percent).

Corbett (1979) surveyed all persons with mental retardation listed in the Camberwell (U.K.) register on 31 December 1971. For each subject in the survey, Corbett had nurses, supervisors, teachers or relatives rate the person on the *Social and Physical Incapacity Scale* (Kushlick, Blunden, & Cox, 1973). A mental health disorder was found for 186 out of 402 subjects, a rate of 46 percent.

Reiss (1990) surveyed a random sample of 205 Chicago-area adolescents and adults who were recipients of community-based mental retardation services. In this study, the *Reiss Screen for Maladaptive Behavior* was completed by caretakers who were familiar with the subject (Reiss, 1988*b*). The results are summarized in Table 1-3:

1. The single most prevalent mental health problem was social inadequacy, which was rated as a "problem" in the lives of 36.5 percent of the sample and as a "major problem" in the lives of an additional 8.9 percent. Thus, nearly 46 out of 100 people were rated as socially inadequate to the extent that it caused a problem or a major problem in their lives.

2. Maladaptive personality traits were especially common in the Chicago sample. Approximately 30 out of 100 people were found to show such traits to the extent that this was either a problem or a major problem in their lives.

3. Approximately one in four persons had either a problem or a major problem with aggressive behavior. Temper tantrums were rated as a "problem" or as a "major problem" for about one in five persons.

TABLE 1-4. CONSUMER DEMAND FOR SERVICES AS A FUNCTION OF AGE (N = 274)[1]

Client Age	Number of Referrals	Percent of Total
5 to 9	18	6.6
10 to 14	21	7.7
15 to 19	59	21.5
20 to 24	63	23.0
25 to 29	53	19.3
30 to 34	31	11.3
35 to 39	11	4.0
40 to 45	9	3.3
46+	9	3.3

[1] Analysis of age of consecutive client referrals to "ISDD Mental Health Program" in Chicago, Illinois during the early 1980s (Reiss & Trenn, 1984).

4. The symptoms of depressive and anxiety disorders were a major problem for about one in 20 to one in 30 people. For example, anxiety was rated as a "major problem" for 6.4 percent of the sample, whereas sadness was rated as a "major problem" for 3.4 percent.

5. The symptoms of psychosis were a major problem for about three to four percent of the sample.

6. Some rare problems included self-injury and suicidal tendencies.

In summary, the available research suggests that people with mental retardation are vulnerable to a wide range of mental health disorders.

C4. MENTAL DISORDERS VS. OTHER DISORDERS. Although some data suggest that children and adolescents with mental retardation may be more anxious or more sad than those without mental retardation, no research has been reported directly comparing the rates of mental disorders in people with mental retardation versus the general population. Presently, there is little evidence to support the commonly held opinion that mental disorders are much more common in people with mental retardation versus the general population. In fact, some mental disorders, such as panic disorder, actually may be less prevalent in persons with mental retardation compared to the general population (Jacobson, 1990).

However, there are data suggesting that people with mental retardation are especially vulnerable to maladaptive personality traits and severe behavior disorders. These data may be summarized as follows:

1. Very high rates have been reported for maladaptive personality traits among persons with IQs between 35 and 70. Craft (1959) diagnosed personality disturbances in 39 of 104 people (37.5 percent) with challenging behavior. Reid and Ballinger (1987) found evidence of mild personality disturbance in 56 percent of a sample of 100 persons with IQs between 35 and 70; the rate for severe personality disturbance was 22 percent. Goldberg, Gitta, and Puddephatt (1992) reported rates for personality disturbance of 80 percent of a community sample of persons with mental retardation seeking psychiatric treatment in Canada. As noted previously, Reiss (1990) found that maladaptive personality traits were present in as many as one in three persons served by Chicago area mental retardation agencies.

2. There is a high rate of severe behavior disorders among persons with IQs below 35. Bruininks, Hill and Morreau (1988) found very high rates of severe behavior problems in persons with mental retardation who resided in institutions: These findings included a 65 percent rate of inappropriate urination; a 32 percent rate of taking objects from others; a 33 percent rate of hitting others; and a 26 percent rate of biting oneself.

In conclusion, the available data suggest that mental health disorders are more common in people with mental retardation versus the general population primarily because of the high prevalence of maladaptive personality traits and severe behavior disorders.

C5. DEFINITION OF MENTAL RETARDATION. The definition of mental retardation may have some impact on measured rates of mental health disorders in persons with mental retardation (Russell, 1985). Specifically, rates for challenging behavior should be higher for definitions of mental retardation that include adaptive behavior versus those based on IQ alone (Borthwick-Duffy, 1994; Russell, 1985).

C6. EFFECTS OF AGE. Mental health disorders have been demonstrated across the life span (Borthwick-Duffy, 1994). Case histories have been reported for children (e.g., Simmons, 1968), adolescents (e.g., Corbett, 1979), adults (e.g., McNally & Calamari, 1989b), and elderly persons (e.g., Day, 1985; James, 1986). As shown in Table 1-4, however, Reiss and Trenn (1984) found that

about two-thirds of the consumer demand for outpatient mental health services was for people with mental retardation between the ages of 15 and 29.

Children. A number of studies have found rates of psychopathology for young children much lower than those reported for adults. This finding emerged from surveys of 76,608 case files in California and 30,578 case files in New York (Rojahn, Borthwick-Duffy, & Jacobson, in press). In a study of 583 children and adolescents, moreover, Reiss and Valenti-Hein (1994) found that mean symptom scores were significantly lower for children under the age of 11 versus children and adolescents aged 11 through 21.

In contrast to these results, some researchers reported high rates of challenging behavior in children. The Isle of Wight studies found very high rates for children aged 9, 10, and 11. High rates were reported in a number of clinical studies (e.g., Chess & Hassibi, 1970; Szymanski, 1977). However, the author could find no studies in which different age groups were directly compared and where higher rates were found for children versus adults.

Although additional research is needed before any firm conclusions can be drawn, mental health disorders appear to be much less prevalent among young children with mental retardation compared with other age groups.

Elderly. Researchers have reported inconsistent results regarding the prevalence rate of mental health disorders in elderly persons with mental retardation. Some researchers have reported high rates for elderly persons (Coyle, 1988; Davidson, Cain, Sloane-Reeves, Kramer, Quijano, Van Heyningen, & Giesow, 1992; Day & Jancar, in press; Harper & Wadsworth, 1990; Jacobson & Harper, 1989). Day (1985) found that, except for dementia, overall rates are lower for elderly persons than for other age groups. Jacobson and Harper (1989) found no differences in rates for elderly versus non-elderly people.

In the Jacobson and Harper (1989) study, questionnaires were sent to 1,000 randomly-selected facilities serving elderly people. A total of 597 questionnaires were returned. A psychiatric diagnosis was reported for 21.6 percent of the 379 people in the sample aged 55 or older. The researchers did not report a breakdown of specific psychiatric diagnoses. The presence of at least one behavior problem had been reported for 77.0 percent of the sample. There were a number of inconsistencies in the data, such as much higher rates for persons aged 60 to 74 than for those aged either 50 to 55 or 75 or higher. Nevertheless, the study provided some support for a significant rate of mental health disorders among elderly persons with mental retardation.

Depression and anxiety states occur in elderly persons in reaction to loss of a close family member or friend (Day, 1985; James, 1986). Day and Jancar (in press) summarized these reactions as follows:

Parents are the only significant persons in the lives of many older men-

tally handicapped people (McLoughlin, 1986). Separation due to infirmity or death can have catastrophic consequences (Emerson, 1977; Day, 1985; McLoughlin, 1986; Seltzer & Seltzer, 1985). The loss is often compounded by a failure to recognize the grieving process, exclusion from the funeral, and precipitous removal from the family home to alternative unfamiliar accommodation and a permanent and fundamental change of lifestyle (Ray, 1978; Bicknell, 1983). Carsrud *et al.* (1980) have pointed to loneliness and lack of social integration as important causative factors in depression and behavior disturbance in institutionalised elderly mentally handicapped people.

James (1986) studied a sample of 50 people, aged 60 or older, with IQs of 50 or less. The subjects were ambulatory and had had a continuous period of admission to an English hospital for developmental disabilities for at least twenty years. Significant rates of behavioral disturbance and affective disorder were found. In some cases, the disorders had persisted for years and even decades. In other cases, affective disorders developed following recent loss such as the death of a family member or a friend. James suggested that elderly persons with mental retardation may be especially vulnerable to loss because of low self-esteem.

Dementia is among the disorders commonly seen in elderly persons. Dementia is indicated by impairments in memory, abstract thinking, judgment, personality change, and other brain functions. Dementia added between two and 22.2 percent to the reported prevalence rates for mental health disorders in elderly persons in the studies reviewed by Jacobson and Harper (1989). Alzheimer type neuropathology, in which there is gross physical deterioration of the brain, is virtually universally present after the age of 35 in people with Down Syndrome and increases in magnitude with age (Dalton & Wisniewski, 1990).

C7. LEVEL OF MENTAL RETARDATION. Some large surveys have reported higher rates for mental health disorders for persons with mild versus severe mental retardation (Borthwick-Duffy, 1994; Jacobson, 1982*a,b*), whereas others have reported lower rates for persons with mild versus severe mental retardation (e.g., Koller *et al.*, 1983; Lund, 1985*a*; Philips & Williams, 1975). In the normative data for the *Reiss Screen for Maladaptive Behavior* (Reiss, 1988*b*), mean symptom item scores varied little as a function of mild versus severe mental retardation (Reiss, 1988*b*). In the normative data for the *Reiss Scales for Children's Dual Diagnosis,* however, mean symptom item scores were significantly higher for children with mild versus severe mental retardation (Reiss & Valenti-Hein, 1994).

Some types of mental illness are more common in mild versus severe mental retardation. For example, both mental disorders and personality disorders seem

to be more prevalent — they are certainly easier to diagnose — in persons with mild versus severe mental retardation. On the other hand, severe behavior disorders, including self-injury, seem to be more common in persons with severe versus mild mental retardation.

C8. DOWN SYNDROME. Collacott, Cooper, and McGrother (1992) evaluated the psychiatric histories of 371 people with Down Syndrome, which represented the total number of adults with that condition living in Leicestershire, England. They used the local health registry to construct a matched sample of people with mental retardation due to other etiologies. The two groups were matched on the basis of age, sex, and type of residence. The results indicated different patterns of mental health disorders in the two groups. Compared to the matched mental retardation controls, the people with Down Syndrome were more likely to have diagnoses of depression and dementia and less likely to have diagnoses of conduct disorder, personality disorder, and schizophrenia/paranoid state. The results are considered preliminary because of the lack of reliability data on the psychiatric diagnoses and the lack of objective assessment instruments. It also was possible that the two groups differed in IQ.

III. DETERMINANTS OF CHALLENGING BEHAVIOR

The research reviewed thus far suggests that mental health disorders have significant consequences, last for long periods of time, and affect a sizeable percentage of the population of people with mental retardation. At this point, we consider the research on risk factors.

Except for some rare genetic disorders that lead to both mental retardation and severe behavior disorders, researchers have not yet identified the causes of challenging behavior. It generally is assumed that for most disorders there is no single cause and that a wide range of factors is involved. A review of the research on each mental health disorder is presented in Chapter 2. The main point discussed here is that biological, psychological, developmental, and social research is relevant to understanding challenging behavior.

A. BIOLOGICAL RISK FACTORS

The search for biological determinants of challenging behavior has focused primarily on genetic and neurochemical theories. These efforts have received considerable impetus from the success of drug therapy with nonretarded populations. Findings of successful drug treatment have led to theories that psy-

chopathology is caused by specific neurotransmitter imbalances in the brain. However, causation cannot be inferred from treatment effects alone. Therefore, researchers are studying neurotransmitters and related brain processes in an effort to evaluate the various hypotheses suggested by drug therapies.

The fragile X syndrome is among the most common example of a genetic abnormality that is linked to challenging behavior (Rogers & Simensen, 1987). This syndrome is indicated by an abnormal constriction or breaking at site Xq27.3, which is at the distal end of the long arm of the X chromosome. The incidence of fragile X mental retardation is approximately one in 1,000. The fragile X syndrome has been linked to genetic predispositions to challenging behavior, autism, and learning disabilities (de la Cruz, 1985; Hagerman & Brunschwig, 1991).

The physical features of fragile X males include large prominent ears, a long face, and large testicles (Hagerman & Brunschwig, 1991; Smith, 1993). The common behavioral features are hand-flapping, hand-biting, tactile defensiveness, poor eye contact, hyperactivity, short attention span, tantrums, and physical aggression:

> In infancy . . . tantrums precipitated by environmental overstimulation are common. Transitions from one activity to another are often difficult, and by the second year, hand-flapping and/or hand-biting when the child is excited or angry is common . . . . . When speech eventually develops, it almost always has a perseverative quality . . . may include mumbling, often of tangential ideas . . . . In the preschool period and throughout grammar school, attentional problems and distractibility are a major difficulty for almost all fragile X boys. This problem is usually associated with hyperactivity . . . . . In adolescence and adulthood, hyperactivity often improves, although a short attention span is usually a persistent problem (Hagerman & Brunschwig, 1991, pp. 168-170).

Another genetic disorder that is associated with challenging behavior is *autism*. This disorder first was described by Kanner (1943), who noted three main features: an inability to relate to people, a peculiar use of language, and a strong desire for sameness. Today, autism is defined in terms of symptoms involving severe problems in the following social, language, and behavior areas (Gillberg, 1993):

1. People with autism have severe problems relating reciprocally to other people. Contrary to prior reports, they can look others in the eyes and may enjoy body contact. However, they cannot show the usual give and take in social interactions.

2. People with autism have severe problems in verbal and non-verbal communication. Although some can speak, they do not understand the meaning of language and its function as a tool for communication. They have major problems with the reciprocity of communications.

3. People with autism have behavioral abnormalities, including stereotypic movements such as hand flapping, adherence to strict routines, and difficulty adjusting behavior to meet the social demands of the moment. Self-injurious behavior is found in some cases of autism.

The prevalence of autism is between two and seven cases per 10,000 (Rutter, 1991; Steffenburg & Gillberg, 1986). Autism is associated with increased risk for challenging behavior, especially self-injury and tantrums. Although autism was once viewed as an emotional disorder and as an early sign of schizophrenia (Hutt & Gibby, 1965), today most authorities agree with Kanner's (1943) hypothesis of biological determinants (Rutter, 1991). Recent research has found that autism has a genetic basis, but the mode of genetic causation has not yet been identified (Rutter, 1991).

Recently, researchers have debated the significance of findings showing a higher prevalence of fragile X in people with autism. Some authorities have suggested that there is no important relationship between fragile X and autism (Einfeld, Molony, & Hall, 1989), whereas others have reviewed the same data and concluded that a relationship does indeed exist (Cohen, Sudhalter, Pfadt, Jenkins, Brown, & Vietze, 1991).

Asperger syndrome is a condition so closely associated with autism that many authorities consider it "high-functioning" autism (Gillberg, 1993). The individual shows severe problems in relating, communicating, and behavior. Mental retardation is usually not present. Asperger syndrome is associated with a poor psychosocial prognosis that can include bizarre crime, atypical depression, suicide, paranoia, and overall social ineptness (Gillberg, 1993).

Lesch-Nyhan syndrome is a severe behavior disturbance in people with mental retardation that is genetically determined. Lesch-Nyhan is a sex-linked disorder in which the child may demonstrate mental retardation, self-mutilation, and aggressive behavior (Lesch & Nyhan, 1964). The person self-mutilates the oral and finger areas; because the self-mutilation causes pain, the child usually welcomes restraint.

Prader-Willi syndrome is a rare chromosomal disorder associated with an insatiable appetite, which leads to excessive eating of practically anything available. The individual must be placed on a strict diet to avoid gross obesity. Most affected individuals have cognitive impairment, with IQs typically in the range of 60 to 90 (Clarke, in press *a*). The associated maladaptive behavior includes self-

injury, sleep disorders, preference for sameness, and explosive temper tantrums. Before Prader-Willi syndrome was identified, it was viewed by some behaviorists as a "bad habit" and by some psychodynamic theorists as an indicator of early insecurity (Kessler, 1988).

Recently, Clarke (in press *a*) has described three cases of Prader-Willi syndrome in which psychotic episodes occurred in adulthood. The psychotic symptoms, which were of sudden onset, included auditory hallucinations and delusions of persecution. There was no obvious social or psychological precipitating factor in any of the cases.

De Lange syndrome has been reported for a very small number of cases. It is associated with mental retardation, autistic-like avoidance and rejection of social interaction, and stereotypic behavior (Menolascino, McGee, & Swanson, 1982). It is believed to be genetically-determined, but this has not yet been proven.

B. PSYCHOSOCIAL RISK FACTORS

Psychologically, it is not difficult to understand why people with mental retardation are vulnerable to maladjustment. People with mental retardation are exposed to stigmatization and other negative social conditions for long periods of time during the developmental, adolescent, and adult phases of life. The life experiences of some people with mental retardation are a prescription for psychological maladjustment.

We need only imagine life through the eyes of a person with mental retardation to appreciate the psychological risk factors for maladjustment. People with mental retardation have been treated as objects to be avoided. They find few friends in life, especially when they live at home and other people with mental retardation do not live nearby. They are likely to be unemployed as adults. They are rarely asked for their opinions because other people erroneously assume that they are not smart enough to have opinions.

B1. PROLONGED EXPOSURE TO NEGATIVE SOCIAL CONDITIONS. The following is a list of six negative social conditions that have been reported to be common in the life experiences of people with challenging behavior (Reiss & Benson, 1984*b*).

Labeling. There are few labels more devastating psychologically than that of "mental retardation." Childish taunts of "retard" create perceptions of inferiority, difference, and exclusion. As noted by Edgerton (1967), many people view mental retardation as forever dooming the individual to incompetence in managing his or her own affairs. People with mental retardation become defensive about their competencies and try to mask their disabilities. They try to "pass" as

nonretarded. This defensiveness sometimes is reinforced by families who deny their child's disabilities (Hagamen, 1980).

Historically, the label "mental retardation" has been associated in the public's mind with "deviance" and "abnormality." For example, consider the following remarks by Walter Fernald, who was one of the pioneers of the mental retardation field in the United States:

> The feebleminded are a parasitic, predatory class, never capable of self-support or of managing their own affairs. . . . They cause unutterable sorrow at home and are a menace and danger to the community. Feebleminded women are almost invariably immoral . . . . Every feeble-minded person, especially the high-grade imbecile, is a potential criminal, needing only the proper environment and opportunity for the development and expression of his criminal tendencies (cited in Zigler, 1971, p. 238).

Rejection and Social Disruption. A number of studies have documented that children with mental retardation often are socially rejected or neglected by their peers and that feelings of loneliness are common (e.g., Luftig, 1988). This rejection was described by Philips (1967) as follows:

> The experience of entering school may present difficulties to the child . . . . The retarded child may be more vulnerable in this situation. He may tend to consider himself different and unwanted and set himself apart from others. He may be shunned and teased by his peers, called names and taunted, be the "fall guy" for the class bully and the victim of jokes. Neighbors may forbid their children to play with him. In reaction . . . he may develop a variety of symptoms of emotional disorder (p. 69).

Some recent studies have found that, although there are wide individual differences, public school children with mental retardation are more lonely than their nonretarded peers (Luftig, 1988; Williams & Asher, 1992). Additional research is needed to evaluate the degree to which this loneliness is a risk factor for depression.

In addition to the rejection and stigmatization that is experienced by the child who lives at home and attends local school, children who live in community or state-operated residential programs also experience rejection and segregation. The placement of a child in a residential program can mean diminished contact with parents, siblings, and friends. Baker, Blacher, and Pfeiffer (1993) found that about one-third of the children in residential treatment settings had

no family contact. The level of family involvement with children with challenging behavior was found to be signficantly less than for children with mental retardation and no mental health disorder or for children with a psychiatric disorder and no mental retardation.

Separation from parents is a particularly difficult psychological experience. Many children perceive separation from parents as a rejection — a child may think that he/she was "sent away" because he/she was unworthy of parental love (Kessler, 1988). Children blame themselves for the loss of parents and family, and this can be psychologically damaging for many years.

After an initial placement in a residential facility, children with mental retardation can experience a high degree of social disruption and loss when they are moved from one residential program to another (Sarason & Gladwin, 1958). Some case studies of people with challenging behavior have documented as many as 19 residential relocations by age 22 (Reiss, 1985). With each residential relocation, there is an abrupt loss of parental figures, peers, and familiar surroundings. At the moment of abrupt loss, moreover, the individual is surrounded by strangers and living in an unfamiliar setting. No wonder residential relocation sometimes is associated with behavioral outbursts.

Berkson and his colleagues were among the first researchers to document the devastating impact of residential relocations on the loss of friendships (Berkson & Romer, 1980). This work called attention to the loss of friendships that occur when people are relocated from one residential facility to another (Berkson & Romer, 1980; Romer & Berkson, 1980*a,b*). As recently as 1980 it was still common in the United States for authorities to relocate people with mental retardation without even considering the potential impact on the individual's social relationships.

Sometimes the first out-of-home placement occurs during adulthood when a parent dies. In such instances, depressive reactions to loss are possible. Depressive reactions may be indicated by sadness or by increased behavioral problems related to anger and irritability (Reiss & Rojahn, 1993).

Segregation. People with mental retardation experience varying degrees of segregation from society. This includes placement in state institutions and in other large congregate residential facilities. In these facilities, individuals live apart from society and may receive segregated services for education, health, and recreation. Although the population of persons living in state institutions in the United States has declined from 1.9 million in 1967 to under 80,000 in 1992, many persons with mental retardation still are served in large congregate residential facilities (Cunningham & Mueller, 1991).

Even people who live at home with their families may experience some significant degree of segregation. There are many community or social situations for which access may be limited; for example, the child may not participate in

little league baseball or go to summer camp with classmates. Additionally, families sometimes control the individual's access to public events in order to protect him or her or to avoid inconvenience or embarrassment.

Segregation can have severe psychological impact. The impact is recognized to be so significant that society uses segregation to punish people who commit serious crimes. In the case of people with mental retardation, the segregation first is experienced as a young child and may last in varying degrees over the life-span. Segregation may have a negative impact on the individual's social development, self-concept, and mood.

Many researchers have documented the negative effects of segregation associated with institutionalization. For example, institutionalization impairs performance on language tasks, tasks of emotional understanding, and learning tasks (Lustman & Zigler, 1982; Zigler, 1971). Institutionalization reduces self-confidence and increases the maladaptive problem-solving strategy of "outerdirectedness," which involves excessive imitation and reliance on others (Zigler, 1971).

Restricted Opportunities. People with mental retardation do not have the usual opportunities for a rewarding life. For example, the vast majority of people with mental retardation will not marry or have a romantic relationship for any length of time. The overwhelming majority will not experience parenthood. Although some people with mental retardation may obtain jobs, their opportunities are restricted. The majority of people with mental retardation will not find competitive employment or satisfying work. Unemployment is very high among people with mental retardation.

Although there are worthwhile leisure programs for people with mental retardation, the opportunities for the overwhelming majority are greatly restricted. People with mental retardation cannot drive themselves wherever they want to go. For the most part, their mobility is limited to places where they can walk or take public transportation.

The transition from high school to adult life is particularly difficult for people with mental retardation (Rusch, DeStefano, Chadsey-Rusch, Phelps, & Szymanski, 1992). When peers obtain a driver's license, start dating, and go to work or college, the person with mental retardation is left behind — no driver's license, no girlfriend or boyfriend, no college, and no job.

The restricted opportunities experienced by people with mental retardation can have significant psychological effects. The absence of romance reduces the potential social support for the individual and may lead to loneliness and depression. Unemployment can lead to boredom and impaired self-esteem. Restricted leisure opportunities can impair psychological growth.

Victimization. Mental retardation is associated with an increased risk of victimization (Edgerton, 1967). This may include physical abuse, robbery, or being taken advantage of by an employer.

Individuals with mental retardation are more vulnerable to sexual exploitation than people in the general population (Valenti-Hein & Mueser, 1990). One survey found abuse rates as high as one-fourth of women with moderate mental retardation and one-third of women with mild mental retardation. In some cases sexual abuse of women with mental retardation has been found to be associated with Posttraumatic Stress Disorder (Ryan, 1993).

One noteworthy example of abuse occurred when researchers from Harvard University and the Massachusetts Institute for Technology conducted U.S. government-funded radiation research on people with mental retardation (Healy, 1994). The subjects were recruited for a "science club" and fed radioactive cereal. People who complained that the food tasted bad were beaten into submission. Neither the subjects nor their parents were informed that research was being conducted. Although it has been suggested that at the time of the experiments the researchers were unaware that small doses of radiation could be harmful, there is no credible evidence to support this view. As one ethicist noted,

> You didn't see them doing it at the Mayo Clinic . . . . these [researchers] didn't experiment on themselves or their families. They said, "Let's round up the insane, the inane, the disabled, debilitated and vulnerable, and experiment on them." They rounded them up and put them on the altar of the Cold War (Healy, 1994).

Infantilization. People with mental retardation often are referred to as "children" even when they are adults (Philips, 1967). They have been treated inconsistently in recent years with regard to the issue of independence. The current generation of people with mental retardation were encouraged to be dependent when they were younger, but today they are encouraged to become independent.

B2. AWARENESS OF NEGATIVE SOCIAL CONDITIONS. Many people with mental retardation are highly aware of the stigmatizing experiences in their everyday lives (Edgerton, 1967; Reiss & Benson, 1984b). For example, in psychotherapy interviews people with mild mental retardation have reported sad memories of being called a "retard," being treated differently, and being viewed as incompetent (Reiss & Benson, 1984b). Whereas people with mild mental retardation can discuss stigmatization experiences in their lives, people with severe mental retardation can only react behaviorally and emotionally to episodes of being treated differently. The awareness of having been stigmatized is one of the most tragic and poignant aspects of mental retardation.

Reiss and Benson (1984b) reported a number of case vignettes in which indi-

viduals discussed stigmatizing experiences. For example, a 27 year-old woman with an IQ of 60 complained that her family "treats me like a baby." A 23 year-old man complained that he could not obtain a driver's license or go to college. A 27 year-old man with an IQ of about 65 recalled childhood experiences of being ridiculed when he took the handicapped bus to school. He also expressed significant loneliness because of his lack of romantic success. "I'm so lonely," he said, "I can see myself as an old man with gray hair — no friends, no family, all by myself" (Reiss & Benson, 1984b).

B3. INADEQUATE SOCIAL SUPPORT. Another risk factor for mental health disorders in persons with mental retardation is inadequate social support from significant others. In the nonretarded population, social support reduces stress, irritability, and sadness. The same seems to hold for people with mental retardation. As Stephens (1953) put it,

> Given ample emotional and social support, many retarded persons do live a marginally normal life without too great inner stress or community disturbance. Without this support, many such boys and girls for obvious reasons are committed to state homes in their early teens. Their defensive reactions against these failures take either an alarmingly aggressive form or lead to retreat from relationships and incapacitating passivity (p. 120).

Unfortunately, people with mental retardation have inadequate access to social support networks. Some children with mental retardation are separated from their parents and raised in community or state-operated residences. Some do not have adequate opportunity to marry and/or to develop a close personal relationship with a member of the opposite sex. People with mental retardation living at home have restricted opportunities for making friends if other people with mental retardation do not live nearby. Thus, some people with mental retardation are forced to cope with their problems without adequate emotional support from significant others.

Krauss, Seltzer, and Goodman (1992) evaluated the social support networks of 418 adults who lived at home. Although the study found wide individual variations in social support, 42.3 percent of the sample had no friends. Instead, the social support networks were comprised mostly of family members. The study provided support for the hypothesis that people with mental retardation who live at home have difficulty finding age-appropriate friends.

Many people with mental retardation who are relocated from an institution to a community residence may have difficulty finding friends (Smith, Valenti-Hein, & Heller, 1985). Schalock, Harper, and Genung (1981) found that one-third

of a sample of 27 former residents of an institution had no friends after having been placed in the community. The remainder of the sample had only one or two friends.

Williams and Asher (1992) evaluated the loneliness of 62 students with mild mental retardation and 62 students with no mental retardation. The study found that boys with mental retardation were significantly more lonely than their non-retarded peers. However, the relationship did not hold for girls.

McKinney and Peterson (1987) found that spouse support and the parent's perceived locus of control were two important factors in the stress level of parents with children with developmental disabilities. The participants in this study were 67 mothers of children aged seven to 41 months. All children had a developmental disability such as Down Syndrome or cerebral palsy. Ninety-seven percent of the participants were living with their spouses. The level of parental stress to which the children were exposed was modulated to a considerable degree by support from the spouse. In families in which spouses helped out and provided support, parent stress was much lower, and mood much higher, than in families in which spouses provided little support.

The *Reiss-Peterson Social Support Scale* is a self-report instrument designed to measure the degree of social support for adolescents and adults with mental retardation (Reiss & Benson, 1985). The scale is divided into two parts. In Part I, the subject can identify up to seven significant others (spouse, mother, father, two family members with whom he/she gets along best, and two best friends). In Part II, an interviewer asks the subject four questions about each of the individuals identified in Part I. The questions are as follows: How often do you see [name]; how often do you talk to [name] about your feelings; how much do you like [name]; and how much does [name] help you with your problems. The test-retest reliability of the scale has been estimated at .53. The instrument has been significantly correlated with informant ratings of social support (Reiss & Benson, 1985).

B4. SOCIAL SKILLS. A number of social skill deficiencies are associated with challenging behavior (Kopp, Baker, & Brown, 1992). Included are difficulty solving everyday social problems (Healey & Masterpasqua, 1992; Greenspan & Granfield, 1992; Philips, 1967), inappropriate assertiveness (Gentile & Jenkins, 1980), and inadequate leisure skills (Adkins & Matson, 1980). Difficulty solving everyday social problems has been related to maladjustment in children with mental retardation (Healey & Masterpasqua, 1992); inappropriate assertiveness has been related to problems in anger management (Benson, 1992; Wolpe, 1958); and inadequate leisure skills increase vulnerability to stress and irritability.

Generalization can be a major problem when teaching social problem solving skills to people with mental retardation. The skills that are learned in an edu-

cational or experimental situation rarely transfer to natural environments. Richard Foxx and his colleagues have been at the forefront of addressing this issue (e.g., Foxx, Bittle, & Faw, 1989; Foxx & Faw, 1992). Foxx trains people with developmental disabilities to ask themselves a set of simple questions such as, "Who should I talk to?", "Where should I look for help?" and "What should I say?" It is hoped that these self-directing questions will help mediate transfer of learning from educational to natural environments.

B5. SELF-CONCEPT. Many people with mental retardation have a negative view of themselves (Zetlin & Turner, 1984). Widaman, MacMillan, Hemsley, Little, and Balow (1992) evaluated the self-concept of a sample of 1,140 eighth-grade students stratified with regard to academic level, ethnicity, and gender. On the *Self-Description Questionnaire* (Marsh & Barnes, 1982), the students with learning handicaps were found to have less positive self-concepts than the general population of eighth graders.

People with mental retardation tend to be defensive about their intellectual disability. They may hide their disability from others and pretend to understand much more than they do. Edgerton (1967) called this behavior the "cloak of competence." Stephens (1953) noted the following:

> [A person with mental retardation] seems unable to accept the fact of his defectiveness. Denial of this handicap, like the denial of an amputation or any other painful reality, can have disastrous consequences. The denial leads the person into discussion and activities that he cannot manage and, as a result, he must marshall further defenses (p. 121).

Stephens (1953) further suggested that the self-concepts of people with mental retardation are influenced by how others view mental retardation. People with mental retardation acquire a sense of being different and may develop a fearfulness of their handicap. There may be strong feelings of inadequacy that motivate identification and closeness to others.

B6. EXPECTATIONS OF FAILURE. Mental retardation has been associated with a generalized expectation of failure (Cromwell, 1963). A vicious circle can occur in which disability leads to failure experiences; failure experiences lead to generalized expectations of failure; and generalized expectations of failure lead to additional failure experiences. The psychological outcomes can include an unsatisfying life and depression.

B7. VULNERABILITY TO STRESS. Although it is widely presumed that people with mental retardation have special difficulties handling stress, the available

research does not consistently support this hypothesis. Researchers have found few differences in how people with and without mental retardation explain a frustrating situation (Angelino & Shedd, 1965; Portnoy & Stacey, 1954; Tebeest & Dickie, 1976; Thorne, 1947). The reaction of persons with mental retardation to frustration also was evaluated in behavioral studies on extinction and nonreinforcement (Libb, 1972; Talkington & Hall, 1968; Viney, Clark, & Lord, 1973). These studies found that people with moderate and severe mental retardation reacted to frustrative nonreinforcement by increasing the rate of responses, which is similar to how nonretarded people react.

Nucci and Reiss (1988) directly tested the hypothesis that people with mental retardation are especially vulnerable to stress. In a 2 (Groups) X 3 (Conditions) factorial experiment, people with mild and no mental retardation waited to perform a counting task under conditions designed to induce stress, no particular emotional state, or relaxation. Physiological, behavioral, and self-report measures confirmed that the Stress Condition actually induced stress. Contrary to prediction, the study found that stress led to similar improvements in task performance for both groups of subjects — those with mild and no mental retardation. The authors concluded the following:

> The idea that mentally retarded people readily fall apart when frustrated or stressed might be an invalid, stereotypic conception. Although some mentally retarded people might have great difficulty handling stress, others might be able to cope very well, so that overall there is little or no association between intelligence and the capacity of handling stress. In this regard, the first author observed an incident in which a mentally retarded woman fell down while leaving the experiment. The woman bruised herself and was in obvious pain. Nevertheless, she kept her wits about her, remained calm during the ride to the university hospital, and was able to respond effectively to the physicians' questions about the incident. . . . The woman handled the stress of the accident quite well, contradicting stereotypic notions that mentally retarded people readily fall apart under conditions of stress (p. 166).

B8. REINFORCER RESPONSIVENESS. High responsiveness to various reinforcers may be risk factors for psychopathology. For example, Reiss, Peterson, Gursky, and McNally's (1986) concept of anxiety sensitivity refers to individual differences in what people believe will happen to them when they experience anxiety. People who have high anxiety sensitivity endorse statements such as, *When I notice that my heart is beating rapidly, I worry that I might have a heart attack.* People with low anxiety sensitivity believe that anxiety is an unpleasant but harmless emotion. High anxiety sensitivity should increase the effectiveness of

anxiety as a negative reinforcer and the person's risk for anxiety disorders, especially panic disorder and phobias. This hypothesis has received some support with nonretarded subjects (e.g., Reiss, 1991).

Bihm, Poindexter, Kienlen, and Smith (1992) evaluated differences in reinforcer preferences among persons scoring high on the various subscales of the *Aberrant Behavior Checklist (ABC)*. The sample consisted of 470 residents of a large state facility. The residents had mostly severe or profound mental retardation. A make-shift instrument called the *Reinforcer Responsiveness Survey* served as the measure of reinforcer preference. The study found differences in patterns of reinforcer preferences among persons scoring high on the *ABC* scales for irritability, lethargy, stereotypy, hyperactivity, and inappropriate speech.

The results of the Bihm *et al.* study are limited by a number of methodological considerations. The study found that a number of uncontrolled variables affected reinforcer preferences, including level of mental retardation and age. Other methodological shortcomings were the lack of demonstrated validity for the measure of reinforcer preferences and the need for replication. Despite these limitations, the study has value in suggesting a new and potentially fruitful area for future research — namely, the possible role of individual differences in reinforcer responsiveness in the occurrence of challenging behavior.

C. DEVELOPMENTAL FACTORS

By definition, children with mental retardation develop slowly and in adulthood do not reach the same levels of cognitive and intellectual functioning seen in the general population. Developmental researchers study the implications of these differences for psychosocial functioning and mental health disorders. For example, the point has been made many times that a description of normative psychosocial development for children with mental retardation is badly needed to understand abnormal psychosocial development.

C1. PSYCHODYNAMIC MODELS. A number of theorists have addressed the issues of psychodynamic development in children with mental retardation. Recently, Dosen (1989a, 1993a, 1993b) has authored book chapters and articles applying Piagetian concepts and theories of psychodynamic development to challenging behavior. For the most part, this work is highly technical and clinical in orientation. For example, Dosen has suggested that children with mental retardation experience abnormal differences in the rate of cognitive versus socioemotional development in a manner that increases the risk of challenging behavior. Although he has published case vignettes, Dosen has not yet published

empirical tests of his ideas.

In the 1950s and 1960s, psychodynamic theorists described people with mental retardation as simplistic and psychologically fragile. The central developmental issues were thought to be separation from parents and the development of a psychological sense of security (Hutt & Gibby, 1965). The child with mental retardation was thought to be more anxiety-prone and rigidly defensive. Denial was suggested to be the most common psychological defense used by people with mental retardation (Stephens, 1953). In particular, the child with mental retardation was thought to deny his or her own differences from others (Stephens, 1953). Feelings of inadequacy were thought to motivate clinging to, and overidentification with, significant others. Although the psychodynamic view has proven insightful at times, researchers have not yet determined if anxiety, denial, and overidentification are in fact associated with mental retardation and/or related to challenging behavior.

Levitas and Gilson (1990, 1994) have provided an updated theory of psychodynamic development. They suggested that children with mental retardation show abnormal psychological development with regard to the sense of self — the children come to view themselves as "faulty" or "broken" and as powerless compared with dominating adults. This idea that disability leads to self-perceptions of being "broken" or "damaged" is common in the psychodynamic literature. Levitas and Gilson suggested further that when the children grow older, they are so insecure they are afraid to become independent of their parents. Levitas and Gilson have theorized that the insecurity can be so significant that many children with mental retardation are afraid to try new behavior and assert themselves. To date Levitas and Gilson have not reported any empirical evaluations of their theory.

Both psychodynamic and experimental theorists have suggested that adolescence poses special adjustment difficulties for people with mental retardation (e.g., Foale, 1956; Sigman, 1985a). During this period rejection from nonretarded peers becomes more open and complete. Children with mental retardation living at home sometimes play with their nonretarded peers and are included in parties and other social events. However, teens with mental retardation rarely go on double dates or interact socially with their nonretarded peers (Foale, 1956; Zetlin & Turner, 1982). Moreover, the usual adolescent adjustment conflicts with parents over sexuality are heightened by parental concerns about sexuality in children who have mental retardation (Zetlin & Turner, 1982).

C2. PERSONALITY DEVELOPMENT. Developmental psychologists have studied the personality development of children with mental retardation. One important consequence of this work is that it has corrected influential misconceptions that mental retardation is associated with degenerate personality traits.

When scientists first studied personality development in mental retardation, there had been a long history of unfortunate stereotypic theories. In the early 1900s, for example, people with mental retardation had been described in the professional literature as immoral, degenerate, lacking in inhibitory controls, impulsive, and depraved (Zigler & Harter, 1969). They were thought to be prone to delinquent behavior and sexual attacks on others.

Over the years, scientists have proposed various maladaptive traits to be characteristic of mental retardation (Zigler & Burack, 1989). These include cognitive rigidity (Lewin, 1936), neuroticism (O'Connor, 1951), excessive attention-seeking (Zeaman & House, 1963), and disassociation between verbal and motor systems (Luria, 1963). Generally, researchers have failed to confirm theories holding that a specific trait is characteristic of all or almost all people with mental retardation. Instead, researchers have found vast individual differences in behavior among persons with mental retardation (e.g., Zigler, 1971).

In the late 1960s, Edward Zigler and his colleagues began a program of research that was to have major impact on our understanding of children with mental retardation. Zigler rejected past stereotypic views and called attention to the fact that people with mental retardation can be as different from one another as are people who do not have mental retardation (Zigler, 1971). He proposed that by itself cognitive disability is not necessarily associated with any particular personality trait. Nevertheless, Zigler observed that many children with mental retardation had common negative social experiences that sometimes led to similar personality traits:

> Over the years, Zigler's thesis on personality development in mentally retarded persons has been a simple one. The individual's experiences, in large part, shape both his or her personality development and motivational factors that characterize the individual's personality structure. By recognizing the importance of both personality-structural and cognitive-structural features, we can view the mentally retarded individual as a whole person . . . (Zigler & Burack, 1989, p. 227).

Zigler (1971) and his colleagues found that social deprivation, institutionalization, and failure can lead to a number of self-concept and motivational deficiencies. They found that children with mental retardation are "outerdirected" in that they lack self-confidence and rely on others too much when attempting to solve experimental tasks. Additionally, institutionalized children with mental retardation were found to be more highly motivated to spend time with adults than matched mental age [MA]-controls. This desire to spend time with adults may be explained as psychological compensation for the social deprivation experienced during institutionalization.

Zigler and Burack (1989) have suggested that the high rate of mental health disorders in persons with mental retardation may be related to maladaptive personality traits resulting from common negative social experiences. These traits include excessive dependency needs, excessive approval-seeking, excessive wariness of strangers, outerdirected problem-solving styles, low expectancy of success, and low aspiration level.

Zigler's findings were based on observations of performance on experimental tasks. This methodology permits an evaluation of only a relatively small number of subjects. To date, there have been no studies based on population surveys using standardized measures of personality. There is a need for future researchers to pursue such research. There is a need to develop standardized personality instruments appropriate for use with persons with mental retardation, and there is a need for epidemiological research on personality traits in persons with mental retardation.

Perhaps Zigler's greatest accomplishment is that he introduced scientific research as a basis for replacing stereotypic views of the personality of people with mental retardation. He called attention to the issues of the "whole child" — that is, the importance of social and emotional development of children with mental retardation.

C3. POOR COMMUNICATION SKILLS. A number of investigators have cited poor communication skills as a possible developmental risk factor for emotional and behavioral problems. As Mundy, Seibert, and Hogan (1985) put it,

> It is plausible that the degree to which children cannot interact effectively with peers and adults is related to the tendency to manifest the symptomatology of emotional disturbance (e.g., depression and conduct disorder). Moreover, the research discussed in this chapter (e.g., Beveridge *et al.*, 1979; Gottman *et al.*, 1975) suggests that level of communication skill is directly related to children's ability to interact effectively with others. Thus, it is reasonable to expect that individual differences in communication skills are related to emotional problems in mentally retarded childen (p. 65).

Carr and Durand (1985*a*, 1985*b*) proposed that some people with mental retardation and poor communication skills develop severe behavior disorders as a substitute means of communication. The behavior problem may communicate a need for sustained adult attention. Another possibility is that behavior problems develop as an expression of frustration over the person's difficulties in effectively communicating. These ideas are discussed in more detail in Chapter 4.

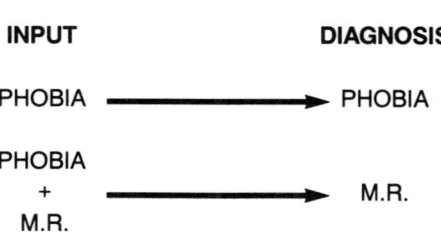

FIGURE 1-1. DIAGNOSTIC OVERSHADOWING

IV. UNDERSERVED POPULATION

People with mental retardation have been underserved with regard to their mental health needs (Reiss, Levitan, & McNally, 1982). Historically, mental illness has been underdiagnosed in this population. Paradoxically, mental retardation has been found to both increase the risk of mental illness and decrease the opportunity for mental health services. As Pollock noted in 1944,

> ordinarily, we regard the mentally ill and mentally defective as distinct groups . . . comparatively little thought is given to mental hygiene needs of mental defectives (as quoted in Nezu, Nezu, & Gill-Weiss, 1992, p.4).

Fletcher (1988) put it this way:

> The mentally retarded have been characterized as worry-free and thus mentally healthy. The severely retarded have been considered to express no feelings and therefore do not experience emotional stress (p. 255).

In 1980 Ludwik S. Szymanski and Peter E. Tanguay published an influential book entitled *Emotional Disorders of Mentally Retarded Persons*. In this book, the following was noted:

> Many mental health clinics still categorically exclude retarded people from their services (p. 4).

A. DIAGNOSTIC OVERSHADOWING

Part of the problem in developing adequate mental health services for people with mental retardation has been conceptual. When a child with mental

retardation behaved inappropriately, people generally viewed the inappropriate behavior as related to the mental retardation rather than as an indication of a separate mental illness. Hence, there was inadequate recognition of the need for services to treat mental health disorders in people with mental retardation.

The experimental phenomenon of diagnostic overshadowing lends support to the hypothesis of a general tendency to attribute maladaptive behavior to mental retardation (Reiss, Levitan, & Szyszko, 1982). As outlined in Figure 1-1, the term *diagnostic overshadowing* refers to instances in which the presence of mental retardation decreases the diagnostic significance of accompanying emotional and behavioral disorders. Just as a six-inch line appears smaller than it really is when viewed next to a ten-inch line, the debilitating effects of mental health disorders appear less significant than they really are when viewed in the context of the debilitating effects of mental retardation. Additionally, the psychological tendency to attribute behavior to the most salient factor (Bem, 1967, 1972) suggests a tendency to explain mental health disorder as a secondary consequence of mental retardation rather than as a primary disorder distinct from the mental retardation.

In the first experimental study on diagnostic overshadowing, a case description of a debilitating fear was presented to three groups of psychologists. The case described a young man who had commuted to and from work at a fast food restaurant for more than a year. One day the man took the wrong bus home, was robbed, and subsequently stopped riding the bus and lost his job. The psychologists were asked to rate the suggested fear on a number of psychological scales and to provide diagnostic impressions and recommendations for interventions.

The three groups differed only in terms of the information that was added to the basic case description. One group rated the fear for an individual who was suggested to have mental retardation; a second group rated the fear for an individual who was suggested to have alcoholism; and a third group rated the fear for an individual who was suggested to have average intelligence.

The results indicated that the same debilitating fear was less likely to be considered an example of a neurosis or an emotional disorder when the subject was suggested to have mental retardation as compared to average intelligence. In other words, the presence of mental retardation overshadowed the diagnostic significance of an accompanying abnormal behavior (avoidance of commuting causing loss of job) that is usually considered indicative of phobia. Additionally, the psychologists were significantly less likely to recommend the appropriate therapy (desensitization) for people with mental retardation. Diagnostic overshadowing also occurred for the alcoholism condition.

The results of subsequent experiments extended the diagnostic overshadowing phenomenon to cases involving schizophrenia and personality disorder

(Reiss *et al.,* 1982). The amount of previous clinical experience with people with mental retardation was found to be unrelated to overshadowing (Reiss & Szyszko, 1983). The phenomenon was demonstrated with both social workers and psychologists (Levitan & Reiss, 1983).

Goldsmith and Schloss (1984) replicated and extended the diagnostic overshadowing findings to case descriptions in which the primary diagnoses were learning disabilities and hearing impairment. They used a hypothetical case of a 17 year-old female who accidentally rode the wrong bus and ended up in an alley where she was accosted by a man. Subsequently, the woman refused to take public transportation and lost her job. The researchers found that school psychologists' ratings of this case differed when the case included a primary diagnosis of hearing impairment or learning disability versus no primary diagnosis. The school psychologists were less likely to apply the diagnosis of mental health disorder to a student previously diagnosed as having a learning disability or hearing impairment and less likely to recommend appropriate services.

Sprengler, Strohmer, and Prout (1990) reported evidence of a diagnostic overshadowing phenomenon at IQ of 58 but not at IQ of 70 or 80. Inspection of their data, however, actually shows a virtual straight line relationship in which diagnoses of schizophrenia are increasingly less likely as IQ decreases. These researchers also replicated the earlier Reiss and Szyszko finding that diagnostic overshadowing is unrelated to professional experience (as measured by the number of clients treated); however, they found that professional experience as measured by longevity in the field diminished the tendency for diagnostic overshadowing.

In comparing the Sprengler *et al.* (1990) results to the Reiss and Szyszko (1983) findings, it is important to appreciate that there was a seven-year difference in time between the studies. During this seven-year period, the occurrence of mental health disorders in people with mental retardation received unprecedented attention in the field in the form of research, numerous workshops and conferences, public policy reviews, and the publication of screening and assessment instruments. The thrust of all this activity was in the direction of educating professionals to recognize diagnostic bias and to diminish overshadowing. The Sprengler *et al.* findings are important in part because they demonstrate that, after all the efforts during the 1980s to move professionals away from diagnostic bias, evidence of diagnostic overshadowing could still be found at the end of the decade, although there may have been some diminishing of the robustness of the phenomenon.

The potential impact of diagnostic overshadowing on mental health services was summarized by Reiss and Szyszko (1983) as follows:

> Service delivery typically requires interdisciplinary staffing leading to a diagnosis of an emotional problem and a recommendation for treat-

ment, a case manager who acts on the recommendation, state administrators who recognize the emotional aspects of mental retardation to be sufficiently important to fund appropriate services, and community clinics capable of providing the relevant services. If overshadowing is interpreted as a tendency to view emotional problems in mentally retarded people as less important than they really are, the phenomenon can influence the delivery of services at any of a variety of points in the case management process. For example, even in instances in which a diagnosis and treatment recommendation are made, the service might not be delivered if the case manager assumes that the recommendation for psychotherapy is less important than the recommendation for other services (p. 401).

B. ISSUE AVOIDANCE

Diagnostic overshadowing is not the only factor that explains the inadequate degree of attention to the mental health aspects of mental retardation. Another factor concerns the natural tendency people have to avoid dealing with tragic issues.

Mental retardation is perceived by the general public as a tragedy for the individual and the individual's family. Psychologically, people try to cope with this perception by de-humanizing the person with mental retardation. De-humanization creates psychological distance between the observer and the person with mental retardation. This enables the observer to avoid having to look at life from the perspective of the individual with mental retardation. It is much less upsetting for the observer to view the person objectively in terms of behavior than subjectively in terms of the individual's feelings and awareness.

Historically, the de-humanization of people with mental retardation has taken the form of denying various aspects of psychological life. For example, it was not until the 1980s that it was recognized that people with mental retardation develop friendships. Although personal freedom and control over one's daily life are fundamental human values, it is a new idea to make them available to people with mental retardation. Even the basic human need for leisure is a relatively recent idea in the field of mental retardation.

The recognition of the emotional life of people with mental retardation is still incomplete. If anything is fundamentally human, it is the person's capacity to have feelings and to develop self-awareness of one's condition. Yet there continues to be inadequate recognition that people with mental retardation have feelings and develop self-awareness. For example, despite numerous policy proclamations demanding that people with mental retardation be recognized as

people, and despite the extraordinary attention to language, including people first language, two words that are almost never seen in reference to people with mental retardation are the words "feelings" and "emotions."

The historical tendency to de-humanize people with mental retardation has contributed to the inadequate attention to the mental health aspects of mental retardation. Since little attention has been paid to the feelings and emotional needs of people with mental retardation, inadequate attention has been paid to the occurrence of emotional disorders. It is difficult enough for many observers to accept the fact that people with mental retardation are exposed to negative social conditions for virtually their entire lives. It is that much more difficult to appreciate that many people with mental retardation have awareness of how they are treated by society (Reiss & Benson, 1984b). It is hard enough for many observers to accept the fact that people with mental retardation tend to be segregated and devalued by the society at large. It is that much harder to appreciate that many people with mental retardation have awareness of when they are being devalued, segregated, and stigmatized.

Since the early 1980s, considerable progress has been made in addressing the mental health aspects of mental retardation. Researchers have documented the occurrence of a wide range of mental health disorders. Hundreds of model service programs have been created. Although diagnostic overshadowing and issue avoidance are still important forces directing attention away from the need for more research and services, a general recognition of the importance of mental health issues exists today.

V. CONCLUDING COMMENT ON MENTAL HEALTH

Mental health should be a goal for all people with mental retardation, not just those who are having difficulties. The two main aspects of mental health are emotional well-being and rewarding social and interpersonal relationships. Emotional well-being implies a basic sense of security and a fundamental satisfaction with one's life. Good social and interpersonal relationships are important for a rich and successful life. People with mental retardation are not in any way handicapped with regard to these essential human needs and values — people with mental retardation are capable of living a rewarding emotional life.

Researchers have identified a number of key factors that contribute to mental health. Perhaps the most important has been social support and inclusive social roles. For example, Ricks and Wessman (1966) conducted an in-depth study of a person chosen for exemplary mental health. The individual was in harmony with a number of key social support units, including family, religion,

and the society at large. The individual was good-looking, very intelligent, and athletic — all of which contributed to a quiet self-confidence. The person also was motivated to achieve and to contribute to the society.

The factors that contribute to mental health are absent for many people with mental retardation. Instead of the history of success and self-confidence that was found for Ricks and Wessman's individual with exemplary mental health, there usually is a history of failure and self-doubt. Instead of the feeling that one is a valued member of society, people with mental retardation often feel excluded and devalued. Thus, even when people with mental retardation do not develop mental illnesses, their overall adjustment and mental health still can be a matter of concern.

CHAPTER 2. PSYCHOPATHOLOGY

The mental health/mental retardation movement represents a significant broadening of clinical interests in the field of mental retardation (Reiss, 1988b). Historically, clinical researchers primarily studied severe behavior disorders such as aggression, stereotypy, and self-injurious behavior. As important as this contribution has been, severe behavior disorders represent only one part of the total mental health needs of people with mental retardation. People with mental retardation are vulnerable to the full range of disorders including personality disorders, mood disorders, anxiety disorders, stress-related disorders, somatoform disorders, substance abuse, and sexual disorders. The initial goal of the mental health/mental retardation movement has been to gain recognition for the total mental health needs of people with mental retardation.

The research literature documents the broadening of clinical interests. Prior to 1980, psychologists published thousands of case studies on the treatment of severe behavior disorders in persons with mental retardation. During this same period, only a few journal articles appeared on depression, anxiety disorders, personality disorders, substance abuse, sexual variance, and stress-related disorders. As late as 1982, many mental retardation authorities questioned or denied the occurrence of depression in people with mental retardation. Since 1982, however, the field has made considerable progress. In the last decade, hundreds of journal articles, one book (Nezu, Nezu, & Gill-Weiss, 1992), and a number of books consisting of edited chapters have been published on the co-occurrence of mental disorders and mental retardation.

This chapter is intended as a comprehensive review of what is known about psychopathology in persons with mental retardation. Some of the thorny issues of the field — such as whether or not schizophrenia can occur in people with severe mental retardation — are addressed. New issues — such as whether or not some subtypes of anxiety disorders are less common in people with mental retardation — are suggested. Apart from providing many details about psychopathology and mental retardation, the chapter is intended to document convincingly the idea that people with mental retardation are vulnerable to the full range of mental health disorders.

I. DEVELOPMENTAL VS. CLINICAL APPROACHES

In consideration of the literature on mental health disorders in persons with mental retardation, it is important to appreciate that many authors are writing from one of two backgrounds. In this book, these two backgrounds will be referred to as the clinical versus developmental approaches. The clinical

TABLE 2-1. DEVELOPMENTAL AND CLINICAL APPROACHES

	DEVELOPMENTAL	CLINICAL
PSYCHOPATHOLOGY	Heavily oriented toward study of hyperactivity and disorders involving activity and motor abnormalities	Oriented toward wide range of mental disorders such as Anxiety Disorder, Mood Disorder, and Schizophrenia
ONSET	Abnormal development	Approximately normal development followed by regression
DIAGNOSIS	Aberrant behavior is identified by comparison with norm	Psychopathology is identified by comparing current behavior to premorbid (predisorder) behavior
CLASSIFICATION	Internal vs. External Disorders	DSM-IV
DISCIPLINES	Pediatrics & Developmental Psychology	Psychiatry & Clinical Psychology

approach is based on the models of adult psychopathology, whereas the developmental approach is based on the models of child psychopathology. The clinical researchers, who are mostly psychiatrists and clinical psychologists, include such persons as Robert Sovner and Johnny Matson. The developmental researchers, who are mostly developmental psychologists, pediatricians, and child psychiatrists, include such persons as Robert Bruininks and Michael Aman.

A summary of key differences between the two approaches is presented in Table 2-1. As shown in this table, one important difference concerns the concept of psychopathology. On the one hand, developmental research has been largely concerned with attention-deficit/hyperactivity (ADHD). Some authorities have estimated that ADHD accounts for as much as 50 percent of the practice of child psychiatrists and behavior pediatricians (cf. Werry & Aman, 1993). This focus helps explain why the *Aberrant Behavior Checklist* reflects a concept of psychopathology that is heavily influenced by disorders of movement and activity

level (Aman, Singh, Stewart, & Field, 1985a). In contrast, clinical research has been largely concerned with the study of mental disorders such as schizophrenia, mood disorders, and anxiety disorders. Disorders of movement and activity level account for only a small percentage of the practice of psychiatrists and clinical psychologists not specializing in children. ADHD is only one of many disorders listed in the *Diagnostic and Statistical Manual* (American Psychiatric Association, 1993). The adult version of the *Reiss Screen for Maladaptive Behavior* has only one item measuring excessive activity and only one scale measuring conduct problems (Reiss, 1988b).

Developmental and clinical researchers differ on the importance of the distinction between internalizing and externalizing disorders. Developmental researchers distinguish between disorders expressed internally, such as depression and anxiety, and disorders expressed externally, such as conduct problems and attention-deficit. However, it sometimes is possible for the same disorder to be expressed both internally and externally. An excellent example of this is the rage/despair phenomenon in which an individual's initial reaction to disability is protest and anger that eventually gives way to resignation and despair. Under the distinction between internal and external disorders, the rage/despair reaction would be considered as an "external" disorder one week (when the person shows rage) and as an "internal" disorder the next (when the person shows despair). In this example, the validity of the distinction is unclear.

Clinical and developmental researchers also differ on the importance of the concept of regression. For example, some developmental researchers have dismissed psychiatric diagnosis in people with mental retardation on the grounds that we need to know more about normative social and emotional development before we can identify abnormal development such as schizophrenia. Although the developmental researchers have made a valid point on the need for more research regarding the social and emotional development of persons with mental retardation, they carry this point too far when they dismiss the current relevance of psychiatric diagnosis. It is a myth that the psychiatric diagnosis of abnormal behavior is based largely on comparisons of an individual's current functioning with normative functioning. On the contrary, the onset of psychopathology produces a gross deterioration in functioning called a *regression*. Regressions often are easy to identify, and when they occur, psychiatric diagnosis can be based on comparisons of an individual's current and past (premorbid) functioning. If an adolescent with an IQ of 60 experiences a gross deterioration in behavior accompanied by hallucinations and delusions, a diagnosis of schizophrenia is suggested, and there is no valid reason to make the diagnosis contingent on future research findings regarding normative emotional and social development in people with mental retardation.

Both the developmental and clinical approaches to psychopathology have

validity. Whereas clinical researchers tend to be familiar with recent advances in psychopathology, developmental researchers tend to be familiar with research on cognitive and social development, the measurement of intelligence, and the diagnosis of mental retardation. Both approaches promise to contribute to our scientific understanding of psychopathology and to the development of new treatments. However, there is a need to recognize the differences between these two approaches to avoid confusion regarding what various authors and researchers are trying to accomplish.

II. ANXIETY DISORDERS

Anxiety is a normal and basically harmless emotional reaction to impending danger. It is indicated by nervousness, arousal, stress, and worry. The common signs of anxiety are as follows:

- Autonomic arousal, which is indicated by rapid heartrate, rapid breathing, sweating, muscle tension, dry mouth, and nausea;

- Behavior such as avoidance, pacing, and shaking; and

- Cognitions of apprehension, impending harm, or impending danger.

Anxiety Disorders are severe disruptions in everyday functioning caused by intense or prolonged anxiety experiences and avoidance behavior. *DSM-IV* recognizes 11 primary subtypes of Anxiety Disorders for adults (American Psychiatric Association, 1993):

Panic Disorder with Agoraphobia
Panic Disorder without Agoraphobia
Agoraphobia without a History of Panic Disorder
Social Phobia
Specific Phobia
Obsessive-Compulsive Disorder (OCD)
Acute Stress Disorder
Posttraumatic Stress Disorder (PTSD)
Generalized Anxiety Disorder (GAD)
Substance-Induced Anxiety Disorder
Anxiety Disorder Not Otherwise Specified

A. EPIDEMIOLOGY

There is conflicting evidence concerning the overall rate of anxiety disorders in persons with mental retardation. Some evidence suggests that rates are low. Jacobson (1990) reported low rates of anxiety and phobic disorders in a sample of 42,479 persons with mental retardation in New York State. Reiss and Trenn (1984) reported very low rates of consumer demand for treatment for phobias in persons with mental retardation — fewer than one percent of the people seen at a developmental disabilities mental health program had been referred for the treatment of phobia. Eaton and Menolascino (1982) reported psychoneurotic anxiety disorder in fewer than one percent of the cases evaluated. On the other hand, there are some findings that rates for anxiety disorders in persons with mental retardation are at least comparable to those for the general population. For example, Craft (1959) reported anxiety states in 10.8 percent of an outpatient sample of persons with mental retardation. Benson (1985) reported that 25 percent of a clinic sample were characterized by "anxious-depressed withdrawal disorder." Reid (1980) reported a 22 percent rate for "neurotic disorders," but it is questionable how many of these persons would have met current *DSM* criteria for anxiety disorder. Bouras and Drummond (1992) reported a 6.6 percent rate for anxiety disorders among a large sample referred for psychiatric evaluation.

One possible reason for the conflicting reports regarding overall rates is that people with mental retardation may be much more vulnerable to some types of anxiety disorders than others. For people with mental retardation, the most commonly reported anxiety disorders are simple phobia, social phobia, and perhaps generalized anxiety disorder. In contrast, there are very few reports of obsessive-compulsive disorder and panic disorder with or without agoraphobia. Posttraumatic stress disorder has been reported, but more research is needed to evaluate possible prevalence.

B. SPECIFIC AND SOCIAL PHOBIAS

Specific phobias are excessive and persistent fears of specific stimuli, such as phobias for snakes or thunderstorms, whereas social phobias are excessive and persistent fears of being embarrassed or humiliated, such as phobias for public speaking or going to parties. In either case, the person invariably experiences intense fear if the phobic stimulus or phobic social situation is encountered. Typically, phobics will go to great lengths to avoid such encounters.

Phobic and subphobic fears have been reported for persons with mental retardation. For example, Matson (1981*a*) reported three cases of long-standing social avoidance in girls with mental retardation aged 8 to 10 years. The fears,

which had been evident for at least six months prior to referral for treatment, limited the ability of the children to function at home and at school. The children scored high on the *Louisville Survey Schedule,* indicating a high level of general fearfulness.

An early research study of fears in persons with mental retardation found four primary themes: fear of separation, fear of natural events, fear of injury, and fear of animals (Guarnaccia & Weiss, 1974). Adults with mental retardation have fears that appear to be similar to those of children matched for mental age (Duff, LaRocca, Lizzet, Martin, Pearce, Williams, & Peck, 1981). Knapp, Barrett, Groden, and Groden (1992) found that the prevalence of ordinary fears in children with mental retardation was approximately equivalent to that reported for children with no mental retardation; however, these investigators also found some preliminary evidence that intense fears may be more common in children with mental retardation. The most commonly feared stimuli for children with mental retardation pertain to small animals, injury, and the unknown. Other researchers have found that persons with mental retardation can develop fears to a very wide range of stimuli. For example, researchers have reported case histories of test anxiety (Knights, 1963), bus phobia (Obler & Terwilliger, 1970), social anxiety (Chiodo & Maddux, 1985), phobia for facial and bodily hair (Rivenq, 1974), fear of heights (Guralnick, 1973), fear of community activities (Matson, 1981*b*), and fear of the toilet (Luiselli, 1977).

The *Reiss Scales for Children's Dual Diagnosis* (Reiss & Valenti-Hein, 1994) is a general screening instrument with empirically-derived, psychometric scales. The Anxiety Disorders Scale on this instrument has five items, four of which refer to specific fears and one of which measures generalized anxiety. The research on the development of the *Reiss Scales* suggests that the best way to screen for anxiety disorders in children with mental retardation may be to screen for high degrees of fearfulness (Reiss & Valenti-Hein, 1990). Screening for general stress or anxiety may be less valid, partially because caretakers have more difficulty judging anxiety than fears, and partially because a high level of stress is seen in a wide range of disorders and is not specific to anxiety disorders.

C. PANIC DISORDER

As the name implies, this disorder is indicated by the occurrence of panic attacks. The attacks must include at least four of the following symptoms: shortness of breath or smothering sensations; dizziness or faintness; palpatations; trembling; sweating; choking; nausea or abdominal distress; depersonalization; numbness or tingling sensations; hot flashes or chills; chest pain or discomfort; fear of dying; and fear of going crazy or doing something uncontrolled. The

attacks must not be a response to a specific external stimulus as in specific or social phobia. If a person also shows widespread avoidance of situations in which panic attacks are embarrassing or incapacitating, *Panic Disorder with Agoraphobia* is diagnosed. Persons with agoraphobia are so afraid of having a panic attack when alone that they may refuse to leave their home unless accompanied by a significant other.

As far as the present author could determine, there are no published cases demonstrating the co-occurrence of panic disorder and mental retardation. In response to the present author's inquiries, however, two colleagues stated that they each have seen at least one case of panic disorder, both involving women with mild mental retardation (McNally, 1993, personal communication; Szymanski, 1993, personal communication). This suggests that panic disorder can occur in people with mental retardation, but in consideration of the absence of published cases, the rate of co-occurrence may be lower than that for the general population.

McNally (1991a) has suggested that persons with mental retardation may develop panic disorder only rarely because they lack the cognitions essential for the development of panic attacks. An example of a cognitive factor strongly associated with panic disorder, but perhaps rarely seen in people with mental retardation, is *anxiety sensitivity*. Anxiety sensitivity refers to individual differences in beliefs about the consequences of experiencing anxiety (Reiss, Peterson, Gursky, & McNally, 1986). People with high anxiety sensitivity believe that anxious arousal leads to heart attacks, mental illnesses, or some other calamity such as frightening loss of control; these people endorse statements such as, *When I notice that my heart is beating rapidly, I worry that I will have a heart attack*. People with low anxiety sensitivity believe anxiety is an unpleasant but harmless emotion that dissipates over time. These people do not worry about having a heart attack, losing control, or going crazy when they notice anxious arousal.

Research on anxiety sensitivity has not yet been extended to persons with mental retardation. However, a *Childhood Anxiety Sensitivity Index* has been developed by Silverman, Flesig, Rabian, and Peterson (1991). The childhood index may be applicable for some adults or children with mild mental retardation.

D. POSTTRAUMATIC STRESS DISORDER (PTSD)

Individuals exposed to traumatic events outside the range of ordinary experience may develop the symptoms of Posttraumatic Stress Disorder (PTSD). These symptoms include a persistent tendency to reexperience traumatic events in flashbacks, intrusive recollections, play (in children), and dreams. The person shows a persistent avoidance of stimuli and symbols associated with the trauma.

Cases of PTSD have been reported for sexually abused children but not as consistently as commonly supposed (McNally, 1993). That is, there were many cases of sexually abused children who did not develop PTSD. However, the best evidence currently available suggests that sexual abuse is more likely than physical abuse to produce PTSD.

Little attention has been paid to the possible occurrence of PTSD in people with mental retardation. Heller (1982) reported PTSD-like behavior in some persons who experienced involuntary residential relocations. Ryan (1993) has made a number of professional presentations on her findings of 51 cases of PTSD in persons with developmental disabilities. The most frequent traumas in Ryan's work were sexual abuse, physical abuse, and life-threatening neglect. Ryan's work, however, is still in preliminary stages. She has not yet provided convincing evidence — such as reliable symptom by symptom evaluations made by at least two observers — that the people she has evaluated in fact suffered from PTSD rather than from depression, fearfulness, or general stress. A clearer picture should emerge when she follows up her preliminary work with a more methodologically-rigorous study.

McNally and Shin (1994) reported a study of intelligence and severity of PTSD symptoms in a group of 105 male Vietnam combat veterans. The study found that PTSD symptom severity increased as intelligence and education decreased, $r = -.33$ and $-.32$, respectively. These trends were evident even after the effects of combat exposure were held constant via the statistical method of partialling out common variance. The results provide some preliminary evidence that low intelligence is a risk factor for severe PTSD symptoms in people exposed to trauma. If these results extend to people with IQs below 70, they would suggest increased vulnerability among persons with mental retardation. Future researchers need to evaluate this possibility.

E. OBSESSIVE-COMPULSIVE DISORDER (OCD)

McNally (1991a) has described obsessions as recurrent, intrusive, anxiety-based thoughts, images, or impulses that often pertain to contamination (e.g., *Might I contract disease from touching a doorknob*) or to worry (e.g., *Did I turn off the oven*). Compulsions are repetitive behaviors and thoughts designed to reduce or to prevent anxiety, objective disasters, or both. True compulsions provide temporary relief from anxiety; they do not produce pleasure. Consequently, frequent gambling or drinking are not considered examples of OCD.

Vitiello, Spreat, and Behard (1989) surveyed 283 residents of the Woodhaven residential facility and found that ten (3.5%) could be diagnosed as having OCD. Although these data have been interpreted as evidence of OCD in people with

mental retardation, the findings are subject to alternative explanation. The rituals seen in OCD are motivated by anxiety. Because the rituals observed in the Vitiello *et al.* study had not been shown to be motivated by anxiety, the study did not demonstrate convincingly that the rituals were related to OCD.

OCD in the general population is associated with above average intelligence (Rasmussen & Tsuang, 1984). Thus, we should expect to find relatively low rates of OCD in people with mental retardation. A number of authors have suggested the possibility of low rates for obsessions and compulsions (Novosel, 1984; McNally & Ascher, 1987).

Only a few case reports of OCD in people with mental retardation have been published. They include the following:

> Matson (1982*b*) reported three men with mild mental retardation whose excessive concerns with personal cleanliness were associated with repeatedly checking clothes and personal appearance. The checking behavior interfered with performance at a sheltered workshop.

> McNally and Calamari (1989*b*) reported a case study of a 51 year-old single, white woman with an IQ of 54 who lived in a group home for persons with mental retardation. She had obsessions about contamination from other people. For example, when an interviewer extended his hand to shake hers, she became visibly anxious, withdrew, and cried out that he was "dirty." She became increasingly anxious during the interview and eventually ran to the bathroom to wash her hands. Her OCD prevented her from making friends and interfered with her productivity at work.

F. GENERALIZED ANXIETY DISORDER (GAD)

GAD is indicated by excessive and uncontrollable worry and anxiety lasting for at least six months. Although the present author could find no studies of GAD in people with mental retardation, there are a number of reports of general anxiety and stress problems. It is possible that what was diagnosed in the past as psychoneurotic disorder might today be diagnosed as GAD. If this is so, future researchers might identify rates of GAD in people with mental retardation at least equal to those for the general population. Presently, however, we need to acknowledge that we do not really know the degree to which the general anxiety and stress problems reported for persons with mental retardation can be diagnosed as GAD.

Evidence that anxiety problems are relatively common among people with mental retardation was provided by Epstein, Cullinan, and Polloway (1986). These researchers asked teachers to rate 360 students with educable mental retardation (EMR) and 360 students with no mental retardation on the *Behavior Problem Checklist*. The ratings were factored into four psychometric scales for aggression, attention disorder, anxiety/inferiority, and social incompetence. Mean scores for anxiety and inferiority problems were significantly higher for the students with EMR than for the students with no mental retardation.

Additional evidence for the prevalence of anxiety problems was reported by Knights (1963). This investigator found higher than average scores on anxiety and defensiveness scales for 128 children with mental retardation compared with 178 children with no mental retardation.

III. MOOD DISORDERS

The primary problem in mood disorders is an aberrant occurrence of "high" and/or "low" mood states. The "high" mood states are called *mania,* and the "low" mood states are called *depression*. In many cases of depression, excessive or inappropriate anger is present. Mood disorders also are called *affective disorders*. (The term "affect" refers to the subjective aspects of emotions.)

A. RECOGNITION OF OCCURRENCE

Researchers and clinicians have been slow to recognize the occurrence of depression in persons with mental retardation. This is partially because behavioral psychologists have focused on overt behavior rather than on underlying emotions. Another reason is that prior to the 1980s many psychologists thought that people with mental retardation lack the cognitive capabilities needed to become depressed (Gardner, 1967). Still another reason is that some influential researchers paid little attention to depression — Frank Menolascino's early work, for example, did not recognize the importance of mood disorders for people with mental retardation (see, e.g., Eaton & Menolascino, 1982). In the early 1980s, some mental retardation experts thought that people with mental retardation are vulnerable to psychosis but not to mood disorder.

A number of researchers published case studies and clinical data to document the occurrence of depression in people with mental retardation (Matson, Barrett, & Helsel, 1988; Reid, 1976; Reiss & Trenn, 1984; Russell & Tanguay, 1981; Szymanski & Biederman, 1984). Matson (1982*a*) reported the first treatment studies using applied behavioral techniques, and Reiss and his

colleagues reported the first psychopathology studies (e.g., Reiss & Benson, 1985). Dosen (1990*a*) has written extensively on mood disorders in both children and adults from the viewpoint of developmental theory. Sovner and Hurley (1983*c*) published a scholarly review that helped establish the fact that people with mental retardation are vulnerable to mood disorders.

B. MOODS

The chief sign of depressed mood is sadness/melancholia. Depressed people also have very low self-esteem and tend to endorse extreme statements such as "I am ugly," "I am incompetent," "I am worthless," and even "I am so worthless I should be killed." They lose interest in formerly enjoyable activities — almost nothing interests them anymore, and they do not want to go anywhere or do anything. They are so preoccupied with their own misery that they show little interest in others. They have low energy and become tired very easily. They show eating disturbances such as a poor appetite or overeating. Changes in usual sleep patterns include difficulty falling asleep, difficulty staying asleep, or oversleeping. Negative thinking is pervasive. Depressed people have a negative view of themselves ("I am worthless"), the future ("things will never get better"), and the environment ("the world stinks; everything is rotten").

The chief signs of mania are sudden bursts of euphoria indicated by excessive activity. The individual may be overly optimistic and overly confident to the point of grandiosity. The individual may be overly talkative and may experience racing thoughts (flight of ideas). Other signs of mania are expansive mood, irritability, excessive seeking of pleasurable activities, distractibility, and a decreased need for sleep.

C. TYPES

The three main types of mood disorder are dysthymia, major depression, and bipolar disorder:

> *Dysthymia* is a chronic state of mild to moderate depressed mood that lasts over an extended period of time. Under *DSM-IV,* a diagnosis of dysthymia can be made only if the mild depression lasts for one year in the case of adolescents and children and for two years in the case of adults.

> In *Major Depression* there is severe sadness, a loss of interest in formerly pleasurable activities, and a disturbance of sleep, appetite, energy level,

and activity level. Major depression is an episode of severe depression lasting two weeks or longer.

Bipolar Disorder is indicated by episodes of mania. The mood swings may include manic and normal phases or manic and depressive phases. When four or more episodes of mood swings occur in a given year, the condition is called *rapid cycling* mood disorder.

Another disorder involving significant disturbance of mood is *schizo-affective disorder*, which is indicated by a combination of psychotic and affective symptoms. This disorder is less common than dysthymia, major depression, or bipolar disorder.

The terms *psychotic depression, neurotic depression, endogenous depression,* and *reactive depression* are no longer used. The old concept of neurotic depression is perhaps most similar to today's concept of dysthymia.

C1. EPIDEMIOLOGY. The prevalence of mood disorder is about three to four percent of the general population (Myers *et al.*, 1984). Dysthymic disorder and major depression are much more common than bipolar disorder, which is relatively rare at a prevalence of about one in every 165 persons (Myers *et al.*, 1984).

Estimated overall rates of mood disorder in persons with mental retardation are roughly equivalent to rates found for the general population (Corbett, 1979; Gostason, 1985; Lund, 1985a; Meins, 1993b). Reiss' (1990) Chicago survey found that sadness was rated as a "major problem" for 3.4 percent of the sample. Meins (1993b) reported a rate of 4.8 percent for *DSM-III-R* depressive disorders for a sample of 798 people with mental retardation in the Hamburg, Germany, metropolitan area.

Although overall rates for mood disorders seem to be about equivalent for people with and without mental retardation, some preliminary evidence has been reported that symptoms of depression and stress may be more common in children with mental retardation. Schloss, Epstein, and Cullinan (1988) reported greater evidence of depressed mood in a large sample of school children with mental retardation versus a large sample of school children with no mental retardation. The results of this study are only preliminary, however, because the rating scale was not specific for the assessment of depression. For example, items such as feelings of inferiority, crying, shyness, daydreaming, and fixed expression either are poor indicators of depression or may indicate other disorders.

A number of mental retardation researchers have reported evidence that depression is more common among females than males. Reiss and Trenn (1984) found that females with depressive mood were proportionately overrepresented

in an outpatient clinic sample compared to males with depressive mood. Reid and Ballinger (1987) found that females with both affective disorder and IQs between 35 and 70 were overrepresented in a hospital sample compared with males. Reiss (1988b) reported that women had significantly higher scores than men on the Depression (Behavioral Signs) Scale of the *Reiss Screen*. Reiss and Valenti-Hein (1990) found that girls scored higher than boys on the children's *Reiss Scales*, but the difference was not statistically significant. Meins (1993b) found that being female was a risk factor for dysthymia.

C2. PRESENTATION IN MENTAL RETARDATION. The cognitive signs of depression — such as hopelessness and negative thinking — can be difficult to assess in persons with IQs below 50. In such cases, a number of clinicians have suggested focusing instead on the behavioral and vegetative signs of depression (Dosen & Gielen, 1993; Sovner, 1986; Szymanski & Biederman, 1984). A general consensus seems to have been reached that behavioral and vegetative symptoms usually are sufficient to permit a confident diagnosis of mood disorder.

Psychometric support for diagnosing depression based on noncognitive symptoms was provided by Reiss (1988b), who successfully developed and validated two rating scales for assessing depression in persons with mental retardation. On the *Reiss Screen*, the psychometric scale Depression (P) evaluates physical symptoms such as eating problems, sleep problems, and low energy, whereas the psychometric scale Depression (B) evaluates behavioral symptoms such as sadness, anxiety, irritability, and crying spells. Reiss (1988b) demonstrated the factorial independence of the Depression (P) and Depression (B) scales using a data base that included both depressed and nondepressed people at all levels of mental retardation from profound to mild.

Charlot, Doucette, and Mezzacappa (1993) evaluated two groups of 30 residents of a large state facility. One group had been diagnosed by a psychiatrist as having affective disorder, and the other group had been diagnosed as having mental health disorders other than affective disorder. The investigators interviewed staff regarding the presence versus absence of *DSM-III-R* criteria. They found that the Affective Disorders Group was significantly more likely to have poor appetite, increased fatigue, increased withdrawn behavior, and more episodic behavior.

A number of authors have discussed the difficulties of diagnosing bipolar disorder in persons with severe mental retardation, who cannot self-report their mood (Berney & Jones, 1988; Reid & Naylor, 1976). It has been suggested that in such cases diagnoses should focus on genetic history, irritability, changes in activity levels, changes in sleep patterns, and the loss of developmental skills such as continence.

Einfeld and Wurth (1989) have questioned the validity of diagnosing bipolar disorder based on activity alone. They have suggested that facial appearance,

interest in activities, social responsiveness, somatic complaints, the cognitive content of play, and the full range of the vegetative symptoms of depression should be taken into account. These authors also have questioned the diagnosis of atypical bipolar disorder on the grounds that *DSM-III* rules out a diagnosis of bipolar disorder if the symptoms are due to organic factors.

Reid (1972*a*, 1976) reported cases of affective disorder with psychotic symptoms in people with mental retardation. He noted that some of the people did not complain of feeling depressed and some had attempted suicide. Reid and Naylor (1976) described cases with short or rapid cycling bipolar disorder. As previously noted, *DSM-IV* permits the use of the phrase "rapid cycling" when at least four discrete manic episodes have occurred within the last 12 months.

Szymanski and Biederman (1984) reported case studies of depression in persons with Down Syndrome. Included was a case of anorexia nervosa in which there was extreme weight loss caused by a refusal to eat. Szymanski and Biederman (1984) also cited unpublished data by Szymanski and Doherty in which there were six cases of affective disorder in people with mild/moderate mental retardation and nine cases of affective disorder in people with severe/profound mental retardation.

Sovner and his colleagues have suggested that persons with Down Syndrome are unable to develop full-blown mania because Down Syndrome affects the neurotransmitter systems that mediate mania (Sovner, Hurley, & Labrie, 1985). Although Sovner (1991) published some case studies to support his views, his hypothesis has been contradicted by recently published cases of mania in people with Down Syndrome (e.g., Collacott, Cooper, & McGrother, 1992; Cooper & Collacott, 1991).

Dosen and Gielen (1993) discussed the impact of developmental level on the presentation of mood disorders. They have suggested the importance of poor communication and expressive skills in the occurrence of frustration, irritability, and depression. They also have suggested that depression in adults with mental retardation may be similar to depression in children with no mental retardation.

Kaminer, Feinstein, Barrett, Tylenda, and Hole (1988) have noted that there are only a few case reports of menstrually-related mood disorders in women with mental retardation. They concluded that this disorder has been largely overlooked and called for greater alertness on the part of the clinician. They also suggested a need for research on this disorder and the development of appropriate assessment instruments.

C3. RESEARCH. The occurrence of depression in people with mental retardation has been linked to conduct problems, poor social skills, and poor social support.

Persistence of Depression. Laman (1989) studied the mood of 36 adults with mental retardation over periods varying between 14 and 30 months (average 21.9 months). The subjects had been selected from either sheltered workshops or a developmental disabilities mental health clinic. The study found a .4 correlation between depressed mood at Time-1 and depressed mood at Time-2. The statistically significant correlation was obtained despite administration of drug and behavioral treatments between Time-1 and Time-2. The findings suggest that for some people depressed mood can persist over periods of at least two and one-half years. For others, there may be substantial variations in mood over time. Because of the small number of subjects in the Laman study, the results should be regarded as preliminary.

Depression and Aggression. The hypothesis that some instances of aggressive behavior may be motivated by depression has been suggested by a number of theorists (e.g., Dosen & Gielen, 1993; Reiss & Rojahn, 1993). Anger and irritability are present in both aggression and depression. In the protest-despair reaction to loss, for example, anger and irritability give way to depression (Suomi, Eiselle, Grady, & Harlow, 1975). Since anger increases irritability, it can lead to aggression, conduct problems, or antisocial behavior. Anger also is present in depression; in fact, some psychoanalysts have described depression as anger/aggression turned against the self (Abraham, 1911).

Evidence that some aggressive incidents may be motivated by depression has been provided by both clinical observations and scientific research. Sovner *et al.* (1993) have reported observations of depression in some persons with conduct problems. Laman and Reiss (1987) found significantly higher levels of antisocial behavior for depressed people with mental retardation versus nondepressed people with mental retardation. The depressed people were significantly more likely to react with excessive anger, take advantage of others, threaten others verbally or physically, get into arguments, manipulate others, and deceive others for personal gain.

Reiss and Rojahn (1993) evaluated the relationship between aggression and depression in 528 adults, adolescents, and children with mental retardation. The subjects had been rated on either the adult or child versions of the *Reiss* instruments for psychopathology in persons with mental retardation. Criterion levels of aggression were found in 40.4 percent of the depressed subjects, but in only 9.9 percent of the nondepressed subjects. For both children and adults, the presence of depression was associated with a fourfold increase in criterion levels of conduct problems and aggressive behavior.

Reiss and Rojahn also found that anger mediated the joint occurrence of depression and aggression. Anger was significantly correlated with both aggression and sadness. However, anger alone did not explain all of the correlational variance between aggression and depression. When the effects of anger were statistically controlled, aggression and depression were still significantly correlated.

FIGURE 2-1. Interrelationships among depressed mood, poor social support, and poor social skills.

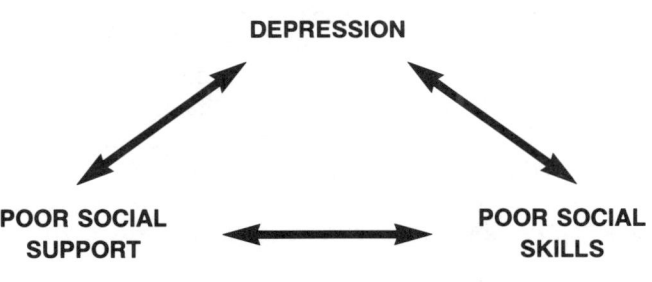

The results suggested that anger is only one of a number of factors that mediate the relationship between aggression and depression.

Meins (1993*b*) found that scores on a modified, German-language *Children's Depression Inventory* (*CDI*; Kovacs, 1981, 1985) were correlated at -.33 with "behavior problems." This finding, which is very similar to the one reported by Reiss and Rojahn (1993), was obtained in a sample of 798 adults in German programs, mostly community-based facilities. The adults with higher *CDI* depression scores had an increased occurrence of some type of behavior or conduct problem.

Benson and Ivins (1992) investigated the relationship among anger, self-concept, and depression for a sample of 130 adults with moderate to mild mental retardation. The study found that depression was related to low self-esteem but not to anger. The absence of a finding regarding anger is inconsistent with the results reported by Reiss and Rojahn (1993). Future research is needed to explore this issue in more detail.

Social Support and Social Skills. Schloss (1982) observed nine depressed and nine nondepressed adult residents of a large mental retardation facility. He found a number of differences in how others interacted with the depressed people. Both staff and peers were less likely to approach the depressed people when there was no specific purpose to the interaction. Avoidance of depressed people can be explained by the fact that it usually is unpleasant to interact with someone who is depressed. Schloss' (1982) findings are consistent with clinical descriptions of depressed people as lonely and socially isolated (Coyne, 1976).

Reiss and his colleagues evaluated the psychosocial correlates of depressed mood in 28 adults with both mental retardation and mental illness and 17 adults who had mental retardation but no mental illness (Reiss & Benson, 1985; Benson, Reiss, Smith, & Laman, 1985). All of the subjects had IQs above 55. The study found that depressed mood was significantly correlated both with low levels of social support and with poor social skills. Evidence also was obtained that

low levels of social support were associated more strongly with depression than with psychopathology in general.

Laman and Reiss (1987) identified some specific social skills deficits that are associated with depressed mood. The subjects were 45 adults with mild mental retardation recruited from either a sheltered workshop or a developmental disabilities mental health outpatient clinic. Compared with the nondepressed people, the depressed people were rated as follows:

preoccupied — they were rated as significantly less likely to get to know others, show appreciation, or show enthusiasm for others' good fortunes;

withdrawn — they were rated as significantly less likely to stay in touch with friends, to make small talk, to help others, or to share responsibility;

insecure — they were rated as significantly more likely to stay too long with others and to put themselves down;

angry — they were rated as significantly more likely to become angry easily, overreact, and get into arguments;

antisocial — they were rated as significantly more likely to manipulate others, to deceive others, and to threaten others verbally or physically.

In a follow-up study, Laman (1989) reevaluated 36 subjects 14 to 30 months after initial assessment. Using sophisticated path analysis statistical techniques, Laman demonstrated that depression, poor social skills, and low levels of social support were correlated over time periods of up to two and one-half years. The hypothesis that best explained the various correlations was that poor social skills was a risk factor for both low levels of social support and depressed mood. Theoretically, poor social skills should lead to low levels of social support, and being alone should lead to depressed mood.

Meins (1993b) found low levels of social support in a group of 38 adults with both a depressive disorder and mental retardation. After a series of multiple regression analyses, Meins (1993b) concluded that, "low social support is specific to depression and not characteristic of behaviour problems in general" (p. 152).

Learned Helplessness. The concept of learned helplessness originally referred to an experimental phenomenon in dogs. When dogs are exposed to preexperimental trials of inescapable electric shock, they become passive and are slow to

learn how to escape future electric shocks when such escape becomes possible. It is as if the pretraining had taught the dogs that there is nothing they can do to escape from electric shock.

Seligman applied the concept of learned helplessness to depression in humans. He proposed that exposure to uncontrollable negative events (such as failure) leads to both learned helplessness and depression (Seligman, 1975). According to this theory, the central feature in depression is a fatalistic belief that there is nothing one can do to control the important events in one's life. This implies that depressed people believe that important outcomes are independent of their effort and behavior. It was proposed that this belief produces the passivity and sadness seen in depression.

A number of researchers have suggested that the concept of learned helplessness is relevant to understanding the experiences of people with mental retardation (Reynolds & Miller, 1985; Weisz, 1979, 1982). Specifically, people with mental retardation have many failure experiences in their everyday lives. Under the concept of learned helplessness, frequent failure experiences may cause people with mental retardation to believe that there is nothing they can do to succeed. Theoretically, this should lead to passivity, sadness, and a tendency to quit easily at the first signs of difficulty in achieving any goal.

Unfortunately, numerous tests of the learned helplessness model of depression have been negative, yielding results inconsistent with the theory. Today, the learned helplessness theory of depression is widely regarded as problematical (see Gargiulo & O'Sullivan, 1986; Huesmann & Morikawa, 1985). This negative opinion prevails despite a number of major attempts at revision of the original theory (e.g., Abramson, Seligman, & Teasdale, 1978). Some of the problems with the learned helplessness model of depression are as follows:

- Depressed people tend to blame themselves when things go wrong when, according to learned helplessness theory, they should perceive success and failure as unrelated to their behavior.

- The induction of learned helplessness in psychological experiments with human subjects does not produce depression or sadness (Huesmann & Morikawa, 1985).

- The learned helplessness theory is too simplistic to explain the many ways in which cognitive factors modify people's reactions to failure.

Although the learned helplessness model of depression is no longer influential among psychopathology researchers, one encouraging line of research to emerge from this tradition is Dweck's (1988) theory of task motivation (Dweck & Leggett, 1988).

Dweck has identified several factors that lead children to quit tasks at the first signs of difficulty. Her theory holds that children differ in their concepts of intelligence as an unchanging (fixed) versus incremental trait. Those who think intelligence is a fixed trait tend to quit at the first signs of difficulty — that is, these children interpret difficulty as evidence that they are incapable of successfully completing the task. In contrast, when children who think that intelligence is incremental encounter difficulty, they increase their effort in the expectation that they are being challenged and have an opportunity to learn and to grow.

The implications of Dweck's theory for mental retardation have yet to be tested. Since the theory addresses individual differences in reaction to task difficulty, it would seem to have potential relevance to the education of children with mental retardation. According to this theory, children who quit easily tend to expect failure. They lack confidence in their ability; they believe they are unintelligent; and they believe that there is nothing they can do to be more successful. If these children can be taught to believe that greater effort will lead to greater success, they may persist longer on educational tasks.

In conclusion, beliefs in fixed traits such as intelligence and expectations of failure may have implications for special education and for how individuals respond to challenging tasks. However, these beliefs do not have the implications for depression that Seligman's theory once predicted. People who quit easily and expect failure often are not depressed. The learned helplessness phenomenon may have relevance for understanding task motivation, but it is not a good model for understanding depression.

Aging. Depression can lead to a decline in cognitive functioning that might be mistaken for a decline related to the aging process (Janicki & Wisniewski, 1985). For example, Harper and Wadsworth (1990) used the term "pseudo-dementia" to refer to cases of depression that were misdiagnosed as dementia. Presently, researchers are attempting to develop ways to help evaluate when cognitive decline is associated with depression, versus aging, in persons with mental retardation.

IV. SUICIDE

Suicide in the general population occurs for a number of reasons: to escape from hopelessness (Beck, 1963; Schuyler, 1974); to get back at others (Shneidman, 1968); to gain attention or fame; altruism, as exemplified by a suicide intended to help one's family collect on a life insurance policy (Durkheim, 1897); and compliance with cultural norms, as exemplified by the Japanese kamikaze pilots during World War II.

It is estimated that about one percent of the population has attempted sui-

cide at some point in their lives (Bootzin & Acocella, 1988). The possibility of suicide always is an issue when mood disorders are present.

A. EPIDEMIOLOGY

In a survey of 205 people with mental retardation, Reiss (1990) found that three people were rated as having a "problem" with suicidal tendencies and that one additional person was rated as having a "major problem." Additional research is needed to follow up on these preliminary findings. Moreover, researchers need to evaluate carefully the possibility that some suicides by persons in residential facilities are being inaccurately recorded as accidental deaths.

B. PRESENTATION IN MENTAL RETARDATION

A number of clinicians have published case studies of suicidal behavior in persons with mental retardation (Barrett & Walters, 1992; Grossi & Brown, 1985; Kaminer, Feinstein, & Barrett, 1987; Menolascino, Lazer, & Stark, 1989; Sternlicht, Pustel, & Deutsch, 1970). These case reports, when coupled with findings that young children are capable of suicidal intent (Hollinger, 1979), suggest that greater attention should be paid to suicidal gestures in persons with mental retardation. As Kaminer *et al.* (1987) put it,

> Low I.Q., the most prominent single factor that differentiates mentally retarded from non-mentally retarded psychiatric patients, may prevent a premeditated and sophisticated suicide attempt, but many suicide attempts are impulsive in nature and therefore do not require elaborate planning (p. 92).

C. RESEARCH

Benson and Laman (1988) compared 22 suicide attempters or ideators with 22 control subjects. The suicide group consisted of persons with IQs in the 60 to 80 range. There were few differences between the suicide and control subjects in terms of demographic variables except that women were overrepresented in the suicide group. All of the subjects were outpatients at a developmental disabilities mental health clinic. Problems with anger and depression were greater for the suicide group than for the control group. Half of the people

in the suicide group made more than one attempt. The most common precipitating factors were problems at school, problems at work, and problems with a girlfriend or boyfriend.

V. SCHIZOPHRENIA

The concept of schizophrenia has undergone a number of changes in the last 130 years. One of the earlier ideas was that of a psychosis beginning in adolescence. This idea dates back to 1860 when the French physician Morel used the term *demence precoce* to describe a case of "stupidity" that degenerated into psychosis. From this phrase, the term *dementia praecox* came into use, indicating that the psychosis was an illness of youth.

In 1896 the great German psychiatrist Kraepelin published case studies and statistical charts to distinguish between two major categories of psychosis. One type was called *dementia praecox*, which is now called *schizophrenia*, and the other was called *manic-depressive illness*, which is now called *bipolar disorder*. According to Kraepelin, the key symptoms for a diagnosis of dementia praecox were hallucinations (false sensory perceptions such as hearing voices), thought disorder (extremely confused, disconnected, or altered ideas), delusions (firmly held false beliefs such as the belief that others are out to get you), emotional blunting (expressionless; restricted range of emotions), and impaired judgment. Although Kraepelin's description of schizophrenia still is regarded as basically accurate, what is remembered most about his work is that he clearly distinguished between thought disorder (schizophrenia; dementia praecox) and mood disorder (bipolar disorder; manic-depression).

In 1911 Bleuler introduced the term *schizophrenia* to replace the term *dementia praecox*. Bleuler argued that the term *dementia praecox* was a misnomer because the disorder is not always premature — many people do not develop the disorder until well into their adult years. Bleuler introduced the term schizophrenia, which means split soul, to suggest that the central feature is the disorganization of personality functioning. In schizophrenia, the person's thoughts, feelings, and perceptions become disorganized and poorly integrated with each other.

Schizophrenia should not be confused with multiple personality disorder — the two disorders are very different from one another. The central problem in multiple personality disorder is that the person has more than one personality; the central problem in schizophrenia is that the person has no well-functioning personality. Schizophrenia is much more common than multiple personality disorder, which some authorities believe to be quite rare.

Schizophrenia is a psychosis. The concept of psychosis implies that the person's behavior is out of touch with reality; that is, in psychosis there is a significant mis-match between objective circumstances and the person's thoughts, feelings, and perceptions. Examples of psychotic behavior include: smiling when angry; hearing voices that are not there; inadequately distinguishing between fantasy and reality; laughing over matters that are serious to others; experiencing depression and guilt over something that never happened; and having ideas of reference (the delusion that events are centered around oneself) and omnipotence (the delusion of being all powerful).

Between 1950 and 1975 hundreds of psychological studies were published documenting the features of schizophrenia (see Reiss, Peterson, Eron, & Reiss, 1977, for a literature review). In any given case, only some of the following features may be present:

- Cognitive features include the presence of delusions, deficits in memory, and the use of overinclusive concepts.

- Communication features include bizarre speech, made-up words, word salad, and informationally redundant speech.

- Perceptual features include hallucinations, attention deficits, and impaired judgment of time. The most common hallucinations are auditory, such as hearing voices. Attention deficits include inattentiveness to other people and the social environment.

- Emotional features include flat or blunted affect (such as rarely smiling), inappropriate affect (such as giggling when remembering a painful experience), and intense resentment and impulsivity.

- Social features include social withdrawal, poor social skills, disdain for social conventions, and strange or bizarre behavior. Severe withdrawal to the point of virtual nonresponsiveness is called *catatonia*.

Researchers have established that schizophrenia has a genetic basis (see Bootzin, Acocella, & Alloy, 1993; Reiss *et al.*, 1977). Brain researchers have identified a number of possible neurotransmitter abnormalities, particularly abnormalities in dopamine.

The onset of schizophrenia is indicated by a gross deterioration in functioning called a *regression*. Typically, the individual presents with deteriorated self-care and is unkempt. Although schizophrenia often develops in adolescence and young adulthood, some cases develop well into adulthood.

Over the years, the formal criteria for diagnosing schizophrenia have changed a number of times. Bleuler suggested that the primary feature of schizoprhenia is thought disorder and that hallucinations and delusions are only secondary features. *DSM-III-R,* however, required the presence of hallucinations and delusions for a diagnosis of Schizophrenic Disorder. In *DSM-IV,* schizoprehnia is diagnosed when any two of a list of five primary symptoms are present for a significant portion of time during a one month period. The five symptoms are:

Hallucinations.
Delusions.
Disorganized Speech.
Grossly Disorganized or Catatonic (withdrawn) Behavior.
Negative Symptoms (e.g., affective blunting).

Using *DSM-IV,* it is possible to diagnose schizophrenia without being able to determine if hallucinations and delusions are present.

A. EPIDEMIOLOGY

Estimates of the lifetime prevalence of schizophrenia in the general population have been decreasing. In the 1970s, the most common estimates were three to four percent of the population of the United States (e.g., Heston, 1970). By the 1980s, most estimates were about one to two percent (Bootzin, Acocella, & Alloy, 1993). Today, it is estimated that at any given time, the prevalence of schizophrenia is about one percent or less of the U.S. population.

The prevalence of schizophrenia among persons with mental retardation has been variously estimated at between one and three percent (Reid, 1993*b*). Since these estimates are based on studies of populations that likely overrepresent people with psychopathology, the true prevalence rate might be one percent or less. The lifetime prevalence has not yet been estimated for people with mental retardation.

B. PRESENTATION IN MENTAL RETARDATION

During the middle of the nineteenth century, a number of eminent European physicians maintained that insanity and mental retardation were caused by a "tainted heredity" (Zilboorg & Henry, 1941). The French physician Morel (1809-1873), a leading exponent of this view, developed detailed tables of diagnostic signs for identifying the presence of hereditary weaknesses. One such weakness was the "degenerative trait"; specifically, it was held that in each suc-

cessive generation of a degenerative line, the manifest symptoms of the tainted heredity become progressively more debilitating. The theory of a degenerative trait holds that mental retardation and psychosis are two variations of the same disease process.

In 1888 Hurd distinguished between insanity and mental retardation. He held that insanity could be recognized in people with mild mental retardation but not in people with severe mental retardation. In the early 1900s Kraepelin suggested that autism was a special type of psychosis called "pfropfschizophrenie." However, he later abandoned this view and held that autism is not a form of schizophrenia. Today, autism and schizophrenia are known to be distinct disorders.

The view that psychosis and mental retardation are distinct disorders is widely accepted today. The possibility of co-morbidity, however, has been a matter of some dispute. Although it generally is accepted that people with mild mental retardation are vulnerable to schizophrenia, some psychiatrists have argued that schizophrenia cannot be diagnosed in people with severe or profound mental retardation. In the past, the basis for the argument concerned the difficulties of identifying hallucinations and delusions in people who cannot self-report them due to severe mental retardation. However, other issues merit consideration, such as the impact of low intelligence on the expression of certain fundamental symptoms of schizophrenia. For example, how can we recognize the symptoms of cognitive dysfunctioning, thought disorder, hallucinations, and delusions in people with severe mental retardation?

C. SCHIZOPHRENIA AND MILD MENTAL RETARDATION

Schizophrenia in people with mild mental retardation presents much like it does in the general population, except that delusions and hallucinations may be more simplistic and unimaginative. Adolescents and adults with mild mental retardation are capable of self-reporting hallucinations and delusions, but they also can report fantasies that are easy to mistake for hallucinations or delusions (see Chapter 3). For example, Szymanski (1980b) reported the case study of a boy who invented an imaginary friend because he was lonely. The boy knew the friend was imaginary, and he showed no other features of schizophrenia. In this case, Szymanski did not consider the imaginary friend to be an hallucination.

D. SCHIZOPHRENIA IN SEVERE MENTAL RETARDATION

Since psychiatrists rely on self-reports to identify hallucinations and delusions, some psychiatrists have suggested that schizophrenia cannot be diagnosed

in people with IQs below 50 (Herskovitz & Plesset, 1941; Reid, 1972b, 1980b, 1993a). In advancing this position, Reid (1993b) cited Batchelor (1964):

> The diagnosis of schizophrenia is clinical and based on various symptoms which tend to be language-based. The significance of these symptoms has to be evaluated against the background of previous personality, the mode of onset of the disability, and the course of the illness. The main symptoms include ideas of influence, made experiences, auditory hallucinations, thought disorder, primary delusions and abnormalities of affect and of motility.

Some authorities disagree with Reid's position and hold that schizophrenia can be diagnosed in persons with IQs below 50. These authorities maintain that schizophrenia can be diagnosed based on psychotic symptoms other than hallucinations and delusions. These symptoms include regression, withdrawal, emotional blunting, inappropriate affect, poor social skills, attention deficits, and possibly some of the newly identified biological markers (Clarke, in press b).

Changes in the definition of schizophrenia from *DSM-III-R* to *DSM-IV* favor the position that schizophrenia can be diagnosed in people with severe mental retardation. As noted previously, in *DSM-IV* it no longer is essential that hallucinations and delusions be present for a diagnosis of schizophrenia. The diagnosis can now be made on the presence of disorganized speech (when such can be considered evidence of thought disorder), catatonic behavior, and emotional blunting.

Clarke (in press b) has provided an excellent discussion of the relevant diagnostic issues. According to Clarke:

> Some authors have concluded that it is usually not possible to establish the diagnosis in people with language development below that seen as about 7 years (Reid, 1972b). Although it may not be possible to establish the diagnosis with certainty, it is sometimes possible to make decisions about likely treatment responses on the basis of observed behaviour. For example, a carer of a person unable to give an account of their symptoms may be able to describe behaviour typical of someone experiencing unpleasant auditory hallucinations.

Clarke (in press b) noted that the overlap in symptoms between mental retardation and schizophrenia can increase the difficulty of diagnosing schizophrenia. Sometimes it can be difficult to distinguish affect that is "out-of-touch" with reality from the distractibility seen in mental retardation. Autistic stereotypies such as hand flapping and string twirling can present as psychotic preoc-

cupations. Clarke suggested the following alternative explanations for specific symptoms:

- False beliefs may be delusions or they may be related to cognitive impairment, social impoverishment, or child-like "magical thinking."

- The behaviors of incoherent speech, irrelevant speech, or neologisms (idiosyncratic language) may indicate communication abnormalities symptomatic of schizophrenia, or they may be related to cognitive impairment, lack of education, distractibility, autism, hearing impairment, or epilepsy.

- The behaviors of apathy, emotional blunting, and social withdrawal may be symptomatic of schizophrenia, or they may be symptomatic of affective disorders, institutionalization, autism, and physical illness.

Because of the possibility of alternative explanations for any one symptom of schizophrenia, it is important to diagnose this condition based on the identification of a number of fundamental symptoms (Reiss, 1992).

The position that schizophrenia can never be recognized in people with IQs below 50 has discouraged needed research. Researchers who believe that it is impossible to know when schizophrenia and severe mental retardation co-occur have not attempted any studies to support their position. Why conduct research into what one believes to be impossible? In contrast, Clarke's hypothesis that schizophrenia can occur in people with severe mental retardation should encourage future research. Future research is needed to determine how the various symptoms of schizophrenia might be affected by low levels of intellectual functioning.

E. RESEARCH

Researchers are still in the early stages of developing the concepts and hypotheses needed to guide future research. Research is needed on how schizophrenia and other mental disorders are expressed in people with severe mental retardation. The following comments concern the conceptual complexities of undertaking such research:

- Some minimal level of cognitive functioning may be essential to the occurrence of schizophrenia.

For example, suppose a germ is inserted into a machine in a spot where there is some dirt so that the germ can survive. The machine would have the germ, but it would not have the disease caused by the germ. To have the disease, an entity must have not only the germ but also the psychological functions that are altered by the germ as part of the disease process.

- When the key genes leading to schizophrenia are identified, it should be possible to find schizophrenic genes in people with IQs below 50. Would such people have schizophrenia? To have schizophrenia, one must have not only the genetic determinants of schizophrenia but also the cognitive functioning that is impaired by schizophrenia. Researchers need to identify the cognitive capabilities that must exist for schizophrenia to occur.

- To what extent can a person who poorly discriminates fantasy from reality because of low IQ have an hallucination in which reality and fantasy are confused because of schizophrenia?

- Imagine a machine that allows an experimenter to lower a person's IQ. If the machine were used with a person with schizophrenia and an IQ of 100, how would various schizophrenic symptoms change as the IQ is progressively lowered? Would the symptoms change slowly as IQ is decreased, or would they remain essentially unchanged until IQ is decreased to the point where there is gross impairment of language, at which point the symptoms would disappear altogether? Would some symptoms remain after IQ is decreased below the point of gross language impairment? Would some symptoms remain but in a distorted fashion?

One possible model for future research may be provided by the observational work of Charles Darwin. Whereas Darwin advanced knowledge on how high and low life forms are related to one another, future mental retardation researchers seek to advance knowledge on how psychopathology varies as a function of high versus low IQs. Detailed descriptions of schizophrenia at various IQ levels might enable researchers to determine which features strengthen or appear, and which features weaken or disappear, as lower IQ levels are considered. A "Darwinian" methodology may be essential to find linkages between schizophrenia in people with mild mental retardation and behavioral disorder in people with severe mental retardation.

VI. PERSONALITY DISORDERS

Personality disorders are deeply ingrained, characteristic styles of inappropriate behavior that significantly impair the individual's quality of life. Because personality disorders describe a life-long pattern of maladaptive behavior, they have no definite onset, course of development, or point of termination. For example, a person with a paranoid personality disorder is unusually suspicious of others. Although the degree of suspicion varies depending on life cicumstances and on situational factors, there is usually no clear point at which one can say that the tendency to be excessively suspicious began.

The consequences of personality disorders may be especially severe for people with mental retardation. In the general population, personality disorders rarely lead to hospitalization, even though they are associated with major problems in the person's marriage, job, or overall social situation. In people with mental retardation, however, adjustment problems related to personality or temperament add to those related to intellectual handicap. In these people, personality disorders may lead to residential placement or increased supervision. For example, personality problems such as irritability and aggressiveness can lead to placement in restrictive residential programs (Reid & Ballinger, 1987).

Maladaptive personality traits are distinguished from personality disorders:

> Personality traits are enduring patterns of perceiving, relating to, and thinking about the environment and oneself, and are exhibited in a wide range of important social and personal contexts. It is only when personality traits are inflexible and maladaptive and cause either significant functioning impairment or subjective distress that they constitute Personality Disorders (American Psychiatric Association, 1987, p.335).

The multiaxial systems of *DSM-IV* code clinical syndromes on Axis I and personality disorders or maladaptive behavior traits on Axis II:

Axis I: Clinical Syndromes
Axis II: Personality Disorders

Note: Clinical syndromes are syndromes or patterns of behavior associated with significant stress, disability, or impairment. They have onsets and can occur in previously well-adjusted people. Onset is usually associated with a deterioration in behavior called a "regression." In contrast, personality disorders are deeply ingrained maladaptive patterns with no definite onset. They cannot occur in previously well-adjusted people, unless following brain injury.

Personality disorders can occur with or without a clinical syndrome (Nestadt, Romanoski, Samuels, Falstein, & McHugh, 1992). Many people with mental retardation who have a personality disorder show no clinical syndrome (e.g., Reiss, 1990); however, some have both a clinical syndrome and a personality disorder. In still other cases, a clinical syndrome is present without any personality disorder.

In past versions of the *DSM* classification system, especially the *DSM-I* and *DSM-II* (American Psychiatric Association, 1952, 1968), personality disorders were poorly described. The classification categories for personality disorders had low interrater reliabilities because the same maladaptive personality trait often was associated with more than one diagnosis. Moreover, past categories seemed to reflect social values rather than any medical or scientific knowledge. For example, homosexuality and sexually variant behavior were considered personality disorders in past versions of the *DSM*. The *DSM-III* and *DSM-III-R* were intended as vast improvements in the description of personality disorders. The improvements were partially the result of Millon's (1981) theories. However, many of the diagnostic categories for personality disorders still have low reliabilities (American Psychiatric Association, 1980).

A. EPIDEMIOLOGY

Significant maladaptive personality traits are by far the most common category of psychopathology seen in persons with mental retardation. Craft (1959) found that 33 percent of the people with mental retardation in a British facility showed maladaptive personality traits. Reid and Ballinger (1987) found marked personality disorder in 22 percent of a Scottish hospital sample of 100 adults with IQs in the range of 35 to 70. Fifty-six percent of the sample were found to show some abnormalities of personality or temperament. Reiss (1990) reported similar results in a survey of a random sample of persons served by community agencies in the Chicago metropolitan area. The Reiss study found evidence of significant maladaptive personality traits in 25 to 45 percent of the research sample. Reiss suggested that maladaptive personality traits and personality disorders are the primary reasons for findings that psychopathology is more common among persons with mental retardation than among the general population.

B. SUBTYPES

A recent factor analytic study of personality in the general population found only three basic types of personality disorders (Bell & Jackson, 1992). Type A was called odd and eccentric; Type B was called emotional, dramatic and erratic; and

Type C was called anxious and fearful. The applicability of these broad categories to people with mental retardation has not yet been explored.

DSM-IV recognizes a number of subtypes of personality disorder. The most important of these for people with mental retardation are briefly summarized here.

B1. AVOIDANT PERSONALITY DISORDER is indicated by a pervasive pattern of avoidance of social situations, feelings of inadequacy, and hypersensitivity to negative evaluation. People with this disorder avoid most social situations. They experience discomfort in social situations unless they are certain of being liked. They lack confidence in their social skills and feel inferior to others.

Social anxiety and avoidance are seen with some frequency in people with mental retardation, perhaps because of frequent experiences with failure and social rejection (Goldberg, Gitta, & Puddephatt, 1992). In the development of the *Reiss Screen for Maladaptive Behavior* (Reiss, 1988*b*), social avoidance emerged as one of eight primary factors accounting for psychopathology in a national sample of 306 people in developmental disabilities mental health programs.

In people with low IQs, avoidant behavior sometimes is expressed by an actual turning away of the head to avoid eye contact or by an actual physical distancing (e.g., walking away) from other people. In people with higher IQs, the avoidance is more subtle and may take the form of inattentiveness to social and interpersonal cues. Sometimes a person with avoidant tendencies will present as "spaced out." When engaged in conversation, the person experiences stress and anxiety related to the possibility of criticism and rejection. The person defends against the anxiety by ignoring the conversation and interaction. However, if the person is aware of the inappropriateness of not listening to someone who is talking to him/her, the person may pretend to be paying attention even when he/she is not.

B2. DEPENDENT PERSONALITY DISORDER is indicated by a pervasive, age-inappropriate need to be taken care of, leading to submissiveness, clinging behavior, and an excessive fear of separation. People who are dependent cannot stand to be alone. They develop relationships quickly and are devastated when relationships are lost. They show excessive concerns over the possibility of being abandoned. They may have difficulty expressing anger for fear it would lead to rejection. They have difficulty making decisions on their own.

Dependent personality traits occur with some frequency in persons with mental retardation. Reiss (1990) found that dependency was rated as a "major problem" for 7.4 percent of his Chicago sample and as a "problem" for an additional 18.1 percent. Dependent behavior is especially common in people with autism, who sometimes develop intense relationships with one or two adult caretakers.

The loss of relationships can be devastating for children with high depen-

dency needs. Reiss and Redd (1970) reported a case of a child with autism who developed self-injurious behavior following the loss of an adult caretaker with whom an intense relationship had developed. The case study suggested the importance of identifying dependent behavior so that the consequences of staff turnover can be anticipated and minimized. When it is known that a dependent child will lose a relationship with a caretaker, a relationship with some other caretaker should be developed so that the child always has somebody to gratify dependency needs.

B3. PARANOID PERSONALITY DISORDER is indicated by excessive suspiciousness of others. People with paranoid traits are easily offended and bear grudges for long periods of time. They overreact when threatened psychologically; they make "mountains out of molehills." They become jealous quickly and are quick to blame others for their own faults.

Paranoid traits are seen with some frequency in people with mental retardation (Bouras & Drummond, 1992; Reiss, 1990; Goldberg *et al.*, 1992). Reiss (1990) found that paranoia was rated as a "major problem" for 3.5 percent of the Chicago sample and as a "problem" for an additional 12.9 percent.

Paranoia sometimes is associated with explosive and violent behavior. Reiss (1992) identified a paranoid trigger in the case of a man with mental retardation who had a tendency for explosive episodes of threatening behavior. The episodes were triggered because the man became jealous and angry when the other residents received attention; Reiss attributed the anger to paranoid beliefs that the caretakers were trying to belittle and demean him by paying attention to the other residents. Ideas such as "How come they do not pay more attention to me?" and "They are trying to make fun of me by paying so much attention to others," were suggested to motivate the explosive episodes.

B4. ANTISOCIAL PERSONALITY DISORDER is indicated by brutality, aggression, stealing, and a total disregard for and violation of the rights of others. People with this disorder show little guilt, anxiety, remorse, and self-doubt. They do not care about others; they do not "bond" to others. Dana (1993) has suggested that this condition should not be diagnosed for persons with mental retardation unless it is clear that the person knows that antisocial behavior is considered to be wrong.

Although aggression occurs with some frequency in people with mental retardation, antisocial personality disorder is much less common. There are no studies of the rate of antisocial personality disorder in this population. However, there are some studies of the prevalence of antisocial behaviors other than aggression. For example, Reiss (1990) found that stealing was rated as a "major problem" for 1.5 percent of his Chicago sample and as a "problem" for an additional 8.9 percent.

Reiss (1985) reported a case history of antisocial personality disorder in a man with mild mental retardation. The individual had a long history of lying, stealing, and brutality and was aware that his behavior was socially unacceptable. In one psychotherapy interview, he told a tall tale of dropping a large rock on someone else's head. The story was told without emotion or concern for the person whose skull was being broken.

B5. BORDERLINE PERSONALITY DISORDER is indicated by excessive instability of interpersonal relationships, poor impulse control, and/or an unstable self-image. Behaviors include impulsiveness, intense anger, and suicidal gestures. The individual is greatly concerned by real or imagined abandonment.

Very little research has been reported on borderline traits in people with mental retardation. No prevalence data have been reported, and case reports have been rare.

Reiss (1985) reported the case history of a 19 year-old woman with mild mental retardation who had a borderline personality disorder and strong dependency needs. When her dependency needs were frustrated, she presented with angry tantrums in which self-destructive behavior was threatened. She was emotionally unstable and volatile. At times she refused to take insulin, which for her was life-threatening. In a mental hospital she called her boyfriend many times each day and made a number of attempts to run away to him. Although some mental health specialists dismissed this behavior as "immaturity" related to mental retardation, a clinical psychologist determined that it actually represented an excessive fear of abandonment (Peterson, 1984).

B6. HISTRIONIC PERSONALITY DISORDER is indicated by excessive attention-seeking. People with this disorder are uncomfortable when they are not the center of attention. They tend to behave in ways that call attention to themselves, as in dramatic behavior or exaggerated expressions of emotion. These people often are perceived by others as emotionally superficial.

Inappropriate attention-seeking is common in people with mental retardation, perhaps because of early childhood experiences in institutions or other residential facilities where their needs for attention were frustrated. Reiss (1990) found that inappropriate attention-seeking was rated as a "problem" for 27.9 percent of a random sample and as a "major problem" for an additional 11.9 percent.

C. PRESENTATION IN MENTAL RETARDATION

Historically, there has been some debate as to the earliest age at which personality disorders can be observed. Some authorities have maintained that per-

sonality disorders develop in adolescence, whereas others have held that personality disorders can be observed in children (cf. Reiss *et al.,* 1977). The issue is particularly relevant to the study of personality disorders in people with mental retardation (Dana, 1993). People with mental retardation are almost always immature for their age. In diagnosing personality disorders, it is important to determine that relevant symptoms are signs of personality disorders and not signs of emotional immaturity.

Ballinger and Reid (1987) evaluated personality disorders in 140 adults with mild or moderate mental retardation. This study used the categories of the 1971 edition of the *International Classification of Diseases.* The most common types of problems were explosive personality disorder, hysterical personality disorder, and affective personality disorder. In *DSM-IV,* explosive personality disorder most likely would be diagnosed as a conduct disorder or as antisocial personality disorder; hysterical personality would be recognized as histrionic personality disorder; and affective personality disorder most likely would be recognized as dysthymic disorder.

The most common personality disorders seen at the ISDD Mental Health Program in Chicago, an outpatient developmental disabilities mental health clinic, were avoidant personality disorder, antisocial personality disorder, paranoid personality disorder, and dependent personality disorder.

VII. SEVERE BEHAVIOR DISORDERS

In this book, the term *severe behavior disorders* is used to refer to persistent behavior difficulties such as aggression, self-injury (SIB), stereotyped behavior, pica, vomiting, and rumination. These behaviors can vary greatly in the frequency and intensity of their expression both within and between individuals (Durand & Crimmins, 1988; National Institutes of Health, 1989). Behavior analysts have conducted extensive clinical research on these problems from the perspective of operant conditioning (Ullmann & Krasner, 1965), nonaversive approaches (LaVigna & Donnellan, 1986), and communication functions (Carr & Durand, 1985a, 1985b). Progress in understanding some of these conditions also has been made by biomedical researchers, such as those researchers investigating fragile X and autism (see Chapter 1).

A. AGGRESSION

Psychological researchers have studied the role of personality versus environment in the occurrence of aggressive behavior. Are the primary causes of

aggression in the person or in the environment? On the one hand, biological, psychoanalytic, and personality theorists have maintained that important determinants of aggressive behavior are person-specific factors such as genetic determinants and personality tendencies to behave aggressively. On the other hand, behavior analysts have maintained that aggressive behavior is situation-specific. These theorists believe that the primary determinants of aggressive behavior are in the environment, as when a child behaves aggressively for attention or to communicate needs.

The importance of innate factors in aggression was suggested by Dollard, Doob, Miller, Mowrer, and Sears' (1939) frustration-aggression hypothesis. This hypothesis suggests an innate relationship between frustration and aggression such that all frustration necessarily leads to some type of aggression, and all aggression is necessarily instigated by some type of frustration. The frustration-aggression hypothesis, as subsequently clarified by Miller (1941), produced an enormous amount of psychological research. Many of the research findings supported the validity of the hypothesis.

In 1963, Bandura and Walters published influential arguments against the frustration-aggression hypothesis. Their central thesis was that the relationship between frustration and aggression is learned and not innate. Bandura and his colleagues subsequently published a number of studies showing that aggressive behavior can be learned by imitation of aggressive models. Because these experiments provided examples of aggression that occurred in people who had not been frustrated, the findings have been cited as evidence against the frustration-aggression hypothesis.

In addition to proposing that aggression is a learned behavior, Bandura and Walters (1963) proposed that aggression is situationally determined. They denied the prevailing view of the times that aggressiveness is a personality trait. Their view became a central part of the behavioral approaches to the treatment of aggression in people with mental retardation (see Chapter 4).

Recently, researchers have obtained evidence that aggression is influenced by personality factors. Leonard Eron and his research team followed a group of bullies from childhood through adulthood and found that aggression was a relatively stable, life-span trait (Eron, Huesmann, Dubow, Romanoff, & Yarmel, 1987; Huesmann & Eron, 1992; Huesmann, Eron, Lefkowitz, & Walder, 1984). The same children who were bullies in elementary school were failures and criminals as adults. Childhood environmental and situational variables did not predict the stability of aggressive behavior over the life-span.

The Eron and Huesmann findings that aggressiveness is a personality trait contradict the ideology that all severe behavior disorders can be understood solely in terms of situational and environmental variables. Situational and environmental variables appear to have mostly short-term influences on aggressive

behavior. Over the long term, aggression is significantly influenced by the individual's personality, upbringing, and emotions.

B. PSYCHOPATHOLOGY

Additional evidence of intra-person, nonsituational determinants of aggression has come from mental retardation/mental health researchers. These researchers have identified examples of aggressive behavior associated with psychopathology. The following categories of psychopathology have been found to be associated with some cases of aggression in people with mental retardation:

- *Psychosis.* Sometimes aggression is associated with schizophrenia. For example, a man with mental retardation may behave aggressively if he hears voices telling him to attack others.

- *Paranoia.* Sometimes aggression is associated with paranoid personality traits or paranoia. As noted previously, Reiss (1992) reported the case history of a man with mental retardation who felt jealous, vulnerable, humiliated, and offended when caretakers paid attention to the other residents.

- *Depression.* Sometimes aggression is associated with mood disorder or with depressed mood. As noted previously, Reiss and Rojahn (1993) found evidence of a strong association between aggression and depression in both children and adults with mental retardation.

- *Antisocial Personality Disorder.* Sometimes aggression is associated with antisocial personality traits. As noted previously, Reiss (1985) reported the case history of a man who brutally attacked others and who fantasized without guilt or anxiety about dropping big rocks on other people's heads.

Only some instances of aggression are related to psychopathology. Other instances may be related to rare conditions such as fragile X or autism. Still other examples may be explained by the communication functions of aggressive behavior.

C. PSYCHOLOGICAL APPROACHES TO STUDY OF AGGRESSION

Psychological research on the study of aggression in mental retardation has focused mostly on situational variables such as stimulus antecedents, conse-

quences, functional analysis, and operant conditioning. Recently, a number of leading researchers have attempted to broaden the range of variables investigated.

C1. INFORMATION PROCESSING AND AGGRESSION. Betsey Benson and her graduate students have initiated a program of cognitive research on aggressive behavior in people with mental retardation. In a recently reported study, Fuchs and Benson (1994) evaluated the social information processing skills of 35 adult males with borderline to moderate mental retardation. Based on formal ratings, 16 of the people were classified as aggressive and 19 were classified as nonaggressive. Aggressive and nonaggressive adults were presented with eight hypothetical conflict situations. It was found that both aggressive and nonaggressive people were equally able to generate multiple solutions including assertive solutions to the conflict situations. However, the aggressive people generated significantly more aggressive solutions and more frequently gave an aggressive solution first. The findings are the first to suggest the relevance of information processing for understanding aggressive behavior in people with mental retardation.

C2. BEHAVIOR ANALYSIS. Gardner and Graeber (1993) have developed a model of aggressive behavior in people with mental retardation that represents a badly needed broadening of the behavior analytic approach. The model suggests that severe behavior disorders are determined by a number of factors, including operant conditioning, genetic disease, personality needs, and psychopathology. Although the model lacks specifics, a general point is that behavior analysts need to abandon the outdated view that *all* aggressive behavior is situationally determined in favor of a more modern view that only some examples of aggressive behavior are situationally determined. Although Gardner and Graeber see situational factors as important for understanding aggressive behavior, they also recognize the importance of nonsituational variables.

D. CRIMINAL OFFENDERS

In the early 1900s, it was widely assumed that mental retardation caused delinquency and criminal behavior. The initial findings of a high rate of mental retardation in prison populations seemed to support the hypothesis of a link between mental retardation and criminality. As researchers developed better measures of IQ and adaptive behavior, however, they found that the prevalence of mental retardation among prisoners is actually quite low. At any given point in time, fewer than one percent of persons with mental retardation are in prison (Day, 1993*a*). Over the life span, fewer than three percent of persons with men-

tal retardation are convicted of criminal conduct (Dyggve & Kodahl, 1979). These findings contradict the view that mental retardation and criminal behavior are strongly associated.

Day (1993a) reviewed gender differences in criminal behavior among persons with mental retardation. He found that male prisoners with mental retardation outnumbered females by about four to one. About one-third of the women prisoners were committed for prostitution.

Koller, Richardson, Katz, and McLaren (1983) and Richardson, Koller, and Katz (1985) reported a significant linear relationship between unstable upbringing and criminal behavior. However, these findings are preliminary because they were based on measures that had not been properly validated.

E. SELF-INJURIOUS BEHAVIOR (SIB)

SIB refers to repeated, self-inflicted, nonaccidental injury. SIB involves activities such as head banging, face slapping, eye poking, ruminative vomiting, and swallowing harmful substances. SIB behaviors vary greatly in frequency and intensity and require some type of intervention to protect the individual (National Institutes of Health, 1989).

Rojahn (1986) surveyed 25,872 persons with mental retardation living in noninstitutional facilities in Germany. He found a prevalence rate of 1.7 percent for SIB and related behavior. This rate is similar to the 2.0 percent rate reported by Reiss (1990) for severe SIB in persons served by community agencies. Borthwick-Duffy and Eyman's (1990) survey of 76,603 service recipients in California found a rate of 3.1 percent for SIB. Higher rates have been reported for surveys of institutions. However, some of the studies that found high rates used broad definitions of SIB (Schroeder, Mulick, & Rojahn, 1980).

SIB is associated with a number of developmental disorders such as autism, Lesch-Nyhan syndrome, and Cornelia deLange syndrome. These findings suggest that there is a strong genetic and neurochemical basis to at least some examples of SIB.

Recent neurochemical theories of SIB have implicated the endogenous opiate system that regulates pain and pleasure (Sandman, 1990). One hypothesis is that SIB is associated with insensitivity to pain (Sandman, 1990). Another hypothesis is that in certain people SIB can release endogenous opiates, essentially producing a euphoric state or "high" (Sokol & Campbell, 1988; Sandman, 1990). These hypotheses have served as a theoretical basis for the use of opiate blockers in the drug treatment of SIB (see Chapter 4). Research on the possible role of the opiate system in the occurrence of SIB is still considered to be preliminary.

Even if future research indicated that opiate blockers or some other medication were effective in the treatment of SIB, this would not provide support for hypotheses that SIB is caused by abnormalities in the opiate system or by neurochemical dysfunctions. Treatment effects are not a basis for inferring the cause of a disorder. For example, it is possible that opiate blockers increase the pain associated with SIB, so that the behavior becomes more self-punitive. Such a finding would not necessarily mean that prior to drug treatment the behavior was less self-punitive than for the average person.

A common logical error is to infer causality from treatment effects. Treatment effects never provide evidence of causation. If a drug X is an effective treatment for SIB, it is a mistake to conclude that SIB is caused by a deficiency in drug X.

E1. PSYCHOLOGICAL MOTIVATION OF SIB. A number of models have been proposed to identify the psychological motivation for SIB. One attractive model was proposed by Napolitan (1979) in his doctoral dissertation. Napolitan's (1979) model posits three different types of SIB distinguished by motivational factors. Socially-reinforced SIB is motivated by attention-seeking. Stereotyped SIB presents as "self-stimulating" or "self-reinforcing" behavior. Avoidance SIB is motivated by negative reinforcement (removal of, or a reduction in, the frequency or intensity of an aversive stimulus). Napolitan (1979) obtained support for this model in two related studies. In Study 1, teachers rated 93 children with severe and profound mental retardation on 25 features of SIB. The ratings were factor analyzed, and the first three factors closely resembled the three types in Napolitan's model. In Study 2, the ten subjects who scored highest on each of the first three factors were observed under six theoretically-relevant, experimental stimulus conditions. The results indicated that for the most part the various types of SIB occurred in accordance with theoretical predictions under the six stimulus conditions. The findings provided some initial support for the Napolitan model.

Similar models have been proposed by other researchers. Carr and Durand (1985a, 1985b) focused on adult attention (what Napolitan called socially-reinforced SIB) and escape from adult demands (what Napolitan called avoidance SIB). According to Carr and Durand's theory, people with mental retardation use aberrant behavior to communicate either a desire for adult attention or a desire to escape from the aversive nature of demands. They hold that adult attention and/or escape reinforce SIB and other forms of severe behavior disorders. Carr and Durand's influential model is considered in Chapter 4 as a treatment approach to severe behavior disorders.

E2. SIB AND PSYCHOPATHOLOGY. Most cases of SIB appear to be determined by complex genetic, biochemical, and learning factors. In some cases, however, psychopathology may be involved. For example, King (1993) has sug-

TABLE 2-2. COMPARISON OF OCD AND SIB

	OCD[1]	SIB[2]
CLASSIFICATION	Anxiety Disorder	Severe Behavior Problem
MOTIVATION	Ritualistic behavior aimed at anxiety reduction	Ritualistic behavior (motivation can be attention-seeking, escape, self-stimulation)
RITUALS	Checking behaviors; rituals related to fears of contamination	Ordering rituals (usually associated with brain disorders)
IQ	Positively correlated with IQ; average person has IQ 115-120	Negatively correlated with IQ; average patient has IQ less than 50
BEHAVIORAL TREATMENT	Behavioral fear exposure therapy effective	Fear exposure therapy not attempted

[1] OCD stands for Obsessive-Compulsive Disorder
[2] SIB stands for self-injurious behavior

gested that some instances of SIB are linked to OCD. This hypothesis is based primarily on the fact that both SIB and compulsive behavior are repetitive in nature. However, the following significant differences between SIB and OCD are noted:

- Rojahn, Borthwick-Duffy, and Jacobson (in press) found a .006 correlation between anxiety disorders and SIB, which is so low it contradicts the hypothesis that OCD and SIB are related.

- OCD is associated with intrusive thoughts, images, or ideas that are anxiety-provoking. Such cognitive processes are difficult to identify in persons with IQs below 50. In addition, SIB has not been shown to be anxiety-reducing, as are compulsions.

- SIB is rare in people with IQs above 70. If SIB is a form of OCD, why is SIB not evident in cases of OCD in the general population?

- The occurrence of OCD is positively correlated with intelligence (Rasmussen & Tsuang, 1984), whereas the occurrence of SIB is negatively correlated with intelligence.

- OCD can be treated effectively with behavioral fear exposure techniques. Nobody has demonstrated that these techniques can be used to treat SIB. It unclear how to attempt to treat SIB with exposure therapy.

In view of these considerations, which are summarized in Table 2-2, future research is needed before it can be concluded that there is any significant relationship between SIB and OCD.

Communication and cognitive consistency theories suggest a possible linkage between some examples of SIB and negative self-esteem. The linkage is suggested by the "rejection of success" phenomenon seen in the general population. For some people with low self-esteem, success and high levels of reward lead to discomfort and behaviors that negate, undo, or reject the success or reward (Haimowitz & Haimowitz, 1966). For example, a child may tear up his or her drawing when a teacher praises it; an adult may say something self-deprecating when praised for some behavior or accomplishment; an adult may do something foolish to insure failure just when success is at hand. Could some examples of mild SIB in people with mental retardation function as behaviors that negate praise or positive evaluative feedback? Are some examples of SIB an attempt to communicate low self-esteem, as if the person were trying to say something like, "Boy, am I incompetent," in order to negate some success or praise?

Reiss, Reiss, and Reppucci (1978) tested the hypothesis that for some children mild SIB such as self-slapping is a rejection of success phenomenon designed to undo or negate reward. In this study, children with severe mental retardation were asked to perform a simple ring-stacking task under conditions of relatively high versus relatively low reward. The High Reward Experimenter gave the child three M&M candies for completing the ring stacking task. The Low Reward Experimenter gave the child only one M&M candy for completing the same ring stacking task. Different college students served as the High and Low Reward Experimenters with appropriate counterbalancing to control for experimenter personality. A discrimination training procedure was used in which each child was given repeated opportunities to perform the task for the High versus Low Reward Experimenter. The prediction was that the children who engaged in mild SIB (self-slapping) would show superior performance under conditions of low versus high reward.

The Reiss *et al.* study found that two children with mild self-injurious behavior performed the ring-stacking task better for the Low Reward Experimenter

than for the High Reward Experimenter. Although these children liked M&M candies and consumed large quantities during a free access period, they preferred one M&M to three M&Ms when the number of M&Ms was symbolic of the quality of the child's performance. The study demonstrated that the two children performed better under conditions of Low versus High Reward. In fact, one child actually started to throw away the three-M&M reward, but not the one-M&M reward, and/or stopped completing the task for the High Reward Experimenter. The results are consistent with the "rejection of success" hypothesis. Sometimes self-injurious behavior can communicate an extremely negative self-esteem so that the individual rejects comparatively high levels of evaluative feedback.

Why do some people show the rejection of success phenomenon? Psychoanalysts believe it is because of a need to reduce the guilt they experience when they are rewarded (Fenichel, 1945). Social psychologists, however, believe it is because of a basic human need for cognitive consistency (Jones, 1973). This view holds that people seek a level of evaluative feedback consistent with their self-esteem. For example, many people feel uncomfortable if praised for skills or attributes they think they do not have — when a boy thinks he is a bad baseball player, he is likely to experience discomfort if others praise him for playing well; a man who feels physically unattractive tends to feel uncomfortable if praised for being handsome. Positive evaluative feedback not only is inconsistent with negative self-esteem but also may create expectations for future success that the person feels he or she cannot fulfill (Maracek & Mettee, 1972).

The Reiss *et al.* study provides only preliminary support for the possibility that SIB sometimes has the communicative function of rejection of success. Much more research is indicated on this issue. For example, the initial results need to be tested for replicability.

VIII. SEXUAL DISORDERS

There are two general types of sexual disorders, called *sexual dysfunctions* and *paraphilias*. Sexual dysfunctions imply problems in the actual performance of sexual behavior. Included are: anxiety problems that inhibit sexual performance, pain during the sex act, and absence of interest or desire. In contrast, paraphilias are indicated by a strong preference for socially disapproved means of sexual gratification. Included are pedophilia (sexual attraction to children); fetishism (the habitual use of a part of the body or an inanimate object to produce sexual gratification); transvestic fetishism (obtaining sexual gratification primarily by cross-dressing); exhibitionism ("indecent exposure"; the attainment of sexual gratification primarily by exposing sex organs to the opposite sex); frotteurism (obtaining sexual gratification primarily by rubbing and touching

against a nonconsenting person); voyeurism (obtaining sexual gratification primarily by observing nudes or others engage in sexual activity); sadism (obtaining sexual gratification primarily by inflicting pain and humiliation on others); masochism (obtaining sexual gratification primarily by receiving pain); and incest (sexual relationships with a member of one's immediate family).

A. EPIDEMIOLOGY

Reiss' (1990) Chicago survey found that sexual activity was rated as a "major problem" for 1.5 percent of the sample and as a "problem" for an additional 11.5 percent. The findings did not distinguish between the occurrence of sexual dysfunctions, paraphilias, and sexually inappropriate behavior.

Day's (1993a) review of studies on criminality among persons with mental retardation included surveys of sex offenders in prison populations. In 12 surveys, sex offenders accounted for 12 to 46 percent of all prisoners with mental retardation. These numbers are much higher than similar counts for the prison population as a whole. Thus, sex offenses seem to account for a disproportionately high percentage of offenders with mental retardation.

B. PRESENTATION IN MENTAL RETARDATION

The literature on sexual problems in persons with mental retardation consists almost entirely of outcome studies of behavioral treatments and some surveys of sex offenders. These studies document the occurrence of a range of sexually inappropriate behaviors, including public masturbation (Barmann & Murray, 1981), pedophilia (Polvinale & Lutzker, 1980), and transvestism (Cooper, Mohamed, & Collacott, 1993). Also documented is the occurrence of frotteurism in a person with severe mental retardation (McNally, 1993) and zoophilic exhibitionism (McNally & Lukach, 1992).

Day (1993a) found a number of similarities in sex offenses committed by people with and without mental retardation. For offenders with mental retardation, about 65 percent of the offenses were trivial and unlikely to harm anyone or offend deeply. Aggression was involved in only nine percent of the sex offenses. Recidivism was common, with some estimates as high as 67 percent. Compared to the offenders with no mental retardation, the offenders with mental retardation were much more likely not to know their victim. However, sex offenders with mental retardation show the same range of adverse psychosocial factors as those shown by other sex offenders. These include growing up in a home with marital disharmony, violence, sexual abuse, and neglect. Nearly two-

thirds of a sample studied by Day had no prior sexual experience with another individual prior to the first sexual offense.

Day (1993a) also studied 197 sexual incidents committed by 47 persons with mental retardation. He found that three of the 47 persons had a mental illness. For the remaining subjects, no mental illness was diagnosed. These findings suggest that psychopathology accounts for only a small percentage of the sexual incidents committed by persons with mental retardaton.

IX. SOMATOFORM DISORDERS

The chief problem in somatoform disorder is a loss or impairment of physical functioning. Although there is an appearance of a physical disorder, no physical disorder is present, and the loss is an expression of psychological needs or conflicts. In *somatization disorder*, the person has numerous and recurrent physical complaints for which there are no medical causes. In *conversion disorder*, the person experiences a medically unexplainable loss or impairment of some motor or sensory function. Examples of *conversion symptoms* include hysterical blindness (a loss of sight that has no medical basis), hysterical paralysis (a paralysis of a limb that has no medical basis), hysterical anesthesias (a loss of sensation that is either medically impossible or has no medical basis), and pseudocyesis (a woman shows all the physical signs of pregnancy except that there is no fetus).

Conversion disorder was previously known as hysteria. Individuals with *hysteria* often are described as unrealistic, romantic, and idealistic. The term "histrionic" refers to the role playing quality and sense of unreality that characterize the hysteric's behavior. Hysterics like the sick role. In about one-third of the people with conversion symptoms, there is a complacent attitude toward illness called *la belle indifference*. Instead of showing concern or alarm over one's disability or illness, the person shows satisfaction related to the attention he/she receives for being disabled or ill.

In *hypochondriasis*, the individual shows excessive fear of becoming ill. The person goes to great lengths to avoid the possibility of becoming ill. People with hypochondriasis tend to be unhappy, if not depressed.

A. EPIDEMIOLOGY

As far as the present author could determine, no studies have been reported on the prevalence of somatoform disorders in persons with mental retardation.

B. PRESENTATION IN MENTAL RETARDATION

The mental retardation literature includes only a few documented cases of somatoform disorder. Matson (1984) published three case studies of middle aged women who made frequent psychosomatic complaints. Brown (1992) reported a case history of a 24 year-old woman with mild mental retardation who had unexplained paralysis. The present author once had a case of a young man with mild mental retardation who had a Factitious Disorder, which in mental retardation may be psychologically equivalent to Somatoform Disorder. The man had numerous emergency hospitalizations related to his persistent habit of swallowing balls and other objects.

The children's *Reiss Scales* has a psychometric scale for somatoform behavior (Reiss & Valenti-Hein, 1994). The items include "avoids by illness," "bodily complaints," "headaches," "seeks medical care," and "stomachaches." Cronbach's alpha coefficient of internal reliability for the scale was estimated at .79. Individuals with mental retardation and psychopathology scored twice as high on the scale as did individuals with mental retardation and no psychiatric disorder.

X. ATTENTION-DEFICIT/HYPERACTIVITY DISORDER

Attention-Deficit/Hyperactivity Disorder (ADHD) is the most commonly diagnosed psychiatric disorder for children with no mental retardation. It is used to diagnose the behavior of elementary school children who fidget a lot and are easily distracted, easily frustrated, and rarely finish anything they start. The essential features of this disorder are developmentally inappropriate degrees of inattention, impulsiveness, and hyperactivity. ADHD has been misused to provide a psychiatric diagnosis for children who are just a nuisance for classroom teachers (Bootzin, Acocella, & Alloy, 1993). The diagnosis should be used only for children who meet the diagnostic criteria and show significant impairment in functioning.

Over the years ADHD has been known by a number of different names. Because a small percentage of children with hyperactive behavior show neurological impairment, the diagnosis of *minimal brain dysfunction* was used. When researchers failed to find evidence of brain damage in most children with the disorder, the disorder was renamed *hyperactivity*. The disorder was renamed again when researchers found that many children were not truly hyperactive. Because researchers found that the basic problem for the vast majority of children was a failure to sustain attention (Douglas & Peters, 1979), the disorder was renamed *Attention-Deficit/Hyperactivity Disorder*.

A. EPIDEMIOLOGY

Reiss' (1990) Chicago survey found that inattentiveness was rated as a "major problem" for 5.4 percent of the sample and as a "problem" for an additional 20.1 percent. The corresponding numbers for overactivity were 3.9 percent and 11.3 percent.

B. PRESENTATION IN MENTAL RETARDATION

The diagnosis of ADHD in people with mental retardation is complicated by the fact that mental retardation is associated with attention deficits even in the absence of ADHD:

- Experimental psychologists have obtained evidence that people with mental retardation show attention deficits on laboratory learning tasks (Ellis, 1962; Zeaman & House, 1963).

- A survey of students with educable mental retardation (EMR) found that mental retardation is associated with attention deficits (Epstein *et al.*, 1986). In this study, the researchers asked teachers to rate 360 students with EMR and 360 students with no mental retardation on the *Behavior Problem Checklist*. Mean scores for attention deficits were significantly higher for the students with EMR than for the students with no mental retardation.

For ADHD to be diagnosed in a person with mental retardation, attention deficits should be present that are greater than those associated with mental retardation *per se*.

C. RESEARCH

Very little research has been reported on ADHD and mental retardation. However, there has been some research on the development of appropriate measures:

- Das (1986) developed a 12-item checklist for measuring attention deficit in persons with mental retardation. The checklist is correlated with the *Conners Rating Scale* and with experimental evaluations on performance tasks sensitive to distractions (Melnyk & Das, 1992).

- The children's *Reiss Scales* has empirically-derived, factorially distinct psychometric scales for impulsivity, conduct disorder, and attention-deficit disorder. The main items on the attention-deficit scale are disobedient, distracted, and overactive. The adult *Reiss Screen* has no ADHD scale but does include items for "overactivity" and "inattentiveness."

XI. SUBSTANCE ABUSE

Substance abuse refers to the habitual use of psychoactive substances to the point that it impairs functioning or causes significant adverse consequences. Excessive use of a number of central nervous system depressant drugs, such as alcohol and heroin, leads to *physical dependency,* or what is commonly called an *addiction.* The physically dependent individual experiences intense withdrawal symptoms if he/she reduces intake of the drug for periods of less than a day. The exact withdrawal symptoms experienced depend on the specific substance, the individual, and the individual's history of abuse of the substance. Typical withdrawal symptoms from alcohol include delirium tremors (DT's), which usually last between three and five days. The DT's include insomnia, terrifying dreams, irritability, fear, and possibly hallucinations.

The most commonly abused substance in the general population is alcohol. Alcohol accounts for more than 30,000 traffic accidents each year. Alcoholism can devastate families. Excessive drinking is a problem with youth, native Americans, and bored workers. Other commonly abused substances are heroin and cocaine.

Recent studies have suggested a link between anxiety sensitivity and alcoholism (Peterson & Reiss, 1992). Apparently, some people drink alcohol and abuse heroin in order to blunt the sensations of anxiety (McNally, in press *b*). These people sometimes are referred to as having a *dual diagnosis* (substance abuse and anxiety disorder) which, of course, is the same term that was used in the past to refer to the co-occurrence of mental retardation and mental illness.

The question of substance abuse by persons with mental retardation has received very little attention. The issue was not even mentioned in some past books on challenging behavior. However, there are a number of important issues for researchers to investigate.

There presently is much confusion regarding the rate of substance abuse among persons with mental retardation. On the one hand, three studies suggest that alcoholism among persons with mental retardation is minimal. On the other hand, there is growing concern among clinicians that this situation may be changing for the worse.

Edgerton (1986) was among the early researchers to report that alcohol abuse was minimal for persons with mental retardation. He reported cases of

adults with mental retardation who did not drink even though they had close friends who were drinkers. Edgerton cited a number of reasons for the low rate of substance abuse among the people he studied. Many could not afford to buy liquor or beer. Some had witnessed the negative impact of drinking on their families. Others had had a history of positive reinforcement for abstinence.

Reiss' (1990) Chicago survey also found low prevalence rates for substance abuse. In this study, drug/substance abuse was rated as a "major problem" for no persons and as a "problem" for only 2.0 percent. Day (1993a) reported that drinking, which is common among sexual offenders generally, is rare among sexual offenders with mental retardation in the United Kingdom.

Despite these findings, there is growing concern that problem drinking may be increasing among persons with mental retardation. In her clinical work, Anne Hurley (1994) is seeing much more problem drinking in the Boston area than was true only a few years ago. Betsey Benson suspects that this also may be true for the Chicago area. Benson notes that more people with mental retardation are in the community now than were even a decade ago. She reported a case of an adult woman with Down Syndrome whose attraction to bars and drinking was related to her desire for acceptance. This woman not only developed a serious drinking problem but also was placing herself in danger by going home from the bar with men.

Much more research is indicated on the issue of substance abuse among persons with mental retardation. The possibility that rates of problem drinking are increasing needs to be evaluated. Researchers also need to consider ways to prevent substance abuse and issues of access to appropriate care.

XII. DISSOCIATIVE DISORDERS

The essential feature of dissociative disorders is a disturbance or impairment in the psychological functions of identity, memory, or consciousness. Examples include *multiple personality disorder, fugue, amnesia,* and *depersonalization.* Historically, these disorders have been reported to be rare in the general population, although in recent years some authorities have suggested that they are not as rare as previously believed. As far as the present author could determine, almost nothing is known about the possible co-occurrence of these disorders in persons with mental retardation.

Lindsley (1989) has reported a case of a woman with mild mental retardation and diagnosed multiple personality disorder. However, the case report is open to questions regarding the occurrence of multiple personalities and the reliability of the diagnosis.

XIII. EATING AND SLEEP DISORDERS

Some textbooks of psychopathology list obesity and eating disorders as stress-related conditions, although they also may result from other factors. The only eating or sleep disorder that has received some attention in people with mental retardation is overeating. Overeating can be a significant health issue — obesity can increase the risk of hypertension and heart disease.

Fox and Rotatori (1982) found rates of obesity varying between 10.1 and 30.8 percent for various groups of people with mental retardation. These rates are higher than those reported for the population as a whole. In a sample of 553 institutionalized adults, Kelly, Rimmer, and Ness (1986) reported rates of obesity of 45.2 percent for males and 50.5 percent for females. Rimmer, Braddock, and Fujiura (1993) surveyed 364 adults in various living arrangements and found overall rates of obesity of 27.5 percent for males and 58.8 percent for females. These investigators concluded that,

> . . . a disproportionate number of adults with mental retardation can be classified as obese. This is especially true for females, whose incidence of obesity was more than double that of males. Comparing our results to one of the largest data bases available for determining the prevalence of obesity in the United States on a nonretarded population . . . our data show that the incidence of obesity among adults with mental retardation is higher than for a nonretarded population . . . . These numbers are alarming and suggest that health-related concerns should be elevated as a priority (p. 108).

Rimmer *et al.* found that living arrangements were associated with obesity. The less restrictive the living environment, the higher the rate of obesity.

Presently, there are very little data on the relationship between obesity and psychopathology in persons with mental retardation (cf. Burkhart, Fox, & Rotatori, 1985). Fox, Burkhart, and Rotatori (1983) found no differences in self-concept and anxiety levels between 18 obese and 19 nonobese adults with mental retardation, but the self-report measures used in this study had not been shown to be valid.

Another eating disorder that has received some attention in people with mental retardation is *anorexia nervosa* (Cottrell & Crisp, 1984; Holt, Bouras, & Watson, 1988; Szymanski & Biederman, 1984). In this disorder, individuals refuse to eat, and they lose weight to the point that poses a danger to health. For example, this author recently learned of a man with mental retardation whose refusal to eat was resulting in a life-threatening weight loss of about one pound per day. One issue that arises in such cases is the degree to which depression,

anxiety, or stress may motivate this condition (Holt *et al.*, 1988; Szymanski & Biederman, 1984). Some preliminary and inconclusive evidence has been presented suggesting that affective disorder may be linked to some cases of anorexia nervosa in people with IQs of 50 or higher (Holt *et al.*, 1988; Szymanski & Biederman, 1984). However, psychiatric evaluation did not find a mood disorder in the case of the man who was losing a pound a day. Future researchers will need to evaluate more completely the relationship between anorexia nervosa and depression, anxiety, or stress in persons with mental retardation.

CHAPTER 3. DIAGNOSIS & ASSESSMENT

There has been significant interest in the diagnosis and assessment of mental health disorders in persons with mental retardation. This is partially because many services cannot be provided until after a diagnosis has been made. Another factor, however, is the discipline interests of psychiatrists and psychologists. Psychiatry has a strong tradition of attention to diagnostic categories, and psychology has excelled in the development of standardized assessment instruments. Our discussion of diagnosis and assessment will focus on the "new" definition of mental retardation, the applicability of psychiatric diagnosis for people with mild versus severe mental retardation, and the specific psychometric instruments that have been developed thus far.

I. AAMR CLASSIFICATION SYSTEM

In 1992 the American Association on Mental Retardation (AAMR) published a new definition of mental retardation (Luckasson, Coulter, Polloway, Reiss, Schalock, Snell, Spitalnik, & Stark, 1992). Whereas the past AAMR definition focused attention on the personal deficiencies of the individual in terms of intellectual behavior, the new definition draws attention to the possibilities of supporting people in inclusive environments.

A. PURPOSE OF NEW DEFINITION

The new definition represents a fundamental shift in attitude from a deficiency to a support model of mental retardation. In the past, when a child with mental retardation learned slowly in a regular education classroom, the tendency was to blame the child's disabilities. People would say things like, "Bill is just too handicapped for a regular classroom." Inadequate expectations were placed on both the teacher and the school for finding ways of supporting children with mental retardation in regular education classrooms. Past ways of thinking led to special education classrooms that we now know stigmatized many children, deprived them of opportunities to learn about their peers, and deprived the average child of having friends who have mental retardation.

It was not just children who were excluded based on past models of mental retardation. Exclusion also was common for adults. Many adults with mental retardation were presumed to be too disabled to work in competitive employment and/or to function as productive members of a community. Unemployment rates have been very high for people with mental retardation.

The AAMR Classification and Terminology Committee addressed the exclusionary aspects of past definitions by suggesting that mental retardation is an interaction between the person and the environment. The locus of the mental retardation is no longer in the person; instead, limitations in personal capabilities are seen as only one of three factors producing mental retardation. The AAMR model holds that mental retardation results from an interaction among the following three factors:

1. Limitations in personal capabilities;

2. The environments in which the person spends time;

3. The supports available to the person.

B. IMPLEMENTATION OF AAMR DEFINITION

One implication of the AAMR model is that clinicians should evaluate more than just the personal capabilities of the individual. Additionally, clinicians should assess the appropriateness of the environments in which the person spends time and the nature and intensity of each support the person needs.

The assessment of personal capabilities consists of an assessment of intelligence and an assessment of adaptive behavior.

- *Intelligence* is assessed by standardized tests with culturally appropriate norms.

- The concept of *adaptive behavior* was broadened to include ten adaptive skills. Presently, there are no instruments to help with this assessment; until appropriate instruments are developed, the assessment must be based on observations, interviews, and data in case files. The AAMR has appointed a task force to develop instruments for assessing adaptive behavior skills.

The new AAMR definition encourages diagnosticians to find ways to support people with mental retardation in inclusive settings. The AAMR recommends assessing the source, nature, and intensity of each needed support. This assessment should be based on detailed knowledge of the person. Presently, there are no psychometric instruments to help with this assessment.

C. CRITICISMS OF NEW AAMR DEFINITION

The new definition has been well-received. Recently, it was cited by the United States Supreme Court and had significant influence on the definition adopted by the American Psychiatric Association (1993). The Arc (formerly, Association for Retarded Citizens/United States) and TASH (The Association for the Severely Handicapped) have joined AAMR in supporting the new definition.

The main objections to the new definition concern some confusion regarding the suggested IQ cutoff scores (MacMillan, Gresham, & Siperstein, 1993). In the past, mental retardation was diagnosed only if the person's true IQ was believed to be 70 or less. The new definition includes language indicating that mental retardation can be diagnosed if the person's IQ is 75 or lower. Hence, there is an appearance that the new definition raised the IQ cutoff score from 70 to 75.

MacMillan, Gresham, and Siperstein (1993) have expressed concern that the new definition will lead to the diagnosis of numerous new cases of mental retardation. This concern is based on the assumption that the new definition raised the IQ cutoff score from 70 to 75. MacMillan et al. argued that this should lead to many new cases of mental retardation because it vastly increases the number of people eligible for consideration for diagnosis. Macmillan et al. also expressed concern about the effects of the new definition on African-American children. Specifically, they asserted that racial differences in IQ norms imply that more African-Americans than Caucasians have IQs between 70 and 75. One likely consequence of raising the IQ limit from 70 to 75 is that African-American children will represent a disproportionate percentage of the new cases of mental retardation.

The following three points have been made in response to the Macmillan et al. criticisms (Reiss, in press; Schalock et al., in press).

1. MacMillan et al.'s assertion that the new definition raised the IQ cutoff from 70 to 75 is based on a misunderstanding of the need for flexibility in interpreting the significance of IQ scores. If IQ tests were perfectly reliable and valid, the AAMR would have set the IQ cutoff at 70. Because IQ tests have some unreliability, however, the AAMR rejected an absolute IQ cutoff score of 70. An absolute IQ cutoff score of 70 would require the automatic diagnosis of a "cure" whenever a person who tested at IQ 68 is retested at IQ 72. The AAMR did not want people to lose services and benefits simply because of a few points difference on an IQ retesting.

The AAMR's position on the need for flexibility in the interpretation of IQ scores did not change from the old to the new definition. In the old

AAMR definition, IQ 70 was suggested to be a guideline, equivalent to a band or zone of IQ scores of 66 to 74 or 62 to 78 (Grossman *et al.*, 1983, p. 24). The authors of the old AAMR definition suggested that it sometimes is necessary to consider IQs of 75 or higher, especially for school children, due to the unreliability of IQ tests. In the new AAMR definition, diagnostic teams have the flexibility of considering IQs as high as 75 if they believe that the "true" IQ is 70 (two standard deviations below the norm.)

In conclusion, the AAMR did not raise the IQ limit in its new definition of mental retardation. The new definition was not intended to increase the numbers of people who could be evaluated for possible mental retardation. Instead, the AAMR simply continued the past practice of allowing diagnosticians some flexibility in interpreting the meaning of IQ scores.

2. Macmillan *et al.* presented no evidence to support their concerns about possible overdiagnosis. No studies have been conducted comparing the old and new AAMR definitions regarding the numbers of people who are diagnosed as having mental retardation. No case study has been published in which the use of the new definition resulted in an inappropriate diagnosis of mental retardation. If the criticisms raised by Macmillan *et al.* were valid, by now some "horror stories" should have come to the attention of the field. This has not happened. The concerns are coming from academic models of IQ, not from research studies, and not from the real world.

3. The MacMillan *et al.* position on race is illogical. If African-Americans score lower than Caucasians on a particular IQ test, the best method for avoiding over-representation of African-Americans in special education would be to use different IQ cutoff scores for the two races. This is exactly what the AAMR proposed — that the "cutoff" score for each race should be two standard deviations below the culturally appropriate norm (Luckasson *et al.*, 1992, p. 45). Yet MacMillan *et al.* did not argue for different cutoff scores for the different races. Instead, they argued that the best way to avoid racial over-representation in special education is to use an inflexible IQ cutoff score of 70 for all races. *MacMillan et al. misunderstood that the cultural bias of certain IQ tests is an argument for, not against, flexibility in interpretation of IQ scores.*

Reiss (in press) has called for the issues to be resolved by empirical research. Absent empirical research, it seems unlikely that any amount of additional

debate will resolve the substantive issues. Researchers need to determine if there is any merit to the criticisms of the new definition. Research also is needed to evaluate the impact of the new definition on support systems and inclusionary practices.

D. IMPLICATIONS FOR PEOPLE WITH CHALLENGING BEHAVIOR

The 1992 AAMR definition has a number of implications for people with challenging behavior. This includes the need for diagnosticians to identify the specific supports this population requires to function in inclusive community environments. Sometimes behavioral supports are needed; sometimes psychopharmacological (drug) supports are needed; sometimes the environment needs to be changed; and often a combination of these interventions is needed.

The 1992 AAMR definition introduced a multidimensional assessment system in which mental health disorders are evaluated on Dimension II. The new system is as follows:

Dimension I: Intellectual Functioning and Adaptive Skills
Dimension II: Psychological/Emotional Considerations
Dimension III: Physical/Health/Etiology Considerations
Dimension IV: Environmental Considerations

In assessing Dimension II issues, professionals are encouraged to use the most recent version of the *DSM*, which should be *DSM-IV* at the time of publication of this book.

The 1992 AAMR definition recognized the importance of social skills for adaptive behavior. Social skills are listed as one of ten adaptive skills, and an assessment of positive and negative social skills is required. As previously noted, poor social skills have been implicated in the development of depression and other mental health disorders in persons with mental retardation.

II. IDENTIFYING PRIMARY VS. SECONDARY DISABILITIES

Historically, the central issue in the assessment of challenging behavior was to distinguish between primary and secondary handicaps (Cutts, 1957; Russell & Tanguay, 1981). Is the person primarily mentally retarded, or is the person primarily mentally ill? Did mental illness cause mental retardation, or did mental

retardation lead to mental illness? The determination of a primary diagnosis had major implications in terms of eligibility for services. People diagnosed as primarily mentally retarded were served by developmental centers, whereas those identified as primarily mentally ill were served by mental hospitals.

Although the distinction between primary and secondary handicaps is still used in many places, it has been criticized on both scientific and practical grounds (Reiss, Levitan, & McNally, 1982; Szymanski & Tanguay, 1980). Specifically, the following three criticisms have been raised:

1. *The criteria for making the distinction are poorly defined.* The distinction is so ambiguous it is almost always possible to argue any position one wants (Reiss, 1993). Mental retardation can be argued to be the primary disability because it creates vulnerability to mental health disorders. Mental illness can be argued to be the primary problem because it increases the person's need for supervision.

2. *Administrators have invalid reasons for requesting assessments of primary versus secondary handicaps.* As Smull (1988) has noted, the issue is basically an administrative one "masquerading as a clinical question. The intent is not to ensure the provision of appropriate services but to determine who gets 'stuck' with responsibility for serving a person for whom appropriate services do not exist" (p. 395).

3. *There are no psychological tests or objective measures that indicate validly when a person has a primary versus a secondary handicap* (Cutts, 1957).

The primary/secondary distinction has been associated with the underfunding of mental health services for people with mental retardation. Obviously, it is unwise to suggest that mental health disorders are of "secondary" significance when asking for funding for mental health services. In order to increase mental health services for people with mental retardation, attention needs to be directed at the primary nature of the need for such services.

Frank Menolascino introduced the concept of *dual diagnosis* as an alternative to the concept of primary versus secondary disabilities. Instead of trying to guess whether the primary disability is emotional or intellectual, both disabilities are diagnosed and appropriate interventions are recommended for each. No effort is made to suggest that it is more important to serve one set of needs rather than the other. Sometimes the person should be referred to specialists in developmental disabilities; sometimes the person should be referred to specialists in mental illness; and sometimes the person should be referred to specialists in both developmental disabilities and mental illness. The underlying philosophy is that all

disabilities should be diagnosed and all important service needs should be addressed. (The term *challenging behavior* is used in this text rather than the term *dual diagnosis;* see Chapter 1.)

III. THE STIGMA OF PSYCHIATRIC DIAGNOSIS

Some concern has been expressed about the effects of adding a psychiatric diagnosis for persons who already have been identified as having mental retardation (Szymanski & Grossman, 1984). Does the second label increase the stigmatization of the person, and if so, by how much and in what ways?

There is some research indicating that psychiatric labels stigmatize nonretarded people (e.g., Langer & Abelson, 1974). However, the implications of this finding may not be what is generally supposed. For example, researchers have found that aberrant behavior also is an important determinant of stigmatization (Sushinsky & Wener, 1975).

Presently, there is no research on whether or not a second diagnosis of mental illness significantly increases the stigmatization of a person who already has been diagnosed with mental retardation. It is theoretically possible that the second diagnosis leads to minimal additional stigmatization. Psychiatric diagnoses generally are less stigmatizing than the diagnosis of mental retardation. For example, Szymanski (1980a) reported that some of his clients asked to be rediagnosed as *mentally ill* rather than as *mentally retarded.*

Diagnosticians always should be sensitive to the stigmatizing impact of diagnostic labels. Diagnoses are recorded in case files, where they may stay for the duration of the person's life. Diagnoses should be kept strictly confidential in order to minimize possible stigmatization. Moreover, diagnosticians should focus on the identification of needed supports rather than on the identification of the person's deficiencies.

However, it will not be possible to avoid altogether the use of diagnostic labels. Diagnostic labels are used because they are necessary to select treatments and justify services, especially services paid for by third parties such as taxpayers or health insurers. Without diagnostic labels, only families who can pay privately would be able to obtain mental health services for people with mental retardation.

IV. PSYCHIATRIC DIAGNOSIS

In 1856 two people were born who would have profound impact on psychiatric diagnosis: Sigmund Freud and Emil Kraepelin (Kirk & Kutchins, 1992).

Freud was a theoretician who developed psychoanalysis, which is a comprehensive attempt to understand psychopathology from a developmental perspective. His ideas provided the basis for the first two official classification systems used in the United States, the *Diagnostic and Statistical Manual (DSM) I* and *II* (American Psychiatric Association, 1952, 1968). In contrast, Emil Kraepelin was an empiricist who categorized psychopathology and authored textbooks with detailed descriptions of each category. His approach to psychiatric classification was adopted by the authors of *DSM-III* (American Psychiatric Association, 1980).

A. RELIABILITY OF PSYCHIATRIC DIAGNOSIS

Whatever one might think of *DSM-II's* psychodynamic approach, it is undeniable that this classification system had serious scientific problems. The diagnostic categories of *DSM-II* were poorly defined. Homosexuality was defined as a mental illness, causing many to wonder if *DSM-II* was a social document rather than a scientific system.

Perhaps the most noteworthy problem with *DSM-II* concerned its poor interrater reliability. (Interrater reliability is the extent to which diagnosticians agree when diagnosing the same cases.) Spitzer and Fleiss' (1974) review of relevant research found satisfactory levels of interrater reliability for only three *DSM-II* categories: mental retardation, organic brain syndrome, and alcoholism. The interrater reliabilities for psychosis and schizophrenia were found to be fair. All other diagnostic categories had low interrater reliability. For the most part, different psychiatrists gave different *DSM-II* diagnoses to the same people.

The authors of *DSM-III* attempted to improve the interrater reliability of psychiatric diagnosis by introducing a multiaxial diagnostic system and by operationally defining diagnostic categories. The criteria for making specific diagnoses were defined much more objectively than had been the case in the past. This was accomplished in part by basing *DSM-III* on a neuroscience model of psychopathology rather than on *DSM-II's* Freudian psychodynamic model. It was claimed that the interrater reliabilities for the *DSM-III* categories were much higher than those for *DSM-II* (Talbott, 1980, p. 27). This claim has been repeated in many textbooks.

Kirk and Kutchins (1992) have raised a number of criticisms of the view that *DSM-III* is more reliable than *DSM-II*. Their major points are as follows:

1. The claim of higher reliability is based on a new statistic called *kappa*. The use of this statistic is controversial. There are no conventional standards for determining high and low kappa values. Kappa is highly unreliable when the prevalence of a disorder is less than five percent of a sample.

Kappa values can move up or down substantially for reasons unrelated to the interrater agreement and validity of psychiatric diagnosis.

2. There are few studies in which the reliability of *DSM-II* and *DSM-III* were compared directly and *DSM-III* was found to be more reliable. On the contrary, a number of independent studies found that the reliability of *DSM-III* is a major problem, much like it was for *DSM-II* (e.g., Bassett & Beiser, 1991; Werry, Methuen, Fitzpatrick, & Dixon, 1983). The problems of co-morbidity and overlapping symptomatology appear to be the main reasons for findings of low interrater reliabilities for *DSM-III*.

3. The *DSM-II* reliability data were reported in terms of *r* values, not kappa values, so that the initial claim of higher reliability for *DSM-III* versus *DSM-II* was based on comparisons of *r* values with kappa values. These two statistics are not directly comparable.

4. The *DSM-III* manual overstated the actual findings regarding the reliability of *DSM-III* diagnoses. Although it was suggested that most kappa values were .70 or higher, this was untrue. Most kappa values were below .70.

5. The reliability of *DSM-III* was investigated by a research program now known as the "*DSM-III* field studies." These studies used biased raters (authors of the *DSM-III*). Many of the raters were present during the same interviews and were not truly independent of one another. There were unexplained discrepancies in the details of various reports on the field studies, including a variance of 25 percent in the number of subjects. Thus, the field studies had methodological shortcomings that biased the results in favor of high interrater reliabilities.

Are these criticisms applicable to the *DSM-III-R* and the new *DSM-IV?* According to Kirk and Kutchins (1992), by the time we find out we will likely have a *DSM-V* and then a *DSM-VI*. Until we have independent and rigorous evaluations of a current version of the *DSM*, Kirk and Kutchins argue that we should be skeptical about the interrater reliabilities of psychiatric diagnoses.

Despite these criticisms, many authorities believe that at least portions of the *DSM-III-R* system are reliable and valid. For example, Matarazzo (1983) has noted that some major psychiatric categories — such as psychosis, epilepsy, alcoholism, senility, and hysteria — have been recognized virtually unchanged since ancient times. These categories tend to have adequate to good interrater reliabilities. Recent data also have indicated that the interrater reliabilities are good for various anxiety disorders (DiNardo, Moras, Barlow, Rapee, & Brown, 1993).

B. PSYCHIATRIC DIAGNOSIS AND MENTAL RETARDATION

Most authorities agree that psychiatric diagnoses are applicable for people with IQs above 50 (MacLean, 1993). However, there is disagreement concerning the applicability of psychiatric diagnosis for people with IQs below 50 (Dosen, 1993a). For people with IQs less than 50, some authorities believe that psychiatric diagnoses can be based on behavioral and biological markers, whereas others believe that it often is impossible to diagnose certain psychiatric disorders.

B1. APPLICABILITY OF PSYCHIATRIC DIAGNOSIS. Macmann and Barnett (1993) evaluated the interrater reliability of psychiatric diagnoses for a sample of 126 people with mental retardation receiving services in a private residential facility. The findings suggested that the interrater reliability of psychiatric diagnosis under real-world conditions may be fairly low. Unfortunately, there were significant methodological shortcomings to the study. One problem was that 84 percent of the subjects were diagnosed as having either organic brain disorder or pervasive developmental disorder. This was a study on the interrater reliability of these two diagnoses rather than an investigation of the interrater reliability of psychiatric diagnosis in general. Moreover, the assessment of interrater reliability was of questionable validity because the diagnoses were made at different points in time.

Bouras, Brooks, and Drummond (1993) also evaluated the applicability of psychiatric diagnosis for people with mental retardation. These investigators examined 356 referrals to a community psychiatric service in England over a period of ten years. The sample included 57.6 percent with mild mental retardation, 27.4 percent with moderate mental retardation, and 15 percent with severe mental retardation. They were able to make a *DSM-III-R* psychiatric diagnosis in only 42.8 percent of the people they evaluated. In the remaining cases, behavioral problems were evident, but it was not possible to determine a specific psychiatric diagnosis.

In conclusion, some preliminary data have been reported concerning the degree to which psychiatric diagnosis can be applied to people with mental retardation. Psychiatric diagnosis seems applicable in some cases but not in others. Much more research is needed, however, before any conclusions can be drawn.

B2. MR FACTORS LIMITING PSYCHIATRIC DIAGNOSIS. A number of factors account for the special difficulties of psychiatric diagnosis in people with mental retardation. Some of these factors are as follows:

UNRELIABLE SELF-REPORT DATA. As noted in Chapter 2, diagnosticians often must rely on the person's self-report to identify the presence of psychiatric

symptoms such as hallucinations, delusions, and obsessional thought. Although nonretarded people can self-report their emotions, experiences, thoughts, and social relationships, people with mental retardation have difficulty doing so. This difficulty increases as the IQ of the person decreases. In people with IQs above 50, disabilities concerning discrimination learning (Zeaman & House, 1963) and emotional recognition (Rojahn, Raboid, & Schneider, in press) can lead to significant unreliability in self-report data. In people with IQs below 50, there is the added problem of significant impairment of language capability. Thus, psychiatric diagnosis in people with mental retardation is difficult partially because subjects often are unable to provide the clinician with reliable self-report data.

CLOAK OF COMPETENCE. Another factor that increases the difficulty of applying psychiatric diagnosis is that people with mental retardation try to hide their disabilities. They pretend to be making problem-free adjustments even when they are making poor adjustments. Edgerton (1967) has referred to this phenomenon as the "cloak of competence." The phenomenon suggests that some people with mental retardation would rather be mis-diagnosed as mentally ill than admit to an interviewer/doctor that they do not understand a question.

PSYCHOSOCIAL MASKING. The symptoms of various psychiatric disorders sometimes are expressed differently in people with mental retardation. Often the symptoms are expressed in simple and unimaginative ways. The expression of symptoms also may be affected by the restricted real-world experiences of people with mental retardation (Sovner, 1986; Szymanski, 1980a). For example, Menolascino observed that:

> When the normal person becomes manic, he thinks he's God. When the mentally retarded person becomes manic, he thinks he's not retarded (as quoted in Sovner, 1986).

Sometimes the life experiences of a person with mental retardation lead to behavior that appears to be symptomatic of a psychiatric condition but which is best attributed to the person's life conditions. For example, Szymanski (1980a) reported the following case vignette:

> A mildly-retarded 14 year-old boy talked during psychological testing about a girl in his head who "controlled" him. He was diagnosed as psychotic, but in psychiatric interviews no evidence of thought disorder was found. The boy told, with a smile, how the girl in his head was, of course, not real but that he had to invent her since, not having any friends, he needed someone to talk to (pp. 77-78).

As the preceding case example illustrates, the diagnosis of mental illness

must take into account the life conditions of people with mental retardation. Their aspirations are much more modest than those of people in the general population. The specific nature of their symptoms reflects the circumstances under which they live. They tend to be segregated from the community and may develop imaginary friends just to escape loneliness.

BASELINE EXAGGERATION. Sovner (1986) has observed that the onset of mental illness can intensify a pre-existing maladaptive behavior. For example, the onset of a major depression may intensify previous problems in the areas of poor social skills, attention deficit, and communication problems. When this occurs, the individual may present with a confusing array of symptoms from the standpoint of psychiatric diagnosis.

C. DIAGNOSTIC GUIDELINES

Reiss (1993) suggested the following guidelines to help in diagnosing psychiatric conditions in persons with mental retardation. The guidelines are designed to help answer the question, "Is this behavior problem an expression of psychopathology or some other condition such as mental retardation or neurological disease?"

C1. DIAGNOSE PATTERNS OF SYMPTOMATOLOGY. For a diagnosis of mental illness, the behavior problem should be one symptom in a defined pattern of symptoms that is considered a psychiatric disorder in the latest version of the *DSM*. In other words, the question, "Is this behavior problem an expression of psychopathology?" should mean the same as the question, "Is this behavior problem part of a correlated pattern of symptoms that is described in the *DSM* as a psychiatric disorder?" When a behavior is associated with a recognizable *DSM* pattern of symptomatology, the appropriate mental illness should be diagnosed. When a behavior is not associated with a recognizable *DSM* pattern of symptomatology, no mental illness should be diagnosed, except where there may be specific knowledge that a particular disorder is expressed differently in mental retardation. By itself, a behavior problem is an insufficient basis for a psychiatric diagnosis.

The principle of diagnosing patterns of symptoms can be applied to Szymanski's (1980a) example of a lonely boy with an imaginary friend. In this case, there were no symptoms of psychosis except for the possible symptom of hallucination. There were no disorganized thoughts, delusions, bizarre behavior, and emotional blunting. Consequently, a diagnosis of psychosis was not indicated.

C2. DIAGNOSE CHANGES IN BEHAVIOR. The onset of many mental disorders is associated with a deterioration in behavior called a *regression*. This fact

can be used to help diagnose psychopathology in people with mental retardation. For example, suppose we need to decide if a man's unkempt appearance is a sign of schizophrenia. If the man's current self-care habits represent a deterioration from prior habits, the behavior may be a sign of regression, and schizophrenia is suggested. If the man's current habits do not represent a deterioration from prior functioning, the behavior is not a sign of regression, and schizophrenia is not suggested.

Generally, mental illness should be diagnosed when an entire category of psychiatric symptoms develops as a deterioration of behavior from prior levels of functioning. For example, when the death of a loved one is followed by regression and changes in activity levels, eating habits, and sleeping habits, there is a basis for a diagnosis of major depression. If during late adolescence a person with mental retardation presents with gross deterioration in functioning and symptoms such as inappropriate affect, increased bizarre behavior, and increased anxiety, there is a basis for diagnosing psychosis even if hallucinations, delusions, and thought disorder cannot be confirmed due to the person's poor verbal abilities.

The phenomenon of regression cannot be used to help diagnose personality disorders in people with mental retardation. As noted in Chapter 2, these disorders develop gradually over the course of a lifetime and have no clear onset.

C3. MAKE ALLOWANCES FOR THE IMPACT OF INTELLECTUAL DISABILITY AND PSYCHOSOCIAL MASKING. As already noted, symptoms sometimes are expressed differently in people with mental retardation. The symptoms tend to be simple, unimaginative, and reflect the social circumstances of the person's life. In diagnosing mental illnesses, diagnosticians sometimes need to make appropriate allowances for these factors in order to recognize psychiatric symptoms.

C4. ADMIT LIMITATIONS OF KNOWLEDGE. Sometimes the behavior problems of people with severe or profound mental retardation are so ambiguous that they cannot be diagnosed with any confidence. In such cases, the best one can do is to acknowledge the diagnostic ambiguity and to make no diagnosis at all. One should not provide diagnostic opinions beyond those that can be based on current knowledge. Speculative diagnoses undermine the credibility of the field and encourage unnecessary doubts about diagnoses that can be made with confidence.

D. SOURCES OF ASSESSMENT INFORMATION

Comprehensive clinical assessments of mental health disorders should be based on the following multiple sources of information.

D1. CASE RECORDS. Case files provide important information about the onset and duration of psychiatric symptoms. Although the case files on people with aberrant behavior tend to be voluminous — containing numerous behavioral incidents, professional reports, medical test data, and intake summaries — a careful reading of the entire file sometimes provides information that cannot be readily obtained anywhere else.

D2. OBSERVATIONS OF BEHAVIOR. Behavior analysis provides information about the current frequency and intensity of maladaptive behavior. Even when a detailed behavior analysis is not possible, diagnosticians should visit the person's everyday environments, including classrooms and residential programs.

D3. CLIENT INTERVIEWS. By spending time interacting with the person, the diagnostician can learn first-hand the ways in which the person relates to other people. For people with mild mental retardation, the interview can be conversational in nature. For people with severe mental retardation, the interview may consist of playing or participating in some activity with the person.

Szymanski (1980*a*) has identified a number of issues in clinical interviews with people with mental retardation. One challenge is to determine early in the interview the level of conversation most appropriate for a particular person. If the language is too complex, the person will not understand the interviewer; if the language is too simple, the person may be insulted. Another challenge is to avoid the perception of the interview as a test or medical procedure. Szymanski advises direct descriptions of the interview process to create appropriate expectations. Szymanski also notes that people with mental retardation find periods of silence to be anxiety provoking.

Sovner and Hurley (1983*b*, 1983*c*) have discussed a special type of interview called the *Mental Status Examination* (MSE). This is a psychological/behavioral assessment that is used for "diagnosis, documentation of behavioral problems, and treatment" (Sovner & Hurley, 1983*b*, p. 5). For persons with mental retardation, the interview may be divided into several brief (10 to 15 minutes) interviews. The interview should be conducted in the setting that is most comfortable to the person. Family members, treatment staff, and direct care workers may be interviewed in addition to the person.

The *MSE* assesses six areas of functioning: general appearance and behavior; speech and thought processes; feeling states; psychotic symptomatology; other psychiatric phenomena (e.g., phobias); and cognitive functioning. Sovner and Hurley offered the following tips for conducting an *MSE:* use objects or tasks to elicit information; avoid questions that have a yes/no answer; and use pictures whenever possible.

Duckworth, Radhakrishnan, Nolan, and Fraser (1993) have developed a rating scale for evaluating psychiatric interview skills. The instrument evaluates nonverbal behavior, vocal behavior, and verbal behavior. Preliminary interrater reliability has been assessed. The scale may be useful as an aid in training interviewers, especially medical interviewers, who all too often focus their interviews on diseases rather than on conversing with individuals to understand how problems relate to people's lives.

D4. STAFF INTERVIEWS. Staff interviews can be an important source of information about maladaptive behavior, interpersonal relationships, and social behavior. The staff should be promised confidentiality and protected from the possibility that work supervisors will attempt to find out what was said.

D5. PSYCHOLOGICAL INSTRUMENTS AND BIOLOGICAL MARKERS. Psychometric instruments, projective techniques, and biological markers sometimes are used to help assess mental illnesses in people with mental retardation. A discussion of these techniques is presented later in this chapter.

V. EVALUATING PSYCHOMETRIC INSTRUMENTS

Many researchers assume that the criteria for developing and evaluating psychometric instruments are well understood. In the opinion of this author, however, this is untrue. There are a number of scientific issues that seem to be widely misunderstood. The following is a discussion of some of these issues.

A. PSYCHOMETRIC EVALUATION CRITERIA

The two most important criteria in evaluating psychometric instruments are *reliability* and *validity*. Reliability refers to the extent to which an instrument provides consistent results for the same individual. Validity refers to the extent to which an instrument measures what it purports to measure. If a measure is unreliable, it measures nothing and has no validity. If a measure is reliable, it may or may not be valid.

A1. TYPES OF RELIABILITY. There are several types of reliability. The reliability most commonly reported in the challenging behavior literature is *interrater reliability*. As previously noted, interrater reliability is an index of the degree of agreement among two or more raters using the same instrument with the same individual. Interrater reliabilities are assessed in terms of correlations or percent

agreement scores.

Another commonly reported statistic is called *test-retest reliability*. This is an index of the extent to which the same test produces the same results with the same person at different points in time. Test-retest reliability is relevant primarily in the assessment of traits that are supposed to change little over time. Test-retest reliability has limited relevance for psychopathology instruments because symptomatology often changes over time.

The most important type of reliability for a psychometric instrument is called *internal reliability*. Internal reliability is the extent to which the items of an instrument all measure the same attribute. Internal reliability is most commonly assessed by the split-half method or by Cronbach's alpha coefficient, which is the average of all possible split-half correlations. Internal reliability is important because it determines the maximum possible validity coefficient.

A2. INTERNAL VERSUS INTERRATER RELIABILITY. Some psychopathology researchers have overestimated the importance of interrater reliability and underestimated the importance of internal reliability. Interrater reliability is affected by many factors unrelated to the specific nature of a diagnostic category or psychological instrument. For example, estimates of the interrater reliability of an instrument can vary greatly depending on factors such as: the pretraining of the raters; the opportunity the raters have to discuss their ratings prior to recording them; the motivation of the raters; the use of individual scores from a single rater versus the use of average scores from two or more raters (Reiss, 1988*b*); the degree of exactness required for agreement in percent agreement scores; and statistical methods such as kappa and weighted kappa that require estimations of reliability attributable to chance versus nonchance causes. (Logically, the estimation of chance reliability should be a validity issue, but with the kappa statistic it is treated as a reliability issue.) Because the method for assessing interrater reliability can vary greatly from one assessment to the next, interrater reliability data often provide a poor basis for comparing different instruments.

On the other hand, internal reliability often provides a good basis for comparing different instruments. Generally, internal reliability is powerfully related to length — the more items on an instrument, the higher is the degree of internal reliability. As noted already, internal reliability is important because it determines the maximum possible validity coefficient.

A3. *r* VERSUS PERCENT EXACT AGREEMENT SCORES. Many behavioral researchers overestimate the value of percent exact agreement scores and underestimate the value of the Pearson product moment statistic, *r*, in the calculation of correlations. For example, Zarcone, Rodgers, Iwata, Rourke, and Dorsey (1991) have suggested that interrater reliability is most meaningfully assessed in terms

of the percentage of exact agreements among raters rather than in terms of *r*. These authors overlooked the fact that the calculation of *r* uses much more information (variance) than the calculation of percent exact agreement scores.

The advantages of the *r* statistic over percent exact agreement scores is documented in the following hypothetical example. Suppose that a researcher finds the following co-variation in noontime Farenheit temperatures in Columbus, Ohio, and Cincinnati, Ohio, over the course of a certain year:

	Columbus, OH	Cincinnati, OH
Jan 1	18.7	19.2
Feb 1	21.1	22.1
Mar 1	36.1	37.1
Apr 1	48.1	48.2
May 1	53.6	53.7
June 1	64.2	67.8
July 1	76.9	79.5
Aug 1	79.5	80.5
Sept 1	72.8	76.5
Oct 1	57.4	62.7
Nov 1	45.3	46.2
Dec 1	35.7	38.6

On the one hand, the Pearson product moment correlation between these two sets of temperatures would reveal a very high correlation, whereas the percent exact agreement score would indicate a zero correlation. In this example, the use of an *r* value produces the correct finding that temperatures in the two cities are highly related, whereas the use of the percent exact agreement score leads to the incorrect finding that temperatures in the two cities are unrelated.

The use of percent "exact" agreement statistics is rarely a good idea. For example, the correlation in temperatures for any two cities could be estimated as zero if the statistic were the percent of days during which the noontime temperatures were within 1/1,000,000th of a degree Centigrade. Agreement is almost never "exact," except where measurement is imprecise.

A4. VALIDITY STATISTICS. In recent years, psychopathology researchers have paid too little attention to validity questions. However, reliability without validity is of no value in a psychometric instrument or a diagnostic category.

The following types of validity are especially relevant to psychopathology instruments:

The *face validity* of a psychopathology measure is the degree to which

the items of the instrument refer to the symptoms of mental illnesses as listed in the *DSM* or in psychopathology textbooks.

The *concurrent validity* of a psychopathology measure is the degree to which it correlates with other validated measures of psychopathology.

The *criterion validity* of a psychopathology instrument is the degree to which test scores can be used to identify different diagnostic groups. For example, on average the total score on the children's *Reiss Scales* (Reiss & Valenti-Hein, 1994) provides a full standard deviation separation between children who do and do not have a mental health disorder.

The *predictive validity* of a psychopathology instrument is its sensitivity to treatment effects and other psychopathology outcomes. Since numerous measures have some sensitivity to treatment effects, predictive validity is best assessed in comparative research that identifies the measures that have the greatest degree of sensitivity to treatment outcomes. Predictive validity also can be assessed in nontreatment contexts. For example, a psychopathology instrument might be developed as part of a specific theory and found to predict events suggested by the theory.

A5. FACTOR VERSUS FACTOR CONTENT VALIDITY. Mental retardation researchers generally have misunderstood the role of *factor analysis* in test development. Many researchers have discussed factor analysis as a validity criterion when, in fact, there is no psychometric criterion called factor validity. If an instrument is shown to have a consistent factor structure across a number of samples, we should conclude that the factor structure has been shown to be reliable. This does not imply that the instrument is valid — it is theoretically possible for an instrument to yield consistent factors, all of which are invalid measures of what they are supposed to measure.

Although factor validity (the consistency of the factor structure across samples) is not validity, Reiss (1988c) has suggested a validity concept called *factor content validity*. Factor content validity refers to the degree to which a psychopathology instrument can be factored into scales that have face validity as a measure of diagnostic categories, such as schizophrenia, or well-defined psychopathological phenomena, such as negative self-concept.

This author believes that factor analysis has been widely over-used by psychopathology researchers. For many years, psychopathology researchers reported numerous factorial studies of symptomatology in the nonretarded population. Literally hundreds of studies have been reported on factor analyses of fears, anxiety, psychotic symptoms, maladaptive personality traits, and so on. Perhaps it is

time to play the devil's advocate and ask what has been discovered from all this research. In this regard, it is difficult to recall an important finding that resulted from factor analytic research. In some research areas, the results of factor analytic studies proved to be misleading by directing attention toward minor differences and away from important similarities. For example, findings from factor analytic studies misled fear researchers' attention away from the major similarities between phobias and panic attacks and toward less important differences among certain fears (Reiss, in press). Perhaps future researchers should rely less on factor analysis or at least understand better its potential limitations.

A6. CONSTRUCT VALIDITY

Construct validity refers to the degree to which an instrument measures a particular construct rather than some other construct. Although numerous scientists believe that construct validity is an important idea, this author holds an alternative view. In the opinion of this author, *construct validity implies a confusing distinction between the validity of a theory and the theoretical validity of the constructs within that theory.*

Because construct validity has been poorly defined, there is widespread confusion as to how it can be demonstrated. Some researchers think that construct validity is demonstrated by providing evidence for the psychological theory underlying the construct. For example, a researcher might test a new theory of intelligence to provide evidence for the construct validity of a particular measure based on that theory. Other researchers think that construct validity is established by factor analysis. For example, the items from a new anxiety test are pooled with those from other anxiety tests, and the pooled items are submitted to a factor analysis to see if the new test emerges as a separate factor.

Criticisms of poor construct validity sometimes degenerate into circular argument. When this author first tried to publish the *Anxiety Sensitivity Index* (Peterson & Reiss, 1992), he was told that it lacked construct validity. But in order to test the theory underlying the construct, it first was necessary to develop a measure. This author has learned to be skeptical whenever construct validity is used as the primary basis for criticizing a new instrument.

A7. SUGGESTED PSYCHOMETRIC CRITERIA. In summary, the following criteria are suggested to be most important in evaluating and comparing various psychopathology instruments:

1. Internal reliabilities (determine maximum validity coefficient).

2. The number of standard deviations separating average scores for various diagnostic groups.

3. The degree to which the instrument can predict psychopathology outcomes or treatment effects better than alternative measures.

The following criteria are relevant but less important:

1. The results of factor analyses (not an estimate of validity).

2. Interrater reliabilities (influenced too much by variables unrelated to the instrument).

3. Test-retest reliability estimates (symptomatology can change over time).

The following criteria should not be used except in special circumstances or with certain types of data:

1. Construct validity (difficult to distinguish clearly between the validity of a theory and the theoretical validity of the constructs within that theory).

2. Percent exact agreement scores (restricts variance; okay to use for non-parametric data).

B. SELF-REPORT VERSUS INFORMANT MEASURES

Both self-report and informant-rated measures of psychopathology have been developed (Matson, 1988; Reynolds & Baker, 1988; Reiss, 1988c). Typically, the self-report measures are administered in an interview format with the interviewer reading the questions and recording the person's responses. In contrast, the informant-rated measures are completed by caretakers, family members, or teachers.

Reiss (1988c, 1993) has discussed the following factors that can bias the results of self-report measures:

- *Denial* — people with mental retardation tend to self-report an overly positive view of themselves (Reiss, Benson, & Szyszko, 1993).

- *Distortion* — psychological defenses can keep people from recognizing

their true feelings (Rogers, 1961). For example, an angry person may self-report an upset stomach but not realize that it is caused by anger.

- *Social desirability* — people with mental retardation tend to self-report what they think will make interviewers like them (Reiss, Benson, & Szyszko, 1993).

- *Expectancy effects* — people with mental retardation tend to answer questions on self-report measures in accordance with the expectations of the interviewers who read the self-report measures (cf. Kirsch, 1990). This is partially because many respondents are motivated to please interviewers.

The results of informant-rated measures cannot always be interpreted at face value (Reiss, 1988c). These measures are subject to the following biasing factors:

- *Rater's Feelings, Personality, and Attitude.* The accuracy of behavior ratings sometimes is distorted by the psychological needs of the rater and/or the specific relationship of the rater and the subject. For example, when a caretaker rates a person with mental retardation as angry, we cannot be sure if the rating is accurate or if the caretaker, not the person, is angry.

- *Rater's Information.* The results of informant-rated measures may be invalidated by a rater's imperfect knowledge of the person (Reiss, 1988b). Raters vary considerably in how well they know a person and in what they know about the person. It is possible for a person's maladaptive behavior to go unreported on a rating scale simply because the rater has not had the opportunity to observe the behavior. For example, a rater may be familiar with the person's behavior at work or at school but not at home. A rater may be familiar with the person's behavior during the day but not at night.

- *Rater's Motivation.* Many raters are minimally motivated to complete an informant-rated scale (Reiss, 1988b). Some raters complete such scales quickly and without much reflection. Some just go through the scale indicating no behavior problems everywhere and hoping that the psychologist will go away and not ask them about their responses. Obviously, inadequate rater motivation produces invalid results.

One way to reduce the bias of informant-rated scales is to ask two or more raters to complete the scale for the same person and then average the ratings (Reiss, 1988b). The average judgment of raters is much less susceptible to rater

bias than is the judgment of a single rater. If a single caretaker rates a person as angry, the anger may be in the person or in the caretaker. If a group of caretakers rate a person as angry, the odds are very high that the anger is in the person and not in all of the raters.

Reiss (1988c) has suggested that informant-rated measures of psychopathology in people with mental retardation generally are superior to self-report measures. There is some evidence to support this hypothesis:

- Laman and Reiss (1987) found that Cronbach's alpha coefficient for a scale combining two supervisor-rated measures of depressed mood was .90 compared with .76 for a scale combining three self-report measures of depressed mood. The finding provided some preliminary support for the superiority of informant-rated versus self-report measures of depressed mood in subjects with mental retardation.

- Reiss, Benson, and Szyszko (1993) found that almost one-third of a sample of people with mild mental retardation could not meaningfully respond to a projective task requiring them to relate details about the feelings and behavior of the story characters.

- A number of psychiatrists have reported clinical observations suggesting that people with mental retardation have difficulty in self-reporting their emotions (e.g., Sovner, 1986).

VI. GENERAL PSYCHOPATHOLOGY INSTRUMENTS

When it became recognized in the mid-1980s that people with mental retardation were vulnerable to the full range of psychopathology, increasing attention was paid to the development of assessment techniques (Reiss, 1988b). Assessment instruments were needed to help identify people eligible for newly created mental health services and to support scientific research. The National Institute of Mental Health (NIMH) convened a workshop in 1986 on the methodological problems of research on psychopathology, including issues in measurement and assessment. The *Reiss Screen for Maladaptive Behavior* was introduced at the 1987 *UIC-NIMH International Research Conference on the Mental Health Aspects of Mental Retardation* held in Evanston, Illinois. (See Figures 3-1 and 3-2). The National Institutes of Health (NIH) and the NIMH jointly sponsored a 1988 workshop on assessment instruments (Dibble & Gray, 1990). The NIMH also issued a contract to fund Aman's (1991a) review of assessment instruments.

FIGURE 3-1.

International Research Conference on the Mental Health Aspects of Mental Retardation

June 8-10, 1987
Orrington Hotel
Evanston, Illinois

Organized by
Professor Steven Reiss
Mental Health Program Director

The Institute for the Study
of Developmental Disabilities

THE
UNIVERSITY
OF
ILLINOIS
AT
CHICAGO

114

FIGURE 3-2.

CONFERENCE AT A GLANCE

Monday, June 8, 1987

8:30 a.m.	Welcome Grand Ballroom			
9:00 a.m.	Keynote Address: George Tarjan Grand Ballroom			
10:00 a.m.	Coffee Break			
10:30 a.m.	**Symposium 1:** "Severe Behavior Disorders" *Heritage*	**Symposium 2:** "Psychiatric Diagnosis" *Mulford*	**Symposium 3:** "Cognitive Therapy" *Evans I & II*	
12:00 p.m.	Lunch			
1:30 p.m.	**Address I:** Andrew H. Reid *Grand Ballroom C*	**Address II:** Edward Zigler *Heritage*	**Address III:** Richard M. Foxx *Grand Ballroom B*	
2:30 p.m.	Student Poster Session & Coffee Break Grand Ballroom			
3:00 p.m.	**Symposium 4:** "Cognition and Emotion" *Grand Ballroom C*	**Symposium 5:** "Public Policy" *Heritage*	**Symposium 6:** "Existential and Play Therapy" *Grand Ballroom B*	**Symposium 18:** "Anxiety Disorders" *Evans I*
5:00 p.m. to 7:00 p.m.	Conference Reception Grand Ballroom			

Tuesday, June 9, 1987

8:45 a.m.	**Address IV:** Frank J. Menolascino *Heritage*	**Address V:** Stephen A. Richardson *Grand Ballroom C*	**Address VI:** Johnny L. Matson *Grand Ballroom B*	
10:00 a.m.	Student Poster Session and Coffee Break Grand Ballroom			
10:30 a.m.	**Symposium 7:** "Depression and Mental Retardation" *Grand Ballroom C*	**Symposium 8:** "Assessment of Emotional Disorders" *Grand Ballroom B*	**Symposium 9:** "Psychotherapy with Mentally Retarded People" *Heritage*	**Symposium 20:** "MR Offender" *Evans I*
12:00 p.m.	Lunch			
1:30 p.m.	**Address VII:** Jaime Rodriguez Sacristan *Heritage*	**Address VIII:** Nirbhay N. Singh *Grand Ballroom B*	**Address IX:** Steven Reiss *Grand Ballroom C*	
2:30 p.m.	Student Poster Session and Coffee Break Grand Ballroom			
3:00 p.m.	**Symposium 10:** "Schizophrenia and Mental Retardation" *Grand Ballroom B*	**Symposium 11:** "Research Ethics" *Grand Ballroom C*	**Symposium 12:** "Behavior Therapy" *Heritage*	**Symposium 19:** "Elderly Persons with Dual Diagnosis" *Evans I*

Wednesday, June 10, 1987

8:30 a.m.	**Symposium 13:** "Children and Families" *Heritage*	**Symposium 14:** "From Research to Improved Services" *Grand Ballroom C*	**Symposium 15:** "Psychopharmacology" *Grand Ballroom B*
10:00 a.m.	Coffee Break Grand Ballroom		
10:30 a.m.	**Symposium 13:** "Children and Families" (Continued from morning) *Heritage*	**Symposium 15:** "Psychopharmacology" (Continued from morning) *Grand Ballroom B*	**Symposium 16:** "Epidemiology" *Grand Ballroom C*
12:00 p.m.	Lunch		
1:30 p.m. to 4:30 p.m.	**Closing Session — Symposium 17:** "International Forum on the Need for Services" *Grand Ballroom*		

A. REISS SCREEN

The *Reiss Screen for Maladaptive Behavior*, published in 1988, was the first standardized measure of psychopathology in persons with mental retardation. It is one of the few measures with empirically-derived cutoff scores. Research on 1,456 people, including normative data broken down by level of mental retardation, was reported in the original test manual.

The *Reiss Screen* provides an objective method of asking caretakers, teachers, and supervisors to identify people with mental retardation who might have a mental health problem. Whenever practical, two or more raters are used in order to reduce the possibility of bias. The informants rate the degree to which each of 36 symptoms currently is *no problem, a problem,* or *a major problem* in the life of the person being evaluated.

The 36 items on the *Reiss Screen* cover the full range of psychopathology. Each item includes a nontechnical definition and common behavioral examples to facilitate understanding by nonprofessional raters. The initial list of symptoms and definitions was based on input from a number of clinical psychologists and psychiatrists with expertise in mental retardation. The final list reflected deletions of some items based on empirical evaluations of interrater reliabilities. One of the most important findings from the reliability research was that caretakers have special difficulty understanding certain mood concepts such as flat affect or excessive mood swings. Generally, the items referring to overt behavior were more reliable than those referring to mood and feelings.

The *Reiss Screen* provides a total score, scores for eight empirically-derived scales, and scores for six significant maladaptive behaviors. The total score on the *Reiss Screen* is viewed as a measure of the severity of psychopathology, whereas the scores for specific scales and maladaptive behaviors are viewed as measures of type of psychopathology. The eight scales include two psychometric measures for depression, one based on behavioral signs of depression and the other on physical signs of depression.

As noted previously, the *Reiss Screen* test manual summarizes research data on 1,456 persons (Reiss, 1988*b*). Only small or statistically unreliable differences were found for adult samples as a function of gender, age, or race. The *Reiss Screen* is standardized for persons with both mild and severe mental retardation.

The total score was found to have the best psychometric properties. Cronbach's alpha coefficient was estimated by Reiss (1988*b*) at .84. Others have obtained much higher estimates (Sturmey & Bertman, 1993; Van Minnen & Hoogduin, 1994, in press *b*). Cronbach's alpha coefficients for the five-item psychometric scales varied between .70 and .85, except for the Depression (Physical Signs) Scale which had lower internal reliability, due in part to the infrequent occurrence of the physical symptoms of depression in the initial research samples.

The *Reiss Screen* has a system of cutoff scores for the total score and for each of the psychometric scales. The cutoff points were set at the estimated value at which Type I and Type II errors are minimized; that is, the intersection of the distributions of scores for persons with and without the criterion psychiatric diagnosis. The system of cutoff scores was suggested to have an overall accuracy of at least 72.9 percent. For five years following the publication of these data, comparable data were not reported for any other mental retardation psychopathology assessment instrument.

The *Reiss Screen* has been validated against psychiatric diagnoses in case files (Reiss, 1988*b*). The correlation between *Reiss Screen* scores and case file diagnoses has been found to improve after the case file diagnoses were updated by psychologists who were unaware of *Reiss Screen* scores. The *Reiss Screen* scores also correlated significantly with the diagnostic results of psychological case studies made by Ph.D.-level clinical psychologists (Reiss, 1988*b*).

Reiss (1988*b*) reported that the mean total score is about three times higher for persons with a mental health disorder than for those with no mental health disorder. Reiss (1988*b*) also reported significant differences for various diagnostic groups on six of the eight psychometric scales. These findings provided preliminary evidence for the criterion validity of the psychometric scales.

The *Reiss Screen* total score is highly correlated with the total scores on both the *Psychopathology Inventory for Mentally Retarded Adults (PIMRA)*, which was intended for people with mild mental retardation, and the *Aberrant Behavior Checklist (ABC)*, which was intended for people with severe mental retardation. Sturmey and Bertman (1993) found a .61 correlation between the total scores on the *Reiss Screen* and the informant-rated version of the *PIMRA*. These researchers also found a .54 correlation between the total scores on the *Reiss Screen* and the *ABC*. These findings provide evidence for the concurrent validity of the *Reiss Screen*.

Van Minnen and Hoogduin (1994, in press *b*) translated the *Reiss Screen* into Dutch. A total of 172 adults with mental retardation were tested on the translated version. Van Minnen and Hoogduin reported a coefficient alpha of .90, which indicated a very high degree of internal reliability. People with psychopathology scored more than a full standard deviation higher than those with no psychopathology.

In 1992, interpretive computer software was published to support the use of the *Reiss Screen* (Gabby, 1992*a*). The interpretive program searches for patterns of symptoms in a hierarchical fashion, so that the search is terminated once a symptom pattern is recognized. For example, the program first evaluates the possibility of autism; if autism is interpreted as likely, the program interprets autism regardless of what other diagnoses might be suggested by test results. That is, when a person scores high on a number of psychometric scales, including autism, the most likely possibility is a diagnosis of autism.

Independent evaluations of the *Reiss Screen* have been favorable (Aman, 1991*b*; Prout, 1993; Sturmey & Bertman, 1993; Van Minnen & Hoogduin, 1994, in press *b*). Aman (1991*b)* recommended use of the instrument for screening purposes:

> The Reiss Screen is the only tool specifically developed for screening purposes in this population [adolescents and adults with mental retardation]; it comes replete with recommended cutoff scores and information about sensitivity and specificity (Aman, 1991*b*, p. 139).

Sturmey and Bertman (1993) obtained favorable validity data independent of those reported by Reiss. Prout (1993) concluded that "both scales [the *Reiss Screen* and *Reiss Scales*] are useful as screening devices" (p. 535).

One criticism of the *Reiss Screen* is the need for more data on the validity of the psychometric scales for diagnosing specific psychiatric conditions. Although the original test manual reported favorable data for a number of diagnoses, this work needs to be extended and replicated. The specific psychometric scales only contain five items each, and this probably limits the use of the instrument to measure specific diagnoses. The idea was to keep the length of the *Reiss Screen* to a minimum in order to maximize use as a quick screening instrument. Even with a length of only five items, however, some of the psychometric scales should prove to be valid indicators of general diagnostic conditions such as mood disorder, psychosis, or avoidant disorder.

The *Reiss Screen* has been one of the most widely used mental retardation psychopathology instruments. An instrument is not usually used and reused as much as the *Reiss Screen* unless practitioners feel it has some value.

B. REISS SCALES

This 60-item instrument was developed as a child and adolescent version of the *Reiss Screen* (Reiss & Valenti-Hein, 1990; Reiss & Valenti-Hein, 1994). As shown in Figure 3-3, the instrument has a total score that is a measure of severity of psychopathology and ten psychometric scales that were empirically derived through factor analysis. The instrument has separate psychometric scales for anger/self-control, attention-deficit, and conduct disorder. There are more psychometric scales on the children's *Reiss Scales* than the adult *Reiss Screen* because mental health professionals consider services for a wider range of adjustment issues in children than in adults. For example, anger and self-concept problems are much more likely to be diagnosed in a child than in an adult because of the possible impact on the child's psychosocial development.

FIGURE 3-3.

Reiss Scales for Children's Dual Diagnosis
(Mental Retardation and Psychopathology)

Child's Name _____ Date Tested _____

Age _____ Sex _____ Race _____

Severity of M.R. (mild, moderate, severe, profound): _____

Previous Psychiatric Diagnoses (if any): _____

Facility/School _____

Rater-1 _____ Rater-2 _____ Scorer _____

Psychometric Scales	**Other Significant Behavior**
_____ Anger/Self-Control	_____ Crying Spells
_____ Anxiety Disorder	_____ Enuresis/Encopresis
_____ Attention-Deficit	_____ Hallucinations
_____ Autism/Pervasive	_____ Involuntary Movements
_____ Conduct Disorder	_____ Lies
_____ Depression	_____ Obese
_____ Poor Self-Esteem	_____ Pica
_____ Psychosis	_____ Sets Fires
_____ Somatoform Behavior	_____ Sexual Problem
_____ Withdrawn/Isolated	_____ Verbally Abusive
_____ SUBTOTAL	_____ SUBTOTAL

_____ TOTAL SCORE (SEVERITY)

THESE DATA ARE INTENDED TO SERVE AS ONE PART OF AN OVERALL EVALUATION. ADDITIONAL EVALUATIONS ARE NECESSARY TO DETERMINE THE VALIDITY OR INVALIDITY OF THESE DATA FOR ANY GIVEN INDIVIDUAL.

© Copyright 1990 IDS Publishing Corporation. All rights reserved.

The *Reiss Scales* test manual summarizes data for 583 children and adolescents (Reiss & Valenti-Hein, 1990). Children with mild mental retardation score higher on the instrument than children with severe mental retardation. Adolescents aged 11 or older scored higher on all psychometric scales than children aged ten or younger. There were no significant differences in scores between boys and girls.

Estimates of internal reliabilities for the *Reiss Scales* were generally higher than those obtained for the *Reiss Screen*. Cronbach's alpha coefficients were estimated at .91 for the total score and between .63 and .86 for the psychometric scales. Internal reliabilities were .80 or higher for four of ten psychometric scales.

Some evidence has been reported for the criterion validity of the total score. The total score provides more than one standard deviation separation between children with and without psychopathology. The overall accuracy of the instrument when used for screening purposes has been estimated at 74.7 percent.

In 1992, interpretive computer software was published to support the use of the *Reiss Scales*. This software functions in much the same manner as that described previously for the *Reiss Screen*.

The *Reiss Scales* has not received as much attention as the *Reiss Screen*, although interest has increased significantly since the publication of Reiss and Valenti-Hein (1994). Since the development of the *Reiss Scales* benefited from the prior experience of developing the *Reiss Screen*, the *Reiss Scales* should be the superior instrument. The only independent review published thus far was Prout's (1993), which drew little distinction between the adult and the child instruments.

C. PIMRA

The *Psychopathology Inventory for Mentally Retarded Adults (PIMRA)* was developed in the mid-1980s to meet the need for a research instrument (Senatore, Matson, & Kazdin, 1985). The *PIMRA* consists of separate self-report and informant versions, each with 56 items. As shown in Figure 3-4, the *PIMRA* has eight psychometric scales.

The initial research data base for the *PIMRA* consisted of 209 adults, aged 18 to 71 years, with IQs in the severe to borderline range (Matson, 1988). The vast majority of the persons in the research samples came from either a university affiliated mental health center or a state hospital. Because of the small size of the data base, the *PIMRA* test manual reports no norms. Presently, the *PIMRA* scales are intended to be used as a structured interview to help assess specific *DSM* diagnostic categories. When used for this purpose, the *PIMRA* is basically a checklist that helps the user evaluate how many symptoms of various disorders

FIGURE 3-4.

The PIMRA

Self-Report

© Copyright 1988 IDS Publishing Corporation

Identifying Information   *Scores*

Subject's
Name _____

_____

Age _____ Sex _____ Race _____

Facility _____

_____

Date of Testing _____

Level of Mental Retardation:
(circle one)

Mild   Moderate   Severe/Profound

Schizophrenia   _____

Affective Disorder   _____

Psychosexual Disorder   _____

Adjustment Disorder   _____

Anxiety Disorder   _____

Somatoform Disorder   _____

Personality Disorder   _____

Inappropriate Adjustment   _____

Total Score   _____

Comments _____
_____
_____

Psychopathology Inventory for Mentally Retarded Adults, Self-Report Scale. By Dr. Johnny L. Matson. All rights reserved. No part of this form may be photocopied or reproduced in any way without prior written permission from the publisher.

are present. It is anticipated that norms will be added in the future so that the *PIMRA* may be used as a standardized instrument.

The internal reliability of the *PIMRA* total score was estimated at .83 by Matson (1988). Preliminary validity tests found that the *PIMRA* total score was significantly higher for persons with psychopathology versus those without psychopathology. Some preliminary evidence has been reported in which a high-low split on the *PIMRA* depression scale was found to be associated with other self-report measures of depression. Evidence for the concurrent validity of the *PIMRA* total score was obtained by Davidson (1988). This investigator studied a sample of 244 adults with mental retardation served by community-based programs. The total scores on the *PIMRA* and a predecessor instrument to the *Reiss Screen* were correlated at .83.

Van Minnen and Hoogduin (1994, in press *a*) translated the *PIMRA* into Dutch. Two samples were studied with 89 and 83 adults with mental retardation. The alpha coefficient for the total score was estimated at .92 and .88 for the two samples. The total scores on the *PIMRA* and *Reiss Screen* were correlated at .87. The subjects with psychopathology scored about twice as high on the total score than those with no psychopathology.

Independent evaluations of the *PIMRA* have indicated both strengths and weaknesses. A number of reviewers have ignored the *PIMRA* total score and focused instead on the eight diagnostic scales. Aman (1991*a*) raised a number of criticisms aimed mostly at the psychometric scales. First, Aman noted that Cronbach's alpha coefficients for the *PIMRA* diagnostic scales varied between .64 and .66, which is lower than the .70 minimally desired value (Aman, Watson, Singh, Turbott, & Wilsher, 1986; Watson, Aman, & Singh, 1988). Second, Aman noted that the *PIMRA* self-report and informant-rated versions are poorly correlated with one another. Third, Aman noted that except for the depression scale, the *PIMRA* scales have not been validated.

Linaker (1991) factor analyzed the *PIMRA* for a sample of 221 mostly institutionalized adults. In this study, the instrument was factored into clinically meaningful scales similar to those reported by Matson *et al.* (1984). However, Linaker (1991) criticized the *PIMRA* because it did not cover the entire spectrum of disorders. In particular, it lacks a scale for mania, and the only kind of depression covered is major depression.

Watson *et al.* (1988) criticized the *PIMRA* because it failed to factor into *DSM* scales for a sample of 160 persons. However, the Watson *et al.* study had some methodological shortcomings. Before it is possible to factor analyze *PIMRA* scores into *DSM* categories, it is essential that the scores be obtained from a subject population in which the full range of psychopathology is well represented. That is, raters cannot be expected to group symptoms into *DSM* categories unless they are rating *DSM* disorders.

On the positive side, the *PIMRA* has been one of the more widely-used mental retardation psychopathology instruments. An instrument usually is not used and reused as much as the *PIMRA* unless practitioners feel it has some value. Although the psychometric properties of the diagnostic scales are somewhat weak, the instrument has attracted a following based largely on the relevance of the content of the scales for *DSM* diagnoses. The face validity of the *PIMRA* may have been underappreciated by the instrument's critics.

D. ABC

The *Aberrant Behavior Checklist (ABC)* was intended to measure psychopharmacology treatment effects in persons with moderate to severe mental retardation (Aman, Singh, Stewart, & Field, 1985a, 1985b). The *ABC* is based on informant ratings and is scored into empirically-derived scales for irritability, lethargy, stereotypic behavior, hyperactivity, and inappropriate speech. Because many psychopharmacological agents affect irritability and activity levels, the *ABC* has face validity as a measure relevant to the evaluation of psychiatric medications.

The *ABC* is a carefully-developed, well-researched, 58-item behavior rating scale. The initial research samples for the instrument included 927 persons in mostly institutional facilities. Cronbach's alpha coefficients were good to high, ranging from .84 to .93. Marshburn and Aman (1992) reported data on an additional 666 students attending special classes. The factor structure of the *ABC* has been carefully identified and independently replicated (Bihm & Poindexter, 1991). There are some validity data for the total score as a measure of behavior problems, but there are less validity data for the individual factors. Separate norms have not been published for various diagnostic or criterion groups.

Although the *ABC* has excellent psychometric properties, the evidence for the validity of the instrument is only preliminary. There are some studies in which the *ABC* has been used successfully to evaluate the effects of psychiatric drugs (Aman, Singh, Stewart, & Field, 1985a). However, this is a simple validity test that many instruments pass. What is needed is evidence that the *ABC* is more sensitive to the effects of psychiatric drugs than are other instruments. Research is needed in which a battery of instruments is administered at pretreatment and posttreatment. The treatment variance that is correlated with the other instruments should be partialled out of the analysis so that the treatment variance that is uniquely explained by the *ABC* can be identified. This important validity research has not yet been conducted.

The *ABC* has a significant following and has been widely used and reused. As noted previously, instruments do not stand this test of time unless users think

they have some value. The *ABC* seems to be especially well-suited for the assessment of severe behavior disorders but may be less well-suited for the assessment of mental disorders.

E. DASH

The *Diagnostic Assessment Instrument of the Severely Handicapped (DASH)* is a 96-item rating scale for assessing psychopathology symptoms in adults with severe or profound mental retardation (Matson, Gardner, Coe, & Sovner, 1991). Because three ratings (severity, frequency, and duration) are required for each item, it takes 288 ratings to complete the *DASH*. This compares to only 36 ratings for the *Reiss Screen* and only 56 ratings for the *ABC*.

The *DASH* was developed by Matson and his colleagues in a manner similar to the way in which the *PIMRA* was developed. The psychometric scales were determined in an *a priori* fashion by studying *DSM-III-R*. The *PIMRA* and *DASH* comprise a package of Matson instruments in which the *PIMRA* was developed to be most relevant for mild mental retardation and the *DASH* was developed to be most relevant for severe mental retardation. However, no evidence has been presented that the *DASH* is superior to the *PIMRA* in the assessment of people with severe mental retardation.

The psychometric data on the *DASH* are based on samples totalling 506 persons with severe or profound mental retardation living in state institutions. Additional data were under analysis at the time of this review.

As previously noted, Matson's practice is to determine the content of psychometric scales on an *a priori* basis rather than through empirical research. This practice does not allow for the deletion of unreliable items or changes in the scoring system based on a factor analysis. In Matson's research, Cronbach's alpha coefficients for the *DASH's* 13 psychometric scales varied between .20 and .84 with a median value of .52. These findings provide a basis for questioning the reliability of the *DASH* in its current form. The *DASH* has by far the lowest degree of internal reliability of any of the psychopathology rating scales. Psychometric scales should have a minimal alpha coefficient of .70. (An average r of .52 accounts for only 55.1 percent of the variance explained by an r of .70; thus, an r of .52 is much below the *minimum* level of .70.)

Since the premise of the *DASH* was that *DSM* is of questionable applicability to severe and profound mental retardation, it is unclear why the *DASH* is scored into *a priori DSM-III-R* scales. The authors of the *DASH* begged the research question with which they began. Instead of basing the *DASH* on empirical findings of how psychopathology is expressed in people with severe mental retardation, the authors constructed the *DASH's* psychometric scales on the assumption that

psychopathology in people with severe mental retardation has the same structure as psychopathology in the general population.

The *DASH* might be strengthened with a new scoring system that resembles more closely its factor structure. In that case, the *DASH's* scoring system would be similar to that of the *ABC*.

Although the *DASH* is intended for people with severe mental retardation, the instrument has 13 items that refer to problems in speech, conversation, or memory. Items such as "speech is harder to understand," "sees things that are imaginary," "speech or sound production lacks emotion," "talks quickly," "verbally abuses people" may not be appropriate for an instrument designed exclusively for persons with severe or profound mental retardation. Some items, such as "talks with imaginary people," are included in the *DASH* as symptoms of psychosis even though Sovner (1986) has held that talking to imaginary people is not a symptom of schizophrenia in persons with severe mental retardation. The *DASH* might be strengthened by deleting this item and the other items that refer to memory and language behavior.

Aman (1991*a*) has criticized the scoring system on the *DASH*. The system requires subjective, fixed ratings for frequency (between 1 and 10 and more than 10 times) for all symptoms. Aman (1991*a*, p.78) suggested that this may be too inflexible:

> To take a specific example, the very essence of stereotypic behavior is that it is performed repetitively, and [the *DASH's*] frequency scale that permits only two levels of gradation (between 1 and 10 times and more than 10 times) may not be sufficiently sensitive to subject differences.

In conclusion, the *DASH* represents a commendable effort to develop a diagnostic instrument explicitly designed for people with severe mental retardation. However, at this point in time we may not know enough about psychopathology in people with severe mental retardation to know how to develop a specialized psychopathology measure. There is no evidence that the *DASH* is superior to, or even as good as, alternative instruments in the assessment of psychopathology in persons with severe mental retardation.

F. PROUT AND STROHMER INSTRUMENTS

The *Prout-Strohmer Personality Inventory (Prout)* and the *Strohmer-Prout Behavior Rating Scale (Strohmer)* were designed for use with people with mild mental retardation and borderline intelligence. The *Prout* is a 147-item self-report instrument, and the *Strohmer* is a 135-item behavior rating scale. The psychometric

scales on the instruments were based on the authors' theoretical views on personality (Strohmer, Prout, & Gorsky, 1994). The authors of the *Prout* and *Strohmer* reported good to excellent reliability for each instrument. In fact, some test-retest reliability data are almost too high to be interpreted without additional research. For example, Strohmer *et al.* (1994) have reported a .88 test-retest correlation for the self-report version of the Depression Scale for a sample of 41 subjects with IQs between 56 and 81. Depression is not sufficiently stable over time for a reliability coefficient of .88 (Laman, 1989), and people with IQs between 50 and 60 have difficulty self-reporting mood in a reliable manner (Laman & Reiss, 1987). A .88 test-retest correlation for depression suggests a strong response bias, such as many subjects always giving the same answer regardless of the question.

The validity data for the *Prout* self-report instrument are based mostly on findings that different treatment procedures are correlated with varying test scores. For example, Strohmer *et al.* (1994) reported that people receiving medications scored higher than those not receiving medications. This is an invalid method of comparison because there is no indication of what types of psychopathology, if any, were present in the subjects with high scores. The evaluation confounded the effects of medication and possible psychopathology so that it is not possible to attribute differences in test scores to personality factors rather than to the consequences of the medications.

As far as this author could determine, the *Strohmer* informant-rating version of this instrument has been published commercially but not in peer-reviewed journals. Aman's (1991*a*) review of the informant-rating version noted strengths in the areas of assessed reliability and standardization. However, Aman also noted a frustrating lack of detail in the reporting of certain statistics. Aman's main critical observation, however, was the very low correlations reported between the self-report and informant-rating versions of the instrument.

Aman (1991*a*) noted that the theoretical rationale for the *Prout* and *Strohmer* instruments is unclear. The instruments have been variously presented as measures of personality and as measures of psychopathology. The authors did not follow the conventional *DSM* system in developing their scales. The authors did not expound clearly their own classification system and their reasons for rejecting the conventional *DSM* approach.

The *Prout* and *Strohmer* instruments represent an enormous amount of work. Aman (1991*a*) concluded that the test developers did a commendable job in standardizing the instrument. On the other hand, there is some confusion regarding the psychometric properties of the instruments. The instruments have been through two commercial publishers, and some items seem to have been deleted in the process. Presently, only one peer-reviewed article has been published, and that article appeared in a journal edited by one of the authors. The

authors have reported numerous statistical tests on so many different subsamples it sometimes is unclear how to interpret the data. The instruments might benefit greatly from additional validity data and from peer-reviewed reports of data on consistent samples and subsamples.

G. EDRS AND DD-CBCL

At the time of this book's publication, research reports had appeared describing the development of two rating instruments for children. The *Emotional Disorders Rating Scale — Developmental Disabilities (EDRS)* was among the first instruments to be reported in a scientific journal, but the article described the instrument in an early stage of development (Feinstein, Kaminer, Barrett, & Tylenda, 1988). Since no new data have appeared in almost six years, it is uncertain if the development of the *EDRS* will be completed.

The *Developmental Disabilities Child Behavior Checklist (DD-CBCL;* Einfeld & Tonge, 1991) is a 91-item instrument that was developed for use with children with IQs of 70 or lower. At the time of publication of this book, the instrument was still in a preliminary stage of development, but the authors were in the process of collecting and analyzing additional data. Einfeld and Tonge (1991) have reported favorable reliability data for the *DD-CBCL*. Cronbach's alpha coefficient of internal reliability was estimated at .90 for the total score. Interrater reliabilities were reported in the range of .78 to .93 for various assessments. Evidence of concurrent validity was reported in the form of statistically significant correlations with other maladaptive behavior rating scales and with clinician ratings of severity of maladaptive behavior. In conclusion, the *DD-CBCL* is among the more carefully researched instruments.

H. COMPARATIVE RESEARCH

Peter Sturmey has been at the forefront of comparative research on mental retardation psychopathology instruments. Sturmey's research has found significant correlations among most of the general instruments (Sturmey & Bertman, 1993; Sturmey, Reed, & Corbett, 1991). There is a need for much more comparative research. The intercorrelations among the instruments need to be assessed further, and the criterion and predictive validity of the various instruments need to be compared for the same samples of persons. Such research might provide empirical data on the comparative strengths and weaknesses of the various instruments.

VII. DIAGNOSTIC INSTRUMENTS

Relatively little attention has been paid to the development of measures of specific psychiatric disorders in people with mental retardation. The following is an overview of the current state of the art.

A. ANXIETY DISORDERS

King, Ollendick, Gullone, Cummins, and Josephs (1990) discussed the assessment of fears in people with mental retardation. They suggested that interviews to assess fears should focus on the individual's actual behavior and that attention needs to be paid to the possibility of acquiescent responses. The most appropriate fear survey schedules are the *Revised Fear Survey Schedule for Children (FSSC-R;* Ollendick, 1988) and the *Louisville Fear Survey for Children* (Miller, Barrett, Hampe, & Noble, 1971).

Gedye (1992) published a checklist for assessing OCD in persons with mental retardation. She presented no psychometric data because her checklist was intended as only a preliminary guide. Researchers interested in developing a measure might consider reviewing the checklist first for ideas for possible items.

Since no technique has been reported for the assessment of posttraumatic stress disorder (PTSD) in people with mental retardation, researchers might wish to consider the instruments available for nonretarded children. According to McNally (1991*b*), the available assessment techniques include structured interviews for children and parents, experimental techniques, and questionnaires. McNally found only preliminary research on the reliability and validity of these measures.

Lindsay and Michie (1988) adapted the *Zung Self-Rating Anxiety Scale* (Zung, 1971) for use with people with mental retardation. The subjects were 29 adults with mild to moderate mental retardation. Various response formats were evaluated, but internal reliabilities were low. A marginal split-half reliability of .69 was found for a no/yes response format. The main conclusion to be drawn from the study is the difficulty of developing reliable self-report measures with people with mental retardation, especially those with IQs below 60.

As shown in Table 3-1, both the adult *PIMRA* and the children's *Reiss Scales* include scales for anxiety disorders. Although these scales have face validity, they have not yet been evaluated for criterion validity.

B. MOOD DISORDERS

Meins (1993*b*) administered a German-translated, modified informant

TABLE 3-1. PSYCHOMETRIC CONTENT ON FOUR MEASURES

	ABC	PIMRA	REISS SCREEN	REISS SCALES
aggressive/conduct			s	s
adjustment disorder		s		
affective disorder		s	s	s
anger				s
anxiety disorder		s		s
attention-deficit				s
autism			s	s
avoidant disorder			s	
drug/alcohol abuse			i	
enuresis/encopresis				i
hyperactivity	s		i	
inappropriate adjustment		s		
inappropriate speech	s			
irritability	s			
lethargy/withdrawn	s			i
motor movements				i
obese				s
paranoia			s	
personality disorder		s		s
pica				i
schizophrenia/psychosis		s	s	s
self-esteem				s
sexual disorder		s	i	i
somatoform disorder		s		s
stereotypic behavior	s			
suicidal			i	

Notes
"s" indicates psychometric scale
"i" indicates standardized screening item

version of the *Children's Depression Inventory (CDI)* to 798 persons with mental retardation aged 20 and older. Approximately 56.9 percent of the sample lived in community-based facilities. The alpha coefficient for the 26-item instrument was estimated at .86. Follow-up psychiatric evaluations indicated that high scores were associated with a psychiatric diagnosis of mood disorder including major depression, dysthymia, and adjustment disorder. These findings need to be replicated by independent research to establish the *CDI* as a reliable and valid measure for depressed mood in persons with mild mental retardation.

Meins' modification of the *CDI* is designed primarily for people with mild mental retardation. The instrument appears to be less applicable for people with severe mental retardation. For example, some of the items (e.g., *pessimism, belief that one is ugly*) may be inappropriate for use with people who are nonverbal.

Reynolds and Baker (1988) developed a 32-item instrument, called the *Self-Report Depression Questionnaire (SRDQ),* for measuring depression in persons with mild mental retardation. The item content relates to the physical, cognitive, and behavioral symptoms of depression. The items are read to the person in an interview format, and the person responds by indicating on a three-point, anchored scale how frequently he/she experiences each symptom.

The initial research sample consisted of 103 persons with mild mental retardation between the ages of 21 and 72 years. Approximately 14 percent of the sample was unable to pass a pretest that evaluated whether or not they could comprehend the items. For the remaining subjects, a coefficient alpha of .90 was found. Test-retest reliability over an 11-week period was .63, or about what should be expected given the episodic nature of depression in persons with mental retardation (Laman, 1989). The *SRDQ* was found to correlate significantly with the *Hamilton Depression Rating Scale.*

The *SRDQ* is a promising, carefully-developed measure from an author who is recognized for assessment work with adolescent school populations. However, the instrument has not attracted a following, perhaps because of an absence of follow-up research.

Reiss and Benson (1985) reported that some of the items on the *Zung Depression Inventory* are inappropriate and confusing for people with mental retardation.

Some preliminary research has been reported on a 14-item self-report measure for loneliness in children with mild mental retardation (Luftig, 1988; Williams & Asher, 1992). The instrument, called the *Loneliness Questionnaire,* was found to have an alpha coefficient of .77 for children.

Benavidez and Matson (1993) administered self-report and informant-rated versions of three depression scales to groups of adolescents with and

without mental retardation. The depression scales were the *CDI*, the *Bellevue Index of Depression* (Petti, 1978), and the *Reynolds Child Depression Scale* (Reynolds, 1989). The three self-report versions were found to be correlated with one another at levels of .64 to .75; the three informant-rated versions were found to be correlated at much higher levels of .80 to .88; the self-report and informant-rated measures were only moderately correlated at levels of .31 to .48. Although the samples in this study were very small, the finding that self-report and informant-rated measures of depression are only moderately correlated should be evaluated further by future researchers.

The *PIMRA* includes a measure for depression that has been criticized by Meins (1993*a*) and others as inadequate, partially because of the low internal reliabilities with some samples. The two *Reiss* instruments include a measure of the behavioral signs of depression in adults, a measure of the physical signs of depression in adults, and a measure of depression in children. There is some evidence for the criterion validity of each of these measures. Moreover, these measures have been found to be associated with conduct problems (Reiss & Rojahn, 1993).

C. SCHIZOPHRENIA

The *PIMRA* has a measure of schizophrenia, and the *Reiss* instruments have measures of psychosis in children and adults. The items on the *PIMRA* Schizophrenia Scale are appropriate primarily for adults with IQs of at least 50. The psychosis scales on the *Reiss* instruments are more generally applicable. There is some preliminary evidence for the criterion validity of the psychosis scales on the *Reiss* instruments.

D. AUTISM

Three commonly used autism scales are the *Autism Behavior Checklist (ABCK;* Krug, Arick, & Almond, 1980), the *Real Life Rating Scale (RLRS;* Freeman, Ritvo, Yokota, & Ritvo, 1986), and the *Childhood Autism Rating Scale (CARS;* Schopler, Reichler, & Renner, 1988). Sturmey, Matson, and Sevin (1992) reported high internal reliabilities between .84 and .87 for the total score of each of these scales. Sevin, Matson, Coe, Fee, and Sevin (1991) found correlations between *DSM-III-R* diagnoses of autism and scores on both the *ABCK* and the *CARS*.

Both *Reiss* instruments have scales for assessing autism. However, these scales are not recommended for any purpose other than general screening. They are among the weakest scales on the *Reiss* instruments.

E. PERSONALITY DISORDERS

Reid and Ballinger (1987) adapted a personality instrument developed by Mann, Jenkins, Cutting, and Cowen (1981) for use with people with mental retardation. During administration of the instrument, the examiner interviews an informant and codes the information in accordance with the nature and severity of the symptoms. The coding categories are based on the 1977 edition of the *International Classification of Diseases*. Initial data were reported for 40 adults with a mean age of 48.5; subsequently, data were reported for an additional 100 institutionalized adults. All subjects had mild or moderate mental retardation. No data were reported on internal reliability or criterion validity; some data were reported indicating satisfactory interrater reliability. The instrument has not yet been standardized on people with mental retardation.

Spirrison (1992) is developing an instrument called the *Personality Traits Checklist (PTC)*. Initial data have been reported for 70 adults with IQs ranging from 20 to 84. The instrument has been factored into scales for agreeableness, social precision, intelligence, extraversion, neuroticism, effective hedonism, and rigidity. Data on internal reliability and validity have not yet been reported.

Both the *PIMRA* and the *Reiss* instruments have psychometric scales for assessing personality disorders in adults. These scales lack the details needed to diagnose subtypes of personality disorder.

F. SEVERE BEHAVIOR DISORDERS

Durand and Crimmins (1988) have published a 16-item rating scale, called the *Motivation Assessment Scale (MAS)*. The *MAS* was designed to assess the underlying motivation for self-injurious behavior. The *MAS* is scored into scales for sensory consequences, escape motivation, attention, and tangible consequences. Newton and Sturmey (1991) reported coefficient alpha values ranging from .67 to .91, with an alpha value of .83 for the total score. These data were obtained on small samples of only 12 and 15 subjects. A number of investigators reported evidence of factor content validity (Bihm, Kienlen, Ness, & Poindexter, 1991; Singh, Donatelli, Best, Williams, Barrera, Lenz, Landrum, Ellis, & Moe, 1993).

Zarcone *et al.* (1991) reported low rates of interrater reliability for the *MAS* and criticized past researchers for assessing the interrater reliability of the *MAS* in terms of the Pearson product moment correlation coefficient, r, rather than the percent of exact agreement between raters. Zarcone *et al.* noted that it is possible to obtain high r values even when there is minimal exact agreement among the raters. Although this is true, it is not a valid argument for the superiority of percent exact agreement scores over r values. As previously noted, the r statistic

is superior to percent exact agreement scores in the evaluation of interrater reliability.

In the criminal justice system, defendants with mental retardation sometimes are not competent to stand trial (Conley, Luckasson, & Bouthilet, 1992). They may not fully comprehend legal proceedings or be capable of adequately assisting in their own defense. In order to help professionals evaluate competence to stand trial, Everington and Luckasson (1992) developed a standardized instrument called *Competence Assessment for Standing Trial for Defendants with Mental Retardation (CAST*MR)*. This instrument is divided into three sections that address understanding of basic legal concepts, skills to assist defense, and understanding of case events. It is hoped that greater use of the instrument will result in fewer prosecutions of defendants who are not competent to stand trial.

Rojahn, Polster, Mulick, and Wisniewski (1989) have reported a 32-item instrument called the *Behavior Problem Inventory (BPI)*. The *BPI*, which was based on an instrument used in a national survey in West Germany, is designed primarily to assess the frequency of self-injurious and stereotypic behavior. Although the instrument is still under development, it holds promise for use in a detailed assessment of severe conduct problems with people with mental retardation.

The *ABC, PIMRA,* and *Reiss* instruments have a number of scales relevant to measuring various aspects of severe behavior disorders. For persons with severe mental retardation, the *ABC* has scales tapping the five dimensions of severe conduct problems. The *Reiss* instruments have scales for conduct problems, anger, and aggressive behavior. The *PIMRA* has an adjustment disorder scale for assessing people with mild mental retardation.

G. SEXUAL DISORDERS

As far as the present author could determine, no instruments have been reported for assessing sexual disorders in persons with mental retardation. However, one of the scales on the *PIMRA* is for the assessment of sexual disorders.

H. ATTENTION-DEFICIT DISORDER

Das and Melnyk (1989) reported a scale for measuring attention deficit. A coefficient alpha of .96 was obtained for 100 people with mild mental retardation. Preliminary evidence for the concurrent validity of the instrument consists of findings of a correlation with the Conners' (1969) *Abbreviated Teacher Rating Scale*.

The *Reiss* instruments have a psychometric scale measuring attention-deficit/hyperactivity disorder in children. Although this scale has face validity, it has not yet been evaluated for criterion validity.

VIII. PROJECTIVE ASSESSMENT OF PERSONALITY

The basic assumption of a projective technique is that people's responses to unstructured (ambiguous) stimuli may be determined in part by personality needs, drives and values. As Zubin, Eron, and Schumer (1965, p. 5) put it:

> Generally, the projection, as applied to projective techniques, seems more likely to be a process by which *S*, when he is presented with a number of ambiguous or semi-ambiguous stimuli and asked to make sense, order or to give meaning to these stimuli, does so while drawing on a reservoir of his own needs, emotions, feelings, or even level of knowledge.

The major examples of projective tests are *apperceptive tests,* which are story-telling techniques (Murray, 1943); drawing tests, such as the *Draw-A-Person* (Machover, 1949); and the Rorschach inkblot technique (Rorschach, 1921). These projective techniques, especially story-telling tests, have been widely used with people with mild mental retardation (Cutts, 1957; Reiss, 1992; Rosen & Weisz, 1983).

One widely used projective test is the *Thematic Apperception Test (TAT;* Morgan & Murray, 1935). In this technique, the subject is shown a series of ambiguous pictures and asked to make up a story about each picture. The story should have a beginning, middle, and end. The *TAT* is widely used with people with mental retardation because of ease of administration, the richness of data, and the absence of a viable alternative (Hurley & Sovner, 1985).

About 50 years ago, Sarason (1943*a,* 1943*b)* reported that the *TAT* was useful for assessing the inner lives of people with mental retardation. Hurley and Sovner (1985) suggested that the *TAT* is an "excellent personality instrument for mentally retarded individuals" (p. 12). Wagner (1991) reported the successful clinical use of the *TAT.* Reiss (1992) reported the successful use of an apperceptive instrument in identifying a paranoid-trigger for a man's explosive behavior incidents. However, Sternlicht and Silverg (1965) found no differences in *TAT* stories for people with mental retardation who were or were not aggressive.

A. FACTORS INFLUENCING STORIES

The *TAT's* popularity in the assessment of people with mental retardation

has received little scientific evaluation. There are very few studies on the use of story-telling techniques for people with mental retardation. However, there is an extensive scientific literature on the *TAT* itself. Research psychologists have learned a great deal about the stories people make up in response to ambiguous stimuli (Rapaport, Gill, & Schafer, 1968; Zubin, Eron, & Schumer, 1965). If there is one conclusion to draw from this literature, it is that *TAT* stories are determined by many factors. Projection of personality needs is at most only one of a number of factors that influence *TAT* stories. The stories people make up on the *TAT* are determined also by culture, social desirability, cognitions, defenses, affect, and interpersonal attitudes.

Because many factors influence *TAT* stories, interpretation of the *TAT* often is difficult and requires clinical expertise. When a subject makes up a story about a child who is extremely poor at athletics, it often is impossible to discern which of the following interpretations, if any, are true: the subject holds an unfavorable attitude toward children; the subject is angry; the subject thinks he is unathletic; the subject thinks the examiner wants him to say the child is unathletic; or the subject's tendency to view matters in extremes suggests immature cognitive development.

Interpretations of the *TAT* need to be considered in the context of all that is known about a person. Because the same stories can be interpreted differently, the *TAT* is best used as an instrument for suggesting hypotheses about personality, with the understanding that the hypotheses need to be confirmed by *non-TAT* data. The *TAT* is neither a personality "test" nor a scientific measure; rather, it is a procedure for generating hypotheses. Although many of the hypotheses generated when interpreting the *TAT* are false, the technique has some value because some hypotheses are true and may have been overlooked if the *TAT* had not been used.

B. APT

Stephen Karp and his colleagues have developed the *Apperceptive Personality Test (APT;* Karp, Silber, & Holmstrom, 1993), which was designed to increase the objectivity of projective assessment. The *APT* is administered in two parts. In Part I, a standard set of stimulus scenes is administered, and the subject makes up a story to each scene. In Part II, a multiple-choice questionnaire is administered about each story. The *APT* questionnaire adds new information and objectivity to the story-telling technique.

C. APT/MR

Reiss, Benson, and Szyszko (1993) developed a projective technique and new

stimulus scenes for use with people with mild mental retardation. The new technique, which is administerd in two parts, is called the *APT/MR*. In Part I, a standardized set of four stimulus cards is administered. (See Figure 3-5.) The themes are: mother-daughter, father-son, damaged toy, and social isolation. In Part II, a questionnaire is administered in an interview format. The questions require the subject to identify the story characters, describe the characters' feelings toward one another, and rate each character for intelligence, happiness, physical appearance, anger, basic goodness, trustworthiness, and aggression. The questions are concretely worded, and innovative rating scales are used to obtain four-point ratings from answers to a pair of "either/or" questions.

The initial normative data base for the *APT/MR* is 160 persons. The *APT/MR*, which is computer-scored, generates hypotheses about self-image, conduct, emotions, cognitions, defenses, interpersonal attitudes, and identification.

The *APT/MR* has a validity scale measuring the degree to which the subject discriminated between pairs of characters in the same stories. The greater the degree to which the subject gives the same descriptions for pairs of characters in the same stories (for example, the subject rates both characters as equally smart, good, happy), the lower is the score on the *APT/MR* validity scale. Subjects with low validity scores have not discriminated story characters sufficiently well to relate meaningful stories and/or they showed a response bias for certain ratings. The *APT/MR* should not be interpreted when subjects score low on the scale for validity.

Although the *APT/MR* offers a number of significant improvements over current practices, it is a new technique and additional evaluation is indicated.

D. HAND-TEST

Panek and Wagner (1993) have reported on a projective technique called the *Hand-Test*. The test was administered to 17 elderly people with both mental retardation and psychopathology and to 17 elderly people with mental retardation but no psychopathology. Most of the people with psychopathology had psychosis. The results indicated that the psychopathology group was higher on the scoring criterion for bizarre responses. This finding extends to persons with mental retardation one of the most established findings in the research literature on projective assessment, namely, that people with psychosis tend to produce bizarre projective responses.

IX. OTHER INSTRUMENTS

As noted in Chapter 1, one of the common consequences of challenging

FIGURE 3-5. Stimulus Scene from *APT/MR*

behavior is an impairment in the individual's quality of life. Therefore, it is relevant to note the recent publication of two instruments for assessing quality of life.

The *Lifestyle Satisfaction Scale* is a 45-item instrument suitable for persons aged 18 or older (Heal & Harner, 1993). The instrument has scales for satisfaction with community life, job, and leisure. The instrument also has an acquiescence (invalidity) scale. The norms are based on 149 persons. Internal reliability was estimated at .87; interrater reliability at .99; and test-retest reliability at .86.

The *Quality of Life Questionnaire* is a 40-item instrument designed to measure overall quality of life (Schalock & Keith, 1993). For the individual with insufficient language skills, the instrument is completed by two raters who know the person well and who are familiar with the person's current activities and living environment. The instrument is scored into scales for Satisfaction, Competence/Productivity, Empowerment/Independence, and Social Belonging/Community Integration. The norms are based on 552 people. Test-retest reliability has been estimated at .80 to .92.

X. BIOLOGICAL TESTS

The identification of biological markers may prove particularly relevant to the diagnosis of mental health disorders in people with severe or profound mental retardation. These people cannot self-report symptoms such as hallucinations and delusions. If biological tests could provide evidence for the presence or absence of mental illnesses, they could be used to help diagnose ambiguous cases.

The *Dexamethasone Suppression Test (DST)* is a laboratory test for identifying hypercortisolema, which is related to depression (Friedenthal & Swartz, 1986). The procedure involves the administration of 1 mg of dexamethasone orally at 11:00 p.m. Blood tests then are performed the next day, and positive or negative results are based on cortisol level.

More than 8,000 articles have been published on the *DST* (Wolkowitz, 1990). Although people with major depression show the highest rates of positive test results, people with other serious mental illnesses also show high rates. Many medical conditions, such as renal failure and cancer, also affect *DST* results. Investigators have not yet reached a consensus on the specificity of the *DST* as a marker for depression (Reus, 1985).

Three studies have been reported on the use of the *DST* as a marker for depression in people with mental retardation. Pirodsky, Gibbs, Hesse, Hsieh, Krause, and Rodriguez (1985) reported the results of this test with 30 people with mental retardation, 28 of whom had severe or profound mental retardation. Five

of the 39 subjects had positive *DST* results. The five subjects were more likely to exhibit stereotypic movements, temper tantrums, and screaming/crying. If it can be assumed that stereotypic movements and temper tantrums are signs of depression in people with severe/profound mental retardation, the data would provide some preliminary evidence that positive *DST* is associated with mood disorder. However, there is little evidence that these severe conduct problems are associated with depression. On the contrary, analysis of the standardization data for the *Reiss Screen* (Reiss, 1988*b*) suggests that there is no correlation between depressed mood and stereotypic behavior.

Ruedrich, Wadle, Sallach, Hahn, and Menolascino (1987) found that 24 percent of 85 persons with mild to profound mental retardation have positive *DST* results. The positive *DST* results were associated with greater severity of mental retardation, greater age, and more behavioral symptoms. Beckwith, Parker, Pawlarczyk, Couk, Schumacher, and Yearwood (1985) found some *post hoc* evidence that a positive *DST* result indicates an increased probability of depression.

Mattes and Amsell (1993) evaluated 12 people with depressive symptomatology, only one of whom met the *DSM-III-R* criteria for a major depressive episode, and 22 others who were aggressive, withdrawn, or displayed self-injurious behavior. Although they found a tendency for more positive *DST* test results in the depressive group, the results were not statistically significant.

Wolkowitz (1990) concluded the following after a review of the literature:

It is uncertain whether the *DST* is a useful tool for diagnosis of depressed mentally retarded patients (p.551).

CHAPTER 4. TREATMENT APPROACHES

The most widely used therapies with people with mental retardation are psychopharmacology and behavior therapy. Other therapies include psychotherapy, cognitive therapy, and play therapy. There is evidence that each of these therapies can benefit some people for at least the period of time during which the therapy is being administered. Historically, therapies have been developed and partially justified in accordance with various theoretical models. These models were first constructed with reference to people who do not have mental retardation and later applied to people who do. The following is an historical review of these models as they apply to people with mental retardation.

I. PSYCHODYNAMIC THERAPY

Psychodynamic models are concerned with intrapsychic phenomena. The two most influential examples are psychoanalysis, which was developed by Sigmund Freud, and client-centered therapy, which was developed by Carl Rogers. Other examples are play therapy, art therapy, and dance therapy, all of which are particularly relevant for use with people with mental retardation.

A. GENERAL MODELS

A1. PSYCHOANALYSIS. Sigmund Freud was born in Moravia in 1856. He earned an M.D. degree in 1881 from the University of Vienna and subsequently studed neurology under the French master Jean-Martin Charcot. In collaboration with Joseph Breuer, he published *On the Psychical Mechanisms of Hysterical Phenomena* in 1893 and *Studies in Hysteria* in 1895. Although his early works reported the success of hypnosis in the treatment of hysteria, Freud gradually abandoned this technique and developed a talking therapy called *psychoanalysis*.

Psychoanalysis is based on the following core assumptions (see Reiss, Peterson, Eron, & Reiss, 1977):

- Freud proposed that all mental life and behavior is ultimately motivated by sexual energy; in his later works, however, Freud modified this view to recognize two types of motivation, sexual (creative) energy and aggressive (destructive) energy. These views are widely credited with having helped liberalize society's attitude toward sexual behavior. From

a therapy standpoint, the main implications concern the individual's need to work through, master, and resolve his/her psychological conflicts so that the energy associated with the conflict can be freed and made available for everyday functioning.

- Freud held that adult personality needs are determined by early childhood experiences. For example, Freudians believe that excessive motivation to succeed might be determined by a childish desire to obtain approval and love from a distant parent. Excessive anger in everyday adult life might have its origin in a child's feelings that father has interfered with the relationship with mother. Attention-seeking ("needy") behavior in adulthood might be related to excessive gratification of dependency needs in childhood.

- How do feelings from childhood determine adult personality? Freudians held that psychologically threatening or anxiety-ridden feelings are repressed into the unconscious mind. Because a person does not know what is in his or her unconscious mind, the childhood feelings are never resolved and continue to influence the person's behavior in adulthood.

- Freud assumed that effective treatment requires the resolution of unconscious conflicts. If a symptom is treated directly without resolving the unconscious, intrapsychic conflict, a new and potentially more debilitating symptom is predicted to appear (symptom substitution hypothesis). For example, before treating fears, psychoanalysts believe it is first necessary to resolve the conflicted sexual desires for the opposite-sex parent.

As noted already, Freud held that important intrapsychic conflicts, wishes, and needs are unconscious. People not only are unaware of their unconscious conflicts and feelings but also resist becoming aware. People have difficulty focusing on unconscious material. When their attention is directed to unconscious feelings, they draw blanks, change the subject, and become anxious. The psychological force that creates the unconscious is called *repression*.

Psychoanalysis has given us the term *defensive behavior*, which refers to an individual's resistance in acknowledging certain feelings. The primary psychological defense mechanism is repression, which is always present in any example of defensive behavior. Other psychological defense mechanisms that can co-occur with repression include the following:

Denial — an individual presents an excessively positive attitude to hide anxiety-ridden thoughts;

Displacement — the object of an impulse is changed from a more threatening to a less threatening source, as when a husband expresses anger toward his wife rather than toward his mother;

Projection — a person attributes his or her impulses to others, as when an angry person thinks that the world is unsafe;

Rationalization — a person uses excuses to make something that is inappropriate appear appropriate;

Intellectualization — a person discusses feelings in an overly intellectual manner.

Most defensive processes are unconscious. All defenses have the function of protecting the individual from overwhelming anxiety associated with unconscious feelings, impulses, ideas, and conflicts.

By 1930, psychoanalysis had become the dominant model of psychopathology. A number of variations were developed, the most influential of which was called *ego psychology*. The ego psychologists rejected Freud's assumption that sexual motivation was the only fundamental human motive. Ego psychologists suggested that fundamental motives include curiosity, the drive to be superior, and the need for self-respect. Some of the best known ego psychologists were Carl Jung, Alfred Adler, Anna Freud, Erik Erickson, and Henry Stack Sullivan.

In-depth psychoanalytic therapy is intended to make unconscious conflicts conscious. In therapy a process called *transference* occurs in which parent/child conflicts are transferred symbolically to the therapist/patient relationship. That is, the patient uses the relationship with the therapist to work through key elements of the conflicts with the parents. The therapist helps the patient gain insight into the conflicts and develop an effective resolution. The process often takes years.

A2. CLIENT-CENTERED MODEL. In the 1950s many clinical psychologists embraced the client-centered approach developed by Carl Rogers (1947, 1961). Like psychoanalysis, client-centered (or nondirective) therapy is a talking therapy that takes place in the context of a series of therapist-client interviews. Unlike psychoanalysis, client-centered therapy is based on the assumption that self-actualization is a fundamental human motive. Human growth (self-actualization) occurs when a person has an experience he/she values and incorporates

into his/her self-concept. Because people have a need for positive self-regard, Rogers suggested that new experiences are incorporated into the self-concept only when they meet the individual's conditions of worth and can be regarded positively by the individual. When a person acts or has feelings that are inconsistent with his or her values (conditions of worth), the defense mechanisms of denial and distortion occur, and personal growth is stunted.

Rogers held that therapists should have an unconditional positive regard for their clients. By providing an accepting, nonthreatening atmosphere, the therapist maximizes the chances that the client will explore the meaning of his or her anxiety-ridden experiences. In the client-centered approach, the therapist is nondirective in the sense that the client is allowed to talk about whatever he or she wishes. The therapist reflects on what the client says in an effort to help the client clarify his or her feelings and values. The therapist's reflections are stated from the viewpoint of the client.

Rogers had a strong commitment to studying the effects of client-centered therapy. Client-centered therapists taperecorded their interview sessions and published numerous studies of the transcripts. They also conducted evaluations of therapy outcomes. Although the methodological rigor of these studies is poor compared to today's standards, the outcome research conducted by client-centered therapists was very important in the context of the 1950s. By accepting the basic principle that therapies need to be evaluated empirically, client-centered therapists contributed to the research development of clinical psychology.

B. APPLICATIONS FOR MENTAL RETARDATION

B1. PSYCHOTHERAPY AND MENTAL RETARDATION. Accomplished therapists such as Anne Hurley, Henry Leland, Manuel Sternlicht, Gary Prouty, and Ludwik Szymanski have identified the following recommendations for psychotherapy with people with mental retardation.

- *Interview techniques need to be adapted to the client's cognitive level.* For example, the therapist should use concrete language and should check frequently for client understanding. Techniques such as play therapy should be favored (Leland & Smith, 1965). Art and music therapy should be considered (Jakab, 1982). Page (1986) used puppets. Hurley and Hurley (1987) suggested relaxing the client with gifts and activities. Sternlicht (1965) used balloons, mirrors, and noisemakers.

- *Therapy needs to be directive.* For example, the session should be structured and limits should be set (Szymanski, 1980a). Hurley and Hurley

(1986) suggested the need to provide specific instructions and to explain the purposes of the meetings and what is expected from the client. Hingsburger (1987) developed a "tell me something good about yourself" technique.

- *The therapist should be supportive* (Prouty, 1976; Sarason, 1953).

- *The therapist should be flexible.* When progress is not made with a nonretarded person, the therapist might assume that the person is resistant. For people with mental retardation, however, the therapist should be more flexible and consider alternative techniques or simpler ways to approach therapy. For example, Deutsch (1985) helped clients grieve by reliving the funeral, eulogy, and burial while they verbalized their feelings about these events. Stavrakaki and Klein (1986) altered the length of therapy sessions.

- *The therapist should intervene in the client's environment* (Menolascino, Gilson, & Levitas, 1986; Szymanski, 1980a). As Fletcher (1993a, p. 337) wrote, "Psychotherapy cannot be done in a vacuum; it must be part of the larger, comprehensive support system involved with the client."

- *Appropriate goals should be set.* Attention should be paid to possible differences in goals between the referring agency and the person (Fletcher, 1993a). The referring agency often is seeking "behavioral compliance" so that the person is easier to manage. However, the person may have very different goals for entering therapy. Szymanski (1980a) suggested the following examples of such goals: improving impulse control, expressing feelings and emotions in a socially acceptable manner, and improving self-esteem.

- *Issues of transference and countertransference need to be managed just as in child therapy.* The person with mental retardation tends to idealize the therapist (Bernstein, 1985; Levitas & Gilson, 1987). A number of therapists have stressed the importance of good rapport (Monfils & Menolascino, 1984). The countertransference is complicated by the therapists' feelings about the disability of mental retardation.

- *The issue of mental retardation as a disability should be addressed explicitly* (Szymanski & Rosefsky, 1980). A large body of literature on disability counseling is applicable.

B2. COUNSELING, GROUP THERAPY, AND MENTAL RETARDATION. Counseling is used much more often than in-depth psychoanalysis when the clients are people with mental retardation (Monfils & Menolascino, 1984; Pfadt, 1991). Counselors help people understand and work out current problems in everyday living. They listen, encourage, and offer advice. They may teach the person the differences between socially appropriate versus socially inappropriate behavior, which can be very helpful for people with mental retardation.

People with mental retardation are much more likely to be offered group therapy instead of individual therapy (Sternlicht, 1965; Szymanski & Kiernan, 1983). Szymanski and Kiernan (1983) have advised group therapists to use a concrete, direct, and structured approach with the active participation of the group leader. These therapists further advised that therapy groups can consist of multiple sets of parents and their adolescent or adult children. The following therapeutic goals might be set: improving communication skills (particularly between adolescents and their parents); learning to verbalize and share feelings; increasing the person's motivation to become more independent; increasing constructive parental support for independent strivings; and learning to understand and to monitor one's own behavior and its social consequences.

Spinner and Pfeifer (1986) discussed the attributes of supportive therapy in a group format. The format was seen as facilitating bonding among the person, peers, and significant others. Desired outcomes included the following: the person acquires feelings of belonging and acceptance; the person learns that others have similar problems and disabilities; and the person has corrective emotional experiences.

B3. CLIENT-CENTERED THERAPY AND MENTAL RETARDATION. Two client-centered approaches have been developed for use with people with mental retardation. One approach, called *gentle teaching* (McGee, 1993), holds that a person's behavior generally will improve if he or she is accepted by the therapist. This approach also holds that the values of the therapist can have an important impact on therapeutic outcomes.

The other client-centered approach is called *pretherapy* (Prouty, 1976). Pretherapy is used with people who lack the skills necessary for psychotherapy. The pretherapist helps the individual gain contact with the world and with inner experience. Reality contact is taught by reflecting on the person's behavior, feelings, and thoughts. For example, affective contact is facilitated by verbalizing the person's feelings and the person's expression of affect through bodily and facial signs. The pretherapist attempts to time these verbalizations at a pace at which the person feels comfortable. The length and frequency of sessions vary with the person's motivation, attention span, and degree of behavioral control.

Of the two applications of client-centered therapy — gentle teaching and

pretherapy — the one that has received the most attention is gentle teaching. Yet pretherapy is by far the more thoughtful, scholarly approach. For example, McGee (1993) does not cite Rogers or anyone else, whereas Prouty (1976) always has been careful to present pretherapy within the context of mainstream Rogerian psychology.

B4. PLAY THERAPY AND MENTAL RETARDATION. Leland and Smith (1965, 1985) stated the general goals for play therapy as strengthening the child's ability to withstand negative factors in the milieu and as helping him/her become happier and more useful as a person. They stressed that the goals of therapy should be consistent with the child's maturational and developmental capabilities and warned against utopian goals that only set the child up for additional failures. They suggested that the play therapist needs to set limits regarding his/her relationship with the child and the child's relationship to both the play materials and the play session.

In order to teach that different behaviors are permitted in different situations, Leland and Smith (1985) suggest that,

> the ideal play therapy suite has two play rooms: an unstructured or "dirty" room and a structured or "clean" room. The "dirty" room has sand, paint, clay, water, and other messy and/or unstructured materials. The client has a great deal of freedom in this room and the walls, ceiling, floors, etc., may become "very dirty." Conversely, the "clean room" has games, a carpet, puzzles, and clean and/or structured materials. The client is expected to help care for this room (p. 22).

Play therapists attempt to modify children's behavior by modifying the amount of structure in the play sessions. Structure is defined as the degree of form or order in the therapeutic setting (Leland & Smith, 1974). The therapist needs to find that mix of structure and unstructure that is causing the greatest difficulty in the child's life, reproduce such in the play sessions, and help the child learn to master the situation.

Four types of play sessions can be created by combining a structured and unstructured therapist approach with structured or unstructured play materials. Leland and Smith (1985) have discussed the goals for each of these various versions of play therapy. Depending on the structure in the play session, specific goals may include learning to recognize self, gaining a sense of personal control over the environment, understanding that impulses can be controlled, living within social boundaries, improved social interactions, dealing with social and cultural realities, evaluating personal goals, improved social maturity through cognitive development, a sense of acceptance, and building realistic levels of aspiration.

According to Leland and Smith (1974), play therapists should adjust the length of the sessions to meet the needs of the child. If progress is not being made, therapy should be terminated and not dragged out indefinitely.

B5. ART, MUSIC, DANCE THERAPY, AND MENTAL RETARDATION. People with developmental disabilities are capable of creative expression (Ludins-Katz & Katz, 1990). In fact, some people with mental retardation have exceptional talent as musicians or artists (Miller & Monroe, 1990). Some individuals prefer to express themselves in drawings or paintings, whereas others prefer sound and movements (e.g., Jarvis, 1988).

The most common examples of artistic therapies are art therapy, music therapy, and dance therapy. In each of these therapies, the focus is on developing creative, nonverbal self-expression in an uncritical, accepting context. It does not matter how well the person draws or even if the person is physically capable of singing or dancing; what matters is how well the person learns to express himself or herself through imagery, sound, and/or movement.

The potential benefits of these therapies include the following (Stamatelos & Mott, 1985):

- Positive self-esteem as the individual develops into a competent artist and/or has positive artistic experiences;

- Reduced anxiety through mastery and contact (Leste & Rust, 1990; Milos & Reiss, 1982);

- Improved self-expression and personal growth (Junge, 1987);

- Increased personal options (LaMore & Nelson, 1993).

C. EVALUATION OF PSYCHODYNAMIC THERAPIES

For many years psychotherapy was accepted on the basis of therapists' and clients' opinions of effectiveness. The therapists thought that most of the clients who had stayed in treatment for a year or longer showed significant improvement even if they had not been completely cured. Many clients seemed to agree, with some providing enthusiatic testimonials of improvements in symptomatology and gains in personal insight. Both therapists and clients seemed generally satisfied with psychotherapy outcomes, and researchers had no evidence to contradict this opinion.

In 1952 Eysenck published his now famous review questioning the effectiveness of psychotherapy outcomes. Eysenck's (1952) basic point concerned the need for controlled observations — in order to evaluate the benefits of psychotherapy, not only do we need to know how many people improve during the course of treatment but also we need to know the numbers who improve without any treatment. Although reports from therapists and clients suggested that people improved during psychotherapy, in 1952 there were little data on how many people improved without psychotherapy.

Eysenck (1952) attempted to estimate the rate of improvement in untreated people, which he called the rate of *spontaneous remission*. He reviewed the available research and concluded that the rate of spontaneous remission was roughly equivalent to the rate of improvement under psychotherapy. Eysenck's review suggested that approximately two-thirds of both psychotherapy and no-therapy groups showed significant improvement after two years. Eysenck concluded that the scientific data were inadequate to establish the effectiveness of psychotherapy.

Bergin (1971) criticized Eysenck's conclusions. Bergin suggested that Eysenck's review of the literature was based on a number of arbitrary assumptions that had the effect of reducing the estimated improvement for psychotherapy groups while increasing the estimated improvement for spontaneous remission groups. For example, Eysenck did not take into account the fact that some therapists refused to consider a client as improved even if the psychotherapy had led to a complete remission in overt symptoms. Moreover, Eysenck did not evaluate the degree to which the people in the "spontaneous remission" group might have received counseling from a minister, priest, or rabbi. According to Bergin, a reanalysis of the data reviewed by Eysenck suggested that psychotherapy is an effective form of treatment for many mental disorders.

Regardless of Bergin's criticisms, Eysenck's article was significant because it stimulated numerous research studies on psychotherapy outcomes. By the mid-1950s, hundreds of outcome studies were presented as evidence for the effectiveness of psychotherapy (Bergin, 1971). Eysenck's basic point that psychotherapy outcomes were inadequately researched had won the day even though his conclusions about the ineffectiveness of psychotherapy have remained highly controversial.

In 1961, Eysenck reviewed the then large literature on psychotherapy outcomes and dismissed almost all of the studies on methodological grounds. Very few studies used appropriate control procedures, and even fewer met high methodological standards. Many psychotherapy researchers did not use valid measures of outcomes. They also did not assign clients randomly to therapy versus no-therapy groups. The researchers rarely conducted long-term followups after therapy had been completed. Because of these and other methodological shortcomings, Eysenck (1961) concluded that, from a scientific perspective, it still had not been proven that psychotherapy is effective.

Eysenck's 1952 paper marked the beginning of an era when researchers made numerous improvements in the methodological rigor of therapy outcome studies. These improvements included the following:

- During the 1950s the necessity of no-therapy control groups gained acceptance.

- During the 1960s significant progress was made in developing objective measures of therapy outcome. Projective testing lost influence as an indicator of therapy outcomes. Standardized tests and behavioral measures gained acceptance.

- During the 1970s researchers studied the relevance of placebo conditions to control for nonspecific therapy effects. The concept of an equally credible placebo control procedure was introduced (Borkovec & Nau, 1972; Kirsch, 1990). This concept requires researchers to use a placebo control condition that creates approximately the same a *priori* expectations of improvement as those associated with the therapy condition.

- During the 1980s attention was paid to evaluating therapy outcomes for specific diagnoses. The criteria for many diagnostic categories were operationalized, and the procedures for determining a diagnosis were made more uniform.

In addition to the question of overall effectiveness, researchers have studied the therapist and client attributes that favor successful outcomes. Good therapists were described as experienced, mentally healthy, empathic, and nonpossessively warm (Truax & Mitchell, 1971). Good candidates for therapy were described as follows: between the ages of 17 and 49; motivated to solve their problems; at least average intelligence; had made successful social adjustments in the past; not seriously disturbed; and well educated (Garfield, 1978). Based on these criteria, people with mental retardation were not considered good candidates for psychotherapy (Rogers, 1942).

Historically, many therapists have questioned the suitability of psychotherapy for people with mental retardation (Chidester & Menninger, 1936). For example, Albini and Dinitz (1965) reported unfavorable outcomes for client-centered therapy with 73 people with mental retardation. Rogers argued that client-centered therapy is not applicable to people with mental retardation (Rogers, 1942). His view discouraged many therapists from attempting psychotherapy with this population. However, Thorne (1948) adapted psychotherapy for use with people with mental retardation and reported beneficial effects for a clinic sample of 500

people. As Levitas and Gilson (1989) concluded,

> The literature critical of psychodynamic psychotherapy with mentally retarded individuals is ultimately . . . useful in focusing attention upon the modifications and adaptations of technique necessary to the successful use of psychotherapy with these patients" (p. 72).

There is a need for outcome research on psychotherapy with people with mental retardation. Benefits and risks need to be quantified in terms of outcomes, diagnosis, length of treatment, durability of treatment benefits, and generalization of improved behavior. Benefits need to be evaluated against appropriate control conditions. The effects of psychotherapy need to be compared to outcomes from alternative therapies. Researchers need to find the most effective combinations of appropriate therapies, such as psychotherapy with behavior therapy and/or medications.

II. BEHAVIORAL APPROACHES

By 1960 many university-based clinical psychologists were searching for an alternative to psychotherapy (Ullmann & Krasner, 1965). They desired an experimental approach based on psychological principles that had been validated in laboratory research. At first, it was suggested that clinical psychology should be based on applications of both learning theory and experimental social psychology (Ullmann & Krasner, 1965). However, applied social psychology never attracted much of a following among clinical psychologists. Consequently, the new clinical psychology was based primarily on applied learning theory. The new approach has been variously named *behavior therapy, behavior modification,* or *behavior analysis.*

In the 1960s the new behavior therapy was presented as the scientific alternative to what was called the "medical model." The "medical model" was said to promote psychiatric diagnosis, psychodynamic therapy, and the study of unconscious events. Adherents of the "medical model" were said to believe that psychiatry (a medical discipline) should be dominant over psychology (a scientific discipline) with regard to the treatment of psychopathology (Ullmann & Krasner, 1965).

A. GENERAL MODELS

Behavior therapists proposed a learning model as an alternative to the medical model (Ullmann & Krasner, 1965). By the late 1960s, two distinguishable

groups had formed to study the learning model. One group, herein called the *behavior therapists,* were interested primarily in the application of Pavlovian conditioning principles to emotions, anxiety, and fear. The other group, herein called the *behavior analysts,* were interested primarily in the application of operant conditioning principles to conduct and severe behavior problems. The two groups have separated from one another and today have separate journals and separate professional societies.

A1. APPLIED PAVLOVIAN MODEL (BEHAVIOR THERAPY)

Behavior therapists once believed that many phobias can be understood in terms of Pavlovian conditioning. The basic idea was that phobias develop when initially neutral stimuli are associated with trauma and/or conflict (Reiss, 1980). When the individual perceives the phobic stimulus, the person automatically experiences fear in anticipation of trauma. For example, a person who has an automobile accident may develop a fear of driving because this activity (initially neutral stimulus) was associated with trauma (the car accident).

A number of clinical techniques were developed based on these ideas. One of the most widely used of the techniques is called *systematic desensitization* (Wolpe, 1958). This procedure pairs increasingly intense phobic stimuli with states of deep muscle relaxation in an effort to countercondition relaxation to the phobic stimuli. A related technique is called *exposure therapy* (Marks, 1971). Essentially, exposure therapy requires people to confront the source of their anxiety or fears. Generally, exposure therapy is thought of as a fear extinction procedure.

When researchers found that expectancy factors can play a powerful role in the effects of systematic desensitization (Kirsch, 1990), some behavior therapists developed an interest in hypnosis, which is believed to work in part because of expectancy factors (Kirsch, 1990). Svec (in press) has suggested the possibility of applying hypnosis for use with people with mental retardation.

A2. APPLIED OPERANT MODEL (BEHAVIOR ANALYSIS)

Behavior analysis is based largely on the work of B. F. Skinner. Skinner's research advanced knowledge on the effects of rewards and punishment on learned behavior. His laboratory research demonstrated that specific patterns of reinforcement are associated with characteristic patterns of responding (Skinner, 1963). The scientific validity of this work is widely accepted.

The first influential clinical applications of operant conditioning were published in the late 1950s and early 1960s. The early pioneers included Ayllon

(1963), Bijou and Baer (1961), Goldiamond (1962), Lovaas, Berberich, Perloff, and Schaeffer (1966), and Ullmann and Krasner (1965). Skinner himself discussed the relevance of his research for human behavior in two influential books: *Walden Two,* which was published in 1948, and *Science and Human Behavior,* which was published in 1953.

B. APPLICATIONS TO MENTAL RETARDATION

Behavior analysis is widely used to treat challenging behavior. It is a treatment of choice for self-injurious behavior, stereotypies, and severe conduct problems. It also is widely used to teach social behavior and social skills.

Behavior analysts have developed the following approaches to the treatment of challenging behavior.

B1. STIMULUS-BASED TREATMENT. These procedures focus on making desirable responses more probable by presenting antecedent events that evoke appropriate behavior or by altering stimuli that evoke high rates of aberrant behavior (National Institutes of Health, 1989). An example of a stimulus-based technique is to have the person spend more time in a setting associated with a low rate of occurrence of aberrant behavior. Stimulus-based treatments are distinguished from procedures involving physical restraint. Physical restraints include restrictive jackets that prevent self-injurious behavior.

B2. CONDITIONING. These techniques make the consequences of aberrant behavior less reinforcing or more punishing. For people with developmental disabilities, the most widely used positive conditioning technique is called *differential reinforcement of other behavior (DRO).* In this procedure, positive reinforcement is provided if the individual does not engage in an undesirable, target behavior for a specified period of time. The intervals can be quite brief, such as five or 15 seconds. In a technique called *differential reinforcement of incompatible behavior (DRI),* systematic reinforcement is given for a positive behavior that is incompatible with the aberrant behavior. As the positive behavior occurs more frequently, the aberrant behavior is inhibited and occurs less frequently.

B3. SKILLS TRAINING. The strategy of teaching skills is to reduce aberrant behavior by enhancing personal competence:

The strategy differs from DRO in that the response that is reinforced is directly specified ahead of time, whereas in DRO any response that hap-

pens to be occurring at the end of the DRO interval is reinforced. The approach differs from DRI in that there is an emphasis on strengthening behaviors that are likely to increase an individual's social competence, whereas in DRI the focus is on choosing responses that are physically incompatible with the problem behavior whether or not the response enhances social competence (National Institutes of Health, 1989, p. 103).

Social skills training includes instruction, modeling of appropriate responses, role-playing of appropriate responses, cognitive rehearsal, performance feedback in the form of televised recordings and/or group discussion, and praise and encouragement (Matson, 1984). Social skills training has been adapted for use with people with mental retardation (Matson & Andrasik, 1982; Matson, Kazdin, & Esveldt-Dawson, 1980). Specific uses include communication training, assertiveness training, and self-management training.

B4. EXTINCTION AND PUNISHMENT. Behavior analysts also have developed the following punishment techniques to reduce the occurrence of severe aberrant behavior:

In *extinction,* the environment is manipulated so that the target behavior has no reinforcing consequence (Lovass, Freitag, Gold, & Kassorla, 1965). For example, the target behavior produces neither tangible nor social reward (attention). People eventually stop performing responses that have no reinforcing consequences.

Overcorrection is a procedure consisting of two parts (Foxx & Bechtel, 1983). First, the individual performs a behavior that undoes the aberrant behavior. For example, a person who has a tantrum might have to clean up the mess caused by the tantrum, or a person who self-injures his face might have to clean the wound. Second, the individual engages in positive practice, which is the repeated performance of behaviors incompatible with the aberrant behavior.

In *punishment* procedures, either aversive stimulation is presented or positive reinforcements are removed immediately following the occurrence of an aberrant behavior. Aversive stimuli used for punishment include electric (faradic) shock, lemon juice, and water mists. The most common procedure for removing positive reinforcement is called *time-out.* During time-out, the individual cannot earn positive reinforcement and may be placed in a "quiet" room.

B5. FUNCTIONAL ANALYSIS. This method of assessment relies on a detailed experimental analysis of behavior (Iwata, Dorsey, Slifer, Bauman, & Richman, 1982). The main purpose of functional analysis is to identify nonarbitrary contingencies. When antecedents are studied, the focus of the analysis is on identifying the actual stimuli and setting events that control a challenging behavior for a particular individual. When consequences are studied, the focus is on identifying the positive and negative reinforcement variables that maintain a challenging behavior for a given individual (Axelrod, 1987).

Functional analysis focuses attention on the consequences of behavior in naturalistic settings and on how treatment could be more economically or optimally implemented.

C. COMMUNICATION THEORY

Carr and Durand (1985a, 1985b) proposed that aberrant behavior sometimes is maintained by its communicative functions. They traced this idea back to the ancient philosopher Plato:

> new born beings, have from the very first a way of screaming . . . So when the nurse would discover its desires she guesses from these indications what to offer it; if the child is quiet when something is offered it, she thinks she has found the right thing, but the wrong if it cries and screams (as quoted in Carr and Durand, 1985a, p. 242).

If newborns can use crying to communicate that they are hungry, cold, or experiencing discomfort, maybe people with mental retardation use aberrant behavior to communicate their needs. If this were so, it might be possible to treat aberrant behavior by determining what the person is trying to communicate and then meeting the person's need.

Carr and Durand (1985b) proposed that people with mental retardation use aberrant behavior to communicate either a desire for adult attention or a desire to reduce task demands. They tested this hypothesis in an experiment with four children who engaged in classroom disruptive behavior such as hitting, poking, and tantrums. Diagnoses included autism, brain damage, and developmental disabilities. Two of the children seemed to use aberrant behavior to communicate a desire to be praised, whereas the other two children seemed to use aberrant behavior to communicate a desire to reduce task demands. The children who seemed to be seeking praise were taught to obtain such by prompting the teacher and saying, "Am I doing good work." The children who seemed to be seeking to reduce task demands were taught to accomplish this by prompting

the teacher and saying, "I don't understand." A counterbalanced research design was used in which the relevant communication prompt for one group of children served as the irrelevant communication prompt for the other group.

The results of the experiment were in accordance with predictions from communication theory. When the children were able to obtain the reinforcement (praise or reduced task demands) they desired through verbal means, they had no need to communicate their needs with aberrant behavior, and the rate of aberrant behavior declined.

Although the Carr and Durand studies have been widely interpreted as supporting the communication hypothesis, the findings are subject to alternative explanation. Specifically, the findings can be reinterpreted as suggesting that children with aberrant behavior have excessive needs. The children in the praise condition may have had an excessive need for adult attention, and the children in the escape conditon may have had an unusually low tolerance for task demands and frustration. Prior to the experiment, the only way the children in the praise condition could have obtained the abnormally high amount of attention they needed was to engage in aberrant behavior. Similarly, the only way the children in the escape condition could have reduced task demands to an abnormally low level was to behave inappropriately when confronted with task demands. According to this view, the central problems are not the communicative contingencies between aberrant behavior and reinforcements but the children's excessive need for attention or reduced task demands.

The key to understanding the alternative hypothesis is the amount of reinforcement the children needed. For example, the children in the praise condition could have obtained teacher praise if they had behaved appropriately, but they could not have obtained the excessive amount of attention they needed by behaving appropriately. In fact, Carr and Durand did not find an appropriate way for the children to obtain high levels of teacher praise. They taught the children to prompt for teacher praise as an alternative to aberrant behavior, but excessive prompting of others for praise is socially inappropriate. It only works in the artificial treatment environments created by behavior analysts; in the real world, it leads to social rejection and perceptions of narcissism, insecurity, and egocentricity.

Excessive needs can be thought of as personality factors. By definition, person-specific, behavioral tendencies that have some generality have been variously referred to as *individual difference variables* or as *personality traits*. The reference here to the Carr and Durand findings as evidence for personality factors is at one level simply descriptive. After all, the entire point of the Carr and Durand study was that two children reacted very differently to praise and demands compared with two other children. The nature of the differences was thought to have some generality. Hence, the Carr and Durand findings fulfill the definition of a personality study.

The Carr and Durand results may be viewed as part of a larger body of research on individual differences in the effectiveness of various reinforcers. Reiss and McNally's (1985) concept of anxiety sensitivity, for example, implies individual differences in the reinforcing effectiveness of anxiety. When the concept of anxiety sensitivity was first introduced, it was criticized by many behavior therapists, partly because behavioral ideology rejects personality constructs. However, the data have been so consistently favorable toward the anxiety sensitivity concept that even the most vigorous critics have reversed their opinion (Peterson & Reiss, 1992). *Just as the concept of anxiety sensitivity holds that anxiety is more negatively reinforcing for some people than for others, Carr and Durand's theories can be reinterpreted as suggesting that praise (or escape) is more reinforcing for some children than for others.*

Successful treatment for some of the children in the Carr and Durand study may require reductions in the effectiveness of praise as a positive reinforcer (or reductions in the effectiveness of demands as a negative reinforcer). That is, treatment should focus on reducing the children's excessive needs, because excessive needs usually are not gratified in normative environments. It should not be sufficient for a durable and generalizable effect to alter response-reinforcement contingencies. There needs to be a desensitization treatment to the reinforcement itself. That is, the therapist needs to teach some of the children to adjust to lower levels of praise and other children to be more tolerant of demands and frustration.

Researchers who disagree with this alternative interpretation of Carr and Durand's work can evaluate the issues empirically. The procedures for identifying personality traits are well established. The central issues are as follows: (1) Is teacher praise a more effective reinforcer for some individuals than for others; and (2) To what degree is aberrant behavior related to a desire for an excessive amount of teacher praise so that this desire must be reduced for a durable and generalizable treatment effect?

Whatever facts may emerge from future research, Carr and Durand's work stands as an important contribution to the behavior analysis literature. Their communication theory is one of the more original ideas in this literature in quite some time, and their research is carefully executed and thoughtfully presented. The possibility of alternative interpretation is not a criticism of Carr and Durand — it is the nature of science for knowledge to be developed through a process of hypothesis, research, and alternative interpretation.

D. EVALUATION

In the 1960s, the behavior analysts revolutionized the field of mental retarda-

tion. They started to arrive in significant numbers in places where few clinical psychologists had previously cared to go. They changed many mental retardation institutions from custodial care facilities to treatment and learning facilities. They addressed forms of human suffering that had been largely ignored, taking an interest in severe behavior disorders such as self-injury, stereotypy, and rumination.

D1. PERCENT OF CASES RESPONDING TO THERAPY. Because operant conditioning research is based on the study of the individual, there is little information as to how the treatment results relate to a given population as a whole. Sometimes it is not even possible to compare treatment results across case studies because of a lack of consistency in the use of outcome measures. Thus, we do not know the percentages of people with various types of behavior problems who show significant improvements lasting a year or longer. For example, researchers have demonstrated that communication training can reduce challenging behavior, but they have not reported the percentage of cases who respond to this therapy and how long treatment effects last.

D2. LONG-TERM BENEFITS. One of the concerns about behavior analysis is the degree to which long-term treatment benefits can be achieved. On the one hand, it is not uncommon for people with mental retardation to show behavioral improvements that are reversed shortly after therapy is discontinued. On the other hand, there is evidence that long-term, durable, and significant behavioral improvements are possible, especially when the behavioral training programs are carefully implemented over periods of years (Foxx, 1990; Foxx & Faw, 1992).

Successful behavior analysis with people with mental retardation often requires a great deal of time and effort. It is not unusual for a behavior treatment program to require hours of intervention on a daily basis for a period of many years. Although such therapy sometimes produces dramatic behavioral improvements, there are practical issues in maintaining quality training over the course of a long period of time. The effectiveness of behavior analysis over a long period of time is of concern partially because behavioral programming relies on direct care staff for implementation and turnover rates among this group are as high as 100 percent per year.

D3. GENERALIZATION ISSUES. Behavioral treatment effects tend to be specific to certain stimulus properties of the environment in which treatment is administered. For example, therapeutic gains may be evident only when certain people are present or only in a particular facility or residential unit (Kazdin & Bootzin, 1972; Matson & Gardner, 1991; Nezu & Nezu, 1994; O'Leary & Drabman, 1971; Reiss, 1973; Whitman, 1990). This issue is variously known as the problem of *generalization* or the problem of *transfer.*

TABLE 4-1. A Comparison of Physical Versus Semantic Similarity

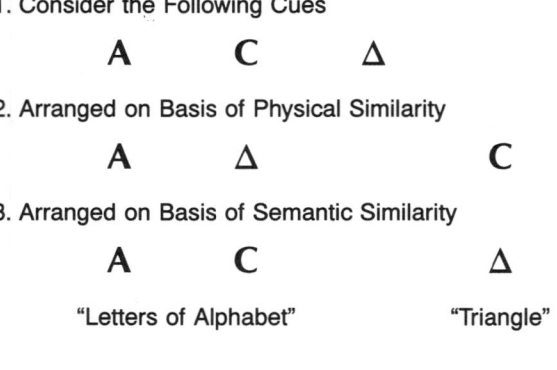

1. Consider the Following Cues

   A   C   Δ

2. Arranged on Basis of Physical Similarity

   A   Δ   C

3. Arranged on Basis of Semantic Similarity

   A   C   Δ

   "Letters of Alphabet"   "Triangle"

Behavior analysts have attempted to program generalization by providing training under a variety of stimulus circumstances. There is some evidence that successive training in different situations requires increasingly less training to produce successful outcomes. For example Reiss and Redd (1970) had college students employ a reinforcement therapy program for a child with persistent screaming and tantrum behavior associated with self-injury. The first reinforcing agent required 22 sessions to reduce the screaming behavior to criterion. Successive reinforcing agents required 14 and six training sessions after which complete transfer was obtained.

As shown in Table 4-1, another approach to the issue of generalization is suggested by the concept of symbolically-mediated transfer, called *secondary generalization* (Dollard & Miller, 1950). There has been very little research on the use of secondary generalization strategies to produce transfer of treatment effects in behavior analysis. However, Reiss (1973) used the concept of symbolically-mediated transfer to explain his findings that success training is more likely than failure training to produce changes in behavior that transfer across reinforcing agents.

D4. SIDE EFFECTS. The *overjustification hypothesis* predicts that tangible rewards undermine intrinsic motivation in the rewarded activity (Lepper, Greene, & Nisbett, 1973). This suggests that if children are taught to behave appropriately in order to get a reward, they will not want to behave appropriately for its own sake, and they may be more likely to behave inappropriately in situations in which they will not be rewarded. For example, the child may think, *I play with others in order to get candy,* instead of thinking, *I play with others because it is fun and I like them.*

Reiss and Sushinsky (1975, 1976) noted a number of shortcomings to the overjustification hypothesis and its prediction of negative side effects for therapies using rewards. First, there are no reliable and valid measures of intrinsic motivation. Second, a number of the studies that demonstrated some undermining effects of rewards actually did not give the children the rewards they were promised (e.g., Lepper, Greene, & Nisbett, 1973). For the most part, the overjustification studies used mildly unpleasant and boring reward procedures such as rewarding people for time spent in an activity regardless of performance. Third, the overjustification hypothesis is not falsifiable and thus is scientifically unacceptable. Fourth, the social psychologists overlooked the potential of tangible rewards to enhance intrinsic motivation, as when rewards are used to teach new skills (Reiss & Sushinsky, 1975). In conclusion, the overjustification researchers did not provide a basis for concern about the possible side effects of behavior analysis.

D5. ETHICS AND NONAVERSIVE THERAPY. Over the years numerous ethical concerns have been expressed regarding the use of applied behavior analysis with people with mental retardation. In the 1960s, it was not uncommon for critics to suggest that applied behavior analysis was a dangerous approach that could make people worse through a process called *symptom substitution* (cf. Ullmann & Krasner, 1965). Later it was suggested that functional analysis is dehumanizing because it ignores the person's inner life (Bootzin, Acocella, & Alloy, 1993). Recently, vigorous concern has been expressed about the tendency to overuse punitive methods of control (Thompson, Gardner, & Baumeister, 1988; Turnbull, 1988). A number of consumer and professional societies have called for a complete ban on the use of aversive behavioral techniques. Some behavior analysts spent much of the 1980s developing nonaversive treatment methods for challenging behavior (e.g., Repp & Singh, 1990).

D6. OUTDATED PAVLOVIAN PRINCIPLES. In the late 1960s and early 1970s, the behavior therapists began to discover scientific problems with applied Pavlovian theory. Perhaps the most notable problem concerned systematic desensitization therapy for fear reduction. This therapy was supposed to reduce fear by counterconditioning relaxation responses to initially phobic stimuli (Wolpe, 1958). It was quite a surprise, therefore, when it was discovered that the therapy was equally effective with or without relaxation (Marks, 1971). Although systematic desensitization is an effective treatment technique, it does not work as originally thought.

By the mid-1970s, influential reviewers had concluded that there were problems with the applied Pavlovian theory of the effectiveness of systematic desensitization (Kazdin & Wilcoxon, 1976). In 1980 Reiss argued that the Pavlovian principles on which behavioral fear reduction techniques were based had

become outdated and no longer explained animal behavior, let alone human behavior. Many behavior therapists abandoned a strict adherence to learning theory and developed the alternatives of cognitive-behavior therapy or cognitive therapy.

III. COGNITIVE APPROACH

Cognitive therapists study mediating processes that affect how each individual uniquely perceives his or her environment. Attention is paid to abnormalities in the encoding and processing of information. Beliefs, expectancies, values, and plans are seen as playing an important role in maintaining abnormal behavior.

In the 1980s cognitive-behavior therapy became the primary model for clinical psychology. Applications to child clinical psychology also were developed (Kanfer & Phillips, 1970; Silverman, Flesig, Rabian, & Peterson, 1991).

A. GENERAL MODELS

A1. RATIONAL-EMOTIVE THERAPY. Ellis' (1962) rational-emotive theory provided the first influential approach to cognitive therapy. Ellis began his career as a psychoanalyst but eventually rejected the psychoanalytic repression hypothesis of how early childhood experiences influence adult behavior. As noted previously, psychoanalysts believe that traumatic childhood experiences become unconscious (repressed). Since people are not aware of their unconscious feelings, they cannot deal with them in an effective manner. For example, a person who does not realize that deep down he/she feels unloved by mother cannot come to terms with this feeling. According to the repression hypothesis, the feeling can remain unconscious, create a life-long sensitivity to rejection, and create an excessive need for love and approval.

Ellis rejected the repression hypothesis and instead suggested that self-talk and irrational beliefs explain the influence of childhood experiences on adult behavior. According to Ellis, neurosis is a twice-told tale. First, a child experiences a trauma (e.g., the parents and the society reject the child). Second, the child learns an irrational idea (e.g., the child says to himself/herself, *I am worthless*). The irrational idea is rehearsed in self-talk over and over again as the child grows older. By the time the child has become an adult, he or she believes that the irrational idea is true and does not consider rational alternatives.

The following are examples of some of the irrational ideas associated with mental health disorders (Ellis, 1962):

1. *The idea that it is a dire necessity for an adult human being to be loved or approved by virtually every significant other person in his community (p. 61).*

2. *The idea that certain people are bad, wicked, or villainous and that they should be severely blamed and punished for their villainy (p. 65).*

3. *The idea that it is awful and catastrophic when things are not the way one would very much like them to be (p. 69).*

The rational-emotive therapist helps people replace irrational beliefs with rational thinking. For example, the therapist might help a person realize that it is irrational to conclude that one is worthless just because one was unloved as a child. It also is irrational to think that it is a catastrophe when things do not always go as one would very much like. By helping people adopt a belief system that is less irrational, rational-emotive therapists hope to improve the person's aberrant behavior.

A2. COVERT SENSITIZATION. Cautela's (1966) covert sensitization represented another early approach to cognitive therapy. Covert sensitization is essentially an attempt at aversive Pavlovian conditioning using symbolic stimuli and images. For example, instead of pairing alcohol stimuli with electric shock in an effort to treat alcoholism, the therapist pairs images of drinking with images of noxious or aversive stimuli. The idea is that alcohol will become so aversive that the person will stop drinking.

A3. COGNITIVE THERAPIES FOR DEPRESSION. In the 1970s cognitive therapy became a major approach to the treatment of depression. Beck's (1963) work was especially influential. Beck suggested that depression is caused by a triad of negative cognitions concerning the environment (e.g., *the world stinks*), the self (e.g., *I am worthless*), and the future (e.g., *the future is hopeless*).

Seligman's (1975) learned helplessness theory of depression, which was discussed in Chapter 2, also stimulated interest in a cognitive approach. However, this theory has been found to have significant shortcomings and no longer is considered to be viable.

B. APPLICATIONS TO MENTAL RETARDATION

Hollon (1984) stated that he would be surprised if cognitive-behavior therapy could be extended to people with mental retardation. However, there is evidence that this can be done, at least for people with IQs above 50.

B1. ANGER MANAGEMENT TRAINING (AMT). Benson (1986, 1992) adapted Novaco's (1975) anger management for use with people with mild mental retardation. In Benson's model, anger is defined as an emotional response to a situation the person perceives as threatening to his or her self-esteem. For example, the self-esteem of some people with mental retardation may be threatened by challenges to their competency (e.g., getting something wrong). People with mental retardation may express anger in the form of aggression, verbal abuse, property destruction, self-abusive behavior, and withdrawal or running away.

Anger is a normal and basic emotion. However, a person has an anger management problem when he/she experiences anger too frequently; when anger interferes with work or school; when anger lasts too long; or when anger poses a danger to self or others.

The goal of AMT is to teach self-control. As Benson (1990) put it,

> The goal of the training program is to teach methods of controlling anger as well as socially acceptable ways to express anger. The goal is not to eliminate anger, because anger is seen as a natural response that everyone experiences at times (p. 6).

An inital step in the assessment of anger management problems is to evaluate the environmental factors that contribute to anger and irritability. These include excessive heat, noise, and crowding. Benson recommends ameliorating any environmental factors prior to starting formal therapy.

Benson's model for AMT recognizes the following four components:

- An external event or situation;

- A cognitive-labelling process;

- Emotional arousal of anger;

- Behavioral reaction.

Benson (1992) summarized her model as follows:

> people are not upset by the external events themselves, but by their interpretation of the events. A filtering, labeling process occurs in which the events may or may not be viewed as a provocation. If anger is experienced, it is accompanied by physiological arousal. The behavioral response that occurs when people are angry can take many forms, aggressive or [withdrawing]. . . (p.7).

AMT addresses several aspects of the model.

1. People are taught to recognize and to identify their emotions. The people self-monitor their mood each day by checking one of four faces representing happy, sad, mad, and neutral.

2. Relaxation training is provided to help people learn to control the physiological components of anger.

3. Self-instructional training is provided to teach people to identify the self-talk that leads them to feel upset versus calm. Trouble statements are defined as self-talk that makes one upset, whereas coping statements are defined as self-talk that keeps one calm. Examples of trouble statements are: *He'd better watch out or he's going to get it* and *Who does he think he is?* Examples of coping statements are: *Be cool* and *Stay calm.* Benson's program teaches people with mental retardation the differences between trouble versus coping statements and has them roleplay provocative situations while practicing aloud coping statements.

4. People are taught to solve problems. A four-step process is used in which people are taught to ask themselves: (1) What is the problem; (2) What are some solutions; (3) What is the best solution; and (4) How did I do?

Benson's program is ideally suited for small groups. She has developed a detailed training manual based on 15 structured sessions. She also has published methods for adapting AMT for use with people who are oppositional.

B2. PROBLEM-SOLVING APPROACH. The problem-solving approach has been adapted for use with people who have mental retardation (D'Zurilla & Goldfried, 1971; D'Zurilla & Nezu, 1982; Nezu, Nezu, & Arean, 1991; Nezu, Nezu, & Perri, 1989). This approach teaches people the following:

- *Problem orientation,* in which people learn to label emotions correctly and to inhibit automatic (impulsive) responding in favor of greater reflection;

- *Problem definition and formulation,* in which people learn to identify the nature of the problem and to set realistic goals;

- *Generation of alternative solutions,* in which people learn to identify possible appropriate solutions to a problem in everyday living;

- *Decision making,* in which people learn to review the consequences of each solution idea and to select the ones that are optimal;

- *Solution implementation and verification,* in which people carry out the solution and monitor its effects.

C. EVALUATION

Benson, Rice, and Miranti (1986) obtained some evidence for the effectiveness of AMT. In this experiment, the subjects were 54 people, aged 17 to 54, with mild or moderate mental retardation. The subjects were assigned to small treatment groups based on their scores on a self-report anger inventory and on the *Peabody Picture Vocabulary Test.* The groups were relaxation training during role-play; self-instructional training during role-play; problem-solving; and anger management training consisting of all treatment components. The dependent measures included a role-play test, an anger self-report inventory, and supervisor ratings. The results indicated that all groups improved as a result of treatment.

Nezu *et al.* (1991) evaluated the effects of problem-solving and assertiveness training with 28 adults with mental retardation. Psychiatric diagnoses were established by use of the *PIMRA* as a structured interview conducted by two independent evaluators. The diagnoses were anxiety disorder, schizoprehenia, intermittent explosive disorder, adjustment disorder, and various personality disorders. The training included a number of components of assertiveness, including voice intensity (loud vs. soft), latency of response (impulsive vs. appropriate), duration of response (brief vs. lengthy), eye contact (focused vs. unfocused), voice quality (angry vs. assertive), body language (threatening vs. appropriate), and listening ability (listening to others vs. talking constantly). Outcome measures consisted of a role-playing test, self-report measures, and Part II of the *AAMR Adaptive Behavior Scales* (Nihira, Foster, Shellhaas, & Leland, 1975). Compared with a waiting-list control, the people who received assertiveness training showed significant improvement in behavior from pretreatment to posttreatment, and the gains were evident at a three-month followup assessment.

Cognitive therapy only recently was adapted for use with people with mental retardation. The research that has been done in this area is promising but still preliminary. Much additional research is needed.

IV. PSYCHIATRIC DRUGS

In 1920, the prognosis for chronic schizophrenia was so poor that many

people who developed this condition were hospitalized for the remainder of their lives. They resided mostly in large state and county institutions that provided custodial care. By 1950, more than one-half of all hospital beds for mental disorders, and about one-fifth of all hospital beds in the United States (including those with physical diseases such as cancer), were occupied by people with schizophrenia (Pugh & MacMahon, 1962).

In 1952 chlorpromazine revolutionalized mental health care for people with schizophrenia. The drug was sufficiently effective that many residents of back wards could be discharged. In the 1960s, chlorpromazine and other drugs were used increasingly to help people with schizophrenia stay out of mental hospitals in accordance with the goals of the community mental health movement. By 1969, the number of people with schizophrenia in state and county hospitals had declined by 31 percent (Mosher, Gunderson, & Buchsbaum, 1973).

A. GENERAL MODEL

Chlorpromazine, which was the first phenothiazine to be synthesized, is considered a *major tranquilizer* or a *neuroleptic*. It was developed after World War II as part of the federal government's effort to find pain-killers for postoperative care. However, it was discovered that the drug is especially effective in controlling the psychotic features of schizophrenia. This discovery eventually led to today's biological psychiatry and to the neuroscience model of psychopathology.

The last 20 years have been a period of considerable research on the identification and synthesis of chemical compounds to treat various types of mental illnesses. Unfortunately, many of the drug studies were done by psychiatrists in private practice who did not have the time or resources needed to conduct methodologically sound research. Despite this limitation, it is undeniable that biological psychiatry has produced many important advances in recent years, including the development of some important new medications.

B. APPLICATIONS TO MENTAL RETARDATION

Surveys show that psychiatric drugs are widely used to manage behavior problems in persons with mental retardation (Aman & Singh, 1991). Hill, Balow, and Bruininks' (1985) national survey found that 25.9 percent of the residents of community facilities, and 37.9 percent of the residents of institutional facilities, were receiving psychiatric drugs. Aman and Singh (1991) concluded that rates of drug therapy were much lower for school-age children, in the range of two to

FIGURE 4-1. Diagram of Professor Michael Aman's Nisonger Center laboratory for evaluating drugs.

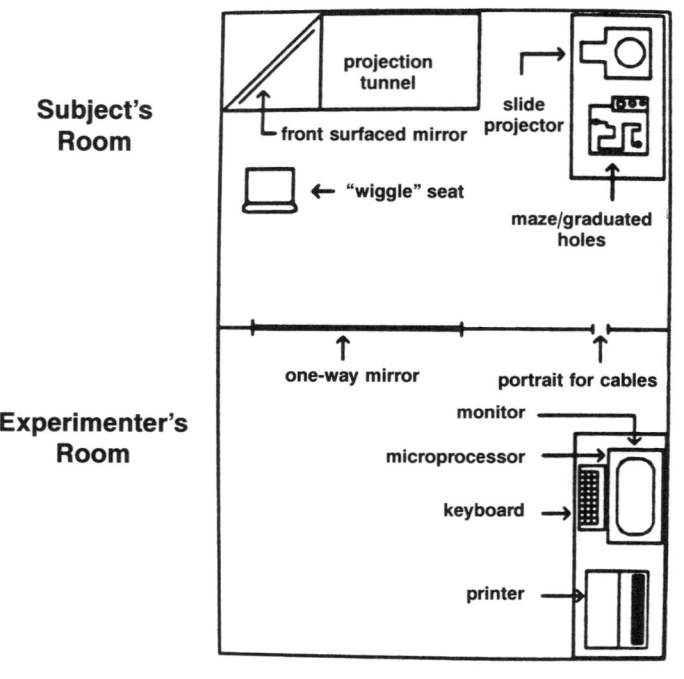

seven percent. The higher rates of drug use for adults versus children is consistent with findings that psychopathology is much more common in adults with mental retardation than in school-age children. Pary (in press *b*) found that rates of psychiatric drug use are higher for elderly persons than for other adults. Tu and Smith (1983) reported that the most common behavioral and psychiatric problems associated with drug treatment in residential faciltiies are aggression, hyperactivity, self-injury, excitability, screaming, anxiety, sadness, destructiveness, and temper tantrums.

B1. NEUROLEPTICS (MAJOR TRANQUILIZERS). These are the most commonly used psychiatric drugs for people with mental retardation (National Institutes of Health, 1989). They are given to control psychosis, schizophrenia, aggression, destructive behavior, and self-injurious behavior (Ruedrich, Grush, & Wilson, 1990). The most commonly used examples are chlorpromazine

(Thorazine), thioridazine (Mellaril), and haloperidol (Haldol). Gadow and Poling (1988) have summarized data for the partial effectiveness of these medications in controlling aggression in persons with mental retardation. There is some evidence that neuroleptics may ameliorate stereotypic behavior, but the evidence is ambiguous regarding effects on self-injurious behavior. Although clinicians generally believe these medications can be partially effective in the treatment of self-injurious behavior, some researchers remain concerned by the absence of compelling evidence (Farber, 1987; Singh & Millichamp, 1985). Significant side effects include Parkinsonian syndrome, tardive dyskinesia, and neuroleptic malignant syndrome (Boyd, 1992; National Institutes of Health, 1989). Neuroleptic malignant syndrome can be fatal. One reason for the concern about side effects is that phenothiazines are eliminated slowly so that blood levels can increase over time with constant dosages.

B2. ANTIDEPRESSANTS. These drugs are used to treat mood disorder. The two main groups are the *monoamine oxidase inhibitors (MAOIs)* and the *tricyclic antidepressants*. The MAOIs can have dangerous side effects with children and with people with mental retardation. The tricyclic antidepressants are used much more often. Examples of tricyclic antidepressants are impiramine, desipramine, amitriptyline, and nortriptyline. There is a need for research on the use of these medications to treat depressive disorders in people with mental retardation (Langee & Conlon, 1992). However, there is some preliminary evidence that impiramine can be effective in controlling irritability and some behavior problems (Aman & Singh, 1991). Recently, interest has developed in the antidepressant drug fluoxetine (Prozac®) as a possible treatment for self-injury.

B3. ANTIMANICS. These drugs are used to treat bipolar disorder. Lithium carbonate is an example of a widely used drug in this group. Craft, Ismail, Krishnamurti, Mathews, Regan, Seth, and North (1987) reported improvements in aggressive behavior for 73% of 42 persons with mental retardation treated with lithium versus only 30% for placebo. Ruedrich, Grush, and Wilson (1990) and Tupin (1978) have summarized the indications as extreme stimulus sensitivity, inability to reflect on the meaning or intent of the stimulus, and little capacity to modulate the expression of anger. A double-blind, cross-over study by Tyrer, Walsh, and Edwards (1984) also produced favorable results with lithium. With lithium, there is a need to monitor serum levels and to observe the person closely for signs of side effects and/or significant toxicity (Sovner & Hurley, 1985). Pary (1991a) has reported side effects in ten out of 15 persons treated with lithium during a 58-week period. The side effects included tremors, gastrointestinal irritation or bleeding, rashes, excessive sedation, and thirst. The side effects were evident in about the same proportion of persons who did, and did

not, receive other psychiatric medications in addition to the lithium. Blood levels must be monitored carefully to prevent possible toxic effects, which were not observed in the Pary study.

B4. ANXIOLYTICS. These drugs are used to treat anxiety. The most widely prescribed anxiolytics are benzodiazepines. This group includes diazepam (Valium), chlordiazepoxide (Librium), and alprazolam (Xanax). The NIH (1989) has suggested that these medications appear to be ineffective in the treatment of stereotypic behavior and self-injurious behavior. Aman and Singh (1980) found the methodological quality of early research in this area to be poor. Ruedrich, Grush, and Wilson (1990) cited paradoxical rage reaction as a potential side effect. However, Ratey and his colleagues have suggested benefits from a new drug called buspirone (Ratey, Sovner, Mikkelsen, & Chmielinski, 1989; Ratey, Sovner, Parks, & Rogentine, 1991). This drug is said to have fewer side effects than the benzodiazepines. Positive outcomes for aggression, anxiety, and self-injurious behavior have been reported for small samples. Much additional research is indicated before any conclusions can be drawn.

B5. ANTICONVULSANTS. These drugs are used primarily to control seizures. However, a number of anticonvulsants have been used with people with mental retardation for their behavioral effects. Included are carbamazepine (Tegretol), valproic acid, and phenobarbital. Carbamazepine has been used especially when aggressive behavior is associated with seizure disorders (Ruedrich *et al.*, 1990; Yudofsky, Silver, & Schneider, 1987); however, the effects of carbamazepine on aggression appear to hold for a variety of diagnoses and are unrelated to EEG brain waves (Mattes, 1986). A number of authors have suggested that carbamazepine is effective for the treatment of depression, affective disorder, bipolar disorder, and chronic irritability in persons with mental retardation. A contrary view has been presented by Aman and Singh (1991), who have concluded that presently there is little methodologically sound evidence for the effectivenesss of anticonvulsant drugs with people with mental retardation. The NIH (1989) cited significant potential for serious side effects with these medications. However, two recent studies suggested that the risk of potential side effects was only about one in 20 (Friedman, Kastner, Plummer, Ruiz, & Henning, 1992; Kastner, Friedman, & Pond, 1992).

B6. STIMULANTS. These drugs are used to treat attention-deficit/hyperactivity disorder. Examples include methylphenidate (Ritalin) and dextroamphetamine (Dexedrine). Although these drugs are widely used with nonretarded children, they are not used very often with persons who have mental retardation. Aman and Singh (1991) cited some unpublished data suggesting that

improvement in behavior associated with methylphenidate may be limited primarily to persons with IQs in the borderline range of intelligence. Brizer (1988) has suggested that amphetamines may increase aggressive behavior. The abuse potential of these drugs is high because they have a short duration of action.

Fenfluramine is an amphetamine analogue that is predominantly serotoninolytic and causes central nervous system depression. It is being evaluated as a possible treatment for autism and attention-deficit in persons with mental retardation.

B7. OPIATE BLOCKERS. These drugs reduce subjective and some physiological effects of opiate narcotics. Examples include naloxone and naltrexone. These medications have been suggested to reduce self-injury (Sandman, 1988, 1990; Sandman & Barron, 1992; Taylor, Hetrick, Neri, Touchette, Barron, & Sandman, 1991). Aman (1991c) reviewed as many as 20 recent studies on these drugs and found that half of them had only one subject and, with one exception, all had fewer than seven subjects. Some of the reported outcomes were based on fewer than two hours of observation. Some of the studies were uncontrolled (e.g., Sandman, Barron, & Colman, 1990). Zingarelli, Ellman, Hom, Wymore, Heidorn, and Chicz-DeMet (1992) found that naltrexone was no more effective than placebo in the treatment of self-injurious behavior and other maladaptive behavior in eight young adults with autism. Much more research is needed to resolve differences of opinion regarding the benefits of these drugs for people with mental retardation (Aman & Singh, 1991).

B8. BETA BLOCKERS. These drugs are used occasionally to treat peripheral signs of anxiety such as palpitations and tremors. They usually are not used to treat anxiety disorders, however, because they do not alter cognitions and other central symptoms of anxiety. Mental retardation researchers have shown some interest in the beta blocker propranolol (Inderal). Ratey, Morrill, and Oxenkrug (1983) reported reductions in aggressive behavior for two persons with mental retardation. Ratey, Bemporad, Sorgi, Bick, Polakoff, O'Driscoll, and Mikkelsen (1987) reported behavioral improvements with eight adults with autism. Calamari, McNally, Benson, and Babington (1990) reported a "dramatic decrease in aggression and a less pronounced improvement in self-injurious behavior" for a 23 year-old woman with an IQ of 27. Ruedrich *et al.* (1990) reported a successful reduction in aggressive behavior related to the use of propranolol in a 25 year-old man with severe mental retardation. An interesting aspect of this case is that the man previously had not responded to a number of medications, including pemoline (a stimulant), carbamazepine, haloperidol, and lithium. Arnold and Aman (1991) reviewed some preliminary data suggesting possible benefits in the treatment of conduct problems in persons with mental retardation.

C. BEST PRACTICES FOR MENTAL RETARDATION

A number of authors have discussed standards for the use of psychiatric drugs with people with mental retardation.

- The use of psychiatric drugs should be based on a diagnosis of a specific psychiatric condition or an identification of a specific behavioral condition.

- The effects of the drug on behavior should be carefully monitored and recorded by a nurse or a trained supervisor.

Unfortunately, these standards often are not met. A number of researchers have found that drugs often are prescribed nonspecifically in the absence of psychiatric diagnosis (Aman & Singh, 1991; Clarke, Kelley, Thinn, & Corbett, 1990). For example, Hill *et al.* (1985) reported that as many as 80 percent of persons in drug therapy are being treated for a condition that has not been formally diagnosed. Moreover, even when drugs are prescribed for diagnosed conditions, the effects of the drugs are not always monitored properly. Although some excellent monitoring systems are available, over long periods of time staff often stop using the systems or stop using them in careful and meaningful ways.

Bishop (1992) has suggested a six-step model for best practices. First, the nature of the problem is assessed and, if possible, diagnosed. Second, behavioral intervention is attempted. Third, appropriate psychotropic medications are selected and administered. Fourth, intensive monitoring of effects is conducted and treatments are adjusted until behavioral stabilization has occurred. Fifth, efforts are made to reduce medication dosages to the point of discontinuance. Sixth, behavior is monitored for at least six months after the drug has been discontinued. Bishop reported having used this program successfully in a large state institution over a period of four years.

Another standard for the use of psychotropic medication is the interdisciplinary team review. Glaser and Morreau (1986) reported some data showing that adoption of this practice can reduce reliance on psychotropic medications without a consequent increase in major injuries, damage to the person, harm to other residents, or property damage. The finding was based on an initial study of 28 residents of a state institution.

The standards for initiating drug treatment vary depending on whether or not a crisis situation is present. In an emergency situation, physicians are not required to consult interdisciplinary teams prior to initiating treatment. In a non-emergency situation, the standards for administering drug therapy have

170

been defined in the context of considerable regulatory agency involvement and litigation (Kalachnik, 1988). Current standards include the following:

(a) interdisciplinary assessment of need for medications;

(b) identification of specific target behaviors (formal psychiatric diagnosis not required);

(c) written, informed consent (individual or guardian must be told in advance of expected benefits and risks);

(d) use of a minimal effective dose;

(e) periodic attempts at dosage reduction;

(f) monitoring for side effects, including tardive dyskinesia if neuroleptics are used;

(g) integration of behavioral, medical, and educational interventions;

(h) periodic, data-based evaluations of drug therapy.

Additional standards suggested by Sovner and Hurley (1985) include: conducting a proper medical assessment prior to drug therapy; avoiding polypharmacy unless medically indicated; avoiding rapid changes in drug therapy; and avoiding overuse of PRNs (standing orders for nurses to administer drugs if certain symptoms emerge).

Because the drugs do not cure psychopathology, they should be used in coordination with psychotherapy, educational interventions, and/or behavior programming. Because some studies have found that a drug can be discontinued or substantially reduced with no adverse effects (e.g., Inoue, 1982; LaMendola, Zabaria, & Carver, 1980), periodic evaluations are required to determine if there is a continued need for the drug. The standards of minimal effective dose and drug holidays are mandated in the United States by regulatory agencies. However, Sovner and Hurley (1986) recommended against the use of abrupt drug holidays for persons with mental retardation:

> Many mentally retarded individuals dislike changes in their daily routines and will react negatively if they suddenly stop receiving their daily drug doses. Instead of drug holidays, lowering daily drug dose to the lowest possible level is a way to decrease cumulative drug exposure and

avoid the negative psychological consequences related to drug holidays (p. 30).

D. EVALUATION

A number of concerns have been expressed about the use of psychiatric drugs with people with mental retardation (e.g., Bates, Smeltzer, & Arnoczky, 1986). Schalock, Foley, Toulouse, and Stark (1985) expressed some of these concerns as follows:

> Clients frequently take multiple drugs prescribed by different physicians who are unaware of one another's prescriptions; personnel are unaware of the initial reason for the prescription, the desired effects, or the possible contraindications; and generic physicians frequently do not provide meaningful data regarding desired effects and time lines within which to evaluate the drug's effects (p. 504).

The following is a discussion of some of the specific concerns.

D1. OVERMEDICATION. As early as 1979, Tu (1979) surveyed five Canadian institutions and found that, although drugs had beneficial effects in many cases, as many as half the people on drugs had been given them inappropriately. Part of the problem was documented by Bates *et al.* (1986), who found that medications often were prescribed by physicians who had no formal training in their use. Bates *et al.* also reported high rates of between 39.1 and 56.4 percent of inappropriate drug use in a survey of 242 patients in an institution. The neuroleptics, which have harmful side effects, were the most widely overused drug group. Schalock *et al.* (1985) have presented some evidence that behavior modification programs can reduce the use of behavior controlling drugs. These authors emphasized the need to integrate drug treatment into an overall habilitative plan.

D2. UNKNOWN EFFECTS. Insufficient research has been conducted on the effects of psychiatric medications on persons who have mental retardation. Too few studies have been reported, and many of the studies that have been conducted do not meet acceptable scientific standards. The methodological limitations common in drug outcome studies include the absence of double-blind procedures to control for powerful expectancy effects; the absence of objective measures of outcome; the absence of placebo control groups; the absence of equally credible placebo control groups; and the absence of random assignment of clients to therapy conditions.

TABLE 4-2. COMMON LOGICAL ERROR IN EVALUATING DRUGS

Drug	Pretreatment Level of Aberrant Behavior	Posttreatment Level of Aberrant Behavior	Difference	Significance
1	A	B	A-B $= D_1$	$p < .05$
2	X	Y	X-Y $= D_2$	not significant

Error: Assume that drug 1 has significantly greater effect than drug 2. In fact, $D_1 - D_2$ (effects of drug 1 vs. drug 2) is not tested by above two tests for significance.

Many of the studies that evaluated the effects of psychiatric drugs in people with mental retardation used only one subject or only a few subjects (Aman, 1991*c*). In some studies, the outcome data are based on only a few hours of observations. Few studies included long-term follow-up data.

Because there are few studies in which alternative drugs are compared directly, conclusions about the relative effectiveness of various drugs must be based on reviews of the literature. However, much of the data is essentially not comparable across studies. If drug X reduces aggression in one study, and if drug Y fails to reduce aggression in another study, it cannot be concluded that drug X is more effective than drug Y in the treatment of aggression. Perhaps the case reported in the drug X study was easier to treat than the one reported in the drug Y study. Moreover, there are important statistical issues in trying to compare different studies. If drug X produces a statistically significant treatment effect for aggression and drug Y does not, as a matter of statistical logic, it is a *non sequitor* to conclude that drug X reduces aggression significantly more than drug Y. As shown in Table 4-2, what is needed is a single statistical test on the difference between two pretreatment/posttreatment differences — this cannot be inferred from two separate tests on each set of pretreatment/posttreatment differences. The statistical data that are needed cannot be obtained from a literature review in which one study evaluated the effects of one drug and another study evaluated the effects of a different drug.

Since the scientific research is inadequate to support the use of many psychiatric drugs with people with mental retardation, these drugs are prescribed on the basis of their effects in people who do not have mental retardation. However, this is not an adequate basis to prescribe drugs. For example, the fact that drug X may reduce psychotic symptoms in people with schizoprhenia does

not necessarily mean that the drug will have the same effects in the treatment of schizophrenia in people with mental retardation. As noted in Chapter 2, the cognitive disabilities associated with mental retardation may interact with psychosis in ways that have led some psychiatrists to conclude that schizophrenia cannot be diagnosed in people with severe mental retardation. Given that there is doubt about extending the diagnosis of schizophrenia from people with no mental retardation to people with severe mental retardation, there should be considerable doubt about extending powerful drug therapies that might have harmful and unpredictable side effects.

In conclusion, there are three primary reasons for our limited knowledge of the effects of psychiatric medications with people with mental retardation:

- The total amount of research reported has been inadequate.

- Few comparative studies have been reported designed to evaluate which drugs are most effective with the fewest side effects. Literature reviews cannot substitute for studies in which alternative drugs are directly compared.

- Because psychopathology has important cognitive determinants, knowledge of the effects of psychiatric drugs in the general population is an insufficient basis for using these drugs with people with mental retardation.

D3. BEST PRACTICES SOMETIMES NOT FOLLOWED. Despite numerous regulations and standards, there is concern about the degree to which best practices are followed on an everyday basis. Many people are given drug therapy without a precise diagnosis or specification of a behavior problem.

D4. SIDE EFFECTS. A number of psychiatric medications have significant side effects. Although side effects are always a concern when drugs are used, the concern is that much greater because many people with mental retardation cannot complain about possible side effects of medications.

One common side effect is called *chemical restraint* (sedation). Because many psychiatric drugs impair consciousness, drug recipients often feel drowsy, disoriented, and confused. The degree of sedation varies with dosage levels.

Future researchers need to evaluate the degree to which psychiatric medications reduce challenging behavior through a general sedation effect. In this regard, it is noteworthy that a range of diverse medications are all reported to have similar effects in reducing aggression. Aggression in people with mental retardation has been treated with neuroleptics, anticonvulsants, antimanics, and beta blockers. Do these diverse drugs reduce aggression in different ways? Why

are so many different drug categories reported to be effective for the same kinds of behavior? To what degree are the various drugs effective because of a general sedation effect?

One side effect of neuroleptic drugs that has received some attention is called *tardive dyskinesia,* which was first reported in 1957 (Kalachnik, 1988). This is a movement disorder indicated by involuntary, rhythmic, and repetitive movements of the face, mouth, and extremities. These movements can include lip smacking, puckering, tics, grimacing, and a variety of jerking movements. The symptoms sometimes are persistent long after drug therapy is terminated. After reviewing the literature, Kalachnik (1988) concluded that persistent tardive dyskinesia is evident in 30 to 40 percent of the persons with mental retardation treated with neuroleptic medication. The *Dyskinesia Identification System: Condensed User Scale (DISCUS)* is a rating instrument designed to assess tardive dyskinesia (Sprague, Kalachnik, & White, 1985).

Another side effect of neuroleptic drugs is called *neuroleptic malignant syndrome.* This syndrome is indicated by fever, severe muscular rigidity, altered consciousness, and autonomic arousal. With nonretarded people, this syndrome is estimated to have an incidence of about one percent and is fatal in 14.3 to 30 percent of cases (Boyd, 1992, 1993; Pope, Keck, & McElroy, 1986). Little attention was paid to the syndrome because it was thought to be rare. However, reports of neuroleptic malignant syndrome in persons with mental retardation have been increasing in recent years. For example, McNally and Calamari (1988) published what appears to be the first report of neuroleptic malignant syndrome in a person with mental retardation. The person was a 23 year-old man with severe mental retardation, seizure disorder, and a diagnosis of paranoid schizophrenia. He had a history of neuroleptic treatment and was the recipient of polypharmacy [multiple medications]. The neuroleptic malignant syndrome was treated successfully by discontinuance of neuroleptic medications. Other cases of neuroleptic syndrome in people with mental retardation have been reported by Boyd (1992) and Ward and Corbett (1989).

Boyd (1992) has suggested a number of procedures to reduce the risk of neuroleptic malignant syndrome:

> First, the use of neuroleptics should be reevaluated, making sure that alternative therapies and classes of drugs have been exhausted prior to returning to them. Second, if neuroleptics are required, they should not be reintroduced until the individual has been free of the symptoms for at least two weeks. . . . Third, close monitoring of the individual should take place for at least 2 weeks after reintroduction of neuroleptics, paying close attention to any changes in mental state, muscle tone, extrapyramidal symptoms, and autonomic functioning. Fourth, caretakers need to be informed

about any prior episode and taught what to look for in a possible recurrence. Finally, consideration should be given to obtaining a MedicAlert bracelet for individuals who have had a prior episode . . . (p. 79).

Kalachnik (1988) has reported a rating scale for monitoring the side effects of psychiatric medications. The scale is called *Monitoring of Side Effects System (MOSES)*. Nurses or caretakers rate each of up to 77 possible side effects on a five-point scale of intensity. At the time of this writing, the MOSES was in a preliminary stage of development.

D5. POLYPHARMACY. The prescription of multiple medications for the same person is called *polypharmacy*. When multiple psychiatric drugs are prescribed, we need to consider not only the effects of each drug but also the interaction effects attributable to the specific combinations of drugs. Unfortunately, there is little knowledge about drug interaction effects in persons with mental retardation.

D6. INADEQUATE TRAINING. Many of the physicians who prescribe psychiatric medications for people with mental retardation have not been adequately trained in mental retardation (e.g., Schalock *et al.*, 1985). Since the doctors have not been properly trained, they are more prone to make mistakes. There has always been a need to train more psychiatrists in mental retardation, but the need is that much greater now that powerful drugs with potentially harmful side effects are being prescribed on a widespread basis.

A number of other training needs can be identified. Nurses should be trained to monitor the effects of psychiatric medications. Psychologists should be trained in psychiatric diagnosis and psychopharmacology. Persons serving on medication review panels should be trained on issues related to the mental health aspects of mental retardation and psychopharmacology.

D7. THE NISONGER-THE Arc INTERNATIONAL CONSENSUS STUDY. In 1993, two Ohio State University Professors of Psychology and Psychiatry, Steven Reiss and Michael Aman, invited approximately 120 eminent medical and scientific authorities from North America, Europe, and Asia to participate on a panel to identify the consensus opinion regarding best practices and the effects of psychiatric drugs for people with mental retardation. It is hoped that the identification of consensus opinion will have the following consequences:

- A reduction in inappropriate uses of medications;

- Greater attention to best practices;

- A reduction in abusive practices.

The consensus panel is co-sponsored by The Ohio State University's Nisonger Center, the national Arc (formerly, Association for Retarded Citizens/United States), the President's Committee on Mental Retardation, and the American Association on University-Affiliated Programs.

V. DIAGNOSTIC CONDITIONS

Very few studies have been reported on the effects of various therapies for specific psychiatric conditions in persons with mental retardation. The following is a summary of the few studies that have been reported.

A. ANXIETY DISORDERS

A number of studies have found evidence for the effectiveness of behavior therapy treatments for phobias. Successful case studies were reported for the use of desensitization therapy in the treatment of a fear of heights (Guralnick, 1973), a psychotic bodily fear related to gender confusion (Rivenq, 1974), and a fear of physical examinations (Freeman, Roy, & Hemmick, 1976). Peck (1977) obtained some preliminary data for the effectiveness of *in vivo* desensitization in the treatment of fears of rats or heights in a group study with 20 people with mild mental retardation. Silvestri (1977) used implosive therapy to provide temporary reductions in anxiety in a group of persons with mental retardation.

Matson (1981*a*) compared the effects of participant modeling (an exposure therapy) against a no-therapy control condition. He used two matched groups of 12 adults with mild or moderate mental retardation who had a phobia for going to the grocery store. The subjects, who lived either in group homes or in independent living, had *DSM-II* diagnoses of mostly schizoprhenia (n = 14) or neurosis (n = 4). The subjects were assessed the week prior to treatment and the 13th week after therapy was completed. Hourly group therapy sessions were conducted for a period of three months. The results indicated that the participant modeling group showed significantly greater fear reduction than the no-therapy controls.

Matson (1981*b*) published three case histories documenting the effectiveness of participant modeling for the treatment of the fear of strangers in children with mental retardation. A six-month follow-up indicated that the reduction in fear had been maintained.

B. MOOD DISORDERS

The primary drug used to treat mood disorders in people with mental retardation is lithium. Due to the possibility of toxicity, however, carbamazepine and valproic acid have been suggested as possible alternatives to lithium (Sovner, 1991).

Sovner (1989) reported the case histories of five adults with mild to moderate mental retardation who were treated with the drug divalproex sodium, a valproate derivative. Four of the individuals had autism. Sovner's clinical diagnoses were bipolar disorder, atypical bipolar disorder (two cases), and rapid cycling bipolar disorder (two cases). Sovner's clinical impression was that four of the persons showed marked improvement and one showed some improvement. Few side effects were noted. No objective indicators of improvement were reported, and no long-term and follow-up data were reported.

Matson and his colleagues reported some success in case studies using reinforcement approaches to treat depression. Matson, Dettling, and Senatore (1981) treated an adult with mild mental retardation with a ten-year history of depression. Behaviors targeted for intervention included body posture, eye contact, poor speech quality, and bland affect. Treatment included instructions, modeling, role playing, self-monitoring, and self-reinforcement. Matson (1982a) treated depression in two additional adults with mild to moderate mental retardation. The behavior modified included words spoken, somatic complaints, irritability, grooming, negative self-statements, flat affect, eye contact, and speech latency.

No studies have been reported on the use of cognitive therapy in the treatment of depression in persons with mental retardation.

No study was found on the use of social skills training for the treatment and/or prevention of mood disorders in persons with mental retardation. However, this treatment is suggested by findings that poor social skills are strongly associated with low levels of social support and with depressed mood (e.g., Laman, 1989; Laman & Reiss, 1987).

C. SCHIZOPHRENIA

Treatments relevant to schizophrenia include social skills training, pretherapy, and play therapy. Social skills training has been used extensively to treat schizophrenia in nonretarded populations, but this author was unable to find outcome studies on the use of social skills training to treat schizophrenia in persons with mental retardation. A number of case studies have been reported doc-

umenting possible benefits from pretherapy (Prouty, 1994, in press; Prouty & Kubiak, 1988). Play therapy has been used with many children with joint schizophrenia and mental retardation, but this author could find no recent outcome evaluations.

Clarke (in press b) cites the importance of family support in recovery from schizophrenia. Efforts to improve the milieu are recommended, including programming occupational therapy and group work. Excessive stimulation should be removed from the environment. However, in some cases music or ear plugs have been tried successfully to interfere with auditory hallucinations (Clarke, in press b). When the individual is at home with his or her family, respite care is needed (Clarke, in press b).

Neuroleptic drugs are the primary treatments for psychosis. Reid (1993b) recommends chlorpromazine to attempt to bring acute episodes under control. He also recommends zuclopenthixol and fluspirilene for maintenance treatment for chronic schizophrenia.

The neuroleptics act predominantly by reducing delusions and hallucinations. They do not affect symptoms such as flat affect (emotional blunting) and lack of drive (Clarke, in press b).

D. PERSONALITY DISORDERS

The psychological therapies that would seem to be most applicable to the treatment of personality disorders are anger management training, problem-solving training, assertiveness training, psychotherapy, and group psychotherapy. However, the relevant therapy outcome studies have not yet been reported.

Tyrer and Seivewright (1988) have noted that therapists are only beginning to identify psychiatric drugs for specific personality disorders in persons with no mental retardation. The situation is even more tentative for people with mental retardation.

E. SEVERE BEHAVIOR DISORDERS

Carr and his colleagues reviewed the behavioral outcome literature for the treatment of severe behavior disorders such as aggression, stereotypies, and self-injurious behavior. They found success rates of 28 percent for DRO, 33 percent for DRI, 51 percent for skills acquisition, and 48 percent for stimulus-based procedures (National Institutes of Health, 1989). Punishment procedures showed higher rates of success. Only a minority of subjects had been evaluated for maintenance of treatment effects.

The four categories of drugs found to have some success in the treatment of aggression are neuroleptics, anticonvulsants (carbamazepine), antimanics (lithium), and beta blockers (propranolol). Currently, antidepressants and opiate blockers are being evaluated to treat SIB.

Sovner, Fox, Lowry, and Lowry (1993) published two cases in which SIB was associated with depression. The symptoms of depression were clearly identified for each case and included episodes of crying, irritability, sleep difficulties, and anxiety (pacing). In each case, the introduction of fluoxetine was correlated with a substantial and rapid decrease in SIB.

> In conclusion, these two case reports highlight an interaction between major depression and SIB in persons with severe and profound developmental disabilities. They make a strong case for the need for a psychiatric assessment of any individual manifesting significant SIB (p. 310).

Ricketts, Goza, Ellis, Singh, Singh, and Cooke (1993) reported four cases of self-injury treated with fluoxetine.

F. EATING DISORDERS

There is an outcome literature documenting benefits of cognitive-behavior therapy for obesity in people with mental retardation (Rotatori & Fox, 1981). Additionally, some case studies have been reported on the treatment of anorexia nervosa. Holt *et al.* (1988) shaped eating behavior in a 33 year-old man with Down Syndrome and anorexia nervosa. Szymanski and Biederman (1984) treated successfully three cases of anorexia nervosa using antidepressant and neuroleptic medications.

G. OTHER DISORDERS

At the time of this review, there were only isolated case studies on the treatment of sexual disorders, attention-deficit disorder, and psychological stress disorders.

VI. CONCLUSIONS

The outcome literature documents temporary benefits from a wide range of therapies. Psychotherapy, play therapy, art/dance therapy, pretherapy, behavior

therapy, behavior analysis, cognitive-behavior therapy, and a wide range of drugs all have been reported to have some benefits with people who have both mental retardation and mental health disorders.

Why have so many different therapies been found to have benefits? Perhaps there are significant nonspecific benefits. Nonspecific treatment factors (placebo effects) include positive therapist expectations for treatment gains, staff expectations for treatment gains, and increased attention from the staff or the therapist. All of these factors often are present when therapies are used with people with mental retardation. When so many diverse therapies are reported to be beneficial, the possibility of a nonspecific effect should be given serious consideration.

Another reason for the favorable outcome literature is that positive results are much more likely to be published than negative results. This is especially true for case studies, which are rarely submitted and accepted for publication when the outcomes are unfavorable. The therapists who publish case studies are not required to report how typical the results are in their practices.

Much additional research is indicated on the effectiveness of all the therapies reviewed in this chapter (Nezu & Nezu, 1994).

CHAPTER 5. COMMUNITY INTEGRATION

Up to this point, the mental health aspects of mental retardation were discussed primarily at the level of the individual. In contrast, the discussion in this chapter will address the level of systems and organizations. Consideration will be given to the role of systems in the possible causes, maintenance, and treatment of challenging behavior.

This author discovered the relevance of systems issues in 1970 while on a psychology internship. The author was assigned the case of a 10 year-old child with autism, Ann, who presented with persistent screaming accompanied by self-injurious behavior (Reiss & Redd, 1970). Ann's neck, underarms, and knees were abraded at the time of referral. In the opinion of an examining physician, these abrasions were so deep that serious infection, and even death, could result if the self-abusive behavior continued.

The author developed an appropriate behavior therapy program for Ann based on a functional analysis of Ann's screaming behavior. The author demonstrated that the use of the behavior program in a special treatment environment brought Ann's aberrant behavior under control. The behavior treatment was so effective that virtually no self-injurious behavior occurred if Ann was in the presence of a person who had used the behavioral program. The reduction in the target behavior was sufficient to allow Ann's self-inflicted wounds to begin to heal. The child's overall condition improved dramatically. She began using language appropriately, smiled more often, and was more relaxed.

Unfortunately, Ann lived in an institution that provided mostly custodial care. The staff to child ratio was about 1 to 20. The direct service staff were adult women who did not think that habilitation of the children was part of their jobs. According to these staff persons, their jobs were to prepare and serve the meals, to keep the children clean, and to supervise the children for safety. They knew nothing about behavioral psychology, and they had little desire to learn. Their attitude was that a child with challenging behavior did not belong in a developmental facility and should be relocated to a mental hospital.

A few weeks after therapy began, Ann caught a flu and was sent to the infirmary. In order to control her screaming, the attending physician had her tied spread-eagled to her hospital bed. Ann stayed in the infirmary for about two weeks. When Ann returned to her unit, her behavior and overall psychological condition had regressed to where they were prior to the use of the behavior therapy program. Her self-injurious behavior reappeared.

This case vignette illustrates the need to change organizations to support positive behavior changes. The behavior treatment program had been found to produce substantial improvement in an experimental classroom. When it was time to implement the behavior program on Ann's ward/unit, however, it

became apparent that the institution was not organized and staffed to accomplish this. It was not enough for the psychologist to improve Ann's behavior in an experimental context. There also was a need to change the job incentives and improve the skills of the direct service staff.

The mistake the author made in the case of Ann — addressing the needs of the individual while overlooking the need to change the institution — is a common mistake. For example, many behavior analysts have developed treatment programs that require years of consistent, quality implementation from trained staff to produce lasting behavior changes. Yet the national rate for job turnover among direct service staff is about 100 percent per year. The result is that numerous behavioral programs are not sustained properly over the years. There is a need to address the incompatibility between a therapy that requires years of consistent implementation and a system with a 100 percent annual rate of staff turnover.

As for Ann, her story is somewhat special. Bruce Baker had changed the children's unit of the institution in which Ann lived into an active treatment program. Ann was moved to the children's unit, where a second trial of behavior therapy reinstated some behavioral improvement. Years later Ann's psychiatrist would be Robert Sovner, who reported that she has made considerable progress.

I. SERVICE BARRIERS

People with challenging behavior face a number of barriers to obtaining adequate mental health services. Our discussion of these barriers begins with an historical review of how the creation of separate organizations for mental health and developmental disabilities services impacted people with challenging behavior.

A. HISTORICAL BARRIERS

The creation of separate organizations for mental health and developmental disabilities services has had important consequences for people who need both types of services. Historically, the creation of separate agencies has led to jurisdictional issues in providing services for people with challenging behavior.

A1. CREATION OF STATE MR UMBRELLA AGENCIES. The National Association for Retarded Children (NARC) was founded in 1950. One of the first goals of the NARC was to improve the coordination and planning of services for people with mental retardation. Services had developed at the state and county levels in response to the local needs and politics of each state. Since there were

few overall plans, the result was a complex array of agencies providing various bits and pieces of the services people needed. Coordination and cross-planning among the agencies were so inadequate that parents and children might have to go to one agency for educational services, another for basic assistance, another for a wheelchair, another for behavior services, and yet another for rehabilitation services.

The need for improved planning and coordination was recognized by the Kennedy administration. President Kennedy established the President's Committee on Mental Retardation (PCMR) in 1961. The PCMR initially consisted of 27 distinguished physicians, scientists, educators, lawyers, and consumers. The PCMR developed a comprehensive set of recommendations that later were enacted into federal law. Federal funding for mental retardation training, research, and service programs was greatly expanded (Braddock, 1987). The states were encouraged to develop coordinating and planning authorities.

The 1970 Developmental Disabilities Act, which introduced the concept of developmental disabilities into federal law, mandated state planning committees and led to additional increases in federal support for mental retardation. By 1976, 37 states had strengthened or created administrative units specifically for mental retardation. Moreover, in 28 states umbrella agencies for human services had been created (Gettings, 1988).

The parent advocacy groups sought separate administrative agencies for developmental disabilities services at both the state and regional level. Separation was sought from both public health and mental health agencies. Some states created cabinet level departments for mental retardation. In other states, a separate administrative division for developmental disabilities was created within a single cabinet level department. State legislatures appropriated separate pools of funds for mental health services versus developmental disabilities services.

By the 1970s, it had become obvious that the creation of separate mental retardation umbrella agencies, although of great benefit to people with mental retardation overall, had led to some service barriers for people with challenging behavior. In states where the advocates for mental retardation took their people and service dollars out from under the mental health umbrella, it was difficult to come back after the separation and ask the mental health system to fund services for people with mental retardation. Since the time when the mental retardation and mental health service organizations were separated, there have been few collaborative programs to help people with challenging behavior.

A2. HISTORY AT FEDERAL LEVEL. The movement for separate mental retardation programs reached the federal level in the 1960s. Prior to that time, the National Institute for Mental Health (NIMH) was the primary agency for funding mental retardation research and demonstration projects. In 1963, however, the National Institute of Child Health and Human Development (NICHD)

was created and given primary responsibility for mental retardation research at the federal level. The creation of the NICHD separated the federal research programs for mental retardation and mental illness.

When the NICHD was created, the NIMH retained the priority of research on the mental health aspects of mental retardation. However, the NIMH currently funds very little mental retardation research. Moreover, many NIMH-funded Community Mental Health Centers (CMHCs) located throughout the United States do not provide services to people with mental retardation. The NIMH has done little to encourage the CMHCs to end this discrimination.

Although both the NIMH and NICHD have budgets for funding research, neither agency funds much research on the use of psychiatric drugs with people with mental retardation (Sprague, 1984). The NIMH has the authority to fund this type of research, but the NICHD is funded as the primary agency for mental retardation research. When research grants are submitted, they are sent to the NIMH, which has the authority but not the funds. Today, very few mental retardation research grants are being funded at NIMH. The NICHD funds very few grants on psychiatric medications because they lack the mandate to fund such research. Consequently, badly needed research on the effects of psychiatric medications on people with mental retardation is not being funded.

In May, 1975, the Directors of the NICHD and NIMH jointly convened a group of six Ad Hoc Consultants on Mental Retardation. They were requested, in light of the history of the prior ten years, "to examine the advisability of NIMH making an explicit policy decision to reenter the field of mental retardation . . . ." (Tarjan, Dornbusch, Fenichel, Graham, Richmond, & Zigler, 1977, p. iv). In February, 1977, this group made the following recommendations in their final report:

- Reintroduce mental retardation into the purview of the Community Mental Health Centers (CMHCs) (p. 55).

- Provide "university training [in mental retardation] for mental health professionals" (p. 56).

- Fund research on the mental health aspects of mental retardation.

Unfortunately, the recommendations were not adopted.

In 1978 another report was filed, this one by the Liaison Task Panel on Mental Retardation, which was a committee of the President's Commission on Mental Health. The committee found that neither the mental health nor the developmental disabilities systems had assumed primary responsibility for services so that people with both mental retardation and mental illness had:

fallen through the cracks . . . [and are] neglected by both mental health and mental retardation systems (President's Commission on Mental Health, 1978, p. 2007).

In 1985 the President's Committee on Mental Retardation (PCMR) and six federal agencies and institutes sponsored a three-day conference on the mental health aspects of mental retardation. The conference, which was organized by the late Frank Menolascino, featured 50 eminent scientists, clinicians, and public policy authorities. The conference found a need for a new national policy on challenging behavior. The PCMR presented the proceedings in the form of a book but took no position on the issues (Stark *et al.*, 1988).

In 1987 the National Institute of Mental Health co-funded an international research conference organized by the present author (Reiss, 1988*a*). The three-day meeting was entitled, "UIC-NIMH International Research Conference on the Mental Health Aspects of Mental Retardation." The conference was attended by 420 persons who listened to 60 research presentations on the need to address the mental health aspects of mental retardation. An outgrowth of the conference was a subsequent NICHD-NIMH workshop on assessment held in Bethesda, Maryland, in 1987 (Dibble & Gray, 1990).

The UIC-NIMH research conference, and the subsequent NICHD-NIMH workshop on assessment, helped stimulate the development of assessment instruments. As these instruments were distributed in significant quantities, thousands of people were identified as needing services. This has contributed to a growing demand for services, and more states and localities have responded by funding special projects, demonstration programs, and clinics.

B. CURRENT BARRIERS

Mental retardation professionals have identified the following barriers to services for people with challenging behavior:

B1. INADEQUATE COMMITMENT. Parent and consumer groups have been insufficiently committed to mental health services for people with mental retardation. Since mental health disorders often do not develop and become recognized until late adolescence or early adulthood, parents are older and beyond the point where many would consider active advocacy. In an era when consumers are becoming empowered, the absence of organized consumer support has been a major barrier to producing needed changes. Consumers must organize to demand improved services or future progress is likely to be minimal.

Professional groups also have shown inadequate commitment. The Association for the Severely Handicapped (TASH) has not advocated strongly for a more adequate level of services. The American Association on Mental Retardation (AAMR) has not developed a policy calling for more services. The National Association for the Dually Diagnosed (NADD) has not made a major commitment to the public policy arena.

B2. INADEQUATE RESOURCES. Thus far, funding has not been available at the levels that are needed. Neither the developmental disabilities nor the mental health system is specifically funded to provide mental health services to people with mental retardation. When resources are inadequate, administrators "tend to draw their boundaries more closely . . . . Hard cases tend to get low priority . . . . " (Boggs, 1988, p. 321).

B3. ORGANIZATIONAL RESISTANCE TO CHANGE. Because systems tend to resist change, it is difficult to create the changes that are needed to increase services for people with challenging behavior. Forces maintaining the status quo include mission statements, official policies, job training programs, and founders who recall how difficult it was to create and to fund the organization (Woodward, 1993).

B4. PROFESSIONAL OPPOSITION. Historically, behavior analysts position against psychiatric diagnosis tended to isolate services for people with developmental disabilities from the larger mental health field. It was not until 1980, when *DSM-III* was introduced, that behavior analysts' opposition to psychiatric diagnosis lessened.

B5. DIFFICULTY FINDING RESIDENTIAL PLACEMENTS. Mental hospitals operate in ways that are incompatible with some of the needs of people with challenging behavior. These hospitals are designed mostly for people who are expected to stabilize, improve, and return to their own families or homes. Many mental hospitals do not want to take people with mental retardation unless they are guaranteed a residential program so that a discharge date can be anticipated (Smull, 1988). In the case of a person with mental retardation, this can be difficult because many mental retardation agencies do not accept people with challenging behavior when they are released from mental hospitals.

B6. LOW STATUS. People with challenging behavior are a low status group in both the mental health and developmental disabilities service communities (Woodward, 1993).

B7. TWO LANGUAGES. The mental health and developmental disabilities service delivery systems use different professional languages. They do not always communicate well with one another.

C. INTERNATIONAL SYSTEMS BARRIERS

The systems barriers that exist in the United States also exist in Canada (Zarfas, 1988), Australia (Parmenter, 1988), and Spain (Sacristan, 1988). For example, Zarfas (1988) drew the following conclusions based on a survey of Canada:

> There is recognition of the dually diagnosed in every Province and Territory. It is evident that some steps are being taken to serve this population, but problems exist. Lack of interest in mentally retarded people by mental health professionals, particularly psychiatrists, is a major stumbling block. A lack of sufficient community resources is seen as a major problem. There remain some jurisdictional disputes between Ministries and some considerable lack of trust between all of the players (p. 6).

Parmenter (1988) wrote the following regarding the situation in Australia:

> Historically the situation in Australia is much the same as developments in countries such as the United States and Canada. The problem of diagnostic overshadowing (Reiss, Levitan, & Szyszko, 1982); the relative lack of interest by psychiatrists; the dearth of training and opportunities for practicum experiences in facilities of psychiatry; the concentration of resources in large institutions . . . . (p. 10).

Here is how Puddephatt and Sussman (1994) summarized the situation in Ontario, Canada:

> . . . the dually diagnosed in the community have been relegated to a psychiatric service netherworld. Few psychiatrists are willing to accept clients with mental retardation. Psychiatric hospitals are reluctant to admit people with a dual diagnosis . . . (p. 356).

II. OVERCOMING SERVICE BARRIERS

Overcoming service barriers will require identifying policy goals and objectives, active support from parent- and self-advocacy groups, and research on

organizational systems and how they change.

A. GOALS AND OBJECTIVES

A number of policy advisors and state task forces have made recommendations for overcoming the service barriers.

A1. GETTINGS' SUGGESTIONS. Robert M. Gettings is Executive Director of the National Association of State Mental Retardation Program Directors, Inc. He offered the following suggestions for effective change at the 1985 PCMR conference on the mental health aspects of mental retardation (Gettings, 1988):

- Interagency cooperation at the state and local levels needs to be increased. The state directors of both systems need to be fully committed to interagency cooperation to bring about lasting improvements.

- Specialists in both systems need to be trained regarding the needs of people with both mental retardation and mental illness.

- The two systems need to develop common diagnostic terminology with regard to people with both mental retardation and mental illness. Within the context of common terminology, the responsibilities of each system need to be delineated and accepted.

- The efficacy of various services needs to be determined.

- Although much improvement will be possible without any new funding, some new funding will be needed.

A2. ILLINOIS STATE TASK FORCE. Benson and Hunter (1993) recently co-lead the "Metro-Area Dual Diagnosis Task Force" for the Chicago metropolitan area. The task force recommended that the developmental disabilities system should take the lead in matters concerning people with both mental retardation and mental illness. Some of the other systems recommendations were as follows:

- There should be a range of residential settings, from community based to institutional.

- Special funding should be provided.

- Crises intervention services are needed.

- A cooperative planning committee is needed between the mental health and developmental disabilities systems.

- The mental health facilities are better suited to provide acute treatment.

- A training institute is needed.

B. CONSUMER ADVOCACY

Consumer advocacy is likely to be essential in any effort to increase services and research pertaining to challenging behavior. There are two main categories of consumer organizations: parent groups and self-advocates.

B1. PARENT GROUPS AND CHALLENGING BEHAVIOR. Scheerenberger (1983) reported that parent groups began in the early 1930s and that the first such group was the Cuyahoga County (Ohio) Council for Retarded Children which was formed in 1933. By 1950, 88 similar local groups had formed with a total membership of 19,300 in 19 states. The parent groups started to hold national meetings in conjunction with the American Association on Mental Retardation, and in 1950 they formed a national organization called the National Association for Retarded Citizens (NARC). In 1980 the name of the organization was changed to "Association for Retarded Citizens of the United States," and in 1992 it was changed again to "The Arc of the United States."

With a membership varying as high as 250,000 at times, the Arc became a powerful lobbying organization for legislation for mental retardation. In 1970 the Arc teamed up with the national United Cerebral Palsy and other groups to pass the Developmental Disabilities Act. This act has been re-authorized a number of times with various amendments intended to promote the community integration, independence, and productivity of persons with mental retardation.

The Arc adopted the principle that it would advocate for all persons with mental retardartion, regardless of other disabilities that may be present (Boggs, 1988). It sought services for individuals with multiple disabilities that were equal in quality to those afforded to individuals with only one disability. The Arc has advocated for persons with challenging behavior.

In the late 1980s the Arc and other developmental disabilities groups supported the efforts of the National Council on Disabilities to pass comprehensive civil rights legislation for people with disabilities. On July 26, 1990, President George Bush signed the Americans with Disabilities Act (ADA). This law makes

illegal certain types of discrimination, exclusion, and segregation. The law affects approximately 43 million Americans with disabilities, including all persons with developmental disabilities. The ADA (PL 101-33) prohibits discrimination against persons with disabilities in the areas of employment (Title I), public services including transportation (Title II), public accommodations and commerce (Title III), and telecommunications (Title IV).

In the 1980s the central policy issue for consumer groups was the elimination of all aversive approaches to challenging behavior. All major consumer organizations have passed resolutions opposing the use of aversive techniques to manage challenging behavior. The development of alternative, nonaversive techniques has been encouraged (e.g., LaVigna & Donnellan, 1986).

In 1989, the National Institute of Child Health and Human Behavior convened a consensus panel that addressed the use of aversive therapy for people with challenging behavior (National Institutes of Health, 1991). The panel consisted of a broad range of eminent scientists, clinicians, and public policy persons. The panel found that alternatives to aversive therapy existed for all but the most extreme cases of destructive behavior. However, the panel did not find scientific support to endorse the view that aversives **never** should be used.

The consumer movement deserves much credit for having reduced the use of aversive techniques to all but the most extreme cases. Presently, there are no more than a few thousand people in the United States for whom any credible person would even consider using aversive therapy. Although the goal of zero aversives has not yet been achieved, a great deal of progress has been made.

As many as 1.5 million Americans may have both mental retardation and a mental health disorder. With the battle against aversives largely won, at this point the single-minded pursuit of the aversive issue to the exclusion of all other issues would be tantamount to basing public policy for 1.5 million people on the needs of just a few thousand.

The national Arc and other consumer groups need to develop a comprehensive policy for people with challenging behavior. Issues that need to be addressed include the overuse of psychiatric medications, inadequate training for psychiatrists and nurses, and inadequate housing.

B2. SELF-ADVOCACY AND CHALLENGING BEHAVIOR. Instead of being represented by parents or family members, people with disabilities are seeking to speak for themselves. This trend toward self-advocacy has been particularly strong among persons with physical disabilities in independent living associations. Self-advocacy is a more recent phenomenon among people with developmental disabilities.

The first developmental disabilities self-advocacy group to form in the United States is called "People First." The name represents the members' desire

to be recognized as people foremost and as having a disability second. Other groups are called "Stand Together" and "Speaking For Ourselves." These are grass-roots organizations (Longhurst, in press). They provide a forum for members to help one another and to try to educate the community about developmental disabilities.

Longhurst (in press) surveyed the self-advocacy groups listed in the 1990 directory compiled by the national Arc. This directory includes groups that are self-directing, have the support of an advisor, and focus on issues pertaining to self-advocacy. Longhurst surveyed 4,125 people in 241 groups in 43 states. Eighty percent of the respondents had mental retardation, ten percent had a learning disability, and 8.8 percent had cerebral palsy. About 83 percent of the respondents were between the ages of 20 and 50. About 85 percent were European-American and 11 percent were African-American. About half of the respondents had been involved for fewer than two years. Activities included information, news, self-advocacy training, and conferences. Financial support came from developmental disabilities councils, state and local Arc chapters, and University-Affiliated Programs.

C. CREATING NEW SERVICES

Sarason's (1972) theory on the creation of settings has implications for overcoming systems barriers and creating new service programs. This theory is intended to identify some of the factors that account for the success versus failure of service programs.

Sarason has taken a somewhat pessimistic view of the chances for success in creating innovative service programs.

> Time and again I have observed the creation of settings (usually in the human service area) with basic values and aims it would be hard to disagree, only to see over time how optimism is replaced by pessimism, consensus by polarization, and passionate concern for values by a desire to exist . . . Why so many new settings fail, and relatively quickly, is not easy to understand and what I have tried to do in very brief fashion in this chapter is to suggest that part of the answer is in how people think: their knowledge, ideas, conceptions (Sarason, 1972, p. 20).

Sarason has recommended a number of strategies to maximize future success in creating new service programs. His advice is directed at how leaders think about creating new services. Sarason believes that leaders need to think about

the new program as an organizational entity and to consider how their program relates to other organizational entities.

C1. CONFRONT HISTORY. Sarason (1972) believes that new programs will inherit the conflicts of the organizations that create or fund them:

> . . . a proposed new setting always arises in relation to existing settings; that there are characteristics of the new setting . . . and concerns of existing ones (such as ideology, concern for resources) which ensure some conflict and competition . . . (p. 46).

For example, a program for challenging behavior that is jointly funded by both mental health and developmental disabilities systems will inherit the conflict between those systems. Unless the leadership of the new program understands this and develops effective strategies, Sarason believes that the new program may not last very long.

Sarason (1972) believes that creators of programs for challenging behavior need to develop an historical perspective on their program:

> If I decided to create a new school for children (or if I decided to start a commune), I should be aware that I was not the first person in history to start such a venture (p. 35).

All too often, the creation of a new service program occurs in the context of optimistic thinking. The focus is on the future, and the hope is that the future will be different from the past. But the past often is the best predictor of the future. Often a more promising future requires that program creators confront the problems of the past.

C2. ADEQUATE RESOURCES. Sarason (1972) has used the phrase the "myth of unlimited resources" to refer to a leader's lack of attention to resource issues when attempting to change a system. All too often social change agents plan programs or services that are prohibitively costly. For example, the present author can recall visiting one demonstration program in which as many as 20 professional staff, including a half dozen medical staff, were present to discuss the mental health status of a single individual. Although the program was successful in demonstrating the potential benefits of the service, it was much too costly for replication.

Some efforts to change service systems are made by people who have little appreciation of resource issues and who demand services as if there were no limit to the taxpayer's willingness to fund them. Instead of developing plans

based on what is possible financially, these leaders develop plans without regard to costs. The consequence is that much more is promised than can be delivered.

C3. REALISTIC TIME PERSPECTIVE. Many advocates and theorists seek rapid, if not immediate, changes. However, it is not possible to produce meaningful change in a period of weeks or months. Even if there were political support and resources to create needed mental health services for people with mental retardation, it would still take years to train the required staff and professionals.

The following anecdote illustrates the issue of time perspective. A site visitor at a mental retardation training program asked how the program planned to meet the priority of expanding mental health services for people with mental retardation. The response was that the program would train future psychiatrists. "This will take years," complained the site visitor, who was looking for a solution with more immediate impact. "But once accomplished the positive benefits will last for decades," came the response.

C4. SUMMARY. In conclusion, Sarason's (1972) theory of the creation of settings offers a number of insights into the factors important for successful new service programs. The theory encourages creators of challenging behavior programs to do all of the following:

(a) To think of the new program as an organizational entity and to consider how it relates to other organizational entities;

(b) To study the history of the organizations that create and fund the new program;

(c) To identify any areas of historical conflict that might be inherited by the new program;

(d) To promise only those services that can be accomplished with available resources;

(e) To allow for realistic time periods for meaningful systems changes to occur.

III. SERVICE MODELS

A number of service models for people with challenging behavior have been created. The various models are based on different philosophies of care and are

designed to meet different needs. Although little outcome data have been reported, descriptive statistics have been published for some of the more widely emulated models.

A. SPECIALIZED VS. GENERIC SERVICES

Opinion has been divided on the need for specialized services for people with challenging behavior. The case against such services was first made by Szymanski and Grossman (1984), who suggested that existing mental health centers should provide the needed mental health services and that existing developmental centers should provide the needed mental retardation services. Szymanski and Grossman suggested that there should be little need for specialized services if authorities representing mental health and developmental disabilities services could learn to cooperate with each other.

Smull and Harrison (1992) have gone beyond the position that specialized services are unnecessary to argue that such services can be harmful and worsen challenging behavior. This view holds that specialized services tend to isolate the individual from the community, resulting in a loss of friends and social supports. Smull and Harrison also have suggested that staff burnout is more likely in specialized than in generic settings.

In contrast to these views, Day (1993b) has been a strong and consistent advocate for some specialized services. He has made the following arguments:

1. Generic psychiatric services are unresponsive to the needs of people with mental retardation who do not fit well into existing programs.

2. The atypical presentation of psychiatric disorders in people with mental retardation requires special expertise.

3. Some treatment techniques are unique to people with mental retardation.

4. Some treatment techniques must be modified to be applicable to people with mental retardation.

5. Special regimes and careful monitoring of drug treatment are necessary.

6. Specialized services increase staff competencies and skills.

7. Specialized services provide an essential base for teaching and research.

Some people with challenging behavior have unique combinations of needs for which there are no pre-existing services. These people require some specialized services. For example, this author recalls the case of a young woman who had mild mental retardation, a borderline personality disorder, and diabetes. Neither the state's mental hospitals nor developmental disabilities centers could meet the woman's needs. The mental hospitals could neither protect her physically nor provide her with appropriate peers with whom to share time. The developmental programs were not staffed to cope with her persistent efforts to run away and her life-threatening refusals to take insulin. The woman needed specialized services that did not exist in her state.

The debate over specialized versus generic services is likely to continue for quite some time. Future research may help decide a number of areas of disagreement. In the meantime, most service systems will likely develop some specialized services while simultaneously seeking ways to utilize existing resources in a more effective manner.

B. FAMILY SERVICES

Very little has been written about the families of people with challenging behavior. For example, Sigman's (1985b) book on children with emotional disorders and developmental disabilities deals extensively with applied developmental psychology but has no subject index listing for families and includes only a nine page chapter on family therapy. Family issues were not included in Matson and Barrett's (1993) book on psychopathology in people with mental retardation. Only one of 41 papers published in Stark et al.'s (1988) book, entitled *Mental Retardation and Mental Health,* is concerned primarily with families.

Baker et al. (1993) evaluated family involvement in the residential treatment of 84 children with challenging behavior. The children were between the ages of 4.4 and 18.8; however, about 70 percent were adolescents. The study found overall family involvement was low for all groups evaluated, including children with challenging behavior.

> To summarize, family involvement was lowest with dually diagnosed children, but it appears that lower involvement was attributable to other characteristics of the dual diagnosis group rather than to the diagnosis *per se* (Baker et al., 1993, p. 565).

Dokecki and Heflinger (1988) have authored one of the few knowledgeable papers on the families of people with challenging behavior. They have noted

that the fragmentation of services between mental health and developmental disabilities systems adds to the families' frustration. Their list of needed services included the following:

- Income support,

- Respite care,

- Transportation,

- Homemaker services,

- Training in parenting skills,

- Counseling.

Some psychologists have developed programs to train parents in behavior modification so children with challenging behavior can live at home. Bruce Baker has been a pioneer in the area of parent training, although his work has focused more on teaching social skills than behavior management (e.g., Baker, Heifetz, & Murphy, 1980; Clark, Baker, & Heifetz, 1982). Baker and his colleagues have helped demonstrate that parent training is an effective component of a service plan for families. Although some have suggested that involving parents might increase the stress and depression in their lives, Baker, Landen, and Kashima (1991) reported some data that were inconsistent with this prediction. Additionally, Napolitan reported successful applications of parent training efforts to foster parents of children with severe behavior disorders (Reiss, McKinney, & Napolitan, 1990).

Allin (1984) has described a successful program for intensive home-based treatment interventions for persons with challenging behavior. The program uses parents or family members to implement behavior modification treatment in the home. The model has been used successfully to treat children with temper tantrums and those with somatic complaints. Allin (1988) concluded the following:

> The program has shown that parents and families can make changes to alleviate problems and that the support of staff working in the natural environment is instrumental in this process. By giving parents a direction, some information, insights, and a practical approach, they are able to impact on a wide range of behavior that otherwise threatens family unity and client independence and places more demands on our community resources (p. 279).

C. CRISIS INTERVENTION

Davidson, Cain, Sloane-Reeves, Giesow, Quijano, Van Heyningen, and Shoham (1993) have described a comprehensive crisis intervention program at the University of Rochester University-Affiliated Program. Because crises cannot be anticipated, some services are needed 24 hours per day every day of the year. The program includes the following components.

1. An interdisciplinary team to respond to behavioral crises. The team has access to both the mental health and developmental disabilities systems.

2. A continuum of inpatient care.

3. Prevention services such as staff training and education.

4. Respite care.

5. Case management.

The treatment team consists of a full-time program director, two full-time behavior modification specialists, a parttime clinical psychologist and a part-time psychiatrist. At this staffing level, the program serves about eight people per month.

A recent survey of 267 Rochester service recipients indicated a mean age of 27. About 60 percent were receiving community-based habilitative day treatment or sheltered employment; 35 percent were enrolled in special education; four percent were in regular education; and one percent were in transitional services. About 52 percent resided with a family member, 22 percent in community residences, and nine percent in Intermediate Care Facilities (ICF/DD). The most common presenting problems were aggression, noncompliance, psychotic symptoms, and self-injury. The most common psychiatric diagnoses were organic brain disorder, conduct disorder, mood disorder, schizophrenia, and adjustment disorder.

For the Rochester program, the re-referral or recidivism rate was estimated as follows:

1.9 percent within one year of discharge;

9.5 percent within two years of discharge;

56.4 percent within four years of discharge.

Gravestock and Bicknell (1992) have reported some data from a crisis intervention program in a south London (England) community. In a six-month period, 40 emergency referrals were made concerning 33 different clients, with 27 (82%) referred once and six (18%) referred more than once. The median age of 25 was similar to that reported for the Rochester program. The most common psychiatric diagnoses, based on the *International Classification of Disorders (ICD-9)*, were manic-depressive psychosis, personality disorder, and atypical childhood psychosis. Aggressive behavior was present in 48 percent of the referrals. A benefit to treatment intervention was suggested for about 82 percent of the referrals.

In conclusion, crises intervention is an important service for the relatively small numbers of people who experience one or more episodes of high intensity challenging behaviors. There is some evidence to suggest effectiveness — recurrence rates are significant but perhaps much lower than what many experts might have expected.

D. OUTPATIENT MODEL

The Mental Health Program of the Institute for the Study of Developmental Disabilities (ISDD Mental Health Program), University of Illinois at Chicago, was among the first outpatient programs to be described in the literature (Reiss & Trenn, 1984). The program was created in 1980 to evaluate consumer demand for outpatient mental health services in a large metropolitan area. The program serves people of all ages and all levels of mental retardation. The program provides diagnostic services, individual psychotherapy, cognitive therapy, reinforcement therapy, and drug therapy. Since the program does not provide services for diagnosing mental retardation or developmental disabilities, all of the referrals to the program are for the purposes of obtaining a mental health service.

The ages of the ISDD clients at time of referral for services were reported in Table 1-4 in Chapter 1. These data provide evidence for consumer demand for mental health services across the life span. However, consumer demand was greatest for adolescents and young adults between the ages of 15 and 29. Approximately two-thirds of all persons referred to the clinic were between these ages. Similar data have been reported at mental health clinics that serve the general population.

Researchers have not yet found the reasons for the high rates of referrals of adolescents and young adults. One possible factor is that adolescents and young adults are challenged by the transition to adulthood, which may be particularly stressful for people with mental retardation. Another possible factor is the loss of the school system as a major support.

TABLE 5-1. Agency Referrals to ISDD Mental Health Program for 27 of 33 Months[1]

TYPE OF AGENCY	Male	Female	Total	Percent
36 Community Agencies	127	54	181	66.1
9 State Facilities	30	15	45	17.2
6 Private Hospitals	10	7	17	6.2
8 Schools	5	5	10	3.6
4 Miscellaneous	5	2	7	2.6
Families	5	5	10	3.6
Private Professionals	4	0	4	1.5
Total	186	88	274	100.0

[1] Based on Reiss and Trenn (1984).

Reiss and Trenn (1984) found that the following four categories of psychopathology accounted for 51 percent of the referrals to the ISDD Mental Health Program: psychosis, antisocial behavior, depression, and personality disorders. The finding of a high rate of depression, which was reported in 1984, is among the earliest reports of depression in people with mental retardation. Depression was reported more frequently for women versus men and more frequently for people with mild versus severe mental retardation.

Table 5-1 provides a breakdown of the sources of referral to the ISDD Mental Health Program. This table shows that approximately two-thirds of the referrals came from community agencies. Most of the remaining referrals came from state facilities. There were relatively few referrals from schools and families. The data suggest that the ISDD Mental Health Program functioned primarily as a support service for community integration.

The ISDD Mental Health Program was followed by a number of programs with outpatient services. One national goal has been to increase outpatient services through the network of federally-funded Community Mental Health Centers (CMHCs). At the University-Affiliated Cincinnati Center for Developmental Disorders, for example, Woodward and Pederson (1991) developed a comprehensive curriculum guide for a program of 100 hours of training

for community mental health professionals. The guide addresses training at both the preservice and inservice levels. The training covers psychotropic medications, generic community services, and mental health consultation. Past trainees gave the program high marks for helping them in the areas of treatment planning, family issues, sexuality, psychopharmacology, case presentations, behavior therapy, collaboration, and consultative role. The trainees also are taught how to consult with community mental health centers to provide services for people with mental retardation.

Bouras, Brooks and Drummond (1993) described a community-based psychiatric service in England. The services included psychiatric assessment, treatment of adults with mental illness, management of behavior problems, home-based intervention, and work with offenders. Bouras et al. reported statistics on 356 referrals to their program over a period of ten years. Although half the referrals presented with physical aggression, only 11 percent of the referrals required admission to an inpatient psychiatric unit.

Bouras et al. (1993) reported that the transition period from adolescence to adulthood was particularly stressful for both individuals and family. These findings are similar to those reported by Reiss and Trenn (1984) for the ISDD Mental Health Program. Bouras et al. recommended increased respite support for families coping with individuals entering the transition period.

Van Minnen, Hoelsgens, and Hoogduin (1993) compared people in the Netherlands who had mental retardation and were receiving either outpatient (n = 81) or inpatient (n = 28) care for mental health services. The only statistically significant difference between the groups was that the outpatients were more likely to have a legal history. Otherwise, the groups did not differ in terms of age, gender, IQ scores, living situation, and psychiatric diagnosis.

In conclusion, outpatient programs function primarily as community-based supports that help people stay out of institutional or congregate-care facilities. The outpatient model provides a relatively cost-effective means of reaching significant numbers of people, especially adolescents and young adults.

E. DAY SERVICES

The Rock Creek Foundation in Silver Springs, Maryland, which was started in 1973, is recognized as the first nationally important day program for people with challenging behavior (Smull, Fabian, & Chanteau, 1984). The program was founded by Michael Smull, who is one of the nation's leading thinkers for program innovation. The program served people with mental retardation who also had a chronic mental illness such as schizophrenia.

The Rock Creek approach included the following elements (Smull et al., 1984):

1. Assessment of the individual in the context of environmental functioning and movement across less restrictive environments;

2. Assessment of habilitation needs and the development of an individual plan in which the client has meaningful input and some control;

3. Interdisciplinary staffing leading to the diagnosis of an emotional problem and a recommendation for treatment;

4. A multidisciplinary blend of professional techniques that meet individual needs.

Rock Creek's day program provided formal psychotherapy, activity programming, and vocational services. Both psychiatric and behavioral services were provided. The therapists were charged with overseeing their clients' multidisciplinary teams and coordinating and implementing treatment plans. When a client progressed psychologically, vocational activities were slowly integrated into the treatment plan.

Another well-known day program is called "Beacon House" (Fletcher, 1988). This is a large psychiatric partial-hospitalization service under the auspices of Ulster County (N.Y.) Community Mental Health Services. The mental retardation day treatment program is a unit of a larger psychiatric day treatment program. Beacon House uses a highly structured group method of treatment in a supportive environment. Both individual and drug therapy are utilized as adjuncts to group therapy. A preliminary outcome study found improvement in the areas of socialization skills, impulse control, self-esteem, and problem-solving skills.

Fletcher (1988) surveyed the service recipients of Beacon House and found an age range of 24 to 46 and an IQ range of 54 to 82. Many of the service recipients experienced dysfunctional families, failure in school, peer rejection, and poor interpersonal skills.

In conclusion, the day program model provides a comprehensive range of nonresidential services for persons with severe or chronic mental illnesses. Several authors have reported that day programs can help keep people with chronic mental illnesses out of state institutions (Fletcher, 1988; Smull *et al.*, 1984).

F. INPATIENT UNITS

Many states have created inpatient observation and stabilization units for people in a behavioral crisis. These units are located in both developmental and

mental health centers. The units in developmental centers usually serve people with severe mental retardation; the units in mental health centers usually serve people with mild mental retardation. Generally, the units in developmental centers are better able to meet the habilitation needs of the individual.

Day (1993b, p. 10) has noted the following difficulties with specialized behavior units:

> It is argued that behaviour therapy units have not been successful (Keene & James, 1986), that it is difficult to maintain management programmes and treatment gains on return to the community (Newman & Emerson, 1991), that it makes more sense to attempt to effect behavioural change in the environment in which it arises (Allin & Allin, 1984; Carr & Durand, 1985b; McBrien, 1987) and that grouping severely disturbed people together creates a chaotic environment for both patients and staff which impairs consistent approaches to treatment and provides inappropriate models of behaviour for individual patients (Blunden & Allen, 1987; Newman & Emerson, 1991).

Since service providers do not want to accept people with a history of challenging behavior, another concern with behavior units is the difficulty of discharging people after their behavior has improved. Once someone is admitted to a behavior unit, they tend to stay for long periods of time, even when they were admitted for temporary observation and stabilization.

Despite these shortcomings, many experts have concluded that the creation of a small number of behavior units is needed. As Bouras (1993) observed,

> Arguments in favor of specialized units include the creation of a secure and controlled environment, the minimisation of disruption to other service users, and the development of enhanced staff expertise (p. 58).

McGee, Folk, Swanson, and Menolascino (1984) argued that,

> A very small percentage of mentally retarded-mentally ill persons require long-term hospitalization. The primary criterion for such a placement is that the person poses a chronic threat to himself or herself or to others (pp. 257-258).

One of the best known inpatient units is located at the Nebraska Psychiatric Institute. This program was founded by the late Frank Menolascino. It served no more than 15 people at any one time. Professional staff included a full-time

clinical psychiatrist, a parttime clinical psychopharmacologist, a charge nurse, three shift nurses, one-to-one staffing of paraprofessionals, an on-staff community liaison person, a parttime social worker, a parttime psychologist, and other specially trained personnel (McGee *et al.*, 1984).

In 1987 Illinois was operating three mental retardation behavior units with 141 beds in state-operated mental hospitals (Reiss, McKinney, & Napolitan, 1990). The system was serving approximately 509 people per year. The age range was five to 72, with the majority being young to middle-aged adults. The most common diagnoses were schizophrenia, personality disorder, organic brain syndrome, atypical psychosis, impulse control disorder, adjustment disorder, substance abuse, conduct disorder, and affective disorder.

A survey of 465 people who had been discharged from the Illinois behavior units found that about half returned to their families (Reiss *et al.*, 1990). The others were discharged to community facilities, including 16 percent to Intermediate Care Facilities for the Developmentally Disabled (ICF/DDs). Only two persons were discharged to independent living.

Day (1993b, 1994) has suggested that a number of different inpatient units are needed to take into account the diversity of mental illness, age, and intellectual level found in the people requiring services. He has argued for separate settings for the mentally ill, behaviorally disturbed, and offenders.

In conclusion, inpatient behavior units are undesirable. They are inconsistent with the philosophy of community integration. They are expensive, may not work very well, and few providers are willing to accept clients being discharged from a behavior unit. Despite all these well-recognized shortcomings, many states have found no satisfactory alternative to the creation of a small number of behavior units to serve people who have high intensity behavior challenges.

G. HOUSING AND SUPPORTED LIVING

There is a need for more community residential supports for people with challenging behavior. These people are overrepresented in state institutions. Some estimates are that people with challenging behavior constitute at least 40 percent of the current institutional population. Addressing the residential needs of people with challenging behavior is an important step toward de-populating and abolishing institutions.

The families of people with challenging behavior have had frustrating experiences finding appropriate housing for their loved ones. Many community residential agencies have closed their doors to people with challenging behavior. Moreover, some families have had the heart-wrenching experience of having

their child terminated from a residential program when destructive behavior emerged or intensified.

One recent innovation in housing is called supported living. In the past, housing for persons with mental retardation was based on a continuum approach in which individuals were supposed to move to the less restrictive alternatives when their community living skills improved. This approach did not work well, however, because the people rarely moved into the less restrictive homes. More recently, it has been suggested that people could move directly into natural/typical settings and be maintained with an array of supports and services (Hitzing, 1980; Taylor, 1987).

People with developmental disabilities want to choose where they live and with whom they live. They prefer places of their own (Kennedy & Olson, 1987; Williams & Shoultz, 1984). In supported living programs, people with mental retardation are treated as if they were living in their own homes. This means that they have considerable choice and control and do not have to adjust to the preferences of direct service staff.

Thus far, supported living programs have been provided primarily to people with no challenging behavior. Persons with challenging behavior usually are offered more restrictive settings. However, a number of advocates have suggested that people with challenging behavior should live, work, and go to school in typical, valued settings (Allin & Allin, 1984; Hitzing, 1987). This might be accomplished by providing a wide array of intensive services and supports so that people with challenging behavior can live in community settings.

H. PERSONAL FUTURES PLANNING

Some theorists have linked challenging behavior both to inadequate control over one's life and to spending too much time in settings that are not valued (Smull & Harrison, 1992). When the individual does not have the personal control and autonomy necessary for his or her lifestyle, behavior problems may emerge as a form of protest. This theory is known as "personal futures planning" or "person centered planning."

> Behaviors that have resulted in a perceived need for treatment should be examined to determine if they are expressions on the part of the individual that the environment is not meeting his or her needs. Unlike the general population, persons with mental retardation cannot change their jobs, move to a new location, or change the people with whom they live. The people with whom they spend their time, where they spend it, and how they spend it are typically matters over which persons

with mental retardation have little or no choice. This lack of control over the basic aspects of life often results in passive compliance. Where the person objects to the decisions made, the only available resource is aggression, destruction, or self-injury (Smull, 1988, p. 397).

Instead of trying to make the needs of a person fit into existing services, personal assistance planners try to design a system of services for each individual. They begin by analyzing a person's lifestyle. They classify aspects of the person's lifestyle as non-negotiable, strong preferences, or highly desirable. This assessment requires looking past the individual's diagnostic labels and viewing matters with empathy from the perspective of the individual (Smull & Harrison, 1992). They find services that support all of the non-negotiable requirements and as many as possible of the strong preferences and highly desirable requirements. The outcome of a personal futures assessment is a plan that supports the individual's essential lifestyle.

Smull and Harrison (1992) recommend training an advocate or personal champion to help the person with challenging behavior choose his or her own lifestyle and plans:

A necessary requirement for people to achieve their desired lifestyle is the presence of one persistent and competent advocate (p. 32).

An aspect of personal assistance planning that has received inadequate attention is its philosophical similarities to Carl Rogers' (1951, 1961) client-centered theory. The following are some of the main points of personal assistance planning followed by the corresponding principles expressed in Rogers' works.

1. Personal assistance planners hold that the service system and community must value people with mental retardation or these people are likely to develop mental health disorders. Rogers held that the therapist must value the client for behavior improvements to occur.

2. Personal assistance planners hold that people with challenging behavior must live in environments they themselves value:

We need to discover what each individual values and what each individual finds to be a hassle (Smull & Harrison, 1992, p. 3).

Rogers held that personal growth is possible only when people value their own experiences. Rogers also believed that psychopathology can occur when people do not value their own experiences.

3. Personal futures planners believe that choice and personal control over one's life are essential for effective treatment of challenging behavior.

> In the current system of service, complete control over all essential choice is in the hands of the professionals. The outcome of this [personal futures] planning process is to re-balance the locus of control (Smull & Harrison, 1992, p. 3).

Similarly, Rogers held that therapy should be nondirective so that people can clarify their own values, make their own choices, and learn to solve their own problems.

4. Personal futures planners hold that advocates and personal champions should develop empathy and understanding of the person's values and what the person is trying to communicate. As Smull and Harrison (1992) put it,

> Plans that are implemented without empathy or insight may appear to offer a reasonable lifestyle but will not support the desired lifestyle (p. 29).

> We are trying to listen to what people want and to help them get it. The simplicity of this statement is deceptively simple and potentially harmful. Understanding others requires empathy and insight (p. 2).

Similarly, Rogers held that therapist empathy is a crucial factor in determining successful outcomes. Rogers also discussed the need for the therapist to understand the client from the client's self-perspective.

H1. EVALUATION OF PERSONAL FUTURES PLANNING. This author could find no research evaluating the effects of personal futures planning on people with challenging behavior. However, there is a substantial body of data evaluating Rogerian therapy. These studies are inconclusive. Some Rogerian researchers believe that the effectiveness of client-centered therapy has been demonstrated in many studies. However, other researchers have noted methodological shortcomings in almost all of the studies. Today, client-centered therapy is not used as often as it was in the past because it is a general approach in an era when therapies are targeted for specific disorders.

Carl Rogers suggested that client-centered therapy is ineffective with people with mental retardation (Rogers, 1942). If he were right in this opinion, personal assistance planning, which is based on many of Rogers' principles, also might be

ineffective for people with mental retardation. However, a number of therapists have challenged Rogers' opinion that client-centered therapy is inappropriate for people with mental retardation. As noted in Chapter 4, John McGee's "gentle teaching" and Gary Prouty's "pretherapy" represent applications of Rogers' therapy to people with mental retardation.

Personal assistance planning is among the very few efforts currently being made to achieve the community integration of persons with challenging behavior. The emphasis on valuing the individual is a needed perspective, especially when working with people with challenging behavior. The idea that some examples of challenging behavior may represent protests over inadequate control of one's life and a nonchosen lifestyle probably has merit for some people. The effort to individualize services is particularly relevant to meet the diverse needs of people with challenging behavior.

Future researchers will need to evaluate the extent to which improvements in lifestyles and personal control lead to fewer instances of challenging behavior and mental illness. In Sweden, where deinstitutionalization and community integration have been implemented to a considerable degree, there has been no noticeable decrease in challenging behavior and mental illness (Gostason, 1985; Kebbon, 1993). However, this may be because community-based services have not led to improved lifestyles. As Smull and Harrison (1992, p.42) have noted, in some instances people living in the community have become more isolated than they had been in institutions.

IV. PROFESSIONAL TRAINING

There is a severe shortage of psychiatrists trained to work with people with mental retardation (Cushna, Szymanski, & Tanguay, 1980). This is true despite numerous efforts to address the issue. For example, in 1965 Potter described mental retardation as the "Cinderella" of psychiatry. In 1966 the American Psychiatric Association (APA) issued a position paper emphasizing the need to train psychiatrists in mental retardation (Tanguay & Szymanski, 1980). The APA statement suggested that every psychiatric trainee should receive some training in mental retardation.

Leaverton and Van Der Heide (1975) surveyed child psychiatry clinics and found that 50 percent did not include any training in mental retardation. In a 1975 survey of 30 University-Affiliated Programs (UAPs), Szymanski found that only 18 had a full or parttime psychiatrist on their teaching staffs.

> Some centers reported that they had had a good psychiatric program, but it was terminated when the psychiatrist left and another one could not be found (Tanguay & Szymanski, 1980, p. 20).

The situation is little improved today. Tanguay and Szymanski (1980) identified the following three areas in which psychiatrists need training:

- Developmental disabilities, including diagnosis and etiology;

- Provision of mental health services to people with mental retardation;

- Experience in an interdisciplinary environment.

Two specific areas in which training is needed are psychiatric diagnosis and psychopharmacology. Currently, there is such a severe shortage of psychiatrists in some areas that psychiatric drugs are prescribed either by psychiatrists with little or no training in mental retardation or by generic physicians. Absent appropriate training, the doctors make errors in diagnosis and/or prescribe psychiatric drugs based on how these drugs work in people who do not have mental retardation. This leads to many problems in diagnosis, drug use, overmedication, and side effects.

In addition to psychiatrists, there is a need to train nurses in the recognition of symptomatology and the use of psychiatric medications. Nurses play a critical role in referring people for professional evaluations. They also play a critical role in monitoring for side effects. However, very few nurses have been adequately trained to perform these critical tasks.

The training of psychologists in mental retardation needs to be upgraded to meet the standards of the American Psychological Association for training clinical psychologists. Too many programs train behavior technicians who have some knowledge of behavior modification but little background in other clinical approaches. Too few Ph.D. programs in clinical psychology provide training in mental retardation.

Supervisor staff at residential programs and case managers also need to be trained to understand the full range of psychopathology seen in people with mental retardation. Staff need to be taught to recognize the major symptoms of psychopathology so that appropriate referrals can be made. Disorders associated with withdrawn behavior may not be recognized and referred for services as often as are disorders associated with conduct problems.

The need for training appears to be as great in the United Kingdom as it is in the United States. Day (1993b) has reported that only 200 U.K. psychiatrists were specializing in mental handicap. In the U.K., mental retardation has been recognized as a specialized area for nurses since 1919.

A. UAPs

The University-Affiliated Programs (UAPs) in mental retardation are well-

suited to provide much of the needed training. In the United States, the UAPs are the primary program for training future mental retardation professionals. Previously, these programs were called University-Affiliated Facilities (UAFs). There are two types of UAPs: those funded by the U. S. Administration for Developmental Disabilities (ADD) and those funded by the U. S. Maternal and Child Health (MCH). Some UAPs, such as the Nisonger Center at The Ohio State University, are jointly funded by both agencies. There is a UAP in almost every state, and there is a national organization called the American Association on University-Affiliated Programs (AAUAP).

The UAPs provide pre-professional training in an interdisciplinary environment. The most common disciplines represented at UAPs are pediatrics, psychology, special education, and nursing. Other disciplines include audiology, nutrition, occupational therapy, physical therapy, and social work. Psychiatry is not mandated and is included in only about one-third to one-half of the UAPs.

Every UAP provides an interdisciplinary training environment. The trainees learn to work with interdisciplinary teams. Historically, interdisciplinary early intervention and diagnostic clinics served as the primary training environment. Today, extensive training occurs in the community.

The UAPs are given a small core grant and are mandated to apply for grants and to obtain other funds to create activities in four areas. These areas are training, exemplary models, technical assistance, and dissemination of information and research. The UAPs must develop these activities in ways that promote the goals of the Developmental Disabilities Act.

The UAP program has worked very well. In most disciplines, the critical shortages of professionals that existed in the 1970s no longer exist today. However, the absence of psychiatry from the UAP network has been a major barrier to supplying the field with personnel trained to work with people with challenging behavior.

B. NADD

Training remains one of the central activities of the National Association for the Dually Diagnosed (NADD). Founded in 1984 and led by Robert Fletcher, the NADD has sponsored many training events pertaining to challenging behavior.

Fletcher (1988) identified six areas of staff training needs, all of which have been addressed in NADD workshops: (1) psychopathology; (2) assessment and diagnosis; (3) individual, group, and family therapy; (4) behavioral analysis; (5) techniques that deal with assaultive and aggressive behavior; and (6) psychosexual dysfunction and deviance.

The NADD annual conference has been one of the few forums professionals

and scientists have to discuss the mental health aspects of mental retardation. The conference attracts about 300 people including 50 to 75 speakers.

V. BRIEFLY NOTED

A. LEGAL ISSUES

People with challenging behavior have the same legal rights and privileges as all other persons with mental retardation (Stark, Menolascino, Albarelli, & Gray, 1988). These include the right to minimally adequate treatment in the least restrictive setting and the right to be free from harm. For these rights to be meaningful, an enforcement mechanism is necessary. Unfortunately, people with challenging behavior have had difficulties in the past finding legal representation and proper advocacy (Herr, 1988).

The U.S. Developmental Disabilities Act establishes a Protection and Advocacy (P&A) authority in each state. The P&A is the primary program of advocacy for persons with challenging behavior. However, Herr (1988) estimated that only a small proportion of the persons served by the P&A have both mental retardation and mental illness. Because other legal service providers, such as Legal Services and law school clinics, also provide few services to this population, Herr (1988) concluded that the population is underserved with respect to legal services.

Litigation on behalf of persons with challenging behavior has been mostly local in impact. The best known lawsuits concerned the inappropriate placement of persons with mental retardation in mental hospitals. *Knox v. Hughes* was one such case brought in Maryland, and *Nathan v. Levitt* was a case brought in Illinois. In the *Nathan v. Levitt* case, a consent decree was entered in October, 1985. The decree protects the rights of persons with both mental retardation and mental illness to both habilitation services and mental health services. Under the terms of the decree, people with severe mental retardation may be admitted to a psychiatric hospital only on an emergency basis. After 72 hours, the person must be discharged to a developmental center. In contrast, people with both a mental illness and mild or moderate mental retardation are served by mental hospitals.

The joint occurrence of mental retardation and mental illness raises a number of legal issues. Ellis (1988) has noted differences in legal criteria for commitment to mental hospitals versus developmental centers. Once admitted into either system, however, the criteria are less stringent for inter-agency transfer. Luckasson (1988) has discussed the issues faced in the criminal justice system, including issues of competence to stand trial. Everington and Luckasson (1992)

have developed an instrument, called *Competence Assessment to Stand Trial * Mental Retardation,* that should have applicability to people with both mental retardation and mental illness.

B. PREVENTION

Very little attention has been given to the possibility of preventing mental health disorders in persons with mental retardation. One reason for this is that prevention generally takes a backseat to treatment when it comes to funding priorities. Treatment is a more immediate issue than prevention. When a person is at risk to develop a mental health disorder, the risk is often invisible and effective prevention is difficult to prove.

Behavior analysts have given very little attention to the possibility of preventing some mental health disorders. The behavioral ideology holds that all measures of behavior must be based on overt behaviors. "If I can't see it and modify it, I don't want to know about it," argued a well-known behaviorist at a national seminar. Since behavioral measures consist almost entirely of measures of observable behavior, the concept of prevention is not suggested. By the time behaviorists measure a maladaptive behavior, it is too late to prevent it.

Various types of prevention are commonly identified. In primary prevention, the effort is to reduce the occurrence of mental health disorders. In secondary prevention, the effort is to prevent a mental health disorder from developing into a more serious condition. In tertiary prevention, the effort is to limit the consequences of a mental health disorder.

One prevention strategy concerns the negative social conditions that surround people with mental retardation. As noted in Chapter 1, the negative social conditions include stigmatization, segregation, social disruption, restricted opportunities, and infantilization. By reducing these negative social conditions, and by creating more positive social conditions, it should be possible to prevent some mental health disorders or at least to keep existing disorders from becoming worse.

Another prevention strategy would be to teach social skills to enhance interpersonal competence. Effective social and interpersonal skills would facilitate the individual's participation in social support groups and networks. This should be particularly relevant to preventing depression or at least preventing a depression from having severe consequences for the individual.

A number of theorists have suggested that improving a person's lifestyle can prevent mental health disorders (Hitzing, 1980; Smull & Harrison, 1992). These theorists have called for increasing the individual's choice and control in their lives. Community integration also has been suggested as a means of preventing mental health disorders (e.g., Smull & Harrison, 1992).

It may be possible to prevent some cases of maladaptive behavior through detailed knowledge of the individual or a diagnostic condition. For example, dependent individuals who quickly develop intense interpersonal relationships may be at risk for developing challenging behavior if the relationship is lost. Where circumstances permit, it may be possible to build a social relationship with a new staff member if it is known that a person is about to lose a close personal relationship with a present staff member.

Future researchers and policy makers need to pay more attention to the possibility of preventing some instances of challenging behavior. It some cases, it may be much easier to prevent challenging behavior than it would be to treat it after the fact.

REFERENCES

Abraham, K. (1911). Notes on the psychoanalytic investigation and treatment of manic-depressive insanity and allied conditions. *Selected papers on psychoanalysis*. New York: Basic Books.

Abramson, L. Y., Seligman, M. E. P., & Teasdale, J. D. (1978). Learned helplessness in humans: Critique and reformulation. *Journal of Abnormal Psychology*, **87**, 49-74.

Adkins, J., & Matson, J. L. (1980). Teaching institutional mentally retarded adults socially appropriate leisure skills. *Mental Retardation,* **189**, 249-252.

Albini, J. L., & Dinitz, S. (1965). Psychotherapy with disturbed and defective children: An evaluation of changes in behavior and attitudes. *American Journal of Mental Deficiency*, **69**, 560-567.

Allin, R. B. (1988). Intensive home based treatment interventions with mentally retarded/ emotionally disturbed individuals and their families. In J. A. Stark, F. J. Menolascino, M. H. Albarelli, & V. C. Gray (Eds.), *Mental retardation and mental health: Classification, diagnosis, treatment, services*. New York: Springer-Verlag.

Allin, R. B., & Allin, D. W. (1984). A home intervention program for mentally retarded emotionally disturbed individuals and their families. In F. J. Menolascino & J. A. Stark (Eds.), *Handbook of mental illness in the mentally retarded*. New York: Plenum Press.

Aman, M. G. (1991*a*). *Assessing psychopathology and behavior problems in persons with mental retardation: A review of available instruments*. Rockville, MD: U.S. Department of Health and Human Services.

Aman, M. G. (1991*b*). Review and evaluation of instruments for assessing emotional and behavioral disorders. *Australia & New Zealand Journal of Developmental Disabilities*, **17**, 127-145.

Aman, M. G. (1991*c*). Pharmacotherapy in the developmental disabilities: New developments. *Australia and New Zealand Journal of Developmental Disabilities*, **17**, 183-199.

Aman, M. G. (1994). Instruments for assessing treatment effects in developmentally disabled populations. *Assessment in Rehabilitation and Exceptionality*, **1**, 1-20.

Aman, M. G., Hammer, D., & Rojahn, J. (1993). Mental retardation. In T. H. Ollendick & M. Hersen (Eds.), *Handbook of child and adolescent assessment*. Boston: Allyn and Bacon. Pp. 321-345

Aman, M. G., & Singh, N. N. (1980). The usefulness of thioridazine for treating childhood disorders. Fact or folklore? *American Journal of Mental Deficiency*, **84**, 331-338.

Aman, M. G., & Singh, N. N. (1982). Methylphenidate in severely retarded residents and the clinical significance of stereotypic behavior. *Applied Research in Mental Retardation, 3*, 345-348.

Aman, M. G., & Singh, N. N. (1991). Pharmacological intervention. In J. L. Matson & J. A. Mulick (Eds.), *Handbook of mental retardation* (2nd ed.). New York: Pergamon Press. Pp. 347-372.

Aman, M. G., Singh, N. N., Stewart, A. W., & Field, C. J. (1985a). The Aberrant Behavior Checklist: A behavior rating scale for the assessment of treatment effects. *American Journal of Mental Deficiency, 89*, 485-491.

Aman, M. G., Singh, N. N., Stewart, A. W., & Field, C. J. (1985b). Psychometric characteristics of the Aberrant Behavior Checklist. *American Journal of Mental Deficiency, 89*, 492-502.

Aman, M. G., Watson, J. E., Singh, N. N., Turbott, S. H., & Wilsher, C. P. (1986). Psychometric and demographic properties of the Psychopathology Instrument for Mentally Retarded Adults. *Psychopharmacology Bulletin, 22*, 1972-1976.

American Psychiatric Association. (1952). *Diagnostic and statistical manual of mental disorders* (1st ed.). Washington, DC: Author.

American Psychiatric Association. (1968). *Diagnostic and statistical manual of mental disorders* (2nd ed.). Washington, DC: Author.

American Psychiatric Association. (1980). *Diagnostic and statistical manual of mental disorders* (3rd ed.). Washington, DC: Author.

American Psychiatric Association. (1987). *Diagnostic and statistical manual of mental disorders* (3rd ed., rev.). Washington, DC: Author.

American Psychiatric Association. (1993). *DSM-IV draft criteria.* Washington, DC: Author.

American Psychological Association. (1985). *Standards for educational and psychological testing.* Washington, DC: Author.

Angelino, R., & Shedd, C. L. (1965). A study of the reactions to "frustration" of a group of mentally retarded children as measured by the Rosenweig Picture-Frustration Study. *Psychological Newsletter, 8*, 49-54.

Arnold, L. E., & Aman, M. G. (1991). Beta blockers in mental retardation/ developmental disabilities. *Journal of Child and Adolescent Psychopharmacology, 1*, 361-373.

Axelrod, S. (1987). Functional and structural analyses of behavior: Approaches leading to reduced use of punishment procedures? *Research in Developmental Disabilities, 8*, 165-178.

Ayllon, T. (1963). Intensive treatment of psychotic behavior by stimulus satiation and food

reinforcement. *Behavior Research and Therapy,* **1**, 53-61.

Ayllon, T. (1965*a*). Some behavioral problems associated with eating in chronic schizophrenic patients. In L. P. Ullmann & L. Krasner (Eds.), *Case studies in behavior modification.* New York: Holt, Rinehart, and Winston, Inc. Pp. 73-77.

Ayllon, T. (1965*b*). Intensive treatment of psychotic behavior by stimulus satisfaction and food reinforcement. In L. P. Ullmann & L. Krasner (Eds.), *Case studies in behavior modification.* New York: Holt, Rinehart, and Winston, Inc. Pp. 77-84.

Baker, B. L., Blacher, J., & Pfeiffer, S. (1993). Family involvement in residential treatment of children with psychiatric disorder and mental retardation. *Hospital and Community Psychiatry,* **44**, 561-566.

Baker, B. L., Heifetz, L., & Murphy, D. M. (1980). Behavioral training for parents of mentally retarded children: One-year follow-up. *American Journal of Mental Deficiency,* **85**, 31-38.

Baker, B. L., Landen, S. J., & Kashima, K. J. (1991). Effects of parent training on families of children with mental retardation: Increased burden or generalized benefit. *American Journal on Mental Retardation,* **96**, 127-136.

Ballinger, B. R., & Reid, A. H. (1987). A standardised assessment of personality disorder in mental handicap. *British Journal of Psychiatry,* **150**, 108-109.

Balthazar, E. E., & Stevens, H. A. (1975). *The emotionally disturbed mentally retarded: A historical and contemporary perspective.* Englewood Cliffs, NJ: Prentice-Hall.

Banavidez, D. A., & Matson, J. L. (1993). Assessment of depression in mentally retarded adolescents. *Research in Developmental Disabilities,* **14**, 179-188.

Bandura, A. (1969). *Principles of behavior modification.* New York: Holt.

Bandura, A., & Walters, R. H. (1963). *Social learning and personality development.* New York: Holt.

Barmann, B. C., & Murray, W. J. (1981). Suppression of inappropriate sexual behavior by facial screening. *Behavior Therapy,* **12**, 730-735.

Barrett, R. P., & Walters, A. S. (1992). Comment. Treating suicidal behavior in the mentally retarded: The case of Kim. *Suicide and Life-Threatening Behavior,* **22**, 506-510.

Barrett, R. P., Walters, A. S., Mercurio, A. F., Klitzke, M., & Feinstein, C. (1992). Mental retardation and psychiatric disorders. In V. B. Van Hasselt & D. J. Kolko (Eds.), *Inpatient behavior therapy for children and adolescents.* New York: Plenum Press. Pp. 113-149.

Bassett, A. S., & Beiser, M. (1991). DSM-III: Use of the multiaxial diagnostic system in clinical practice. *Canadian Journal of Psychiatry,* **36**, 270-274.

Batchelor, I. R. C. (1964). The diagnosis of schizophrenia. *Proceedings of the Royal Society of Medicine, 57*, 417-419.

Bates, W. J., Smeltzer, D. J., & Arnoczky, S. M. (1986). Appropriate and inappropriate use of psychotherapeutic medications for institutionalized mentally retarded persons. *American Journal of Mental Deficiency, 90*, 363-370.

Beck, A. T. (1963). Thinking and depression: I. Idiosyncratic content and cognitive distortions. *Archives of General Psychiatry, 9*, 324-335.

Beckwith, B. E., Parker, L., Pawlarczyk, D., Couk, D., Schumacher, K., & Yearwood, K. (1985). The Dexamethasone Suppression Test in depressed retarded adults: Preliminary findings. *Biological Psychiatry, 20*, 825-831.

Begab, M. (1966). The mentally retarded and his family. In I. Philips (Ed.), *Prevention and treatment of mental retardation.* New York: Basic Books.

Beier, D. C. (1964). Behavioral disturbances in the mentally retarded. In H. Stevens & R. Huber (Eds.), *Mental retardation.* Chicago: University of Chicago Press.

Bell, R. C, & Jackson, H. J. (1992). The structure of personality disorders in DSM-III. *Acta Psychiatrica Scandinavica, 85*, 279-287.

Bem, D. J. (1967). Self-perception: An alternative interpretation of cognitive dissonance phenomena. *Psychological Review, 74*, 536-557.

Bem, D. J. (1972). Self-perception theory. In L. Berkowitz (Ed.), *Advances in experimental social psychology* (Vol. 6). New York: Academic Press.

Benavidez, D. A., & Matson, J. L. (1993). Assessment of depression in mentally retarded adolescents. *Research in Developmental Disabilities, 14*, 179-188.

Benson, B. A. (1985). Behavior disorders and mental retardation: Associations with age, sex, and level of functioning in an outpatient clinic sample. *Applied Research in Mental Retardation, 6*, 79-85.

Benson, B. A. (1986). Anger management training. *Psychiatric Aspects of Mental Retardation Reviews, 5*, 51-55.

Benson, B. A. (1990). Anger management training. In A. Dosen, A. Van Gennep, & G. Zwanikken (Eds.), *Proceedings of the International Congress on Treatment of Mental Illness and Behavioral Disorders in the Mentally Retarded.* Leiden, The Netherlands: PAOS.

Benson, B. A. (1992). *Teaching anger management to persons with mental retardation.* Worthington, OH: IDS Publishing Corporation.

Benson, B. A. (1994, personal communication). Conversation on substance abuse and mental

retardation.

Benson, B. A., & Hunter, R. H. (1993). *Summary recommendations of the Metro-Area Dual Diagnosis Task Group*. Unpublished report to the Illinois Department of Mental Health and Developmental Disabilities.

Benson, B. A., & Ivins, J. (1992). Anger, depression and self-concept in adults with mental retardation. *Journal of Intellectual Disability Research, 36*, 169-175.

Benson, B. A., & Laman, D. S. (1988). Suicidal tendencies of mentally retarded adults in community settings. *Australia and New Zealand Journal of Developmental Disabilities, 14*, 49-54.

Benson, B. A., & McKinney, B. E. (1989). *Residential services indicator manual*. Worthington, OH: IDS Publishing Corporation.

Benson, B. A., Reiss, S., Smith, D., & Laman, D. (1985). Psychosocial correlates of depression in mentally retarded adults: II. Poor social skills. *American Journal of Mental Deficiency, 89*, 657-659.

Benson, B. A., Rice, C. J., & Miranti, S. V. (1986). Effects of anger management training with mentally retarded adults in group treatment. *Journal of Consulting and Clinical Psychology, 54*, 728-729.

Bergin, A. E. (1971). The evaluation of therapeutic outcomes. In S. L. Garfield & A. E. Bergin (Eds.), *Handbook of psychotherapy and behavior change*. New York: Wiley.

Berkson, G., & Romer, D. (1980). Social ecology of supervised communal facilities for mentally disabled adults: I. Introduction. *American Journal of Mental Deficiency, 85*, 219-228.

Berney, T. P., & Jones, P. M. (1988). Manic depressive disorder in mental handicap. *Australia and New Zealand Journal of Developmental Disabilities, 14*, 219-225.

Bernstein, N. (1985). Psychotherapy and the retarded adolescent. *Adolescent Psychiatry, 12*, 406-413.

Beveridge, M., Spencer, J., & Mittler, P. (1979). Self-blame and communication failure in retarded adolescents. *Journal of Child Psychology and Psychiatry, 21*, 175-181.

Bialer, I. (1970). Emotional disturbance and mental retardation: Etiologic and conceptual relationships. In F. J. Menolascino (Ed.), *Psychiatric approaches to mental retardation*. New York: Basic Books.

Bicknell, J. (1983). The psychopathology of handicap. *British Journal of Medical Psychology, 56*, 167-178.

Bihm, E. M., Kienlen, T. L., Ness, M. E., & Poindexter, A. (1991). Factor structure of the

Motivation Assessment Scale for persons with mental retardation. *Psychological Reports*, **68**, 1235-1238.

Bihm, E. M., & Poindexter, A. R. (1991). Cross-validation of the factor structure of the Aberrant Behavior Checklist for persons with mental retardation. *American Journal on Mental Retardation*, **96**, 209-211.

Bihm, E. M., Poindexter, A. R., Kienlen, T., & Smith, B. L. (1992). Staff perceptions of reinforcer responsiveness and aberrant behaviors in people with mental retardation. *Journal of Autism and Developmental Disorders*, **22**, 83-93.

Bijou, S. W., & Baer, D. M. (1961). *Child development I: A systematic and empirical theory*. New York: Appleton-Century-Crofts, Inc.

Bishop, A. C. (1992). Empirical approach to psychopharmacology for institutionalized individuals with severe or profound mental retardation. *Mental Retardation*, **30**, 283-288.

Blunden, R., & Allen, D. (1987). *Facing the challenge: An ordinary life for people with learning difficulties and challenging behavior*. Kings Fund Project Paper No. 74. London: Kings Fund Centre.

Boggs, E. M. (1988). The role of legislation. In J. A. Stark, F. J. Menolascino, M. H. Albarelli, & V. C. Gray (Eds.), *Mental retardation and mental health. Classification, diagnosis, treatment, services*. New York: Springer-Verlag, pp. 317-325.

Bootzin, R., & Acocella, J. R. (1988). *Abnormal psychology: Current perspectives*. (5th ed.). New York: Random House.

Bootzin, R., Acocella, J. R., & Alloy, L. B. (1993). *Abnormal psychology*. New York: McGraw-Hill.

Borkovec, T. D., & Nau, S. D. (1972). Credibility of analogue therapy rationale. *Journal of Behavior and Experimental Psychiatry*, **3**, 257-260.

Borthwick-Duffy, S. A. (1994). Epidemiology and prevalence of psychopathology in persons with mental retardation. *Journal of Consulting and Clinical Psychology*, **62**, 17-27.

Borthwick-Duffy, S. A. (in press). Prevalence of destructive behaviors: A study of aggression, self-injury, and property destruction. In D. Gray & T. Thompson (Eds.), *Destructive behavior: Epidemiology, measurement, and information management* (Vol. 1). Newbury Park, CA: Sage Publishing.

Borthwick-Duffy, S. A., & Eyman, R. K. (1990). Who are the dually diagnosed? *American Journal on Mental Retardation*, **94**, 586-595.

Bouras, N. (1993) . Policies, practices and perspectives of mental health care for people with learning disabilities in the U.K. *Journal of Intellectual Disability Research*, **37**, 57-60.

Bouras, N., Brooks, D., & Drummond, K. (1993). Community psychiatric services for people

with mental retardation. In N. Bouras (Ed.), *Mental health in mental retardation.* New York: Cambridge University Press.

Bouras, N., & Drummond, C. (1992). Behavior and psychiatric disorders of people with mental handicaps living in the community. *Journal of Intellectual Disability Research, 36,* 349-357.

Bouras, N., Kon, Y., & Drummond, C. (1993). Medical and psychiatric needs of adults with a mental handicap. *Journal of Intellectual Disability, 37,* 177-182.

Bouras, N., Holt, G., & Gravestock, S. (1994). *Psychiatric services for adults with learning disabilities: Current issues and practices.* Unpublished manuscript, University of London.

Boyd, R. D. (1992). Recurrence of neuroleptic malignant syndrome via an inadvertent rechallenge in a woman with mental retardation. *Mental Retardation, 30,* 77-79.

Boyd, R. D. (1993). Neuroleptic malignant syndrome and mental retardation: Review and analysis of 29 cases. *American Journal on Mental Retardation, 98,* 143-155.

Braddock, D. (1987). *Federal policy toward mental retardation and developmental disabilities.* Baltimore, MD: Paul H. Brookes Publishing Co.

Brizer, D. A. (1988). Psychopharmacology and the management of violent patients. *Psychiatric Clinics of North America, 9,* 745-754.

Brown, M. G. (1992). Conversion disorder in persons with developmental disabilities. *The Habilitative Mental Healthcare Newsletter, 11,* 23-27.

Bruininks, R. H., Hill, B. K., & Morreau, L. E. (1988). Prevalence and implications of maladaptive behaviors and dual diagnosis in residential and other service programs. In J. A. Stark, F. J. Menolascino, M. H. Albarelli, & V. C. Gray (Eds.), *Mental retardation and mental health. Classification, diagnosis, treatment, services.* New York: Springer-Verlag. Pp. 3-29.

Bruininks, R. H., Hill, B. K., Weatherman, R. F., & Woodcock, R. W. (1986). *Technical summary for the Inventory for Client and Agency Planning.* Allen, TX: DLM Teaching Resources.

Bruininks, R. H., Olson, K. M., Larson S. A., & Lakin, K. C. (in press). Challenging behaviors among persons with mental retardation in residential settings: Implications for policy, research, and practice. In D. Gray & T. Thompson, (Eds.), *Destructive behavior: Epidemiology, measurement, and information on management.* Newbury Park, CA: Sage.

Bullard, W. N. (1915). Mental disturbances in the feeble-minded. *The Journal of Nervous and Mental Diseases, 42,* 818-823.

Burgio, L. D., Willis, K., & Burgio, K. L. (1986). Operantly based treatment procedure for stair avoidance by a severely mentally retarded adult. *American Journal of Mental Deficiency, 91,* 308-311.

Burkart, J. E., Fox, R. A., & Rotatori, A. F. (1985). Obesity of mentally retarded individuals: Prevalence, characteristics, and intervention. *American Journal of Mental Deficiency,* **90**, 303-312.

Calamari, J. E., McNally, R. J., Benson, D. S., & Babington, C. M. (1990). Case study: Use of propranolol to reduce aggressive behavior in a woman who is mentally retarded. *Behavioral Residential Treatment,* **5**, 287-296.

Carr, E. G. (1977). The motivation of self-injurious behavior: A review of some hypotheses. *Psychological Bulletin,* **84**, 800-816.

Carr, E. G., & Durand, V. M. (1985a). The social-communicative basis of severe behavior problems in children. In S. Reiss & R. R. Bootzin (Eds.), *Theoretical issues in behavior therapy.* New York: Academic Press.

Carr, E. G., & Durand, V. M. (1985b). Reducing behavior problems through functional communication training. *Journal of Applied Behavior Analysis,* **18**, 111-126.

Carsrud, A. L., Carsrud, K. I., & Standifer, J. (1980). Social variables affecting geriatric mentally retarded individuals: An explorative study. *Mental Retardation,* **18**, 80-90.

Cautela, J. R. (1966). Treatment of compulsive behavior by covert sensitization. *Psychological Record,* **16**, 33-41.

Charlot, L. R., Doucette, A., & Mezzacappa, E. (1993). Affective symptoms of institutionalized adults with mental retardation. *American Journal on Mental Retardation,* **98**, 408-416.

Chess, S. (1962). Psychiatric treatment of the mentally retarded child with behavior problems. *American Journal of Orthopsychiatry,* **32**, 863-869.

Chess, S. (1970). Emotional problems in mentally retarded children. In F. J. Menoloascino (Ed.), *Psychiatric approaches to mental retardation.* New York: Basic Books. Pp. 55-67.

Chess, S., & Hassibi, M. (1970). Behavior deviation in mentally retarded children. *Journal of the American Academy of Child Psychiatry,* **9**, 282-297.

Chidester, L., & Menninger, K. (1936). The application of psychoanalytic methods to the study of mental retardation. *American Journal of Orthopsychiatry,* **6**, 616-624.

Chiodo, J., & Maddux, J. E. (1985). A cognitive and behavioral approach to anxiety management of retarded individuals: Two case studies. *Journal of Child and Adolescent Psychotherapy,* **2**, 16-29.

Chitty, D., Boo, S., & Jamieson, J. (1993). Prevalence of dual diagnosis in an institution for individuals who are developmentally handicapped. *Behavioral Residential Treatment,* **8**, 55-66.

Clark, D. B., Baker, B. L, & Heifetz, L. J. (1982). Behavioral training for parents of mentally

retarded children: Production of outcome. *American Journal of Mental Deficiency,* **87**, 14-19.

Clarke, C. M., & Davis, R. (1963). The families of mentally retarded children. *Developmental Medicine Child Neurology,* **5**, 270-286.

Clarke, D. J. (in press *a*). Prader-Willi syndrome and psychoses: Three case reports. *British Journal of Psychiatry.*

Clarke, D. J. (in press *b*). Treatment of schizophrenia. In A. Dosen & K. Day (Eds.), *The treatment of mental illness and behavioral disorders in mentally retarded children and adults.*

Clarke, D. J., Kelley, S., Thinn, K., & Corbett, J. A. (1990). Psychotropic drugs and mental retardation: 1. Disabilities and the prescription of drugs for behavior and for epilepsy in three residential settings. *Journal of Mental Deficiency Research,* **34**, 385 395.

Clarke, D. J., & MacLeod, M. (in press). Recurrent brief depression and mild learning disability: Successful community management. *Mental Handicap.*

Cohen, I. L., Sudhalter, V., Landon-Jimenez, D., & Keogh, M. (in press). A neutral network approach to the classification of autism. *Journal of Autism and Developmental Disorders.*

Cohen, I. L., Sudhalter, V., Pfadt, A., Jenkins, E. C., Brown, W. T., & Vietze, P. M. (1991). Why are autism and the fragile X syndrome associated? Conceptual and methodological issues. *American Journal of Medical Genetics,* **48**, 195-202.

Cohen, I. L., Vietze, P. M., Sudhalter, V., Jenkins, E. C., & Brown W. T. (1991). Effects of age and communication level on eye contact in fragile X males and non fragile X autistic males. *American Journal of Medical Genetics,* **38**, 498-502.

Collacott, R. A., Cooper, S. A., & McGrother, C. (1992). Differential rates of psychiatric disorders in adults with Down's syndrome compared with other mentally handicapped adults. *British Journal of Psychiatry,* **161**, 671-674.

Conley, R. W., Luckasson, R., & Bouthilet, G. N. (1992). *The criminal justice system and mental retardation.* Baltimore: Paul H. Brookes Publishing Co.

Conners, C. (1969). A teacher ratings scale for use in drug studies with children. *American Journal of Psychology,* **126**, 884-888.

Cooper, S. A., & Collacott, R. A. (1991). Manic episodes in Down's syndrome: Two case reports. *Journal of Nervous and Mental Disease,* **179**, 635-636.

Cooper, S. A., Mohamed, W. N, & Collacott, R. A. (1993). Possible Asperger's syndrome in a mentally handicapped transvestite offender. *Journal of Intellectual Disability Research,* **37**, 189-194.

Corbett, J. A. (1979). Psychiatric morbidity and mental retardation. In F. E. James & R. P. Snaith

(Eds.), *Psychiatric illness and mental handicap*. London: Gaskell Press, Pp. 11-25.

Cottrell, D. J., & Crisp, A. H. (1984). Anorexia nervosa in Down's syndrome. *British Journal of Psychiatry*, **145**, 195-196.

Coyle, J. T. (1988). Psychiatry, neuroscience, and the double disabilities. In J. A. Stark, F. J. Menolascino, M. H. Albarelli, & V. C. Gray (Eds.), *Mental retardation and mental health: Classification, diagnosis, treatment, services*. New York: Springer Verlag.

Coyne, J. C. (1976). Depression and the response of others. *Journal of Abnormal Psychology*, **85**, 186-193.

Craft, M. (1959). Mental disorder in the defective: A psychiatric survey of in-patients. *American Journal of Mental Deficiency*, **63**, 329-834.

Craft, M., Ismail, I. A., Krishnamurti, D., Mathews, J., Regan, A., Seth, R. V., & North, P. M. (1987). Lithium in the treatment of aggression in mentally handicapped patients. *British Journal of Psychiatry*, **150**, 685-689.

Cromwell, R. L. (1963). A social learning approach to mental retardation. In N. R. Ellis (Ed.), *Handbook of mental deficiency*. New York: McGraw-Hill. Pp. 41-91.

Cullinan, D., Epstein, M., & Olinger, E. (1983). School behavior problems of mentally retarded and normal females. *The Mental Retardation and Learning Disability Bulletin*, **11**, 104-109.

Cunningham, P. J., & Mueller, C. D. (1991). Individuals with mental retardation in residential facilities: Findings from the 1987 national medical expenditure survey. *American Journal on Mental Retardation*, **96**, 109-117.

Cushna, B., Szymanski, L. S., & Tanguay, P. E. (1980). Professional roles and unmet manpower needs. In L. S. Szymanski & P. E. Tanguay (Eds.), *Emotional disorders of mentally retarded persons*. Baltimore, MD: University Park Press.

Cutts, R. A. (1957). Differentiation between pseudo-mental defectives with emotional disorders and mental defectives with emotional disturbances. *American Journal of Mental Deficiency*, **61**, 761-772.

Dalton, A. J., & Wisniewski, H. M. (1990). Down's syndrome and the dementia of Alzheimer's disease. *International Reviews of Psychiatry*, **2**, 43-52.

Dana, S. (1993). Personality disorder in persons with mental retardation: Assessment and diagnosis. In R. Fletcher & A. Dosen (Eds.), *Mental health aspects of mental retardation*. New York: Lexington Books. Pp. 130-140.

Das, J. P. (1986). *Attention Checklist*. Unpublished psychometric instrument, University of Alberta, Edmonton, Developmental Disabilities Centre.

Das, J. P., & Bower, A. C. (1973). Autonomic responses of retarded adolescents during anticipation and feedback in probability learning. *Journal of Mental Deficiency Research*, 17, 171-175.

Das, J. P., & Melnyk, L. (1989). Attention Checklist: A rating scale for mentally handicapped adolescents. *Psychological Reports*, 64, 1267-1274.

Davidson, M. (1988). *Psychometric characteristics of the checklist of functional problems with mentally retarded adults.* Unpublished doctoral dissertation, Department of Psychology, University of Illinois at Chicago.

Davidson, P. W., Cain, N. N., Sloane-Reeves, J. E., Giesow, V. E., Quijano, L.. E., Van Heyningen, J., & Shoham, I. (1993). *Crisis intervention for community-based persons with developmental disabilities and concomitant behavioral and psychiatric disorders.* Unpublished manuscript, University of Rochester.

Davidson, P. W., Cain, N. N., Sloane-Reeves, J. E., Kramer, B., Quijano, L .E., Van Heyningen, J., & Giesow, V. E. (1992). *Aging effects on severe behavior disorders in community-based clients with mental retardation.* Paper presented at the annual meeting of the Gerontological Society of America, Washington, DC.

Davidson, P. W., Cain, N. N., Sloane-Reeves, J. E., Van Speybroech, A., Segel, J., Gutkin, J., Quijano, L. E., Kramer, B., Porter, B., Shoham, I., & Goldstein, E. (1993). Characteristics of community-based clients with mental retardation and aggressive behavioral disorders. [update: to appear in *American Journal on Mental Retardation.*]

Day, K. (1983). A hospital based psychiatric unit for mentally handicapped adults. *Mental Handicap*, 11, 137-140.

Day, K. (1985). Psychiatric disorders in the middle-aged and elderly mentally handicapped. *British Journal of Psychiatry*, 147, 660-667.

Day, K. (1993a). Crime and mental retardation: A review. In C. R. Hollin & K. Howells (Eds.), *Clinical approaches to the mentally disordered offender.* New York: John Wiley & Sons Ltd. Pp. 111-144.

Day, K. (1993b). Mental health services for people with mental retardation: A framework for the future. *Journal of Intellectual Disability Research*, 37, 7-16.

Day, K. (1994). Psychiatric services in mental retardation: Generic or specialized provision. In N. Bouras (Ed.), *Mental health in mental retardation.* New York: Cambridge University Press.

Day, K., & Jancar, J. (in press). Mental and physical health and aging in mental handicap - A review. *Journal of Intellectual Disability Research.*

de la Cruz, F. (1985). Fragile X syndrome. *American Journal of Mental Deficiency*, 90, 119-123.

Deutsch, H. (1985). Grief counseling with the mentally retarded client. *Psychiatric Aspects of*

Mental Retardation Reviews, **4**, 17-20.

Dewan, J. G. (1948). Intelligence and emotional stability. *American Journal of Psychiatry,* **104**, 548-554.

Dibble, E., & Gray, D. B. (Eds.) (1990). *Assessment of behavior problems in persons with mental retardation living in the community.* Rockville, MD: National Institute of Mental Health.

DiNardo, P. A., Moras, K., Barlow, D. H., Rapee, R. M., & Brown, T. A. (1993). Reliability of DSM-III-R anxiety disorder categories using the Anxiety Disorder Interview Schedule — Revised (ADIS-R). *Archives of General Psychiatry,* **50**, 251-256.

Doherty, M., & Szymanski, L. S. (1981). Mental disorders in severely and profoundly retarded. *American Psychiatric Association Annual Meeting 1981 Syllabus and Scientific Proceedings.* Washington, DC: American Psychiatric Association.

Dokecki, P. R., & Heflinger, C. A. (1988). Families and developmental needs. In F. J. Menolascino, & J. A. Stark (Eds.), *Handbook of mental illness in the mentally retarded.* New York: Plenum Press.

Dollard, J., Doob, L. W., Miller, N. E., Mowrer, O. H., & Sears, R. R. (1939). *Frustration and aggression.* New Haven, CT: Yale University Press.

Dollard, J., & Miller, N. E. (1950). *Personality and psychotherapy.* New York: McGraw-Hill.

Dosen, A. (1989*a*). The developmental - dynamic approach applied to psychiatric diagnosis and treatment of mentally ill mentally retarded children. *Italian Journal of Intellectual Impairment,* **2**, 111-122.

Dosen, A. (1989*b*). Diagnosis and treatment of mental illness in mentally retarded children: A developmental model. *Child Psychiatry and Human Development,* **20**, 73 84.

Dosen, A. (1990*a*). Psychotherapeutic approaches in the treatment of depression in mentally retarded children. In A. Dosen & F. J. Menolascino (Eds.), *Depression in mentally retarded children and adults.* Leiden, the Netherlands: Logon Publications. Pp. 255-264.

Dosen, A. (1990*b*). Depression in mentally retarded children and adults. In A. Dosen & F. J. Menolascino (Eds.), *Depression in mentally retarded children and adults.* Leiden, the Netherlands: Logon Publications.

Dosen, A. (1990*c*). Developmental psychosis: A developmental-dynamic view of the theories, diagnostics and treatment. *Italian Journal of Intellectual Impairment,* **3**, 1-9.

Dosen, A. (1990*d*). Developmental-dynamic relationship therapy. In A. Dosen, A. Van Gennep, & G. J. Zwanikken (Eds.), *Treatment of mental illness and behavioral disorders in the mentally retarded.* Leiden, The Netherlands: Logon Publications. pp. 37-41.

Dosen, A. (1992). Psychotic conditions in mentally retarded children and adolescents. In G.

Nissen (Ed.), *Endogene psychosyndrome und ihre therapie im kindes — Und jugend alter.* Verlag Hans Huber, Bern.

Dosen, A. (1993a). Mental health and mental illness in persons with retardation: What we are talking about? In R. Fletcher & A. Dosen (Eds.), *Mental health aspects of mental retardation - Progress in assessment and treatment* (pp. 3-17). New York: Lexington Books.

Dosen, A. (1993b). Self injury behavior in the mentally retarded — A developmental psychiatric approach. In R. Fletcher & A. Dosen (Eds.), *Mental health aspects of mental retardation — Progress in assessment and treatment.* New York: Lexington Books.

Dosen, A. (1993c). *A Developmental-Psychiatric Approach in the Diagnosis of Psychiatric Disorders of Persons with Mental Retardation.* Frank J. Menolascino, M.D. Memorial Lecture at the International Congress on the Dually Diagnosed, Boston.

Dosen, A. (1993d). Diagnosis and treatment of psychiatric and behavioral disorders in mentally retarded individuals. The state of the art. *Journal of Intellectual Disability Research, 37,* 1-7.

Dosen, A., & Bojanin, S. (1990). Developmental and biological factors in the mentally retarded and vulnerability to depression. In A. Dosen & F. J. Menolascino (Eds.) *Depression in mentally retarded children and adults.* Leiden, the Netherlands: Logon Publications. Pp. 63-79.

Dosen, A., & Gielen, J. (1993). Depression in the mentally retarded — Assessment and diagnosis. In R. Fletcher & A. Dosen (Eds.), *Mental health aspects of mental retardation — Progress in assessment and treatment.* New York: Lexington Books.

Dosen, A., & Menolascino, F. J. (Eds.). (1990). *Depression in mentally retarded children and adults.* Leiden, the Netherlands: Logon Publications.

Dosen, A., & Petry, D. (1993). Treatment of depression in the mentally retarded. In R. Fletcher & A. Dosen (Eds.), *Mental health aspects of mental retardation - Progress in assessment and treatment.* New York: Lexington Books.

Douglas, V. I., & Peters, K. G. (1979). Toward a clearer definition of the attentional deficits of hyperactive children. In G. A. Hale & M. Lewis (Eds.), *Attention and cognitive development.* New York: Plenum Press.

Duckworth, M. S., Radhakrishnan, G., Nolan, M. E., & Fraser, W. I. (1993). Initial encounters between people with a mild mental handicap and psychiatrists: An investigation of a method of evaluating interview skills. *Journal of Intellectual Disability Research, 37,* 263-276.

Duff, R., La Rocca, J. l, Lizzet, A., Martin, P., Pearce, L., Williams, M., & Peck, C. (1981). A comparison of the fears of mildly retarded adults with children of their mental age and chronological age matched controls. *Journal of Behavior Therapy and Experimental Psychiatry, 12,* 121-124.

Duncan, A. G., Penrose, L. S., & Turnbull, R. C. (1936). A survey of patients in a large mental hospital. *Journal of Neurology and Psychopathology, 16,* 225-238.

Dupont, A. (1980). A study concerning the time-related and other burdens when severely handicapped children are reared at home. *Acta Psychiatrica Scandinavica, 62,* 249-257.

Durand, V. M., & Crimmins, D. B. (1988). Identifying the variables maintaining self injurious behavior. *Journal of the Association for the Severely Handicapped, 6,* 17-22.

Durkheim, E. (1897). *Suicide* (Translated by J. A. Spaulding & G. Simpson). New York: Free Press, 1951.

Dweck, C. S. (1991). Self-theories and goals: Their role in motivation, personality, and development. In R. A. Dienstbier (Ed.), *Nebraska symposium on motivation, 1990.* Lincoln: University of Nebraska Press.

Dweck, C. S., & Leggett, E. L. (1988). A social-cognitive approach to motivation and personality. *Psychological Review, 95,* 256-273.

Dyggve, H., & Kodahl, T. (1979). Disease patterns among 942 mentally retarded persons in a Danish county. *Acta Psychiatrica Scandinavica, 59,* 381-394.

D'Zurilla, T. J., & Goldfried, M. R. (1971). Problem solving and behavior modification. *Journal of Abnormal Psychology, 78,* 107-126.

D'Zurilla, T. J., & Nezu, A. (1982). Social problem solving in adults. In P. C. Kendall (Ed.), *Advances in cognitive-behavioral research and theory* (Vol. 1). San Diego: Academic Press. pp. 202-274.

Eaton, L. F., & Menolascino, F. J. (1982). Psychiatric disorders in the mentally retarded: Types, problems, and challenges. *American Journal of Psychiatry, 139,* 1297-1303.

Edgerton, R. B. (1967). *The cloak of competence: Stigma in the lives of the mentally retarded.* Berkeley: University of California Press.

Edgerton, R. B. (1986). Alcohol and drug use by mentally retarded adults. *American Journal of Mental Deficiency, 90,* 602-609.

Einfeld, S. L. (1984). Clinical assessment of 4500 developmentally delayed individuals. *Journal of Mental Deficiency Research, 28,* 129-142.

Einfeld, S., Molony, H., & Hall, W. (1989). Autism is not associated with fragile X syndrome. *American Journal of Medical Genetics, 30,* 655-663.

Einfeld, S., & Tonge, B. (1991). Psychometric and clinical assessment of psychopathology in developmentally disabled children. *Australia & New Zealand Journal of Developmental*

Disabilities, 17, 147-154.

Einfeld, S., & Wurth, P. (1989). Manic depressive disorder in mental handicaps. *Australia & New Zealand Journal of Developmental Disabilities, 15*, 155-156.

Ellis, A. (1962). *Reason and emotion in psychotherapy.* Secaucus, NJ: Lyle Stuart.

Ellis, J. W. (1988). Residential placement of "dual diagnosis" clients: Emerging legal issues. In J. A. Stark, F. J. Menolascino, M. H. Albarelli, & V. C. Gray (Eds.), *Mental retardation and mental health, Classification, diagnosis, treatment, services* (pp. 326-337). New York: Springer-Verlag.

Ellis, J. W., & Luckasson, R. A. (1985). Mentally retarded criminal defendants. *The George Washington Law Review, 53*, 414-493.

Ellis, N. R. (1963). The stimulus trace and behavioral inadequacy. In N. R. Ellis (Ed.), *Handbook of mental deficiency: Psychological theory and research.* New York: McGraw-Hill. Pp. 134-158.

Emerson, P. (1977). Covert grief reactions in mentally retarded clients. *Mental Retardation, 15*, 46-47.

Epstein, M. H., Cullinan, D., & Polloway, E. A. (1986). Patterns of maladjustment among mentally retarded children and youth. *American Journal of Mental Deficiency, 91*, 127-134.

Eron, L. D., Huesmann, L. R., Dubow, E., Romanoff, R., and Yarmel, P. W. (1987). Aggression and its correlates over 22 years. In D. H. Crowell, I. M. Evan, & C. R. O'Donnell (Eds.), *Childhood aggression and violence.* New York: Plenum. Pp. 249-262.

Everington, C. T., & Luckasson, R. (1992). *Competence assessment for standing trial for defendants with mental retardation.* Worthington, OH: IDS Publishing Corporation.

Eyman, R. K., & Borthwick, S. A. (1980). Patterns of care for mentally retarded persons. *Mental Retardation, 18*, 63-66.

Eyman, R. K., Borthwick, S. A., & Miller, C. (1981). Trends in maladaptive behavior of mentally retarded persons placed in community and institutional settings. *American Journal of Mental Retardation, 85*, 473-477.

Eyman, R. K., & Call, T. (1977). Maladaptive behavior and community placement of mentally retarded persons. *American Journal of Mental Deficiency, 82*, 137-144.

Eyman, R. K., O'Connor, G., Tarjan, G., & Justice, R. S. (1972). Factors determining residential placement of mentally retarded children. *American Journal of Mental Deficiency, 76*, 692-698.

Eysenck, H. J. (1943). Neurosis and intelligence. *The Lancet,* 362-363.

Eysenck, H. J. (1952). The effects of psychotherapy: An evaluation. *Journal of Consulting Psychology, 16*, 319-324.

Eysenck, H. J. (1961). The effects of psychotherapy. In H. J. Eysenck (Ed.), *Handbook of abnormal psychology: An experimental approach.* New York: Basic Books.

Eysenck, H. J. (1979). The conditioning model of neurosis. *The Behavioral and Brain Sciences, 2,* 155-199.

Farber, J. M. (1987). Psychopharmacology of self-injurious behavior in the mentally retarded. *Journal of American Academy of Child and Adolescent Psychiatry, 26,* 296- 300.

Feinstein, C., Kaminer, Y., Barrett, R. P., & Tylenda, B. (1988). The assessment of mood and affect in developmentally disabled children and adolescents: The Emotional Disorders Rating Scale. *Research in Developmental Disabilities, 9,* 109-122.

Fenichel, O. (1945). *The psychoanalytic theory of the neurosis.* New York: Norton.

Ferrell, D., & Madison, C. (1986). *Mental health and the developmentally disabled in California. The final report on the Mental Health Pilot Project of Far Northern Regional Center.* Unpublished report. Redding, CA.

Ferster, C. B., & Demyer, M. K. (1965). A method for the experimental analysis of autistic children. In L. P. Ullman & L. Krasner (Eds.), *Case studies in behavior modification* (pp. 121-129). New York: Holt, Rinehart, and Winston, Inc.

Fine, R. (1965). Psychotherapy with the mentally retarded adolescent. *Current Psychiatric Therapy, 5,* 58-66.

Fletcher, R. (1988). A county systems model: Comprehensive services for the dually diagnosed. In J. A. Stark, F. J. Menolascino, M. H. Albarelli, & V. C. Gray (Eds.), *Mental retardation and mental health. Classification, diagnosis, treatment, services.* New York: Springer-Verlag. Pp. 254-264.

Fletcher, R. (1993a). Individual psychotherapy for persons with mental retardation. In R. Fletcher & A. Dosen (Eds.), *Mental health aspects of mental retardation.* New York: Lexington Books.

Fletcher, R. (1993b). Mental illness-mental retardation in the United States: Policy and treatment challenges. *Journal of Intellectual Disability Research, 37,* 25-33.

Fletcher, R., & Dosen, A. (1993). *Mental health aspects of mental retardation.* New York: Lexington Books.

Fletcher, R. & Menolascino, F. J. (Eds.) (1989). *Mental retardation and mental illness, Assessment, treatment, and services for the dually diagnosed.* Lexington, MA: D. C. Heath and Company.

Foale, M. (1956). The special difficulties of the high grade mental defective adolescent. *American Journal of Mental Deficiency,* **60**, 867-877.

Fox, R., Burkhart, J. E., & Rotatori, A. F. (1983). Eating behavior of obese and nonobese retarded adults. *American Journal of Mental Deficiency,* **87**, 570-573.

Fox, R., & Rotatori, A. F. (1981). Regression including anorexia nervosa in a Down's syndrome adult: A seven year follow-up. *Journal of Behavior Therapy and Experimental Psychiatry,* **12**, 351-354.

Fox, R., & Rotatori, A. F. (1982). Prevalence of obesity among mentally retarded adults. *American Journal on Mental Deficiency,* **87**, 228-230.

Foxx, R. M. (1989). *Decreasing severe behaviors with punishment procedures: Discontinuing their use while maintaining long-term treatment effects.* Paper presented at NIH Consensus Development Conference, Bethesda, Maryland.

Foxx, R. M. (1990). Harry: A ten-year follow-up of the successful treatment of a self-injurious man. *Research in Developmental Disabilities,* **11**, 67-76.

Foxx, R. M., & Bechtel, D. R. (1983). Overcorrection: A review and analysis. In S. Axelrod & J. Apsche (Eds.), *The effects of punishment on human behavior.* New York: Academic Press.

Foxx, R. M., Bittle, R. G., & Faw, G. D. (1989). A long-term maintenance strategy for discontinuing aversive procedures: A 52-month follow-up of the treatment of aggression. *American Journal on Mental Retardation,* **94**, 27-36.

Foxx, R. M., & Faw, G. D. (1992). An eight-year follow-up of three social skills training studies. *Mental Retardation,* **30**, 63-66.

Foxx, R. M., Faw, G. D., Taylor, S., Davis, P. K., & Fulia, R. (1993). Would I be able to. . . ? Teaching clients to assess the availability of their community living life style preferences. *American Journal on Mental Retardation,* **98**, 235-248.

Foxx, R. M., Kyle, M. S., Faw, G. D., & Bittle, R. G. (1989). Problem-solving skills training: Social validation and generalization. *Behavioral Residential Treatment,* **4**, 269-288.

Fraser, W. I., Leudar, I., Gray, J., & Campbell, I. (1986). Psychiatric and behavior disturbance in mental handicap. *Journal of Mental Deficiency Research,* **30**, 49-57.

Frazier, J. A., Barrett, R. P., Feinstein, C., & Walters, A. S. (in press). Moderate to profound mental retardation. In J. Noshpitz (Ed.), *Handbook of child and adolescent psychiatry.* New York: Basic Books.

Freeman, B. J., Ritvo, E. R., Yokota, A., & Rivto, A. (1986). A scale for rating symptoms of patients with the syndrome of autism in real life settings. *Journal of the American Academy of*

Child Psychiatry, 25, 130-136.

Freeman, B. J., Roy, R. R., & Hemmick, S. (1976). Extinction of a phobia of physical examination in a seven-year-old mentally retarded boy — A case study. *Behavior Research and Therapy, 14*, 63-64.

Friedenthal, S. B., & Swartz, C. M. (1986). A milestone for the Dexamethasone Suppression Test. *American Journal of Psychiatry, 143*, 1198.

Friedman, D. L., Kastner, T., Plummer, A. T., Ruiz, M. Q., & Henning, D. (1992). Adverse behavioral effects in individuals with mental retardation and mood disorders treated with Carbamazepine. *American Journal on Mental Retardation, 96*, 541-546.

Fuchs, C., & Benson, B. A. (1994). *Social information processing in aggressive and nonaggressive adult males with mental retardation.* Paper presented at the national meeting of the American Association on Mental Retardation.

Gabby, S. (1992*a*). Interpretive software for the *Reiss Screen.* Worthington, OH: IDS Publishing Corporation.

Gabby, S. (1992*b*). Interpretive software for the *Reiss Scales.* Worthington, OH: IDS Publishing Corporation.

Gadow, K. D., & Kalachnick, J. (1981). Prevalence and pattern of drug treatment or behavior and seizure disorders of TMR students. *American Journal of Mental Deficiency, 85*, 588-595.

Gadow, K. D., & Poling, A. D. (1988). *Pharmacotherapy and mental retardation.* Boston: College-Hill Press.

Gardner, W. I. (1967). Occurrence of severe depressive reactions in the mentally retarded. *American Journal of Psychiatry, 124*, 386-388.

Gardner, W. I., & Graeber, J. L. (1993). Treatment of severe behavioral disorders in persons with mental retardation: A multimodal behavioral treatment model. In R. Fletcher & A. Dosen (Eds.), *Mental health aspects of mental retardation.* New York: Lexington Books. Pp. 45-69.

Garfield, S. L. (1963). Abnormal behavior in mental deficiency. In N. Ellis (Ed.), *Handbook of mental deficiency: Psychological theory and research.* New York: McGraw-Hill. Pp. 574-602.

Garfield, S. L. (1978). Research on client variables in psychotherapy. In S. L. Garfield & A. E. Bergin (Eds.), *Handbook of psychotherapy and behavior change* (second edition). New York: Wiley.

Garfield, S. L., Wilcott, J. B., & Milgram, N. A. (1961). Emotional disturbance and suspected mental deficiency. *American Journal of Mental Deficiency, 62*, 23-29.

Gargiulo, R. M., & O'Sullivan, P. S. (1986). Mildly mentally retarded and nonretarded

children's learned helplessness. *American Journal of Mental Deficiency, 91*, 203-206.

Gedye, A. (1992). Recognizing obsessive—compulsive disorder in clients with developmental disabilities. *The Habilitative Mental Healthcare Newsletter, 11*, 73-77.

Gentile, C., & Jenkins, J. O. (1980). Assertive training with mildly mentally retarded persons. *Mental Retardation, 18*, 315-217.

Gettings, R. M. (1988). Service delivery trends: A state-federal policy perspective. In J. A. Stark, F. J. Menolascino, M. H. Albarelli, & V. C. Gray (Eds.), *Mental retardation and mental health. Classification, diagnosis, treatment, services.* New York: Springer-Verlag. Pp. 385-393.

Gillberg, C. (1993). Autism and related behaviours. *Journal of Intellectual Disability Research, 37*, 343-372.

Gillberg, C. (1987). Psychiatric disorders in mildly and severely mentally retarded urban children and adolescents. *Psychiatry Digest, 3*, 2-4.

Gillberg, C., Persson, E., Grufman, M., & Themner, U. (1986). Psychiatric disorders in mildly and severely mentally retarded urban children and adolescents: Epidemiological aspects. *British Journal of Psychiatry, 149*, 68-74.

Gillberg, C., & Steffenburg, S. (1987). Outcome and prognostic factors in infantile autism and similar conditions: A population-based study of 46 cases followed through puberty. *Journal of Autism and Developmental Disorders, 17*, 273-287.

Gilson, S., Levitas, A., & Meade, C. (1987). *Psychiatric disorders in community-based mentally retarded adults: A statewide study.* Paper presented at the 1987 UIC-NIMH International Research Conference on the Mental Health Aspects of Mental Retardation, Evanston, IL.

Glaser, B. A., & Morreau, L. E. (1986). Effects of interdisciplinary team review on the use of antipsychotic agents with severely and profoundly mentally retarded persons. *American Journal of Mental Deficiency, 90*, 371-379.

Goldberg, B., Gitta, M. Z., & Puddephatt, A. (1992). *Personality and trait disturbances in an adult mental retardation population: Significance for psychiatric management.* Presented at the International Association for the Scientific Study of Mental Deficiency, Gold Coast, Australia.

Goldiamond, I. (1962). The maintenance of ongoing fluent verbal behavior and stuttering. *Journal of Mathematics, 1*, 57-96.

Goldsmith, L., & Schloss, P. J. (1984). Diagnostic overshadowing among learning-disabled and hearing-impaired learners with an apparent secondary diagnosis of behavior disorders. *International Journal of Partial Hospitalization, 2*, 209-217.

Gostason, R. (1985). Psychiatric illness among the mentally retarded: A Swedish population

study (Supplement No. 318). *Acta Psychiatricia Scandinavica*, 71, 1-117.

Gottman, J., Gonso, J., & Rasmussen, B. (1975). Social interaction, social competence, and friendship in children. *Child Development*, 46, 706-728.

Gravestock, S., & Bicknell, J. (1992). Emergency referrals to a south London community mental handicap team (CMHT). *Psychiatric Bulletin*, 16, 475-477.

Greenspan, S. B., & Granfield, J. M. (1992). Reconsidering the construct of mental retardation: Implications of a model of social competence. *American Journal of Mental Deficiency*, 96, 442-453.

Greenspan, S., & Shoultz, B. (1981). Why mentally retarded adults lose their jobs: Social competence as a factor in work adjustment. *Applied Research in Mental Retardation*, 2, 23-38.

Grossi, V., & Brown, R. I. (1985). Suicide attempts among mentally handicapped individuals: A pilot study. *Alberta Psychology*, 14, 12-13.

Grossman, H. J., Begab, M. J., Cantwell, M. D., Clements, J. D., Eyman, R. K., Meyers, C. E., Tarjan, G., & Warren, S. A. (1983). *Classification in mental retardation*. Washington, DC: American Association on Mental Deficiency.

Guarnaccia, V. J., & Weiss, R. L. (1974). The structure of fears in the mentally retarded. *Journal of Clinical Psychology*, 30, 540-545.

Guralnick, M. J. (1973). Behavior therapy with an acrophobic mentally retarded young adult. *Journal of Behavior Therapy and Experimental Psychiatry*, 4, 263-265.

Hagamen, M. B. (1980). Family adaptation to the diagnosis of mental retardation in a child and strategies of intervention. In L. Szymanski & P. Tanguay (Eds.), *Emotional disorders of mentally retarded persons*. Baltimore, MD: University Park Press.

Hagerman, R., & Brunschwig, A. (1991). Fragile X syndrome: A clinical perspective. *Comprehensive Mental Health Care*, 1, 157-176.

Hagerman, R., & McKenzie, P. (Eds.) (1992). *International fragile X conference proceedings*. Snowmass, CO.

Haimowitz, M. L., & Haimowitz, N. R. (1966). The evil eye: Fear of success. In M. L. Haimowitz & N. R. Haimowitz (Eds.), *Human development: Selected readings*. New York: Cromwell.

Harper, D. C., & Wadsworth, J. S. (1990). Dementia and depression in elders with mental retardation: A pilot study. *Research in Developmental Disabilities*, 11, 177-191.

Heal, L. W., & Harner, C. J. (1993). *The lifestyle satisfaction scale manual (LSS)*. Worthington, OH: IDS Publishing Corporation.

Healey, K. N., & Masterpasqua, F. (1992). Interpersonal cognitive problem-solving among children with mental retardation. *American Journal of Mental Deficiency, 96*, 367-372.

Healy, M. (1994, January 9). Radiation tests left chilling legacy. *Columbus (OH) Dispatch.*

Heaton-Ward, A. (1977). Psychosis in mental handicap. *British Journal of Psychiatry, 130*, 525-533.

Heller, T. (1982). Social disruption and residential relocation of mentally retarded children. *American Journal of Mental Deficiency, 87*, 48-55.

Herr, S. (1988). Clients in limbo: Asserting the rights of persons with dual diagnosis. In J. A. Stark, F. J. Menolascino, M. H. Albarelli, & V. C. Gray (Eds.), *Mental retardation and mental health. Classification, diagnosis, treatment, services.* New York: Springer-Verlag. Pp. 338-353.

Herskovitz, H. H., & Plesset, M. R. (1941). Psychoses in adult mental defectives. *Psychiatric Quarterly, 15*, 574-588.

Heston, L. L. (1970). The genetics of schizophrenic and schizoid disease. *Science, 167*, 249-256.

Hill, B. K., Balow, E. A., & Bruininks, R. H. (1985). A national survey of prescribed drugs in institutions and community residential facilities for mentally retarded people. *Psychopharmacology Bulletin, 21*, 279-284.

Hill, B. K., & Bruininks, R. H. (1984). Maladaptive behavior of mentally retarded individuals in residential facilities. *American Journal of Mental Deficiency, 88*, 380-387.

Hingsburger, D. (1987). Sex counseling with the developmentally handicapped: The assessment and management of seven critical problems. *Psychiatric Aspects of Mental Retardation Reviews, 6*, 41-46.

Hitzing, W. (1980). ENCOR and beyond. In T. Appolloni, J. Cappuccili, & T. P. Cooke (Eds.), *Toward excellence: Achievements in residential services for persons with disabilities.* Baltimore: University Park Press. Pp. 71-93.

Hitzing, W. (1987). Living options for persons with severe behavior problems. In A. Donnellan & R. Raul (Eds.), *The handbook of autism.* New York: Wiley.

Hollinger, P. C. (1979). Violent deaths among the young: Recent trends in suicide, homocide, and accidents. *American Journal of Psychiatry, 136*, 1144-1147.

Hollon, S. D. (1984). Cognitive therapy for depression: Translating research into practice. *the Behavior Therapist, 7*, 125-127.

Holmstrom, R. W., Silber, D. E., & Karp, S.A. (1990). Development of the Apperceptive Personality Test. *Journal of Personality Assessment, 54*, 252-264.

Holt, G., Bouras, N., & Brooks, D. (1993). Medical students' evaluation of their experience of

the psychiatry of mental handicap. *Psychiatric Bulletin, 17*, 21-22.

Holt, G. M., Bouras, N., & Watson, J. (1988). Down's syndrome and eating disorders. A case study. *British Journal of Psychiatry, 152*, 847-848.

Huesmann, L. R., & Eron, L. D. (1992). Childhood aggression and adult criminality. In J. McCord (Ed.), *Advances in criminological theory, 3*, 137-156.

Huesmann, L. R., Eron, L. D., Lefkowitz, M. M., & Walder, L. O. (1984). The stability of agression over time and generations. *Developmental Psychology, 20*, 1120-1134.

Huesmann, L. R., & Morikawa, S. (1985). Learned helplessness and depression. Cognitive factors in treatment and inoculation. In S. Reiss & R. Bootzin (Eds.), *Theoretical issues in behavior therapy.* New York: Academic Press.

Hurley, A. D. (1994, personal communication). Conversations on substance abuse and mental retardation.

Hurley, A. D., & Hurley, F. J. (1986). Counseling and psychotherapy with mentally retarded clients: I. The initial interview. *Psychiatric Aspects of Mental Retardation Reviews, 5*, 22-26.

Hurley, A. D., & Hurley, F. J. (1987). Counseling and psychotherapy with mentally retarded clients: II. Establishing a relationship. *Psychiatric Aspects of Mental Retardation Reviews, 6*, 15-20.

Hurley, A. D., & Sovner, R. (1979). Anorexia nervosa and mental retardation: A case report. *Journal of Clinical Psychiatry, 40*, 480-482.

Hurley, A. D., & Sovner, R. (1985). The use of the Thematic Apperception Test in mentally retarded persons. *Psychiatric Aspects of Mental Retardation, 4*, 9-12.

Hutt, M., & Gibby, R. G. (1965). *The mentally retarded child: Development, education and treatment* (2nd ed.). Boston: Allyn and Bacon, Inc.

Inoue, F. (1982). A clinical pharmacy service to reduce psychotropic medication use in an institution for mentally handicapped persons. *Mental Retardation, 20*, 70-74.

Iwata, B. A., Dorsey, M. F., Slifer, K. J., Bauman, K. E., & Richman, G. S. (1982). Toward a functional analysis of self-injury. *Analysis and Intervention in Developmental Disabilities, 2*, 3-20.

Jacobson, J. W. (1982*a*). Problem behavior and psychiatric impairment within a developmentally disabled population. I. Behavior frequency. *Applied Research in Mental Retardation, 3*, 121-139.

Jacobson, J. W. (1982*b*). Problem behavior and psychiatric impairment within a developmentally disabled population II. Behavior severity. *Applied Research in Mental Retardation, 3*, 369-381.

Jacobson, J. W. (1988). Problem behavior and psychiatric impairment within a developmentally disabled population. III. Psychotropic medication. *Research in Developmental Disabilities, 9*, 23-38.

Jacobson, J. W. (1990). Do some mental disorders occur less frequently among persons with mental retardation? *American Journal on Mental Retardation, 94*, 596-602.

Jacobson, J. W., & Harper, M. S. (1989). Mental health status of older persons with mental retardation in residential care settings. *Australia and New Zealand Journal of Developmental Disabilities, 15*, 301-309.

Jakab, I. (1982). Psychiatric disorders in mental retardation: Recognition, diagnosis, and treatment. In I. Jakab (Ed.), *Mental retardation*. New York: Kargan. Pp. 270-322.

James, D. H. (1986). Psychiatric and behavioral disorders amongst older severely mentally handicapped inpatients. *Journal of Mental Deficiency Research, 30*, 341-345.

Janicki, M. A., & Wisniewski, H. M. (1985). *Aging and developmental disabilities: Issues and approaches*. Baltimore: Paul H. Brookes Publishing Co.

Jarvis, J. (1988). Guided imagery and music (GIM) as a primary psychotherapeutic approach. *Music Therapy Perspectives, 5*, 69-72.

Jones, S. C. (1973). Self and interpersonal evaluations: Esteem theories versus consistency theories. *Psychological Bulletin, 79*, 185-199.

Junge, M. (1987). *Art therapist: Model job description*. Unpublished fact sheet, The American Art Therapy Association, Mundelein, Illinois.

Kalachnik, J. E. (1988). Medication monitoring procedures: Thou shall, here's how. In K. D. Gadow & A. G. Poling, (Eds.), *Pharmacotherapy and mental retardation*. Boston: Little Brown. Pp. 231-268.

Kaminer, Y., Feinstein, C., & Barrett, R. P. (1987). Suicidal behavior in mentally retarded adolescents: An overlooked problem. *Child Psychiatry and Human Development, 18*, 90-94.

Kaminer, Y., Feinstein, C., Barrett, R. P., Tylenda, B., & Hole, W. (1988). Menstrually related mood disorder in developmentally disabled adolescents: Review and current status. *Child Psychiatry and Human Development, 18*, 239-249.

Kanfer, F. H., & Phillips, J. S. (1970). *Learning foundations of behavior therapy*. New York: Wiley.

Kanner, L. (1943). Autistic disturbances of affective contact. *The Nervous Child, 2*, 217-250.

Karp, S. A., Holmstrom, R. W., & Silber, D. E. (1989). *Apperceptive Personality Test manual*. Worthington, OH: IDS Publishing Corporation.

Karp, S. A., Silber, D. E., & Holmstrom, R. W. (1993). *Apperceptive Personality Test consolidated manual.* Worthington, OH: IDS Publishing Corporation.

Kastner, T., Friedman, D. L., & Pond, W. S. (1992). Carbamazepine-induced hyponatremia in patients with mental retardation. *American Journal on Mental Retardation, 96,* 536-540.

Kazdin, A. E., & Bootzin, R. (1972). The token economy: An evaluative review. *Journal of Applied Behavior Analysis, 5,* 343-372.

Kazdin, A. E., Matson, J. L., & Senatore, V. (1983). Assessment of depression in mentally retarded adults. *American Journal of Psychiatry, 140,* 1040-1043.

Kazdin, A. E., & Wilcoxon, L. A. (1976). Systematic desensitization and nonspecific treatment effects: A methodological evaluation. *Psychological Bulletin, 83,* 729-758.

Kebbon, L. (1993). Sweden. *Journal of Intellectual Disability Research, 37,* 62-65.

Keene, N., & James, H. (1986). Who needs hospital care? *Mental Handicap, 14,* 101-103.

Kelly, L. E., Rimmer, J. H., & Ness, R. A. (1986). Obesity levels in institutionalized mentally retarded adults. *Adapted Physical Activity Quarterly, 3,* 167-176.

Kennedy, M., & Olson, D. (1987). Living in the community: Speaking for yourself. In S. J. Taylor, D. Biklen, & J. Knoll (Eds.), *Community integration for people with severe disabilities.* New York: Teachers College Press. Pp. 202-208.

Kessler, J. W. (1987). *Psychopathology of childhood.* Englewood Cliffs, NJ: Prentice-Hall, Inc.

Kessler, J. W. (1988). *Psychopathology of childhood* (2nd ed.). Englewood Cliffs, NJ: Prentice-Hall, Inc.

King, B. H. (1993). Self-injury by people with mental retardation: A compulsive behavior hypothesis. *American Journal on Mental Retardation, 98,* 93-112.

King, N. J., Ollendick, T. H., Gullone, E., Cummins, R. A., & Josephs, A. (1990). Fears and phobias in children and adolescents with intellectual disabilities: Assessment and intervention strategies. *Australia and New Zealand Journal of Developmental Disabilities, 16,* 97-108.

Kirk, S. A., & Kutchins, H. (1992). *The selling of DSM.* Hawthorne, NY: Aldine de Gruyter.

Kirsch, I. (1990). *Changing expectations.* Pacific Grove, CA: Brooks/Cole Publishing Company.

Knapp, L. G., Barrett, R. P., Groden, G., & Groden, J. (1992). The nature and prevalence of fears in developmentally disabled children and adolescents: A preliminary investigation. *Journal of Development and Physical Disabilities, 4,* 195-203.

Knights, R. M. (1963). Test anxiety and defensiveness in institutionalized and noninstitutionalized normal and retarded children. *Child Development,* **34**, 1019-1026.

Koller, H., Richardson, S., Katz, M., & McLaren, J. (1983). Behavior disturbance since childhood among a 5-year birth cohort of all mentally retarded young adults in a city. *American Journal of Mental Deficiency,* **87**, 386-395.

Kopp, C. B., Baker, B. L., & Brown, K. W. (1992). Social skills and their correlates: Preschoolers with developmental delays. *American Journal of Mental Deficiency,* **96**, 357-366.

Kovacs, M. (1981). Rating scales to assess depression in school aged children. *Acta Paedopsychiatrica,* **46**, 305-215.

Kovacs, M. (1985). The Children's Depression Inventory (CDI). *Psychopharmacology Bulletin,* **21**, 995-998.

Krauss, M. W., Seltzer, M. M., & Goodman, S. J. (1992). Social support networks of adults with mental retardation who live at home. *American Journal of Mental Deficiency,* **96**, 432-441.

Krug, D. A., Arick, J., & Almond, P. (1980). Behavior checklist for identifying severely handicapped individuals with high levels of autistic behavior. *Journal of Child Psychology and Psychiatry,* **21**, 221-229.

Kushlick, A., Blunden, R., & Cox, G. (1973). A method of rating behavior characteristics for use in large scale surveys of mental handicap. *Psychological Medicine,* **3**, 466-478.

Lakin, K. C., Hill, B. K., Chen, T. H., & Stephens, S. A. (1989). *Persons with mental retardation and related conditions in mental retardation facilities: Selected findings from the 1987 National Medical Expenditure Survey* (Report No. 29). Minneapolis: University of Minnesota, Center for Residential and Community Services.

Lakin, K. C., Hill, B. K, Hauber, F. A., Bruininks, R. H., & Heal, L. W. (1983). New admissions and readmissions to a national sample of public residential facilities. *American Journal of Mental Deficiency,* **88**, 13-20.

Laman, D. S. (1989). *A longitudinal investigation of the relationship among depressed mood, social support, and social skills in mentally retarded adults.* Unpublished doctoral dissertation, Department of Psychology, University of Illinois at Chicago.

Laman, D. S., & Reiss, S. (1987). Social skill deficiencies associated with depressed mood of mentally retarded adults. *American Journal of Mental Deficiency,* **92**, 224-229.

LaMendola, W., Zabaria, E. S., & Carver, M. (1980). Reducing psychotropic drug use in an institution for the retarded. *Hospital and Community Psychiatry,* **31**, 271-272.

LaMore, K. L., & Nelson, D. L. (1993). The effects of options on performance of an art project

in adults with mental disabilities. *The American Journal of Occupational Therapy, 47*, 397-401.

Langee, H. R., & Conlon, M. (1992). Predictors of response to antidepressant medications. *American Journal on Mental Retardation, 97*, 65-70.

Langer, E. J., & Abelson, R. P. (1974). A patient by any other . . . : Clinician group differences in labelling bias. *Journal of Consulting and Clinical Psychology, 42*, 4-9.

Larson, S. A., & Lakin, K. C. (1992). *Quality of life for people with challenging behavior living in community settings.* This study was presented at the 1992 annual AAMR National Convention in New Orleans.

LaVigna, G. W., & Donnellan, A. M. (1986). *Alternatives to punishment.* New York: Irvington Press.

Leaverton, D. R., & Van Der Heide, C. (1975, May). *Lip service no longer.* Paper read at the national meeting of the American Academy on Mental Retardation. Cited in Tanguay & Szymanski (1980).

Leland, H. (1973). Adaptive behavior and mentally retarded behavior. In G. Tarjan, R. K. Eyman, & C. E. Meyers (Eds.), *Sociobehavioral studies in mental retardation.* Washington, DC: Monographs of the American Association on Mental Deficiency, Whole No. 1. Pp. 91-100.

Leland, H., & Smith, D. E. (1965). *Play therapy with mentally subnormal children.* New York: Grune and Stratton.

Leland, H., & Smith, D. E. (1972). Psychotherapeutic considerations with mentally retarded and developmentally disabled children. In E. Katz (Ed.), *Mental health services for the mentally retarded.* Springfield, IL: Charles C. Thomas. Pp. 38-65.

Leland, H., & Smith, D. E. (1974). *Mental retardation: Present and future perspectives.* Worthington, OH: Charles A. Jones Publishing Co.

Leland, H., & Smith, D. E. (1985). *Play therapy with developmentally disabled children.* Unpublished manuscript, Nisonger Center, The Ohio State University.

Lepper, M. R., Greene, D., & Nisbett, R. E. (1973). Undermining children's intrinsic interest with extrinsic reward: A test of the "overjustification" hypothesis. *Journal of Personality and Social Psychology, 28*, 129-137.

Lesch, M., & Nyhan, W. (1964). A familial disorder of uric acid metabolism and central nervous system function. *American Journal of Medicine, 36*, 561-570.

Leste, A., & Rust, J. (1990). Effects of dance on anxiety. *American Journal of Dance Therapy, 12*, 19-25.

Levitan, G. W., & Reiss, S. (1983). Generality of diagnostic overshadowing across disciplines. *Applied Research in Mental Retardation, 4*, 59-64.

Levitas, A., & Gilson, S. (1987). Transference, countertransference, and resistance. *National Association for the Dually Diagnosed Newsletter,* 1, 2-7.

Levitas, A., & Gilson, S. (1989). Psychodynamic psychotherapy with mildly and moderately retarded patients. In R. Fletcher & F. J. Menolascino (Eds.), *Mental retardation and mental illness: Assessment, treatment and service for the dually diagnosed.* Lexington, MA: Lexington Books. Pp. 71-110.

Levitas, A., & Gilson, S. (1990). Toward the developmental understanding of the impact of mental retardation on the assessment of psychopathology. In *Assessment of behavior problems in persons with mental retardation living in the community.* Rockville, MD: National Institute of Mental Health (DHHS Publication No. ADM 90-1642). Pp. 71-106.

Levitas, A., & Gilson, S. F. (1994). Psychosocial development of children and adolescents with mild mental retardation. In N. Bouras (Ed.), *Mental health in mental retardation.* New York: Cambridge University Press.

Lewin, K. (1936). *A dynamic theory of personality.* New York: McGraw-Hill.

Lewis, G. A., Kleven, K. B., & Melcher, W. A. (1988). *A comprehensive service delivery model for dually diagnosed persons.* Unpublished report. Great Falls, MT.

Libb, W. J. (1972). Stimuli previously associated with reinforcement: Reinforcing or frustrating to the mentally retarded. *Journal of Experimental Child Psychology,* 14, 1-10.

Linaker, O. (1991). DSM-III diagnoses compared with factor structure of the Psychopathology Instrument for Mentally Retarded Adults (PIMRA), in an institutionalized, mostly severely retarded sample. *Research in Developmental Disabilities,* 12, 143-154.

Linden, B. E., & Forness, S. R. (1986). Post-school adjustment of mentally retarded persons with psychiatric disorders: A ten-year follow-up. *Education and Training of the Mentally Retarded,* 21, 157-164.

Lindsay, W. R., & Michie, A. M. (1988). Adaptation of the Zung self-rating anxiety scale for people with a mental handicap. *Journal of Mental Deficiency Research,* 32, 485-490.

Lindsley, H. L. (1989). Multiple personality disorder in persons with developmental disabilities. *Psychiatric Aspects of Mental Retardation Reviews,* 8, 65-71.

Longhurst, N. A. (in press). *The self-advocacy movement by persons with developmental disabilities: A demographic study and directory of groups in the United States.* Washington, DC: American Association on Mental Retardation.

Lovaas, O. I., Berberich, J. P., Perloff, B. F., & Schaeffer, B. (1966). Acquisition of imitative speech by schizophrenic children. *Science,* 151, 705-707.

Lovaas, O. I., Freitag, G., Gold, V., & Kassorla, I. (1965). Experimental studies in childhood

schizophrenia: Analysis of self-destructive behavior. *Journal of Experimental Child Psychology*, **2**, 67-84.

Luckasson, R. (1988). The dually diagnosed client in the criminal justice system. In J. A. Stark, F. J. Menolascino, M. H. Albarelli, & V. C. Gray (Eds.), *Mental retardation and mental health. Classification, diagnosis, treatment, services*. New York: Springer-Verlag. Pp. 354-360.

Luckasson, R., Coulter, D., Polloway, E., Reiss, S., Schalock, R. L., Snell, M., Spitalnik, D., & Stark, J. A. (1992). *Mental retardation: Definition, classification, and systems of supports*. Washington, DC: American Association on Mental Retardation.

Ludins-Katz, F., & Katz, E. (1990). *Art and disabilities*. Brookline, MA: Brookline Books.

Luftig, R. L. (1988). Assessment of the perceived school loneliness and isolation of mentally retarded and nonretarded students. *American Journal on Mental Retardation*, **92**, 472-475.

Luiselli, J. K. (1977). Case report: An attendant-administered contingency management programme for the treatment of a toileting phobia. *Journal of Mental Deficiency Research*, **21**, 283-288.

Lund, J. (1985*a*). The prevalence of psychiatric morbidity in mentally retarded adults. *Acta Psychiatrica Scandinavica*, **72**, 563-570.

Lund, J. (1985*b*). Mentally retarded admitted to psychiatric hospitals in Denmark. *Acta Psychiatrica Scandinavica*, **72**, 202-205.

Luria, A. (1963). Psychological studies of mental deficiency in the Soviet Union. In N. R. Ellis (Ed.), *Handbook of mental deficiency*. New York: McGraw-Hill.

Lustman, N., & Zigler, E. (1982). Imitation by institutionalized and noninstitutionalized mentally retarded children and nonretarded children. *American Journal of Mental Deficiency*, **87**, 252-258.

Machover, K. (1949). *Personality projection in the drawing of the human figure*. Springfield, IL: Charles C. Thomas.

MacLean, Jr., W. E. (1993). Overview. In J. L. Matson & R. P. Barrett (Eds.), *Psychopathology in the mentally retarded* (2nd ed.). Needham Heights, MA: Allyn and Bacon. Pp. 1-16.

Macmann, G. M., & Barnett, D. W. (1993). Reliability of psychiatric and psychological diagnoses of mental retardation severity: Judgments under naturally occurring conditions. *American Journal on Mental Retardation*, **97**, 559-567.

MacMillan, D. L., Gresham, F. M., & Siperstein, G. N. (1993). Conceptual and psychometric concerns about the 1992 AAMR definition of mental retardation. *American Journal on Mental Retardation*, **98**, 325-335.

Mann, A. H., Jenkins, R., Cutting, J. C., & Cowen, P. J. (1981). The development and use of a standardized assessment of abnormal personality. *Psychological Medicine, 11*, 839-847.

Maracek, J., & Mettee, D. R. (1972). Avoidance of continued success as a function of self-esteem, level of esteem certainty, and responsibility for success. *Journal of Personality and Social Psychology, 22*, 98-107.

Marks, I. M. (1971). Behavioral psychotherapy of adult neurosis. In S. Garfield & A. Bergin (Eds.), *Handbook of psychotherapy and behavior change*. New York: Wiley.

Marsh, H. W., & Barnes, J. (1982). *Self-description questionnaire*. II. Unpublished manuscript. University of Sydney, Sydney, Australia.

Marshburn, E. C., & Aman, M. G. (1992). Factor validity and norms for the Aberrant Behavior Checklist in a community sample of children with mental retardation. *Journal of Autism and Developmental Disorders, 22*, 357-373.

Matarazzo, J. D. (1983). The reliability of psychiatric and psychological diagnosis. *Clinical Psychology Review, 3*, 103-145.

Matson, J. L. (1981*a*). A controlled outcome study of phobias in mentally retarded adults. *Behavior Research and Therapy, 19*, 101-107.

Matson, J. L. (1981*b*). Assessment and treatment of clinical fears in mentally retarded children. *Journal of Applied Behavior Analysis, 14*, 287-294.

Matson, J. L. (1982*a*). The treatment of behavioral characteristics of depression in the mentally retarded. *Behavior Therapy, 13*, 209-218.

Matson, J. L. (1982*b*). Treating obsessive-compulsive behavior in mentally retarded adults. *Behavior Modification, 6*, 551-567.

Matson, J. L. (1983*a*). Depression in the mentally retarded: Toward a conceptual analysis of diagnosis. In M. Hersen, R. Eisler, & P. N. Miller (Eds.), *Progress in behavior modification*. Vol. 15. New York: Academic Press. Pp. 57-79.

Matson, J. L. (1983*b*). The treatment of behavioral characteristics of depression in the mentally retarded. *Behavior Therapy, 13*, 209-218.

Matson, J. L. (1984). Psychotherapy with persons who are mentally retarded. *Mental Retardation, 22*, 170-175.

Matson, J. L. (1985). Biosocial theory of psychopathology: A three by three factor model. *Applied Research in Mental Retardation, 6*, 199-227.

Matson, J. L. (1988). *The PIMRA manual*. Worthington, OH: IDS Publishing Corporation.

Matson, J. L. (1990). *The MESSY test manual*. Worthington, OH: IDS Publishing Corporation.

Matson, J. L., & Adkins, J. (1980). A self-instructional social skills training program for mentally retarded persons. *Mental Retardation, 18*, 245-248.

Matson, J. L., & Andrasik, F. (1982). Training leisure time social interaction skills to mildly mentally retarded adults. *American Journal of Mental Deficiency, 86*, 533-542.

Matson, J. L.., & Barrett, R. P. (Eds.) (1993). *Psychopathology in the mentally retarded* (2nd ed.). Needham Heights, MA: Allyn and Bacon.

Matson, J. L., Barrett, R. P., & Helsel, W. J. (1988). Depression in mentally retarded children. *Research in Developmental Disabilities, 9*, 39-46.

Matson, J. L., & Coe, D. A. (1992). Applied behavior analysis: Its impact on the treatment of mentally retarded emotionally disturbed people. *Research in Developmental Disabilities, 13*, 171-189.

Matson, J. L., Coe, D. A., Gardner, W. I., & Sovner, R. (1991). A factor analytic study of the diagnostic assessment for the severely handicapped scale. *The Journal of Nervous and Mental Disease, 179*, 553-557.

Matson, J. L., Dettling, J., & Senatore, V. (1981). Treating depression of a mentally retarded adult. *British Journal of Mental Subnormality, 16*, 86-88.

Matson, J. L., & Gardner, W. I. (1991). Behavioral learning theory and current application to severe behavior problems in problems with mental retardation. *Clinical Psychology Review, 11*, 175-183.

Matson, J. L., Gardner, W. I., Coe, D. A., & Sovner, R. (1991). A scale for evaluating emotional disorders in severely and profoundly retarded persons. *British Journal of Psychiatry, 159*, 404-409.

Matson, J. L., Kazdin, A. E., & Esveldt-Dawson, K. (1980). Training interpersonal skills among mentally retarded and social dysfunctional children. *Behavior Research and Therapy, 18*, 419-427.

Matson, J. L., Kazdin, A. E., & Senatore, V. (1984). Psychometric properties of the Psychopathology Inventory for Mentally Retarded Adults. *Applied Research in Mental Retardation, 5*, 881-889.

Matson, J. L., Rotatori, A. F., & Helsel, W. J. (1983). Development of a rating scale to measure social skills in children: The Matson Evaluation of Social Skills with Youngsters (MESSY). *Behavior Research and Therapy, 21*, 335-340.

Mattes, J. A. (1986). Psychopharmacology of temper outbursts: A review. *Journal of Nervous and*

Mental Disease, **174**, 464-470.

Mattes, J. A., & Amsell, L. (1993). The Dexamethasone Suppression Test as an indication of depression in patients with mental retardation. *American Journal on Mental Retardation,* **98**, 354-359.

McBrien, J. (1987). The Haytor Unit: Specialized day care for adults with severe mental handicaps and behavior problems. *Mental Handicap,* **15**, 77-80.

McGee, J. (1993). Gentle teaching for persons with mental retardation: The expression of a psychology of interdependence. In R. J. Fletcher, & A. Dosen (Eds.), *Mental health aspects of mental retardation.* New York: Lexington Books.

McGee, J., Folk, L., Swanson, D. A., & Menolascino, F. J. (1984). In F. J. Menolascino & J. A. Stark (Eds.), *Handbook of mental illness in the mentally retarded.* New York: Plenum Press.

McKinney, B., & Peterson, R. A. (1987). Predictors of stress in parents of developmentally disabled children. *Journal of Pediatric Psychology,* **12**, 133-150.

McLoughlin, I. J. (1986). A study of mortality experiences in a mental handicap hospital. *British Journal of Psychiatry,* **154**, 645-649.

McNally, R. J. (1991*a*). Anxiety and phobias. In J. L. Matson & J. A. Mulick (Eds.), *Handbook of mental retardation.* New York: Pergamon. Pp. 413-423.

McNally, R. J. (1991*b*). Assessment of posttraumatic stress disorder in children. *Journal of Consulting and Clinical Psychology,* **3**, 531-537.

McNally, R. J. (1992). Anxiety sensitivity distinguishes panic disorder from generalized anxiety disorder. *Journal of Nervous Mental Disease,* **180**, 737-738.

McNally, R. J. (1993). Stressors that produce posttraumatic stress disorder in children. In J. R. T. Davidson & E. B. Foa (Eds.), *Posttraumatic stress disorder: DSM-IV and beyond.* Washington, DC: American Psychiatric Press. Pp. 57-74.

McNally, R. J. (1993, November). Personal communication.

McNally, R. J. (in press *a*). Anxiety sensitivity is distinguishable from trait anxiety. In R. M. Rapee (Ed.), *Current controversies in anxiety disorders research.* New York: Guilford.

McNally, R. J. (in press *b*). *Panic disorder: A critical analysis.* New York: Guilford.

McNally, R. J., & Ascher, L. M. (1987). Anxiety disorders in mentally retarded people. In L. Michelson & L. M. Ascher (Eds.), *Anxiety and stress disorders.* New York: Guilford.

McNally, R. J., & Calamari, J. E. (1988). Neuroleptic malignant syndrome in a man with mental

retardation. *Mental Retardation, 26,* 385-386.

McNally, R. J., & Calamari, J .E. (1989*a*). Preventing water intoxication: A reply. *Journal of Behavioral Therapy & Experimental Psychiatry, 20,* 89-90.

McNally, R. J., & Calamari, J. E. (1989*b*). Obsessive-compulsive disorder in a mentally retarded woman. *British Journal of Psychiatry, 155,* 116-117.

McNally, R. J., Calamari, J. E., Hansen, P. M., & Kaliher, C. (1988). Behavioral treatment of psychogenic polydipsia. *Journal of Behavioral Therapy & Experimental Psychiatry, 19,* 57-61.

McNally, R. J., & Lukach, B. M. (1992). Behavioral treatment of zoophilic exhibitionism. *Journal of Behavioral Therapy & Experimental Psychiatry, 22,* 281-284.

McNally, R. J., & Shin, L. M. (1994). *Intelligence predicts severity of posttraumatic stress disorder symptoms in Vietnam combat veterans.* Unpublished manuscript, Department of Psychology, Harvard University.

McNally, R. J., & Steketee, G. S. (1985). The etiology and maintenance of severe animal phobias. *Behaviour Research and Therapy, 18,* 3-11.

McQueen, P. C., Spence, M. W., Garner, J. B., Pereira, & Winsor, E. J. (1987). Prevalence of major mental retardation and associated disabilities in the Canadian Maritime Provinces. *American Journal of Mental Deficiency, 91,* 460-471.

Meins, W. (1993*a*). Assessment of depression in mentally retarded adults: Reliability and validity of the Children's Depression Inventory (CDI). *Research in Developmental Disabilities, 14,* 299-312.

Meins, W. (1993*b*). Prevalence and risk factors for depressive disorders in adults with intellectual disability. *Australia and New Zealand Journal of Developmental Disabilities, 18,* 147-156.

Melnyk, L., & Das, J. P. (1992). Measurement of attention deficit: Correspondence between rating scales and tests of sustained and selective attention. *American Journal on Mental Retardation, 96,* 599-606.

Menolascino, F. J. (1965). Emotional disturbance and mental retardation. *American Journal of Mental Deficiency, 70,* 248-256.

Menolascino, F. J. (1969). Emotional disturbances in mentally retarded children. *American Journal of Psychiatry, 126,* 54-62.

Menolascino, F. J., Gilson, S. F., & Levitas, A. (1986). Issues in the treatment of mentally retarded patients in the community mental health system. *Community Mental Health Journal, 22,* 314-327.

Menolascino, F. J., Lazer, J., & Stark, J. A. (1989). Diagnosis and management of depression and suicidal behavior in persons with severe mental retardation. *Journal of the Multihandicapped Person,* 2, 89-103.

Menolascino, F. J., McGee, J. J., & Swanson, D. A. (1982). Behavioral dimensions of the de Lange syndrome. *Journal of Mental Deficiency Research,* 26, 259-261.

Menolascino, F. J., & Stark, J. A. (Eds.), (1984). *Handbook of mental illness in the mentally retarded.* New York: Plenum Press.

Miller, L. C., Barrett, C., Hampe, E., & Noble, H. (1971). Revised anxiety scales for the Louisville Behavioral Checklist. *Psychology Reports,* 29, 503-511.

Miller, L. K., & Monroe, M. J. (1990). Musical aptitude and adaptive behavior of people with mental retardation. *American Journal on Mental Retardation,* 95, 220-227.

Miller, N. E. (1941). The frustration-aggression hypothesis. *Psychological Review,* 48, 337-342.

Millon, T. (1981). *Disorders of personality.* New York: Wiley.

Milos, M. E., & Reiss, S. (1982). Effects of three play conditions on separation anxiety in young children. *Journal of Consulting and Clinical Psychology,* 50, 389-395.

Molony, H. (1993). Mental health services for people with intellectual disability: Current developments. *Australia and New Zealand Journal of Developmental Disabilities,* 18, 169-176.

Monfils, M., & Menolascino, F. (1984). Modified individual and group treatment approaches for the mentally retarded-mentally ill. In F. J. Menolascino & J. A. Stark (Eds.), *Handbook of mental illness in the mentally retarded.* New York: Plenum Press. Pp. 155-170.

Morgan, C., & Murray, H. (1935). A method for investigating fantasies: The Thematic Apperception Test. *Archives of Neurology and Psychiatry,* 434, 289-306.

Mosher, L. R., Gunderson, J. G., & Buchsbaum, S. (1973). Special report on schizophrenia: 1972. *Schizophrenia Bulletin,* 7, 10-52.

Mueser, K. T., Valenti-Hein, D., & Yarnold, P. R. (1987). Dating-skills groups for the developmentally disabled. Social skills and problem-solving versus relaxation training. *Behavior Modification,* 11, 200-228.

Mundy, P. C., Seibert, J. M., & Hogan, A. E. (1985). Communication skills in the mentally retarded. In M. Sigman (Ed.), *Children with emotional disorders and developmental disabilities.* Orlando, FL: Grune & Stratton.

Murray, H. A. (1943). *Thematic Apperception Test.* Cambridge, MA: Harvard University Press.

Myers, B. A. (1986). Psychopathology in hospitalized developmentally disabled individuals. *Comprehensive Psychiatry, 27*, 115-126.

Myers, B. A. (1987). Patterns of withdrawal and avoidance in developmentally disabled adolescents. *American Academy of Child and Adolescent Psychiatry,* 738-743.

Myers, B. A., & Pueschel, S. M. (1991). Psychiatric disorders in persons with Down Syndrome. *Journal of Nervous and Mental Disease, 179,* 609-613.

Myers, J. K., Weissman, M. M., Tischler, G. L., Hozer, C. E. III, Leaf, P. J., Orvaschel, H., Anthony, J. C., Boyd, J. H., Burke, J. D., Kramer, M., & Stoltzman, R. (1984). Six-month prevalence of psychiatric disorders in three communities. *Archives of General Psychiatry, 41,* 959-967.

Napolitan, J. T. (1979). *The classification of self-injurious behavior in mentally retarded children.* Unpublished doctoral dissertation. Department of Psychology, University of Illinois at Chicago.

National Institutes of Health. (1989). *Final report of the consensus development panel on treatment of destructive behaviors in persons with developmental disabilities.* Bethesda, MD: Author.

National Institutes of Health. (1991, July). *National Institutes of Health consensus development conference statement.* Bethesda, MD: Author. Publication No. 91-2410.

Nestadt, G., Romanoski, A. J., Samuels, J. F., Folstein, M. F., & McHugh, P. R. (1992). The relationship between personality and DSM-II Axis I disorders in the population: Results from an epidemiological survey. *American Journal of Psychiatry, 149,* 1228-1233.

Newman, I., & Emerson, E. (1991). Specialized treatment units for people with challenging behaviors. *Mental Handicap, 19,* 113-119.

Newton, J. T., & Sturmey, P. (1991). The Motivation Assessment Scale: Inter-rater reliability and internal consistency in a British sample. *Journal of Mental Deficiency Research, 35,* 472-474.

Nezu, A. M. (1987). A problem-solving formulation of depression: A literature review and proposal of a pluralistic model. *Clinical Psychology Review, 7,* 121-144.

Nezu, A. M., Nezu, C. M., & Perri, M. G. (1989). *Problem-solving therapy for depression: Theory, research, and clinical guidelines.* New York: Wiley.

Nezu, C. M., & Nezu, A. M. (1994). Outpatient psychotherapy for adults with mental retardation and concomitant psychopathology: Research and clinical imperatives. *Journal of Consulting and Clinical Psychology, 62,* 34-42.

Nezu, C. M, Nezu, A. M, & Arean, P. (1991). Assertiveness and problem-solving training for mildly mentally retarded persons with dual diagnoses. *Research in Developmental Disabilities,*

12, 371-386.

Nezu, C. M., Nezu, A. M., & Gill-Weiss, M.J. (1992). *Psychopathology in persons with mental retardation, Clinical guidelines for assessment and treatment.* Champaign IL: Research Press.

Nihira, K., Foster, R., Shellhaas, M., & Leland, H. (1975). *AAMD Adaptive Behavior Scale 1975 revision manual.* Washington, DC: American Association on Mental Deficiency.

Nolan, M. E. (1992). Generic services for people with a mental handicap. *Psychiatric Bulletin,* 16, 212-213.

Novaco, R. W. (1975). *Anger control: The development and evaluation of an experimental treatment.* Lexington, MA: Lexington Books.

Novosel, S. (1984). Psychiatric disorder in adults admitted to a hospital for the mentally retarded. *British Journal of Mental Subnormality,* 30, 54-58.

Nucci, M., & Reiss, S. (1988). Mental retardation and emotional disorders: A test for increased vulnerability to stress. *Australia and New Zealand Journal of Developmental Disabilities,* 13, 161-166.

Obler, M., & Terwilliger, R. F. (1970). Pilot study on the effectiveness of systematic desensitization with neurologically impaired children with phobic disorders. *Journal of Consulting and Clinical Psychiatry,* 34, 445-452.

O'Connor, N. (1951). Neuroticism and emotional instability in high-grade male defectives. *Journal of Neurology, Neurosurgery, and Psychiatry,* 14, 226-230.

O'Leary, K. D., & Drabman, R. (1971). Token reinforcement programs in the classroom: A review. *Psychological Bulletin,* 4, 379-398.

Ollendick, T. H. (1988). Reliability and validity of the revised Fear Survey Schedule for Children (FSSC-R). *Behaviour Research and Therapy,* 21, 685-692.

Page, F. (1986). The therapeutic use of puppetry with mentally handicapped people. *Occupational Therapy,* 16, 122-125.

Pagel, S., & Whitling, C. (1978). Readmissions to a state hospital for mentally retarded persons: Reasons for community placement failure. *Mental Retardation,* 16, 164-166.

Panek, P. E., & Wagner, E. E. (1993). Hand test characteristics of dual diagnosed mentally retarded older adults. *Journal of Personality Assessment,* 61, 324-328.

Parmenter, T. R. (1988). An analysis of Australian mental health services for people with mental retardation. *Australia and New Zealand Journal of Developmental Disabilities,* 14, 9-13.

Pary, R. J. (1991a). Side effects during lithium treatment for psychiatric disorders in adults with

mental retardation. *American Journal on Mental Retardation, 96,* 269-273.

Pary, R. J. (1991*b*). Towards defining adequate lithium trials for individuals with mental retardation and mental illness. *American Journal on Mental Retardation, 95,* 681-691.

Pary, R. J. (in press *a*). Psychiatric hospitalization of persons with mental retardation, mental illness and seizure diagnosis. *American Journal on Mental Retardation.*

Pary, R. J. (in press *b*). Survey of psychoactive drugs in persons with mental retardation: Comparison of elders to adults 20-54 years. *American Journal on Mental Retardation.*

Peck, C. L. (1977). Desensitization for the treatment of fear in the high level adult retardate. *Behaviour Research and Therapy, 15,* 137-148.

Penrose, L. S. (1938). *A clinical and generic study of 1,280 cases of mental defect.* London: Medical Research Council Special Report No. 229.

Peterson, R. A. (1984, personal communication). Psychological case report. Institute for the Study of Developmental Disabilities, University of Illinois at Chicago.

Peterson, R. A., & Reiss, S. (1992). *Anxiety Sensitivity Index revised test manual.* Worthington, OH: IDS Publishing Corporation.

Petti, T. A. (1978). Depression in hospitalized child psychiatry patients: Approaches to measuring depression. *Journal of the American Academy of Child Psychiatry, 17,* 49-59.

Pfadt, A. (1991). Group psychotherapy with mentally retarded adults: Issues related to design, implementation, and evaluation. *Research in Developmental Disabilities, 12,* 261-285.

Pfeiffer, S. I. (1992). Psychology and mental retardation: Emerging research and practice opportunities. *Professional Psychology: Research and Practice, 23,* 239-243.

Philips, I. (1965). Mental hygiene and mental retardation: Implications for planning. *Mental Hygiene, 49,* 525-533.

Philips, I. (1967). Psychopathology and mental retardation. *American Journal of Psychiatry, 124,* 67-73.

Philips, I., Jeffres, M., Koch, E. (1962). The application of psychiatric clinic services for the retarded child and his family. *Journal of American Academy of Child Psychiatry, 1,* 297-313.

Philips, I., & Williams, N. (1975). Psychopathology and mental retardation: A study of 100 mentally retarded children: I. Psychopathology. *American Journal of Psychiatry, 132,* 1265-1271.

Pirodsky, D. M., Gibbs, J. W., Hesse, R. A., Hsieh, M. C., Krause, R. B., & Rodriguez, W. H. (1985). Use of dexamethasone suppression test to detect depressive disorders. *American Journal*

of Mental Deficiency, 90, 245-252.

Pollock, H. M. (1944). Mental disease among mental defectives. *American Journal of Psychiatry,* **191,** 361-363.

Pollock, H. M. (1945). Mental disease among mental defectives. *American Journal of Mental Deficiency,* **49,** 477-480.

Polvinale, R. A., & Lutzker, J. R. (1980). Elimination of assaultive and inappropriate sexual behavior by reinforcement and social restitution. *Mental Retardation,* **18,** 27-30.

Pope, H. G., Keck, P. E., & McElroy, S. L. (1986). Frequency and presentation of neuroleptic malignant syndrome in a large psychiatric hospital. *American Journal of Psychiatry,* **143,** 1227-1233.

Portnoy, B., & Stacey, C. L. (1954). A comparative study of Negro and white subnormals on the children's form of the Rosensweig Picture-Frustration Test. *American Journal of Mental Deficiency,* **59,** 272-278.

Potter, H. (1964). The needs of mentally retarded children for child psychiatric services. *Journal of American Academic Child Psychiatry,* **3,** 352-374.

Potter, H. (1965). Mental retardation: The Cinderella of psychiatry. *Psychiatric Quarterly,* **39,** 537-549.

Potter, H. (1992). Personality in the mental defective with a method for its evaluation. *Mental Hygiene,* **6,** 487-497.

President's Commission on Mental Health. (1978). *Liaison task panel on mental retardation,* **4,** 2001-2006.

President's Committee on Mental Retardation. (1977). *Mental retardation: Past and present.* Washington, DC: U.S. Government Printing Office.

Prout, H. T. (1993). Assessing psychopathology in persons with mental retardation: A review of the Reiss Scales. *Journal of School Psychology,* **31,** 535-540.

Prout, H. T., & Strohmer, D. C. (1989). *Prout-Strohmer Personality Inventory manual.* Schenectady, NY: Genium Publishing Corporation.

Prouty, G. (1976). Pre-therapy—A method of treating preexpressive psychotic and retarded patients. *Psychotherapy: Theory, Research and Practice,* **13,** 290-294.

Prouty, G. (1994, in press). *Theoretical evolutions in person-centered/experiential therapy: Applications to schizophrenic and retarded psychoses.* Westport, CT: Praeger Publishing.

Prouty, G., & Kubiak, M. A. (1988). Pre-therapy with mentally retarded clients. *Psychiatric*

Aspects of Mental Retardation Reviews, 7, 62-66.

Puddephatt, A., & Sussman, S. (1994). Developing services in Canada: Ontario vignettes. In N. Bouras (Ed.), *Mental health in mental retardation*. New York: Cambridge University Press.

Pugh, T. F., & MacMahon, B. (1962). *Epidemiologic findings in United States mental hospital data*. Boston: Little, Brown.

Rapaport, D., Gill, M. N., & Schafer, R. (1968). *Diagnostic psychological testing*. New York: International Universities Press.

Rasmussen, S. A., & Tsuang, M. T. (1984). The epidemiology of obsessive- compulsive disorder. *Journal of Clinical Psychology, 45*, 450-457.

Ratey, J. J., Bemporad, J., Sorgi, P., Bick, P., Polakoff, S., O'Driscoll, G., & Mikkelsen, E. (1987). Brief report: Open trial effects of beta-blockers on speech and social behavior in 8 autistic adults. *Journal of Autism and Developmental Disorders, 17*, 439-446.

Ratey, J. J., Mikkelsen, E. J., Smith, G. S., Upadhyaya, A., Zuckerman, S., Martell, D., Sorgi, P., Polakoff, S., & Bemporad, J. (1986). Beta blockers in the severely and profoundly mentally retarded. *Journal of Clinical Psychopharmacology, 2*, 103-107.

Ratey, J. J., Mikkelsen, E. J., Sorgi, P., Zuckerman, S., Polakoff, S., Bemporad, J., Bick, P., & Kadish, W. (1987). Autism: The treatment of aggressive behaviors. *Journal of Clinical Psychopharmacology, 7*, 35-41.

Ratey, J. J., Morrill, R., & Oxenkrug, G. (1983). Use of propranolol for provoked and unprovoked episodes of rage. *American Journal of Psychiatry, 140*, 1356-1357.

Ratey, J. J., Sovner, R., Mikkelsen, E., & Chmielinski, H. (1989). Buspirone therapy for maladaptive behavior and anxiety in developmentally disabled persons. *Journal of Clinical Psychiatry, 50*, 382-384.

Ratey, J. J., Sovner, R., Parks, A., & Rogentine, K. (1991). Buspirone treatment of aggression and anxiety in mentally retarded patients: A multiple-baseline placebo lead-in study. *Journal of Clinical Psychiatry, 52*, 159-162.

Ray, R. (1978). The mentally handicapped child's reaction to bereavement. *Health Visitor, 51*, 333-334.

Reid, A. H. (1972a). Psychoses in adult mental defectives. I. Manic depressive psychosis. *British Journal of Psychiatry, 120*, 205-212,

Reid, A. H. (1972b). Psychoses in adult mental defectives. II. Schizophrenic and paranoid psychoses. *British Journal of Psychiatry, 120*, 213-218.

Reid, A. H. (1976). Psychiatric disturbances in the mentally handicapped. *Proceedings of the Royal Society of Medicine, 69,* 509-512.

Reid, A. H. (1980*a*). Diagnosis of psychiatric disorders in the severely and profoundly retarded patient. *Journal of the Royal Society of Medicine, 73,* 607-609.

Reid, A. H. (1980*b*). Psychiatric disorders in mentally handicapped children: A clinical and follow-up study. *Journal of Mental Deficiency Research, 24,* 287-298.

Reid, A. H. (1993*a*). Schizophrenic and paranoid syndromes in persons with mental retardation: Assessment and diagnosis. In R. Fletcher & A. Dosen (Eds.), *Mental health aspects of mental retardation - Progress in assessment and treatment.* New York: Lexington Books. pp.98-110.

Reid, A. H. (1993*b*). Schizophrenic and paranoid syndromes in persons with mental retardation: Treatment and assessment. In R. Fletcher & A. Dosen (Eds.), *Mental health aspects of mental retardation.* New York: Lexington Books.

Reid, A. H., & Ballinger, B. R. (1987). Personality disorder in mental handicap. *Psychological Medicine, 17,* 983-987.

Reid, A. H., Ballinger, B. R., & Heather, B. B. (1978). Behavioral syndromes identified by cluster analysis in a sample of 100 severely and profoundly retarded adults. *Psychological Medicine, 8,* 399-412.

Reid, A. H., Ballinger, B. R., Heather, B. B., & Melvin, S. J. (1984). The natural history of behavioral symptoms among severely and profoundly mentally retarded patients. *British Journal of Psychiatry, 145,* 289-293.

Reid, A. H., & Naylor, G. J. (1976). Short cycle manic depressive psychosis in mental defectives: A clinical and physiological study. *Mental Deficiency Research, 20,* 67-76.

Reiss, S. (1973). Transfer effects of success and failure training from one reinforcing agent to another. *Journal of Abnormal Psychology, 82,* 435-445.

Reiss, S. (1980). Pavlovian conditioning and human fear: An expectancy model. *Behavior Therapy, 11,* 380-396.

Reiss, S. (1982). Psychopathology and mental retardation: Survey of a developmental disabilities mental health program. *Mental Retardation, 20,* 128-132.

Reiss, S. (1985). The mentally retarded, emotionally disturbed adult. In M. Sigman (Ed.), *Children with emotional disorders and developmental disabilities, Assessment and treatment.* Orlando, FL: Grune & Stratton, Inc. Pp. 171-192.

Reiss, S. (1988*a*). Dual diagnosis in the United States. *Australia and New Zealand Journal of Developmental Disabilities, 14,* 43-48.

Reiss, S. (1988*b*). *The Reiss Screen for Maladaptive Behavior test manual*. Worthington, OH: IDS Publishing Corporation.

Reiss, S. (1988*c*). The development of a screening measure for psychopathology in people with mental retardation. In E. Dibble & D. B. Gray (Eds.), *Assessment of behavior problems in persons with mental retardation living in the community*. Rockville, MD: National Institute of Mental Health.

Reiss, S. (1989*a*). Cross-cultural images of mental retardation. *News and Notes, 2*.

Reiss, S. (1989*b*). Assessment of dual diagnosis. *The NADD Newsletter, 7*, 1-3.

Reiss, S. (1990). Prevalence of dual diagnosis in community-based day programs in the Chicago metropolitan area. *American Journal on Mental Retardation, 94*, 578-585.

Reiss, S. (1991). Expectancy model of fear, anxiety, and panic. *Clinical Psychology Review, 11*, 141-153.

Reiss, S. (1992). Assessment of a man with a dual diagnosis. *Mental Retardation, 30*, 1-6.

Reiss, S. (1993). Assessment of psychopathology in persons with mental retardation. In J. L. Matson & R. P. Barrett (Eds.), *Psychopathology in the mentally retarded* (2nd ed.). Needham Heights, MA: Allyn and Bacon.

Reiss, S. (in press). Issues on defining mental retardation. *American Journal on Mental Retardation*.

Reiss, S., & Benson, B. A. (1984*a*). *Stability and measurement of depression in mentally retarded adults*. Paper presented at the 17th Annual Gatlinburg Conference on Research in Mental Retardation and Developmental Disabilities.

Reiss, S., & Benson, B. A. (1984*b*). Awareness of negative social conditions among mentally retarded, emotionally disturbed outpatients. *American Journal of Psychiatry, 141*, 88-90.

Reiss, S., & Benson, B. A. (1985). Psychosocial correlates of depression in mentally retarded adults: I. Minimal social support and stigmatization. *American Journal of Mental Deficiency, 89*, 331-337.

Reiss, S., Benson, B. A., & Szyszko, J. (1993). *Apperceptive Personality Test Mental Retardation (APT/MR) manual*. Worthington, OH: IDS Publishing Corporation.

Reiss, S., & Bootzin, R. (Eds.) (1985). *Theoretical issues in behavior therapy*. Orlando, FL: Academic Press, Inc.

Reiss, S., Levitan, G. W., & McNally, R. J. (1982). Emotionally disturbed mentally retarded people. An underserved population. *American Psychologist, 37*, 361-367.

Reiss, S., Levitan, G., & Szyszko, J. (1982). Emotionally disturbed, mentally retarded people: An underserved population. *American Psychologist, 37*, 361-367.

Reiss, S., McKinney, B., & Napolitan, J. T. (1990). Three new mental retardation service models: Implications for behavior modification. In J. Matson (Ed.), *Handbook of behavior modification with the mentally retarded* (2nd ed.) New York: Plenum Press, Pp. 51-70.

Reiss, S., & McNally, R. J. (1985). Expectancy model of fear. In S. Reiss & R. Bootzin (Eds.), *Theoretical issues in behavior therapy.* New York: Academic Press Co. Pp. 107-121.

Reiss, S., Peterson, R. A., Eron, L. D., & Reiss, M. M. (1977). *Abnormality: Experimental and clinical approaches.* New York: Macmillan.

Reiss, S., Peterson, R. A., Gursky, D. M., & McNally, R. J. (1986). Anxiety sensitivity, anxiety frequency, and the prediction of fearfulness. *Behavior Research and Therapy, 24*, 1-8.

Reiss, S., & Redd, W. H. (1970). Generalization of the control of screaming behavior in an emotionally disturbed, mentally retarded female. *APA Proceedings,* 741-742.

Reiss, S., Reiss, M. M., & Reppucci, N. D. (1978). Rejection of success in two severely retarded children. *Cognitive Therapy and Research, 2*, 293-297.

Reiss, S., & Rojahn, J. (1993). Joint occurrence of depression and aggression in children and adults with mental retardation. *Journal of Intellectual Disability, 37*, 287-294.

Reiss, S., & Sushinsky, L. W. (1975). Overjustification, competing responses, and the acquisition of intrinsic interest. *Journal of Personality and Social Psychology, 31*, 1116-1125.

Reiss, S., & Sushinsky, L. W. (1976). The competing response hypothesis of decreased play effects: A reply to Lepper and Greene. *Journal of Personality and Social Psychology, 33*, 233-244.

Reiss, S., & Szyszko, J. (1983). Diagnostic overshadowing and professional experience with retarded persons. *American Journal of Mental Deficiency, 87*, 396-402.

Reiss, S., & Trenn, E. (1984). Consumer demand for outpatient mental health services for mentally retarded people. *Mental Retardation, 22*, 112-115.

Reiss, S., & Valenti-Hein, D. (1990). *Reiss Scales for Children's Dual Diagnosis: Test manual.* Worthington, OH: IDS Publishing Corporation.

Reiss, S., & Valenti-Hein, D. (1994). Development of a psychopathology rating scale for children with mental retardation. *Journal of Consulting and Clinical Psychology, 62*, 28-33.

Repp, A. C., & Singh, N. N. (1990). *Perspectives on the use of nonaversive and aversive interventions*

for persons with developmental disabilities. Sycamore, IL: Sycamore Publishing Company.

Reus, V. I. (1985). Toward an understanding of cortisol dysregulation in major depression: A review of studies of the Dexamethasone Suppression Test and urinary free-cortisol. *Psychiatric Medicine, 3,* 1-21.

Reynolds, W. M. (1989). *Reynolds Child Depression Scale.* Odessa, FL: Psychological Assessment Resource.

Reynolds, W. M., & Baker, J. A. (1988). Assessment of depression in persons with mental retardation. *American Journal on Mental Retardation, 93,* 93-103.

Reynolds, W. M., & Miller, K. L. (1985). Depression and learned helplessness in mentally retarded and nonmentally retarded adolescents: An initial investigation. *Applied Research in Mental Retardation, 6,* 295-306.

Richardson, S. A., Koller, H., & Katz, M. (1985). Relationship of upbringing to later behavior disturbance of mildly retarded young people. *American Journal of Mental Deficiency, 90,* 1-8.

Richardson, S. A., Koller, H., Katz, M., & McLaren, J. (1981). A functional classification of seizures and its distribution in a mentally retarded population. *American Journal of Mental Deficiency, 85,* 457-466.

Ricketts, R. W., Goza, A. B., Ellis, C. R., Singh, Y. N., Singh, N. N., & Cooke, J. C. (1993). Fluoxetine treatment of severe self-injury in young adults with mental retardation. *Journal of the American Academy of Child and Adolescent Psychiatry, 32,* 865-869.

Ricks, D. F. & Wessman, A. E. Winn. (1966). A case study of a happy man. *Journal of Humanistic Psychology, 6,* 2-16.

Rimmer, J. H., Braddock, D., & Fujiura, G. (1993). Prevalence of obesity in adults with mental retardation: Implications for health promotion and disease prevention. *Mental Retardation, 31,* 105-110.

Rivenq, B. (1974). Behavioral therapy of phobias: A case with gynecomastia and mental retardation. *Mental Retardation, 12,* 44-45.

Rogers, R. (1942). *Counseling and psychotherapy.* Boston: Houghton Mifflin Co.

Rogers, R. (1947). Some observations on the organization of personality. *American Psychologist, 2,* 358-368.

Rogers, R. (1951). *Client-centered therapy.* Boston: Houghton Mifflin Co.

Rogers, R. (1957). The necessary and sufficient conditions of therapeutic personality change. *Journal of Consulting Psychology, 21,* 95-103.

Rogers, R. (1961). *On becoming a person.* Boston: Houghton Mifflin Co.

Rogers, R., & Simensen, R. J. (1987). Fragile X syndrome: A common etiology of mental retardation. *American Journal of Mental Deficiency, 91,* 445-449.

Rojahn, J. (1986). Self-injurious and stereotypic behavior of noninstitutionalized mentally retarded people: Prevalence and classification. *American Journal of Mental Deficiency, 91,* 268-276.

Rojahn, J., Aman, M. G., Marshburn, E., Moeschberger, M., King, E., Logsdon, D., & Schroeder, S. (1993). Biological and environmental risk for poor developmental outcome of young children. *American Journal on Mental Retardation, 97,* 702-708.

Rojahn, J., Borthwick-Duffy, S. A., & Jacobson, J. (in press). The association between psychiatric diagnoses and severe behavior problems in mental retardation. *Annals of Clinical Psychiatry.*

Rojahn, J., Kroeger, T. L., & McElwain, D. C. (in press). Performance on the Penn facial discrimination task by adults with mental retardation. *American Journal on Mental Retardation.*

Rojahn, J., Polster, L., Mulick, J., & Wisniewski, J. (1989). Reliability of the Behavior Problem Inventory. *Journal of the Multihandicapped, 2,* 283-293.

Rojahn, R., Rabold, D., & Schneider, F. (in press). The emotion specificity hypothesis in adults with mental retardation. *American Journal on Mental Retardation.*

Romer, D., & Berkson, G. (1980*a*). Social ecology of supervised communal facilities for mentally disabled adults: II. Predictors of affiliation. *American Journal of Mental Deficiency, 85,* 229-242.

Romer, D., & Berkson, G. (1980*b*). Social ecology of supervised communal facilities for mentally disabled adults: III. Predictors of social choice. *American Journal of Mental Deficiency, 85,* 243-252.

Rorschach, H. (1921). *Psychodiagnostics.* New York: Grune & Stratton.

Rosen, M., & Weisz, S. (1983). Personality constructs in the evaluation of mentally retarded persons. *Mental Retardation, 21,* 116-118.

Rotatori, A. F., & Fox, R. (1981). *Behavioral weight reduction program for mental handicapped persons.* Baltimore, MD: University Park Press.

Ruedrich, S. L. (1993). Treatment of bipolar mood disorders in persons with mental retardation. In R. Fletcher & A. Dosen (Eds.), *Mental health aspects of mental retardation.* New York: Lexington Books. Pp. 268-280.

Ruedrich, S. L., Grush, L., & Wilson, J. (1990). Beta adrenergic blocking medications for

aggressive or self-injurious mentally retarded persons. *American Journal on Mental Retardation,* **95**, 110-119.

Ruedrich, S. L., Wadle, C. V., Sallach, H. S., Hahn, R. K., & Menolascino, F. J. (1987). Adrenocortical function and depressive illness in mentally retarded patients. *American Journal of Psychiatry,* **144**, 597-602.

Rusch, F. R., DeStefano, L., Chadsey-Rusch, J., Phelps, L. A., & Szymanski, E. M. (1992). *Transition from school to adult life: Models, linkages and policy.* Sycamore, IL: Sycamore Publishing.

Russell, A. T. (1985). The mentally retarded, emotionally disturbed child and adolescent. In M. Sigman (Ed.), *Children with emotional disorders and developmental disabilities: Assessment and treatment.* Orlando, FL: Grune & Stratton, Inc. Pp. 111-135.

Russell, A. T. (1988). The association between mental retardation and psychiatric disorder: Epidemiological issues. In J. A. Stark, F. J. Menolascino, M. H. Albarelli, & V. C. Gray (Eds.), *Mental retardation and mental health, Classification, diagnosis, treatment, services.* New York: Springer-Verlag. Pp. 42-49.

Russell, A.T., & Tanguay, P. E. (1981). Mental illness and mental retardation: Cause or coincidence? *American Journal on Mental Deficiency,* **85**, 570-574.

Rutter, M. (1991). Autism: Pathways from syndrome definition to pathogenesis. *Comprehensive Mental Health Care,* **1**, 5-26.

Rutter, M., Tizard, J., & Whitmore, K. (1970). *Education, health and behavior.* New York: Wiley.

Rutter, M., Tizard, J., Yule, W., Graham, P., & Whitmore, K. (1976). Isle of Wight studies, 1964-1974. *Psychological Medicine,* **6**, 313-332.

Ryan, R. (1993). *Posttraumatic stress disorder in persons with developmental disabilities.* Unpublished manuscript. Department of Psychiatry, University of Colorado Health Sciences Center.

Sacristan, J. R. (1988). Mental health in Spanish-speaking mentally retarded people: The state of the art. *Australia and New Zealand Journal of Developmental Disabilities,* **14**, 27-30.

Sandman, C. A. (1988). B-endorphin dysregulation in autistic and self-injurious behavior: A neurodevelopmental hypothesis. *Synapse,* **2**, 193-199.

Sandman, C. A. (1990). The opiate hypothesis in autism and self-injury. *Journal of Child and Adolescent Psychopharmacology,* **1**, 237-248.

Sandman, C. A., & Barron, J. L. (1992). Paradoxical response to sedative/hypnotics in patients with self-injurious behavior and stereotypy. *Journal of Developmental and Physical Disabilities,* **4**,

307-316.

Sandman, C. A., Barron, J. L., & Colman, H. (1990). An orally administered opiate blocker, naltrexone, attenuates self-injurious behavior. *American Journal of Mental Retardation, 95*, 93-102.

Sarason, S. B. (1943*a*). The use of the Thematic Apperception Test with mentally deficient children. I. A study of high grade boys. *American Journal of Mental Deficiency, 47*, 169-173.

Sarason, S. B. (1943*b*). The use of the Thematic Apperception Test with mentally deficient children. II. A study of school grade girls. *American Journal of Mental Deficiency, 47*, 415-421.

Sarason, S. B. (1953). *Psychological problems in mental deficiency.* New York: Harper & Brothers.

Sarason, S. B. (1972). *The creation of settings and the future societies.* San Francisco: Jossey-Bass.

Sarason, S. B., & Doris, J. (1969). *Psychological problems in mental deficiency* (Ed. 4). New York: Harper and Row.

Sarason, S. B., & Gladwin, T. (1958). Psychological and cultural problems in mental subnormality. In R. Masland, S. Sarason, & T. Gladwin (Eds.), *Mental subnormality.* New York: Basic Books.

Scanlon, P. L. (1978). Social work with the mentally retarded client. *Social Casework, 8*, 161-166.

Schalock, R. L., Foley, J., Toulouse, A., & Stark, J. A. (1985). Medication and programming in controlling the behavior of mentally retarded individuals in community settings. *American Journal of Mental Deficiency, 89*, 503-509.

Schalock, R. L., & Harper, R. (1978). Placement from community-based mental retardation programs: How well do clients do? *American Journal of Mental Deficiency, 83*, 240-247.

Schalock, R. L., Harper, R. S., & Genung, T. (1981). Community integration of mentally retarded adults: Community placement and program success. *American Journal of Mental Deficiency, 85*, 478-488.

Schalock, R. L., & Keith, K. D. (1993). *Quality of Life Questionnaire Manual.* Worthington, OH: IDS Publishing Corporation..

Schalock, R. L., Stark, J. A., Snell, M. G., Coulter, D. L., Polloway, E. A., Luckasson, R., Reiss, S., & Spitalnik, D. M. (in press). The changing conception of mental retardation: Implications for the field. *Mental Retardation.*

Scheerenberger, R. C. (1980). *Public residential services for the mentally retarded, 1979.* Madison, WI: National Association of Superintendents of Public Residential Facilities for the Mentally Retarded.

Scheerenberger, R. C. (1983). *A history of mental retardation.* Baltimore, MD: Paul H. Brookes Publishing Co.

Schloss, P. J. (1982). Verbal interaction patterns of depressed and nondepressed institutionalized mentally retarded adults. *Applied Research in Mental Retardation, 3,* 1-12.

Schloss, P. J., Epstein, M. H., & Cullinan, D. (1988). Depression characteristics among mildly handicapped students. *Journal of the Multihandicapped Person, 1,* 293-302.

Schopler, E., Reichler, R., & Renner, B. R. (1988). *The Childhood Anxiety Rating Scale.* Los Angeles: Western Psychological Services.

Schroeder, S. R., Kanoy, R. C., Mulick, J. A., Rojahn, J., Thios, S. J., Stephens, M., & Hawk, B. (1982). In J. H. Hollis & C. E. Meyers (Eds.), *Life threatening behavior: Analysis and intervention.* Washington, DC: American Association on Mental Deficiency. Pp. 105-159.

Schroeder, S. R., Mulick, J. A., & Rojahn, J., (1980). The definition, taxonomy, epidemiology, and ecology of self-injurious behavior. *Journal of Autism and Developmental Disorders, 10,* 417-432.

Schuyler, D. (1974). *The depressive spectrum.* New York: Jason Aronsin.

Seligman, M. E. P. (1975). *Helplessness: On depression, development and death.* San Francisco: W. H. Freeman.

Seltzer, M. M., & Seltzer, G. B. (1985). The elderly mentally retarded: A group in need of service. In G. Getzei & J. Mellor (Eds.), *Gerontological social work practice in the community.* New York: Haworth Press. Pp. 99-119.

Senatore, V., Matson, J. L., & Kazdin, A. E. (1985). An inventory to assess psychopathology of mentally retarded adults. *American Journal of Mental Deficiency, 89,* 459-466.

Sevin, J. A., Matson, J. L., Coe, D. A., Fee, V. E., & Sevin, B. M. (1991). A comparison and evaluation of three commonly used autism scales. *Journal of Autism and Developmental Disorders, 21,* 417-432.

Sheard, M. H. (1988). Clinical pharmacology of aggressive behavior. *Clinical Neuropharmacology, 11,* 483-492.

Shneidman, E. S. (1968). Classification of suicidal phenomena. *Bulletin of Suicidology.* Washington, DC: U.S. Government Printing Office.

Sigman, M. (1985*a*). Individual and group psychotherapy with mentally retarded adolescents. In M. Sigman (Ed.), *Children with emotional disorders and developmental disabilities: Assessment and treatment.* Orlando, FL: Grune & Stratton, Inc. Pp. 259-276.

Sigman, M. (Ed.) (1985*b*). *Children with emotional disorders and developmental disabilities:*

Assessment and treatment. Orlando, FL: Grune & Stratton, Inc.

Silver, J. M., & Yudofsky, S. C. (1985). Propanolol in the treatment of chronically hospitalized violent patients. In C. Shasass, R. C. Josiassen, W. H. Bridger, K. J. Weiss, D. Stoff, & G. M. Simpson (Eds.), *Biological psychiatry.* New York: Elsevier Science. Pp. 174-176.

Silverman, W. K., Flesig, W., Rabian, B., & Peterson, R. A. (1991). Childhood Anxiety Sensitivity Index. *Journal of Clinical Child Psychology, 20,* 162-168.

Silvestri, R. (1977). Implosive therapy treatment of emotionally disturbed retardates. *Journal of Consulting and Clinical Psychology, 45,* 14-22.

Simmons, J. Q. (1968). Emotional problems in mental retardation — Utilization of psychiatric services. *Pediatric Clinics of North America, 15,* 957-967.

Singh, N. N., Donatelli, L. S., Best, A., Williams, D. E., Barrera, F. J., Lenz, M. W., Landrum, T. J., Ellis, C. R., & Moe, T. L. (1993). Factor structure of the Motivation Assessment Scale. *Journal of Intellectual Disability Research, 37,* 65-74.

Singh, N. N., & Millichamp, C. J. (1985). Pharmacological treatment of self-injurious behavior in mentally retarded persons. *Journal of Autism and Developmental Disorders, 15,* 257-267.

Skinner, B. F. (1948). *Walden two.* New York: Macmillan.

Skinner, B. F. (1953). *Science and human behavior.* New York: Macmillan.

Skinner, B. F. (1963). Operant behavior. *American Psychologist, 18,* 503-515.

Skinner, B. F. (1969). *Contingencies of reinforcement: A theoretical analysis.* Englewood Cliffs, NJ: Prentice-Hall.

Smith, D. C., Valenti-Hein, D., & Heller, T. (1985). Interpersonal competence and community adjustment of retarded adults. In M. Sigman (Ed.), *Children with emotional disorders and developmental disabilities: Assessment and treatment.* Orlando, FL: Grune & Stratton, Inc. Pp. 71-94

Smith, S. E. (1993). Cognitive deficits associated with Fragile X sydrome. *Mental Retardation, 31,* 279-283.

Smull, M. W. (1988). Systems issues in meeting the mental health needs of persons with mental retardation. In J. A. Stark, F. J. Menolascino, M. H. Albarelli, & V. C. Gray (Eds.), *Mental retardation and mental health: Classification, diagnosis, treatment, services.* New York: Springer-Verlag. Pp. 394-398.

Smull, M. W., Fabian, E. S., & Chanteau, F. B. (1984). A special program for mentally retarded/mentally ill citizens: The Rock Creek Foundation. In F. J. Menolascino & J. A. Stark

(Eds.), *Handbook of mental illness in the mentally retarded.* New York: Plenum. Pp. 235-248.

Smull, M. W., Fabian, E. S, & Chanteau, F. B. (1984). Value-based programming for the dually diagnosed. The Rock Creek Model. In F. J. Menolascino & J. A. Stark (Eds.), *Handbook of mental illness in the mentally retarded.* New York: Plenum. Pp. 235-248.

Smull, M. W., & Harrison, S. B. (1992). *Supporting people with severe reputations in the community.* Alexandria, VA: National Association of State Mental Retardation Program Directors, Inc.

Sokol, M. S., & Campbell, M. (1988). Novel psychoactive agents in the treatment of developmental disorders. In M. G. Aman & N. N. Singh (Eds.), *Psychopharmacology of the developmental disabilities.* New York: Springer-Verlag. Pp. 146-167.

Sovner, R. (1986). Limiting factors in the use of DSM-III criteria with mentally ill/mentally retarded persons. *Psychopharmacology Bulletin, 22,* 1055-1059.

Sovner, R. (1989). The use of valproate in the treatment of mentally retarded persons with typical and atypical bipolar disorders. *Journal of Clinical Psychiatry, 50,* (3rd supplement), 40-43.

Sovner, R. (1991). Divalproex-response rapid cycling bipolar disorder in a patient with Down syndrome: Implications for the Down's syndrome-mania hypothesis. *Journal of Mental Deficiency Research, 35,* 171-173.

Sovner, R., Fox, C. J., Lowry, M. J., & Lowry, M. A. (1993). Fluoxetine treatment of depression and associated injury in two adults with mental retardation. *Journal of Intellectual Disability Research, 37,* 301-311.

Sovner, R., & Hurley, A. D. (1983*a*). The mental status examination. Part I: Behavior, speech and thought. *Psychiatric Aspects of Mental Retardation, 2,* 5-8.

Sovner, R., & Hurley, A. D. (1983*b*). The mental status examination. Part II. *Psychiatric Aspects of Mental Retardation, 2,* 9-12.

Sovner, R., & Hurley, A. D. (1983*c*). Do the mentally retarded suffer from affective illness? *Archives of General Psychiatry, 40,* 61-67.

Sovner, R., & Hurley, A. D. (1985). Assessing the quality of psychotropic drug regimens prescribed for mentally retarded persons. *Psychiatric Aspects of Mental Retardation Reviews, 8/9,* 31-38.

Sovner, R., & Hurley, A. D. (1986). Drug profiles II Mesoridazine and Thioridazine. *Psychiatric Aspects of Mental Retardation Reviews, 5,* 27-37.

Sovner, R., Hurley, A. D., & Labrie, R. (1985). Is mania incompatible with Down syndrome? *British Journal of Psychiatry, 46,* 319-320.

Spinner, D., & Pfeifer, G. (1986). Group psychotherapy with ego impaired children: The

significance of peer group culture in the evaluation of a holding environment. *International Journal of Group Psychotherapy, 36,* 427-446.

Spirrison, C. L. (1992). *Personality and adults with mental retardation: Structure and independence from intelligence.* Paper presented at the annual meeting of the American Association on Mental Retardation, New Orleans.

Spitzer, R. L., & Fleiss, J. L. (1974). A reanalysis of the reliability of psychiatric diagnosis. *British Journal of Psychiatry, 125,* 341-347.

Sprague, R. L. (1984). *The sad saga of support for research on the psychopharmacology of developmentally disabled people.* Paper presented at the 1984 annual meeting of the American Association on Mental Deficiency in Minneapolis, Minnesota.

Sprague, R .L., Kalachnik, J. E., & White, D. M. (1985). *Dyskinesia Identification System: Condensed User Scale (DISCUS).* Unpublished instrument, Institute for Child Behavior and Development, University of Illinois at Urbana-Champaign.

Sprengler, P. M., Strohmer, D. C., & Prout, H. T. (1990). Testing the robustness of diagnostic overshadowing bias. *American Journal on Mental Retardation, 95,* 204-273.

Stamatelos, T., & Mott, D. (1985). Creative potential among persons labeled developmentally delayed. *The Arts in Psychotherapy, 12,* 101-113.

Stark, J. A., Menolascino, F. J., Albarelli, M. H., & Gray, V. C. (Eds.). (1988). *Mental retardation and mental health: Classification, diagnosis, treatment, services.* New York: Springer-Verlag.

Stavrakaki, C., & Klein, J. (1986). Psychotherapies with the mentally retarded. *Psychiatric Clinics of North America, 9,* 733-743.

Steffenburg, S., & Gillberg, C. (1986). Autism and autistic-like conditions in Swedish rural and urban areas: A population study. *British Journal of Psychiatry, 149,* 81-87.

Stephens, E. (1953). Defensive reactions of mentally retarded adults. *Social Casework, 34,* 119-124.

Sternlicht, M. (1965). Psychotherapeutic techniques useful with the mentally retarded: A review and critique. *Psychiatric Quarterly, 39,* 84-90.

Sternlicht, M. (1966). Psychotherapeutic procedures with the retarded. In N. R. Ellis (Ed.), *International review of research in mental retardation.* New York: Academic Press.

Sternlicht, M. (1979). Fears of institutionalized mentally retarded adults. *The Journal of Psychology, 101,* 67-71.

Sternlicht, M., Pustel, G., & Deutsch, M. R. (1970). Suicidal tendencies among institutionalized

retardates. *Journal of Mental Subnormality,* **16**, 93-102.

Sternlicht, M., & Silverg, E. F. (1965). The relationship between fantasy aggression and overt hostility in mental retardation. *American Journal of Mental Deficiency,* **70**, 819-821.

Strohmer, D. C., Prout, H. T., & Gorsky, J. (1994). The development of a personality inventory for adolescents and adults with mild mental retardation and borderline intelligence. *Assessment in Rehabilitation and Exceptionality,* **1**, 78-89.

Sturmey, P., & Bertman, L. J. (1993). *The validity of the Reiss Screen for Maladaptive Behavior.* Unpublished manuscript, Abilene (Texas) State School.

Sturmey, P., & Ley, T. (1990). The Psychopathology Instrument for Mentally Retarded Adults: Internal consistencies and relationship to behavior problems. *British Journal of Psychiatry,* **156**, 428-430.

Sturmey, P., Matson, J. L., & Sevin, J. A. (1992). Brief report: Analysis of the internal consistency of three autism scales. *Journal of Autism and Developmental Disorders,* **22**, 321-328.

Sturmey, P., Reed, J., & Corbett, J. (1991). Psychometric assessment of psychiatric disorders in people with learning difficulties (mental handicap): A review of measures. *Psychological Medicine,* **21**, 143-155.

Sudhalter, V., Scarborough, H. S., & Cohen, I. L. (1991). Syntactic delay and pragmatic deviance in the language of fragile X males. *American Journal of Medical Genetics,* **38**, 493-497.

Suomi, S. J., Eiselle, C. D., Grady, S. A., & Harlow, H. F. (1975). Depressive behavior in adult monkeys following separation from family environment. *Journal of Abnormal Psychology,* **84**, 576-578.

Sushinsky, L. W., & Wener, R. (1975). Distorting judgments of mental health. *Journal of Nervous and Mental Disease,* **161**, 82-89.

Svec, H. J. (in press). Use of hypnosis as a technique for persons with dual diagnosis. *NADD Newsletter.*

Szymanski, L. S. (1977). Psychiatric diagnostic evaluation of mentally retarded individuals. *Journal of the American Academy of Child Psychiatry,* **16**, 67-87.

Szymanski, L. S. (1980a). Individual psychotherapy with retarded persons. In L. S. Szymanski & P. E. Tanguay (Eds.), *Emotional disorders of mentally retarded persons: Assessment, treatment, and consultation.* Baltimore, MD: University Park Press. Pp. 131-148.

Szymanski, L. S. (1980b). Psychiatric diagnosis in retarded persons. In L. S. Szymanski, & P. E. Tanguay (Eds.), *Emotional disorders of mentally retarded persons: Assessment, treatment, and consultation.* Baltimore, MD: University Park Press.

Szymanski, L. S. (1985). Diagnosis of mental disorders in mentally retarded persons. In M. Sigman (Ed.), *Children with emotional disorders and developmental disabilities: Assessment and treatment.* Orlando, FL: Grune & Stratton, Inc. Pp. 249-258.

Szymanski, L. S. (1993, November). Personal communication.

Szymanski, L. S., & Biederman, J. (1984). Depression and anorexia nervosa of persons with down syndrome. *American Journal of Mental Deficiency, 89,* 246-251.

Szymanski, L. S., & Doherty, M. (1981). Mental illness in mildly-moderately retarded adults. *American Psychiatric Association Annual Meeting 1981 Syllabus and Scientific Proceedings.* Washington, DC: American Psychiatric Association. Pp. 84-85.

Szymanski, L., & Grossman, H. (1984). Dual implications of "dual diagnosis." *Mental Retardation, 22,* 155-156.

Szymanski, L. S., & Kiernan, W. E. (1983). Multiple family group therapy with developmentally disabled adolescents and young adults. *International Journal of Group Psychotherapy, 33,* 521-534.

Szymanski, L. S., & Rosefsky, Q. B. (1980). Group psychotherapy with retarded persons. In L. S. Szymanski & P. E. Tanguay (Eds.), *Emotional disorders of mentally retarded persons: Assessment, treatment, and consultation.* Baltimore: University Park Press. Pp. 173-194.

Szymanski, L. S., & Tanguay, P. E. (1980). *Emotional disorders of mentally retarded persons.* Baltimore: University Park Press.

Talbott, J. (1980). An indepth look at DSM-III: An interview with Robert Spitzer. *Hospital and Community Psychiatry, 31,* 25-32.

Talkington, L. W., & Hall, S. M. (1968). Use of a frustration technique to reinstate speech in non-verbal retarded. *American Journal of Mental Deficiency, 73,* 496-499.

Tanguay, P. E., & Szymanski, L. S. (1980). Training mental health professionals in mental retardation. L.. S. Szymanski & P. E. Tanguay (Eds.), *Emotional disorders of mentally retarded persons: Assessment, treatment, and consultation.* Baltimore: University Park Press.

Tarjan, G. (1977). Mental retardation and clinical psychiatry. In P. Mittler (Ed.), *Research to practice in mental retardation: Care and intervention.* Vol. 1. Baltimore: University Park Press. Pp. 401-407.

Tarjan, G., Dornbusch, S. M, Fenichel, G., Graham, F., Richmond, J., & Zigler, E. (1977). *Federal research activity in mental retardation: A review with recommendations for the future.* Unpublished report to Directors of NICHD/NIMH.

Taylor, D. V., Hetrick, W. P., Neri, C. L., Touchette, P., Barron, J. L., & Sandman, C. A. (1991).

Effect of naltrexone upon self-injurious behavior, learning and activity: A case study. *Pharmacology, Biochemistry & Behavior, 40,* 79-82.

Taylor, S. J. (1987). Continuum traps. In S. J. Taylor, D. Biklen, & J. Knoll (Eds.), *Community integration for people with severe disabilities.* New York: Teachers College Press. Pp. 25-35.

Taylor, S. J. (1991). Community living in three Wisconsin counties. In S. J. Taylor, R. Bogdan, & J. A. Rocino (Eds.), *Life in the community: Case studies of organizations supporting people with disabilities.* Baltimore: Paul H. Brookes Publishing Co.

Tebeest, D. L., & Dickie, J. R. (1976). Responses to frustration: Comparison of institutionalized and noninstitutionalized retarded adolescents and nonretarded children and adolescents. *American Journal of Mental Deficiency, 80,* 407-413.

Thompson, T., Axtell, S., & Schaal, D. W. (1993). Self-injurious behavior: Mechanisms and intervention. In J. L. Matson & R. P. Barrett (Eds.), *Psychopathology in the mentally retarded* (2nd ed.). Needham Heights, MA: Allyn and Bacon.

Thompson, T., Gardner, W. I., & Baumeister, A. (1988). Ethical issues in interventions for persons with retardation, autism, and related developmental disorders. In J. A. Stark, F. J. Menolascino, M. H. Albarelli, & V. C. Gray (Eds.), *Mental retardation and mental health: Classification, diagnosis, treatment, services.* New York: Springer-Verlag.

Thorne, F. C. (1947). The problem of institutional elopements. *American Journal of Mental Deficiency, 51,* 637-643.

Thorne, F. C. (1948). Counseling and psychotherapy with mental defectives. *American Journal of Mental Deficiency, 52,* 263-271.

Tonge, B., & Einfeld, S. (1991). Intellectual disability and psychopathology in Australian children. *Australia & New Zealand Journal of Developmental Disabilities, 17,* 155-167.

Truax, C. B., & Mitchell, K. M. (1971). Research on certain therapist interpersonal skills in relation to process and outcome. In A. E. Bergin & S. L. Garfield (Eds.), *Handbook of psychotherapy and behavior change.* New York: Wiley.

Tu, J. B. (1979). A survey of psychotropic medication in mental retardation facilities. *Journal of Clinical Psychiatry, 40,* 125-128.

Tu, J. B., & Smith, J. T. (1983). Factors associated with psychotropic medications in mental retardation facilities. *Comprehensive Psychiatry, 20,* 289-295.

Tupin, J. P. (1978). Usefulness of lithium for aggressiveness. *American Journal of Psychiatry, 135,* 11-18.

Turnbull, H. R. (1988). Fifteen questions: Ethical inquiries in mental retardation. In J. A. Stark,

F. J. Menolascino, M. H. Albarelli, & V. C. Gray (Eds.), *Mental retardation and mental health: Classification, diagnosis, treatment, services*. New York: Springer-Verlag. Pp. 368-377.

Tyrer, P., & Seivewright, N. (1988). Pharmacological treatment of personality disorders. *Clinical Neuropharmacology, 11*, 493-499.

Tyrer, P., Walsh, P., & Edwards, D. E. (1984). Factors associated with a good response to lithium in aggressive mentally handicapped subjects. *Progress in Neuropsychopharmacology and Biological Psychiatry, 8*, 751-755.

Ullmann, L. P., & Krasner, L. (Eds.) (1965). *Case studies in behavior modification*. New York: Holt, Rinehart, and Winston, Inc.

Valenti-Hein, D. C., & Mueser, K. T. (1990). *The dating skills program: Teaching social-sexual skills to adults with mental retardation*. Worthington, OH: IDS Publishing Corporation.

Van Minnen, A., Hoelsgens, I., & Hoogduin, K. A. (1993). *Decisions in inpatient versus outpatient treatment of mildly mentally retarded adults with psychiatric disorders*. Unpublished manuscript, University of Nijmegen.

Van Minnen, A., & Hoogduin, K. (1994, in press *a*). *Dutch version of the PIMRA*. Worthington, OH: IDS Publishing Corporation.

Van Minnen, A., & Hoogduin, K. (1994, in press *b*). *Dutch version of the Reiss Screen*. Worthington, OH: IDS Publishing Corporation.

Viney, L., Clark, A., & Lord, J. (1973). Resistance to extinction and frustration in retarded and non-retarded children. *American Journal of Mental Deficiency, 78*, 308-315.

Vitiello, B., Spreat, S., & Behard, D. (1989). Obsessive-compulsive disorder in mentally retarded patients. *Journal of Nervous and Mental Disease, 177*, 233-235.

Wagner, P. (1991). Developmentally based personality assessments of adults with mental retardation. *Mental Retardation, 29*, 87-92.

Ward, M. R., & Corbett, J. A. (1989). Neuroleptic malignant syndrome with hypomania and mental retardation. *Journal of Mental Deficiency Research, 33*, 339-342.

Watson, J. E., Aman, M. G., & Singh, N. N. (1988). The Psychopathology Instrument for Mentally Retarded Adults: Psychometric characteristics, factor structure, and relationship to subject characteristics. *Research in Developmental Disabilities, 9*, 277-290.

Weaver, T. R. (1946). The incident of maladjustment among mental defectives in military environment. *American Journal of Mental Deficiency, 51*, 238-246.

Webster, T. (1963). Problems of emotional development in young retarded children. *American*

Journal of Psychiatry, 120, 37-43.

Webster, T. (1970). Unique aspects of emotional development in mentally retarded children. In F. J. Menolascino (Ed.), *Psychiatric approaches to mental retardation.* New York: Basic Books. Pp. 3-54.

Weisz, J. (1979). Perceived control and learned helplessness among mentally retarded and nonretarded children: A developmental analysis. *Developmental Psychology, 15,* 311-319.

Weisz, J. (1981). Effect of the "mentally retarded" label on adult judgments about child failure. *Journal of Abnormal Psychology, 90,* 371-374.

Weisz, J. (1982). Learned helplessness and the retarded child. In E. Zigler & D. Balla (Eds.), *Mental retardation: The developmental-difference controversy.* Hillsdale, NJ: Erlbaum. Pp. 27-40.

Werry, J., & Aman, M. G. (1993). *Practitioner's guide to psychoactive drugs for children and adolescents.* New York: Plenum.

Werry, J., Methuen, R., Fitzpatrick, J., & Dixon, H. (1983). The interrater reliability of DSM-III in children. *Journal of Abnormal Child Psychiatry, 11,* 341-354.

White, C. C., Latkin, K. C., Bruininks, R. H., & Li, X. (1991). *Persons with mental retardation and related conditions in state-operated residential facilities: Year ending June 30, 1989 with longitudinal trends from 1950 to 1989.* Unpublished manuscript, Center for Residential and Community Studies, University of Minnesota.

Whitman, T. L. (1990). Self-regulation and mental retardation. *American Journal on Mental Retardation, 94,* 347-363.

Widaman, F. J., MacMillan, K. F., Hemsley, D. L., Little, R. E., & Balow, I. H. (1992). Differences in adolescents' self-concept as a function of academic level, ethnicity, and gender. *American Journal on Mental Retardation, 96,* 387-403.

Williams, G. A., & Asher, S. R. (1992). Assessment of loneliness at school among children with mild mental retardation. *American Journal on Mental Retardation, 96,* 357-366.

Williams, P., & Shoultz, B. (1984). *We can speak for ourselves: Self-advocacy by mentally handicapped people.* Bloomington: Indiana University Press.

Wolkowitz, O. (1990). Use of the Dexamethasone Suppression Test with mentally retarded persons: Reviews and recommendations. *American Journal on Mental Retardation, 94,* 509-514.

Wolpe, J. (1958). *Psychotherapy by reciprocal inhibition.* Palo Alto: Stanford University Press.

Woodward, H.L. (1993). *One community's response to the multi-system needs of individuals with mental stress and developmental disabilities.* Unpublished manuscript, University Affiliated Cincinnati Center for Developmental Disabilities, University of Cincinnati.

Woodward, H. L., & Pederson, E. L. (1991). *A model for developing mental retardation/mental illness intervention services in existing community mental health centers.* Cincinnati, OH: University Affiliated Cincinnati Center for Developmental Disabilities.

Wright, B. A. (1948). Counseling and psychotherapy with mental defectives. *American Journal of Mental Deficiency,* 52, 263-271.

Wright, E. C. (1982). The presentation of mental illness in mentally retarded adults. *British Journal of Psychiatry,* 141, 496-502.

Yudofsky, S. C., Silver, J. M., & Schneider, S. E. (1987). Pharmacologic treatment of aggression. *Psychiatric Annals,* 17, 397-406.

Zarcone, J. R., Rodgers, T. A., Iwata, B. A., Rourke, D. A., & Dorsey, M .F. (1991). Reliability analysis of the Motivation Assessment Scale: A failure to replicate. *Research in Developmental Disabilities,* 12, 349-360.

Zarfas, D. E. (1988). Mental health systems for people with mental retardation: A Canadian perspective. *Australia and New Zealand Journal of Developmental Disabilities,* 14, 3-7.

Zeaman, D., & House, B. J. (1963). The role of attention in retardate discrimination learning. In N. R. Ellis (Ed.), *Handbook of mental deficiency: Psychological theory and research.* New York: McGraw-Hill. Pp. 159-223.

Zetlin, A. G., & Turner, J. L. (1982, March). *Coping with adolescence: Perspectives of retarded individuals and their families.* Paper presented at the Gatlinburg Conference on Research in Mental Retardation, Gatlinburg, TN.

Zetlin, A. G., & Turner, J. L. (1984). Self-perspectives on being handicapped: Stigma and adjustment. In R. Edgerton (Ed.), Lives in progress: Mentally retarded adults in a large city. *AAMD Monograph,* 6, 93-120.

Zigler, E. (1967). Familial mental retardation: A continuing dilemma. *Science,* 155, 292-298.

Zigler, E. (1971). The retarded child as a whole person. In H. E. Adams & W. K. Boardman (Eds.), *Advances in experimental clinical psychology.* New York: Pergamon Press. Pp. 47-121.

Zigler, E., & Burack, J. (1989). Personality development and the dually diagnosed person. *Research in Developmental Disabilities,* 10, 225-240.

Zigler, E., & Harter, S. (1969). The socialization of the mentally retarded. In D. A. Goslin (Ed.), *Handbook of socialization theory and research.* Chicago: Rand McNally. Pp. 1065-1102.
Zilboorg, G., & Henry, G. (1941). *A history of medical psychology.* New York: W. W. Norton.

Zingarelli, G., Ellman, G., Hom, A., Wymore, M., Heidorn, S., & Chicz-DeMet, C. (1992). Clinical effects of naltrexone on autistic behavior. *American Journal on Mental Retardation,* 97, 57-63.

Zubin, A., Eron, L.D., & Schumer, F. (1965). *An experimental approach to projective techniques.* New York: John Wiley & Sons.

Zung, W. (1965). A self-rating depression scale. *Archives of General Psychiatry, 29,* 328-337.

Zung, W. (1971). A rating instrument for anxiety disorders. *Psychosomatics, 12,* 371-379.

SUBJECT INDEX

AAUAP, 176

Abbreviated Teaching Rating Scale, 132

Aberrant Behavior Checklist, 31, 42, 122-123, 128

abuse, 25-26

adaptive behavior, new AAMR concept, 92

Administration on Developmental Disabilities, 209

advocacy, 182-185, 187, 189-191, 204

affect, 50

aggression, 70-71, 73-76, 166-168, 178-179, 197-198, 208

aging
  depression, 59

agoraphobia (see Panic Disorder)

alcoholism (see substance abuse)

alprazolam, 167

American Association on Mental Retardation, 91-92, 186, 189

Americans with Disabilities Act, 189-190

amitriptyline, 166

amphetamines, 168

anger, 56-57, 71, 140, 161

anger management therapy, 28, 161-163, 178

anorexia nervosa, 54, 88-89, 179

anticonvulsants, 167, 179

antidepressant drugs, 166, 179

antimanics, 166, 179

antisocial behavior, 4, 57, 109

Antisocial Personality Disorder, 71-72, 75

anxiety, 13, 44, 49-50, 167

Anxiety Disorders, 4, 44-50
  assessment, 127
  DSM-IV, 44
  epidemiology, 45

treatment, 176

anxiety sensitivity, 30, 47, 155

anxiolytics, 167

Apperceptive Personality Test, 134

Apperceptive Personality Test/Mental Retardation, 134-136

Arc, 93, 176, 182-183, 189, 191

artistic therapies, 142, 145-146, 179

Asperger syndrome, 21

assertiveness
  inappropriate, 28

assessment information (also see psychiatric diagnosis), 103-106

Attention-Deficit Disorder, 42, 84-86, 132, 167, 179

attention-seeking, 33, 72, 140

Australia, 187

autism, 5, 20-21, 64, 71, 130, 168, 177

Autism Behavior Checklist, 130

aversives/nonaversives, 158, 190

Avoidant Personality Disorder, 70

baseline exaggeration, 102

Beacon House, 201

behavior analysis (also see behavior therapy), 50, 76, 181-182, 186, 196, 211

Behavior Problem Checklist, 11, 86

Behavior Problem Inventory, 132

behavior therapy, 149-159, 170, 177, 179

Bellevue Index of Depression, 130

benzodiazepines, 167

beta blockers, 168, 179

Bipolar Disorder, 50, 52-53, 61, 101, 166-167

blunted affect, 62, 65

Borderline Personality Disorder, 72

buspirone, 167

Canada, 187
carbamazepine, 167-168, 177, 179
catatonia, 62, 65
causality, 78
cerebral palsy, 191
challenging behavior (also see
    epidemiology & specific
    disorders)
    broadening concept, 41
    consequences, 4-5
    persistence over time, 5-6
chemical restraint, 173
Childhood Anxiety Sensitivity Index,
    47
Childhood Autism Rating Scale, 130
Children's Depression Inventory, 129
chlordiazepoxide, 167
chlorpromazine, 164-165, 178
choice, 205
client-centered model/therapy, 141-
    142, 144-145, 205-207
client outcome factors, 148
clinical psychology, 41-43
clinical syndrome, 2, 68-69
cloak of competence phenomenon,
    101
cognitive consistency, 80
cognitive rigidity, 33
cognitive therapy, 159-163, 177, 179
co-morbidity, 1, 63-64
Competence Assessment to Stand
    Trial, 132, 211
communication theory, 34, 78, 153-
    155
Community Mental Health Centers,
    184
conditions of worth, 141-142
Conners Rating Scale, 85
construct validity (see validity
    concepts)

consumer demand, 15, 198
conversion symptoms, 83
coping statements, 162
correlation statistics (see kappa
    statistic & Pearson product
    moment coefficient)
counseling (also see psychodynamic
    model), 144
countertransference, 143
covert sensitization, 160
creation of settings, 191-193
criminal offenders, 76-77, 82-83, 203
crises intervention, 189, 197-198

dance therapy (see artistic therapies)
day services, 200-201
defensiveness, 50, 139-141
    denial, 29, 110, 141
    distortion, 110
    feelings of inadequacy, 29
    intellectualism, 141
    projection, 141
    rationalization, 141
    repression, 140
degenerative trait, 63-64
De Lange syndrome, 21, 77
delusions, 62-63, 66, 178
dementia, 59
dementia praecox, 61
denial (see defensiveness)
Dependent Personality Disorder, 70,
depression (see Mood Disorder)
desipramine, 166
Developmental Disabilities Act, 183,
    189, 209, 210
Developmental Disabilities Child
    Behavior Checklist, 126
developmental psychology
    depression, 54

psychoanalysis, 140
psychopathology, 41-43
Dexamethasone Suppression Test, 137-138
Diagnostic Assessment Instrument for the Severely Handicapped, 123-124
diagnostic overshadowing, 9-10, 36-38, 187
Diagnostic & Statistical Manuals (see psychiatric diagnosis & specific psychopathology categories)
Dissociative Disorders, 87
diazepam, 167
divalproex sodium, 177
dopamine, 62
Down Syndrome, 19, 28, 54, 87
Draw-A-Person Test, 133
DRI, 151-152, 178
DRO, 151-152, 179
drugs (see psychopharmacology)
dual diagnosis, 2, 96
DISCUS, 174
Dysthymia, 51

Eating Disorders, 88-89, 179
ego psychologists, 141
Emotional Disorders Rating Scale, 126
epidemiology, 6-19
    age, 15-18
    children, 17
    definition of MR, 16
    Down Syndrome, 19
    elderly, 17
    levels of MR, 18-19
    mental disorders, 16
    personality disorders, 16
    research methods, 9
    residential setting, 12

special vulnerability of MR, 10-11
    types, 12-15
exhibitionism, 81
expectations (also see placebo)
    behavior therapy, 150
    failure, 29, 58-59
    interviewing, 111
exposure therapy, 150, 176
extinction, 152

Factitious Disorder, 84
factor analysis, 108-109
factor content validity (see validity concepts)
families, 24-25, 178, 195-196, 200
fear (see anxiety sensitivity, phobia)
fear of abandonment, 72
federal funding, 183
feelings of inadequacy (see defensiveness)
fenfluramine, 168
fetishism, 81
fluspirilene, 178
fluoxetine, 179
foster parents, 196
Fragile X syndrome, 19-20
friendship, 24, 27-28
froteurism, 81-82
frustration-aggression hypothesis, 74
functional analysis, 153

gender differences
    criminal behavior, 77
    depression, 52-53
generalization of training effects, 28-29, 156-157
Generalized Anxiety Disorder, 49-50
gentle teaching, 144-145, 207

group therapy (also see
    psychodynamic models), 144

Haldol (see haloperidol)
hallucinations, 62-63, 66-67, 178
haloperidol, 166, 168
Hand-Test, 135
Hamilton Depression Rating Scale,
    129
Histrionic Personality Disorder, 72
home-based treatment, 196
homosexuality, 69
housing, 203-204
hyperactivity, 84
hypochondriasis, 83
hypnosis, 150
hysteria, 83

impiramine, 166
implosive therapy (see exposure
    therapy)
impulsiveness, 72
incest, 82
inclusion, 91-92
Inderal (see propranolol)
infantilization, 26
informant measures (also see specific
    instruments), 110-112
inpatient services, 201-203
institutionalization, 24-25, 181-182,
    203
intellectualization (see defensiveness)
intelligence & IQ tests, 93-94
interagency cooperation, 188-189
internal vs. external disorders, 42-43
internal reliability (see reliability
    concepts & specific instruments)
International Classification of

Diseases, 73, 131
interrater reliability (see reliability
    concepts & specific instruments)
interviewing, 104-105, 142
ISDD Mental Health Program, 15,
    198-199
issue avoidance, 38-39

jealousy, 71

kappa statistic, 98-99
Knox v. Hughes, 210

la belle indifference, 83
labels, 22-23, 26
learned helplessness, 57-59, 160
legal issues, 210-211
legal services, 210
leisure, 25
Lesch-Nyhan syndrome, 21, 77
Librium, 167
Lifestyle Satisfaction Scale, 137
lithium carbonate, 166, 168, 177, 179
locus of control, 28
loneliness, 26-28
Loneliness Questionnaire, 129
Louisville Survey Schedule, 46, 127

Major Depression, 51
maladaptive behavior (also see
    challenging behavior), 2
MAOIs, 166
mania (see Bipolar Disorder)
masochism, 82
Maternal and Child Health, 209
Mellaril (see thioridazine)

mental health, 39-40
mental health clinics (see outpatient services)
mental health disorders (see challenging behavior)
mental hospitals, 186-187, 195
mental illness (also see specific disorders), 2
mental retardation, AAMR definitions, 91-95
Mental Status Exam, 104
methylphenidate, 167-168
Metro-Area Dual Diagnosis Task Force, 188
minimal brain dysfunction, 84
monoamine oxidase inhibitors (see MAOIs)
Mood Disorders, 4-6, 50-59, 75, 197, 199, 208
    aggression, 55-56
    assessment, 127, 129-130, 137-138
    dementia, 59
    drug therapy, 166-168
    DSM-IV, 51-52
    epidemiology, 13, 52-53
    recognition of occurrence, 50-51
    treatment, 177
MOSES, 175
motivation, 32-34, 58-59
Motivation Assessment Scale, 131
music therapy (see artistic therapies)

NADD, 186, 209-210
naloxone, 168
naltrexone, 168
Nathan v. Levitt, 210
National Association of State Mental Retardation Program

Directors, 188
National Council on Disabilities, 189
Nebraska Psychiatric Institute, 202-203
neologisms, 66
neuroleptic malignant syndrome, 166, 174-175, 179
neuroleptics, 164-166, 171, 178-179
neuroticism, 33
NICHD, 184-185, 190
NIMH, 183-185
Nisonger-The Arc Consensus Study, 175
nonspecific treatment effects (see placebo)
nortriptyline, 166
nurses, 208

obesity
    health, 86
    Prader-Willi syndrome, 21
Obsessive-Compulsive Disorder, 48-49
    assessment, 127
    intelligence, 49
    SIB, 78-80
opiate blockers, 77-78, 168
organic brain syndrome, 208
outpatient services, 198-200
outcome research methods, 147-148
outerdirectedness, 33
overcorrection, 152
overjustification hypothesis, 157-158

panic attacks, 46-47
Panic Disorder, 46-47
Paranoid Personality Disorder, 4, 71, 75
paraphilias, 81

Parkinsonian syndrome, 166
participant modeling, 176
Pavlovian conditioning, 150, 158-159
Peabody Picture Vocabulary Test, 163
Pearson product moment coefficient, 99, 106-107
pedophilia, 81, 82
pemoline, 168
People First, 190-191
percent exact agreement reliability, 106-107
personal futures planning, 204-206
personality development, 32-34, 199
personality disorders, 2, 4, 68-73, 131, 178, 195
personality traits, 2, 13, 68, 154-155, 208
Personality Traits Checklist, 131
phenobarbital, 167
phenothiazines, 166
phobias, 45-46, 127, 176
physical abuse
PTSD, 48
Piaget, 31
placebo, 148, 166, 168, 179
play therapy (see artistic therapies)
polypharmacy, 171, 175
positive self-regard, 142
Posttraumatic Stress Disorder, 47-48, 127
Prader-Willi syndrome, 21
President's Commission on Mental Health, 184-185
President's Committee on Mental Retardation, 176, 183, 185, 188
pretherapy, 144-145, 178-179, 207
prevention, 211-212
primary disabilities, 95-97
PRNs, 170
problem-solving, 162-163

projection (see defensiveness)
projective assessment, 133-135
propranolol, 168, 179
Prosac®, 166
Protection & Advocacy, 210
Prout-Strohmer Personality Inventory, 125-126
psychiatric diagnosis, 97-103, 186, 208
    mental retardation, 100-102
    reliability, 98-99
psychoanalysis (also see psychodynamic models), 139-141
psychodynamic models, 31-32, 139-141, 142-144, 146-149, 179
psychodynamic therapy (see psychodynamic models)
psychometric evaluation criteria, 105-110
psychopathology (also see specific disorders), 2
Psychopathology Inventory for Mentally Retarded Adults, 116, 119-122, 123, 128, 130, 131, 163
psychopharmacology, 163-175, 208
psychosis (also see Schizophrenia), 62, 75, 199, 208
psychosocial masking, 101, 103
punishment, 152

Quality of Life Questionnaire, 137

rapid cycling, 52
rational emotive therapy, 159-160
rationalization (see defensiveness)
Real Life Rating Scale, 130
recidivism, challenging behavior, 197
regression, 42-43, 62, 102-103

Reinforcer Responsiveness Survey, 31
Reiss-Peterson Social Support Scale, 28
Reiss Scales for Children's Dual
    Diagnosis, 6, 53, 84, 117-119, 128
Reiss Screen for Maladaptive Behavior,
    14-15, 18, 43, 70, 112, 115-117,
    128, 131
reliability concepts (also see
    psychiatric diagnosis), 105-107
rejection, 23-24
rejection of success, 80-81
repression (see defensive behavior)
research methods, 67
residential services (also see housing
    & supported living), 186, 188
respite care, 196-197
Revised Fear Survey Schedule for
    Children, 127
Reynolds Child Depression Scale, 130
risk factors
    biological, 19-22
    developmental, 31-34
    personality, 32-34
    psychological, 22-31
Ritalin, 167
Rock Creek Foundation, 200
role-play, 162-163

sadism, 82
Schizophrenia (also see psychosis), 4,
    13, 61-67, 197, 200, 208
    assessment, 130
    drug therapy, 163-164
    therapy, 177-179
secondary disabilities, 95-97
segregation, 24
self-actualization, 141
self-advocacy, 190-191
self-awareness

stigma, 26-27
self-concept, 29, 32, 51, 56, 146
Self-Description Questionnaire, 29
self-injurious behavior, 73, 78-81,
    151, 165-168, 178-179, 181-182,
    197
self-report data, 110-112
Self-Report Depression Questionnaire,
    129
self-report measures (also see specific
    instruments), 110
service barriers, 182-187
service models, 193-203
severe behavior disorders, 2, 13, 73-
    81, 131-132, 151, 165-168, 178-
    179
sex offenders (see criminal offenders)
sexual abuse, 26, 48
Sexual Disorders, 81-83, 132, 179
sexual dysfunction, 81
Sleep Disorders, 88
social desirability, 111
social phobias (see phobias)
social skills, 5, 13, 28-29, 95, 152,
    177, 211
    depression, 54-57
    generalization, 29
    schizophrenia, 65
social support, 27-28, 56, 194
Somatoform Disorder, 83-84
Spain, 187
Speaking for Ourselves, 191
specialized services, 194-195, 202
spontaneous remission, 147
staff burnout, 194
Stand Together, 191
state MR/DD agencies, 182-183, 188-
    189
stereotypies (see self-injurious
    behavior & severe behavior

disorders)
stigmatization, 26-27, 91, 97, 186, 211
stimulants, 167-168
stimulus-based treatment, 151
stress (also see anxiety), 28, 30, 179
Strohmer-Prout Behavior Rating Scale (see Prout-Strohmer Personality Inventory)
substance abuse, 13, 86-87, 160, 208
success motivation, 140
supported living, 204
supportive therapy (see counseling)
supports (see mental retardation, AAMR definitions)
suicide, 59-62, 72
symptom substitution, 158
systematic desensitization (also see exposure therapy), 150, 158-159

tardive dyskinesia, 166, 174
TASH, 93, 186
Tegretol (see carbamazepine)
terminology, 1-4, 187-188
test-retest reliability (see reliability concepts & specific instruments)
Thematic Apperception Test, 133-134
therapist outcome variables, 148
thioridazine, 166
Thorazine (see chlorpromazine)
time-out, 152
training issues, 105, 175, 187-189, 193, 196-197, 199-200, 207-210
tranquilizers (see neuroleptics)
transfer (see generalization)
transference, 141, 143
transitions, 25, 200
transvestism, 82
tricyclic antidepressants, 166

trouble statements, 162

UIC-NIMH International Research Conference, 112-114
unconditional positive regard, 142
unconscious mind (see defensiveness)
underserved population, 1, 35-38
unemployment, 25
United Cerebral Palsy, 189
University-Affiliated Programs, 191, 207-209

validity concepts, 107-110
Valium (see diazepam)
valproic acid, 167, 177
victimization, 25

Xanax, 167

zuclopenthixol, 178
Zung Anxiety Rating Scale, 127
Zung Depression Inventory, 129

AUTHOR INDEX

Abelson, R. P., 97
Abraham, K., 55
Abramson, L. Y., 58
Acocella, J. R., 60, 62-63, 84, 158
Adkins, J., 28
Adler, A., 141
Albarelli, M., 210
Albini, J.L., 148
Allen, D., 202
Allin, D. W., 202, 204
Allin, R. B., 202, 204
Alloy, L. B., 62-63, 84, 158
Almond, P., 130
Aman, M. G., 42, 43, 112, 117, 121-122, 124-125, 164-169, 172, 175
Amsell, L., 138
Andrasik, F., 152
Angelino, R., 30
Anthony, J. C., 52
Arean, P., 162-163
Arick, J., 130
Arnoczky, S. M., 171
Arnold, L. E., 168
Ascher, L. M., 49
Asher, S. R., 23, 28, 129
Axelrod, S., 153
Ayllon, T., 150

Babington, C. M., 168
Baer, D. M., 151
Baker, B. L., 23, 28
Baker, J. A., 110, 129
Ballinger, B. R., 5, 8, 16, 53, 68-69, 73, 131
Balow, E. A., 29, 169
Balow, I. H., 164
Balthazar, E. E., 3
Banavidez, D. A., 129
Bandura, A., 74
Barlow, D. H., 99
Barmann, B. C., 82
Barnes, J., 29

Barrera, F. J., 131
Barrett, R. P., 46, 54, 60, 126
Barron, J. L., 168
Bassett, A. S., 99
Batchelor, I. R. C., 65
Bates, W. J., 171
Bauman, K. E., 153
Baumeister, A., 158
Bechtel, D. R., 152
Beck, A. T., 59, 160
Beckwith, B. E., 138
Begab, M. J., 94
Behard, D., 48-49
Beier, D. C., 5
Beiser, M., 99
Bell, R. C., 69
Bem, D. J., 36
Bemporad, J., 168
Benavidez, D. A., 129
Benson, B. A., 6, 22, 26, 28, 39, 45, 50-51, 56, 60, 76, 110-112, 129, 134, 160, 163, 168, 188
Berberich, J. P., 151
Bergin, A. E., 146
Berkson, G., 24
Berney, T. P., 53
Bernstein, N., 143
Bertman, L. J., 115-117, 125
Best, A., 131
Beveridge, M., 34
Bialer, I., 1
Bick, P., 168
Bicknell, J., 18, 198
Biederman, J., 50, 53-54, 88-89, 179
Bihm, E. M., 31, 122, 131
Bijou, S. W., 151
Bishop, A. C., 169
Bittle, R. G., 29
Blacher, J., 23
Bleuler, E., 61
Blunden, R., 14, 202
Boggs, E. M., 186
Boo, S., 8

Bootzin, R., 60, 62-63, 84, 156, 158
Borkovec, T. D., 148
Borthwick-Duffy, S. A., 5, 7, 9, 12, 16-18, 77, 79
Bouras, N., 45, 71, 88-89, 100, 179, 200, 202
Bouthilet, G. N., 132
Boyd, J. H., 52
Boyd, R. D., 166, 174
Braddock, D., 88
Brizer, D. A., 168
Brooks, D., 100, 200
Brown, K. W., 28
Brown, M. G., 84
Brown, R. I., 60
Brown, T. A., 99
Brown, W. T., 21
Bruininks, R. H., 5, 7, 12, 16, 42, 164, 169
Brunschwig, A., 20
Buchsbaum, S., 164
Burack, J., 33, 34
Burkhart, J. E., 88
Burke, J. D., 52

Cain, N., 17
Calamari, J. E., 16, 49, 168, 174
Call, T., 5
Campbell, I., 2
Cantwell, M. D., 94
Carr, E. G., 34, 73, 78, 153, 202
Carsrud, A. L., 18
Carsrud, K. I., 18
Carver, M., 170
Cautela, J. R., 160
Chacot, J. M., 139
Chadsey-Rusch, J., 25
Chanteau, F. B., 200-201
Charlot, L. R., 53
Chess, S., 8, 17,
Chicz-DeMet, C., 168

Chidester, L., 148
Chiodo, J., 46
Chitty, D., 8
Clark, A., 30
Clark, D. B., 196
Clarke, D. J., 21, 65, 169, 178
Clements, J. D., 94
Coe, D. A., 6, 123, 130
Cohen, I. L., 21
Collacott, R. A., 19, 54, 82
Colman, H., 168
Conley, R. W., 132
Conlon, M., 166
Conners, C., 132
Cooke, J. C., 179
Cooper, S. A., 19, 54, 82
Corbett, J. A., 8, 14, 16, 50, 52, 126, 169, 174
Cottrell, D.J.
Couk, D., 138
Coulter, D., 1, 91, 93-94
Cowen, P. J., 131
Cox, G., 14
Coyle, J. T., 17
Coyne, J. C., 56
Craft, M., 8, 16, 45, 166
Crimmins, D. B., 73, 131
Crisp, A. H., 88
Cromwell, R. L., 29
Cullinan, D., 11, 50, 52, 85
Cummins, R. A., 127
Cunningham, P. J., 12, 24
Cushna, B., 207
Cutting, J. C., 131
Cutts, R. A., 95-96, 133

Dalton, A. J., 18
Dana, S., 71, 73
Darwin, C., 67
Das, J. P., 85, 132
Davidson, M., 128

Davidson, P. W., 17
Day, K., 7, 16-18, 76-77, 82-83, 87, 202-203, 208
de la Cruz, F., 20
DeStefano, L., 25
Dettling, J., 177
Deutsch, H., 143
Deutsch, M. R., 60
Dewan, J. G., 8, 11
Dibble, E., 112
Dickie, J. R., 30
DiNardo, P. A., 99
Dinitz, S., 148
Dixon, H., 99
Doherty, M., 54
Dokecki, P. R., 195
Dollard, J., 74, 157
Donatelli, L. S., 131
Donnellan, A. M., 73
Doob, L. W., 74
Doris, J., 1
Dorsey, M. F., 106, 131, 153
Dosen, A., 31, 51, 53-55, 100
Doucette, A., 53
Douglas, V. I., 84
Drabman, R., 156
Drummond, C., 45, 71, 100, 200
Dubow, E., 74
Duckworth, M. S., 105
Duff, R., 46
Duncan, A. G., 11
Dupont, A., 7
Durand, V. M., 34, 73, 78, 131, 153, 202
Durkheim, E., 59
Dweck, C. S., 58-59
Dyggve, H., 77
D'Zurilla, T. J., 162

Eaton, L. F., 7, 14, 45, 50
Edgerton, R. B., 22, 25-26, 29, 86, 101
Edwards, D. E., 166

Einfeld, S. L., 7, 21, 53, 126
Eiselle, C. D., 55
Ellis, A., 85, 159
Ellis, C. R., 131, 179
Ellis, J. W., 210
Ellman, G., 168
Emerson, E., 18
Emerson, P., 202
Epstein, M. H., 50, 52, 85
Erickson, E., 141
Eron, L. D., 62, 74, 133-134, 139
Esveldt-Dawson, K., 152
Everington, C. T., 132, 210
Eyman, R. K., 5, 12, 77, 94
Eysenck, H. J., 10, 147-148

Fabian, E. S., 200-201
Farber, J. M., 162
Faw, G. D., 29, 156
Fee, V. E., 130
Feinstein, C., 54, 60, 126
Fenichel, O., 81
Ferrell, D., 7
Field, C. J., 43, 122
Fitzpatrick, J., 99
Fleiss, J. L., 98
Flesig, W., 47, 159
Fletcher, R., 35, 143, 201, 209
Foale, M., 32
Foley, J., 171, 175
Folk, L., 202-203
Folstein, M., 69
Forness, S. R., 5
Foster, R., 6, 163
Fox, C. J., 179
Fox, R., 88, 179
Foxx, R. M., 38, 114, 152, 156
Fraser, W. I., 2
Frazier, J. A., 105
Freeman, B. J., 130, 176
Freud, A., 141

Freud, S., 97-98, 139-140
Friedenthal, S. B., 137
Friedman, D. L., 167
Freitag, G., 152
Fuchs, C., 76,
Fujiura, G., 88

Gabby, S., 116
Gadow, K. D., 166
Gardner, W. I., 6, 50, 76, 123, 156, 158
Garfield, S. L., 148
Gargiulo, R. M., 58
Gedye, A., 127
Gentile, C., 28
Gettings, R. M., 188
Gibbs, J. W., 137
Gibby, R. G., 21, 32
Gielen, J., 53-55
Giesow, V. E., 17
Gill, M. N., 134
Gill-Weiss, M. J., 6, 9, 35, 41
Gillberg, C., 5, 8, 20-21
Gilson, S. F., 8, 32, 143, 149
Gitta, M. Z., 8, 16, 70-71
Gladwin, T., 24
Glaser, B. A., 169
Gold, V., 152
Goldberg, B., 8, 16, 70-71
Goldiamond, I., 151
Goldsmith, L., 37
Goldfried, M. R., 162
Gonso, J., 34
Goodman, S. J., 27
Gorsky, J., 125
Gostason, R., 8 , 52, 207
Gottman, J., 34
Goza, A. B., 179
Graham, P., 10
Gravestock, S., 198
Gray, D. B., 112, 210
Gray, J., 2

Granfield, J. M., 28
Greene, D., 157-158
Greenspan, S. B., 5, 28
Gresham, F. M., 93-94
Grush, L., 165-168
Groden, G., 46
Groden, J., 46
Grossi, V., 60
Grossman, H. J., 1, 3, 90, 97
Guarnaccia, V. J., 46
Gullone, E., 120
Gunderson, J. G., 164
Guralnick, M. J., 46, 176
Gursky, D. M., 30, 47

Hagamen, M. B., 23
Hagerman, R., 20
Hahn, R. K., 138
Haimowitz, M. L., 80
Haimowitz, N. R., 80
Hall, S. M., 30
Hall, W., 21
Hampe, E., 127
Harlow, H. F., 55
Harner, C. J., 137
Harper, D. C., 17-18
Harper, R. S., 5, 27, 59
Harrison, S. B., 204-206, 211
Harter, S., 33
Hassibi, M., 8, 17
Hauber, F. A., 12
Heal, L. W., 12, 137
Healey, K. N., 28
Healy, M., 26
Heather, B. B., 5
Heaton-Ward, A., 7
Heflinger, C. A., 195
Heidorn, S., 168
Heifetz, L. J., 196
Heller, T., 27, 48
Helsel, W. J., 50

Hemmick, S., 176
Hemsley, D. L., 29
Henning, D., 167
Henry, G., 63
Herr, S., 210
Herskovitz, H. H., 65
Hesse, R. A., 137
Heston, L. L., 63
Hetrick, W. P., 168
Hill, B. K., 5, 7, 12, 16, 164, 169
Hingsburger, D., 143
Hitzing, W., 204, 211
Hoelsgens, I., 200
Hogan, A. E., 34
Hole, W., 54
Hollinger, P. C., 60
Hollingworth, 10
Hollon, S. D., 160
Holmstrom, R. W., 134
Holt, G., 88-89, 179
Hom, A., 168
Hoogduin, K. A., 115-117, 121, 200
House, B., 33, 85, 101
Hozer, C.E., 52
Hsieh, M. C., 137
Huesmann, L. R., 58, 74
Hunter, R. H., 188
Hurd, H. M., 64
Hurley, A. D., 51, 54, 87, 104, 133, 142, 170
Hurley, F. J., 142, 166
Hutt, M., 21, 32

Inoue, F., 170
Ismail, I. A., 166
Ivins, J., 56
Iwata, B. A., 106, 131, 153

Jackson, H. J., 69
Jacobson, J. W., 7, 9, 15, 17-18, 45, 79

Jakab, I., 142
James, D. H., 5, 16, 17, 18
James, H., 202
Jamieson, J., 8
Jancar, J., 17
Janicki, M. A., 59
Jarvis, J., 146
Jenkins, E. C., 21
Jenkins, J. O., 28
Jenkins, R., 131
Jones, P. M., 53
Jones, S. C., 81
Josephs, A., 127
Jung, C., 141
Junge, M., 146

Kalachnik, J. E., 170, 174-175
Kaminer, Y., 54, 60, 126
Kanner, L., 20, 21
Kanfer, F. H., 159
Karp, S. A., 134
Kashima, K. J., 196
Kastner, T., 167
Kassorla, I., 152
Katz, E., 146
Katz, M., 8, 11, 18, 77
Kazdin, A. E., 121, 152, 156, 158
Kebbon, L., 207
Keck, P. E., 174
Keene, N., 202
Keith, K. D., 137
Kelly, L. E., 88
Kelley, S., 169
Kennedy, M., 204
Kessler, J. W., 22, 24
Klein, J., 143
Kleven, K. B., 7
Kienlen, T. L., 31, 131
Kiernan, W. E., 144
King, B. H., 78
King, N. J., 127

Kirk, S. A., 97-99
Kirsch, I., 146, 150
Knapp, L. G., 46
Knights, R. M., 46, 50
Kodahl, T., 77
Koller, H., 8, 11, 18, 77
Kopp, C. B., 28
Kovacs, M., 56
Kraepelin, E., 61, 64, 97-98
Kramer, B., 17
Kramer, M., 52
Krasner, L., 73, 149, 151, 158
Krause, R. B., 137
Krauss, M. W., 27
Krishnamurti, D., 166
Krug, D. A., 130
Kubiak, M. A., 178
Kushlick, A., 14
Kutchins, H., 97-99

Labrie, R., 54
Laggert, E. L., 58
Lakin, K. C., 4, 8, 12
Laman, D. S., 6, 55-57, 60, 112, 125, 129, 177
LaMendola, W., 170
LaMore, K. L., 146
Landen, S. J., 196
Landrum, T. J., 131
Langee, H. R., 166
Langer, E. J., 97
La Rocca, J., 46
Larson, S. A., 3
LaVigna, G., 73
Lazer, J., 60
Leaf, P. J., 52
Leaverton, D. R., 207
Lefkowitz, M. M., 74
Leggett, E. L., 58
Leland, H., 6, 142, 145-146, 163
Lepper, M. R., 157-158

Lesch, M., 21
Leste, A., 146
Leudar, I., 2
Levitan, G. W., 1-2, 9, 35-37, 96
Levitas, A., 8, 32, 143, 149
Lewin, K., 33
Lewis, G. A., 7
Li, X., 12
Libb, W. J., 30
Linaker, O., 121
Linden, B. E., 5
Lindsay, W. R., 127
Lindsley, H. L., 87
Little, R. E., 29
Lizzet, A., 46
Longhurst, N. A., 191
Lord, J., 30
Lovaas, O. I., 151-152
Lowry, M. A., 179
Lowry, M. J., 179
Luckasson, R., 1, 91, 93-94, 132, 210
Ludins-Katz, F., 146
Luftig, R. L., 23, 129
Luiselli, J. K., 46
Lukach, B. M., 82
Lund, J., 7, 18, 52
Luria, A., 33
Lustman, N., 25
Lutzker, J. R., 82

Machover, K., 133
MacLean, Jr., W. E., 100
MacMahon, B., 164
Macmann, G. M., 100
MacMillan, D. L., 93-94
MacMillan, K. F., 29
Maddux, J. E., 46
Madison, C., 7
Mann, A. H., 131
Maracek, J., 81
Marks, I. M., 150, 158

Marsh, H. W., 29
Marshburn, E. C., 122
Martin, P., 46
Masterpasqua, F., 28
Matarazzo, J. D., 99
Mathews, J., 166
Matson, J. L., 6, 28, 42, 45-46, 49-50,
    84, 110, 114, 119-121, 123, 129-130
    152, 156, 176, 177
Mattes, J. A., 138, 167
McBrien, J., 202
McElroy, S. L., 174
McGee, J., 22, 144-145, 202-203, 207
McGrother, C., 19, 54
McHugh, P. R., 69
McKinney, B. E., 28, 203
McLaren, J., 8, 11, 77
McLoughlin, I. J., 18
McNally, R. J., 1, 16, 30, 35, 47-49, 82,
    86, 96, 127, 155, 168
McQueen, P. C., 7
Meade, C., 18
Meins, W., 52-53, 56-57, 127, 130
Melcher, W. A., 7
Melnyk, L., 85, 132
Melvin, S. J., 5
Menninger, K., 148
Menolascino, F. J., 7-8, 14, 22, 45, 50, 60,
    96, 114, 138, 143-144, 202-203, 210
Methuen, R., 99
Mettee, D. R., 81
Meyers, C. E., 94
Mezzacappa, E., 53
Michie, A. M., 127
Mikkelsen, E. J., 168
Miller, K. L., 58
Miller, L. C., 127
Miller, L. K., 146
Miller, N. E., 74, 157
Millichamp, C. J., 166
Millon, T., 69
Milos, M. E., 146

Miranti, S. V., 163
Mitchell, K. M., 148
Moe, T. L., 131
Mohamed, W. N., 82
Molony, H., 21
Monfils, M., 143, 144
Monroe, M. J., 146
Moras, K., 99
Morel, D., 61, 63
Morgan, C., 133
Morikawa, S., 58
Morreau, L. E., 5, 169
Morrill, R., 5, 16, 168
Mosher, L. R., 164
Mott, D., 146
Mowrer, O. H., 74
Mueller, C. D., 12, 24
Mueser, K. T., 26
Mulick, J. A., 77, 132
Mundy, P. C., 34
Murphy, D. M., 196
Murray, H. A., 133
Murray, W. J., 82
Myers, B. A., 1
Myers, J. K., 52

Napolitan, J. T., 78, 203
Nau, S. D., 148
Naylor, G. J., 53-54
Nelson, D. L., 146
Neri, C. L., 168
Ness, M. E., 88, 131
Nestadt, G., 69
Newman, I., 202
Newton, J. T., 131
Nezu, A. M., 6, 9, 35, 41, 156,
    162-163, 179
Nezu, C. M., 6, 9, 35, 41, 156,
    162-163, 179
Nihira, K., 163
Nisbatt, R. E., 157-158

Noble, H., 127
Nolan, M. E., 105
North, P. M., 166
Novaco, R. W., 160
Novosel, S., 49
Nucci, M., 30
Nyhan, W., 21

Obler, M., 46
O'Connor, G., 168
O'Connor, N., 33
O'Leary, K. D., 156
Olinger, E., 11
Ollendick, T. H., 127
Olson, D., 204
Orvaschel, H., 52
O'Sullivan, P. S., 58
Oxenkrug, G., 168

Page, F., 142
Pagel, S., 5
Panek, P. E., 135
Parker, L., 138
Parks, A., 167
Parmenter, T. R., 187
Pary, R. J., 165-167
Pawlarczyk, D., 138
Pearce, L., 46
Peck, C. L., 46, 176
Pederson, E. L., 199
Penrose, L. S., 11
Perloff, B. F., 151
Perri, M. G., 162
Persson, E., 8
Peters, K. G., 84
Peterson, R. A., 28, 30, 47, 62, 72, 86,
    109, 139, 155, 159
Petti, T. A., 130
Pfadt, A., 21
Pfeiffer, S. I., 23, 144

Phelps, L. A., 25
Philips, I., 8, 14, 18, 23, 26, 28, 159
Pirodsky, D. M., 137
Plummer, A. T., 167
Poindexter, A. R., 31, 122, 131
Polakoff, S., 168
Poling, A. D., 166
Pollock, H. M., 11, 35
Polloway, E. A., 1, 11, 50, 85, 91, 93-94
Polster, L., 132
Polvinale, R. A., 82
Pond, W. S., 167
Pope, H. G., 174
Portnoy, B., 30,
Potter, H., 207
Primrose, D.A.
Prout, H. T., 37, 117, 119, 125
Prouty, G., 142-145, 178, 207
Puddephatt, A., 8, 16, 70-71
Pueschel, S. M., 1
Pugh, T. F., 164
Pustel, G., 60

Quijano, L. E., 17

Rabian, B., 47, 159
Rabold, D., 101
Radhakrishnan, G., 105
Rapaport, D., 134
Rapee, R. M., 99
Rasmussen, S. A., 34, 49, 80
Ratey, J. J., 167-168
Ray, R., 18
Redd, W. H., 71, 157
Reed, J., 126
Regan, A., 166
Reichler, R., 130
Reid, A. H., 5, 8, 16, 45, 50, 53-54, 63,
    65, 68-69, 73, 114, 131, 178
Reiss, M. M., 139

Reiss, S., (author of this book)
Renner, B. R., 130
Repp, A. C., 158
Reppucci, N. D., 80
Reus, V. I., 137
Reynolds, W. M., 58, 110, 129-130
Rice, C. J., 163
Richardson, S. A., 8, 11, 18, 77, 114
Richman, G. S., 153
Ricketts, R. W., 179
Ricks, D. F., 39
Rimmer, J. H., 88
Rivenq, B., 46, 176
Ritvo, E. R., 130
Rivto, A., 130
Rodgers, T. A., 106, 131
Rodriguez, W. H., 137
Rogentine, K., 167
Rogers, C., 111, 139, 141, 148, 205-207
Rogers, R., 20
Rojahn, J., 17, 24, 55-56, 77, 79, 101, 130, 132
Romanoff, R., 74
Romanoski, A., 69
Romer, D., 24
Rorschach, H., 133
Rosefsky, Q. B., 143
Rosen, M., 133
Rotatori, A. F., 88, 179
Rourke, D. A., 106, 131
Roy, R. R., 176
Ruedrich, S. L., 38, 165-168
Ruiz, M. Q., 167
Rusch, F. R., 25
Russell, A. T., 4, 9, 16, 50, 95
Rust, J., 146
Rutter, M., 8, 10, 21
Ryan, R., 26, 48

Sacristan, J. R., 114
Sallach, H. S., 138

Samuels, J., 69
Sandman, C. A., 77, 168
Sarason, S. B., 1, 24, 143
Schaeffer, B., 151
Schafer, R., 134
Schalock, R. L., 2-3, 5, 27, 91, 93-94, 137, 171, 175
Scheerenberger, R., 5
Schloss, P. J., 37, 52, 56
Schneider, F., 101
Schopler, E., 130
Schroeder, S. R., 77
Schumacher, K., 138
Schumer, F., 133-134
Schuyler, D., 59
Sears, R. R., 74
Seibert, J. M., 34
Seivewright, N., 178
Seligman, M. E. P., 58-59, 160
Seltzer, G. B., 18
Seltzer, M. M., 18, 27
Senatore, V., 121, 177
Seth, R. V., 166
Sevin, J. A., 130
Shedd, C. L., 30
Shellhaas, M., 6, 163
Shneidman, E. S., 59
Shoultz, B., 5, 204
Sigman, M., 32
Silber, D. E., 134
Silver, J. M., 167
Silverg, E. F., 133
Silverman, W. K., 47, 159
Silvestri, R., 176
Simensen, R. J., 20
Simmons, J. Q., 16
Singh, N. N., 42, 114, 121-122, 131, 158, 166-169, 179
Singh, Y. N., 179
Siperstein, G. N., 93, 94
Skinner, B. F., 150-151
Slifer, K. J., 153

Sloane-Reeves, J. N., 17
Smeltzer, D. J., 171
Smith, B. L., 31
Smith, D. C., 27
Smith, D. E., 56, 142, 145-146
Smith, J. T., 165
Smith, S. E., 20
Smull, M. W., 96, 200, 201, 204-206
Snell, M., 1, 91, 93
Sokol, M. S., 77
Sorgi, P., 168
Sovner, R., 6, 42, 51, 53-55, 101-102,
    104, 112, 123-124, 133, 166, 170,
    177, 179
Spreat, S., 48-49
Spinner, D., 149
Spirrison, C. L., 131
Spitalnik, D. M., 1, 91, 93-94
Spitzer, R. L., 98
Sprague, R. L., 174
Spreat, S., 48-49
Sprengler, P. M., 37
Stacey, C. L., 30
Stamatelos, T., 146
Stark, J., 1, 60, 91, 93-94, 171, 175, 210
Stavrakaki, C., 143
Steffenburg, S., 5, 21
Stephens, E., 27, 29, 32
Sternlicht, M., 133, 142, 144
Stevens, H. A., 3
Stewart, A. W., 43, 122
Stoltzman, R., 52
Strohmer, D. C., 37, 125
Sturmey, P., 115-117, 126, 130-131
Sudhalter, V., 21
Sullivan, H. S., 141
Suomi, S. J., 55
Sushinsky, L. W., 97, 158
Svec, H. J., 150
Swanson, D. A., 202-203
Swartz, C. M., 137
Szymanski, L. S., 3, 7, 17, 25, 35, 47, 50,

53-54, 64, 88-89, 96-97, 101-102,
    104, 142-144, 179, 207-208
Szyszko, J., 2, 9, 36-37, 110-112, 134

Talbott, J., 98
Talkington, L. W., 30
Tanguay, P. E., 4, 35, 50, 95-96, 207-208
Tarjan, G., 1, 94, 114
Taylor, D. V., 168
Taylor, S. J., 204
Teasdale, J. D., 58
Tebeest, D. L., 30
Terwilliger, R. F., 46
Thinn, K., 169
Thompson, T., 158
Thorne, F. C., 30
Tischler, G. L., 52
Tizard, J., 8, 10
Tonge, B., 126
Touchette, P., 168
Toulouse, A., 171, 175
Trenn, E., 15-16, 45, 50, 57, 109-199
Truax, C. B., 148
Tsuang, M. T., 49, 80
Tu, J. B., 165, 171
Tupin, J. P., 166
Turbott, S. H., 121
Turnbull, H. R., 158
Turnbull, R. C., 11
Turner, J. L., 29, 32
Tylenda, B., 54, 125
Tyrer, P., 166, 178

Ullmann, L. P., 73, 149, 151, 158

Valenti-Hein, D., 17-18, 26-27, 46, 53,
    84, 108, 117-118
Van der Heide, C., 207
Van Heyningen, J., 17

Van Minnen, A., 115-117, 121, 200
Vietze, P. M., 21
Viney, L., 30
Vitiello, B., 48, 49

Wadle, C. V., 138
Wadsworth, J. S., 17, 59
Wagner, E. E., 135
Wagner, P., 133
Walder, L. P., 74
Walsh, P., 166
Walters, R. H., 60, 74
Ward, M. R., 174
Warren, S. A., 94
Watson, J. E., 88-89, 121, 179
Weatherman, R. F., 12
Weaver, T. R., 8
Weiss, R. L., 46
Weissman, M. M., 52
Weisz, J., 58
Weisz, S., 133
Wener, R., 97
Werry, J., 42, 99
Wessman, A. E., 39
White, C., 12
White, D. M., 174
Whitling, C., 5
Whitman, T. L., 156
Whitmore, K., 8, 10
Widaman, F. J., 29
Wilcoxon, L. A., 158
Wilson, J., 165-168
Williams, C.D.
Williams, D. E., 131
Williams, G. A., 23, 28, 129
Williams, M., 46
Williams, N., 8, 18
Williams, P., 204
Wilsher, C. P., 121
Wisniewski, H. M., 18, 59
Wisniewski, J., 132

Wolkowitz, O., 137-138
Wolpe, J., 28, 150, 158
Woodward, H.L., 199
Wright, E. C., 7
Wurth, P., 53
Wymore, M., 168

Yarnold, P. R., 74
Yearwood, K., 138
Yokota, A., 130
Yudofsky, S. C., 167
Yule, W., 10

Zabaria, E. S., 170
Zarcone, J. R., 106, 131
Zarfas, D. E., 187
Zeaman, D., 33, 85, 101
Zetlin, A. G., 29, 32
Zigler, E., 23, 32-34, 114
Zilboorg, G., 63
Zingarelli, G., 168
Zubin, A., 133-134
Zung, W. K., 127